国际税收

(双语版)

主　编　邓廷梅
副主编　王晓芳　巴　英　梅雅洁

北京理工大学出版社
BEIJING INSTITUTE OF TECHNOLOGY PRESS

内 容 简 介

本教材在内容上力求全面、系统地阐述国际税收理论和实务。国际税收理论篇介绍了国际税收导论和所得税的税收管辖权问题；国际税收实务篇介绍了国际重复征税、消除国际重复征税、国际避税及其一般方法，还有避税港避税模式、国际反避税方法和措施及国际税收协定等具体的国际税收现象。

本教材具有以下特点：第一，基本覆盖了国际税收学科的主要内容；第二，语言规范、通俗易懂，内容深入浅出、适用面广；第三，结合我国高等教育发展的要求和趋势，融入课程思政内容；第四，编写体例、形式和内容适用于对应用型人才的培养。

本教材对培养具有国际社会经济文化知识、懂外语、熟悉国际税收和商业管理的高级管理人才，以及具有良好外语能力和知识结构的国际化税务人员有相当重要的作用，既可以作为应用型院校的教材，供高等学校财政学、税收学、经济学及国际经济与贸易等专业本科或专科学生使用，也可以作为各种财税培训机构的培训教材，供企业董事长、经理、财务主管、税务经理、律师、注册会计师、税务师、会计师、纳税筹划师等各类关心财税的人士阅读及自学使用。

版权专有　侵权必究

图书在版编目（CIP）数据

国际税收：双语版：英、汉 / 邓廷梅主编. --北京：北京理工大学出版社，2023.7

ISBN 978-7-5763-2635-2

Ⅰ.①国… Ⅱ.①邓… Ⅲ.①国际税收-高等学校-教材-英、汉 Ⅳ.①F810.42

中国国家版本馆 CIP 数据核字（2023）第 136766 号

责任编辑：封　雪	**文案编辑**：毛慧佳
责任校对：刘亚男	**责任印制**：李志强

出版发行	/ 北京理工大学出版社有限责任公司
社　　址	/ 北京市丰台区四合庄路6号
邮　　编	/ 100070
电　　话	/ （010）68914026（教材售后服务热线）
	（010）68944437（课件资源服务热线）
网　　址	/ http://www.bitpress.com.cn
版 印 次	/ 2023年7月第1版第1次印刷
印　　刷	/ 河北盛世彩捷印刷有限公司
开　　本	/ 787mm×1092mm　1/16
印　　张	/ 19
字　　数	/ 440千字
定　　价	/ 95.00元

图书出现印装质量问题，请拨打售后服务热线，负责调换

前　言

国际税收是财政学、税收学、国际税收等专业的一门重要的必修课程，在我国设有财政学及税收学专业的院校中广为开设。它是研究跨国税收关系的一门课程，包括对跨国课税对象征税的国际规范、所得的国际重复征税及其消除方法、国际避税与反避税、国际税收协定等内容。

随着我国对外开放的不断深入，与国际经济发展密切相关的国际税收问题也越来越被人们重视，政府部门面临着加强涉外税务管理以及制定开放经济条件下税收政策的紧迫任务，众多向国际市场进军的国内企业也亟待了解跨国经营的国际税收环境和国际税务筹划方法。此外，当今世界经济的发展趋势也使得国际税收成为一个不可忽略的问题，这就不可避免地产生了对具有国际社会经济文化知识、懂外语、熟悉国际税收和商业惯例的高级管理人才的大量需求。与此同时，中国税收的国际化进程正在加快，对税务从业人员的要求越来越高，因此，如何培养具有良好的外语能力和知识结构的国际化税务人员也是我国高等教育面临的一个紧迫课题。

国际税收在国外许多大学的经济学院和工商管理学院及法学院都是一门很重要的课程，我国许多高等院校也把国际税收作为财经类、会计类、国际经济与贸易等专业本科生或研究生的一门必修课。

国际化人才的培养方式主要包括：推行双语教学形式，重整全球性知识体系，选用国际化通用教材及培训国际化水平的教师等。其中，推行双语教学是高等院校经济管理教学改革走向国际化的切入点，教育部早在2001年就制定了推动双语教学的文件，又在2005年强调要求高等院校继续推广双语课程，尤其是经济管理类专业。可见，双语教学早已成为高校教学改革的热点。

推行双语教学，首先应该推进教材的双语化。纵观国内外的国际税收方面的教材可知，一方面，国外原版教材体系庞大，内容丰富，习题案例充实齐全，理论与实务的阐述深度与广度并举，但篇幅过大，不适合目前经济管理类专业教学学时的安排，且价格昂贵，加重学生经济负担；另外，国外原版教材中的部分内容与中国目前的经济管理实践尚有差距。另一方面，国内国际税收双语教材历来鲜见，可供参考的很少。因此，编写一本既能吸收西方国际税收理论与实务之精华，又能符合我国经济管理发展的实情，还能适合当前高校经济管理教育体制与教学计划的双语教材势在必行，这也是国际税收双语教师的职业使命。本教材正是在高等院校经济管理类专业教学改革的背景下酝酿而成的。

本教材共分9章，着重介绍国际税收专业知识及专业词汇，具有以下特点：第一，基本覆盖了国际税收学科的主要内容，通过学习，学生可以掌握国际税收领域的专业知识和大量核心词汇，在提高专业素养的同时，也提高了专业英语水平。第二，语言规范、通俗易懂，内容深入浅出、适用面广，教材采用英汉对照的双语格式，是适应全面推行教育国际化的需要，也是走向双语教育模式的过渡。教材基本素材选自原版教材，但表述形式力求符合中国人的思维习惯、价值观念与文化特征，适应不同层面学生的学习需求。第三，结合新时代我国高等教育发展的要求和趋势。教材融入了课程思政的内容，体现了"立德树人、为国育才"的理念，在潜移默化中增强学生的民族自信心和自豪感，使其认同社会主义核心价值观和为人民服务的崇高信念。第四，编写体例、形式和内容适用于对应用型人才的培养。本教材在每章开头设置"时政观点"，落实立德树人的根本任务；接着设置"学习目标"，让学生明确每章的学习目的；在学习每章具体内容之前设置"课程导入"，激发学生的学习兴趣；在具体章节中引入大量的"教学案例"和"模拟演示"，实现教学内容的理实一体，让学生体验案例学习的趣味；在每章的最后设置"复习思考题"，让学生进一步理解和掌握所学知识。

本教材由贵州大学经济学院邓廷梅副教授担任主编，由贵州大学经济学院王晓芳、巴英、梅雅洁担任副主编。

其中，邓廷梅负责拟定大纲，对教材内容进行统稿和审定，并编写第1章、第2章、第4章、第6章和第8章；王晓芳编写第3章和第9章；巴英编写第5章；梅雅洁编写第7章。

本教材精选国内外财税教科书、报纸及互联网的材料，对国际税收理论与实务的阐述受许多教科书的启发和影响，诸多案例参考了许多经典的原版国际税收著作。特别感谢中国人民大学财政金融学院的朱青教授。自朱老的《国际税收》教材出版以来，编者就成为朱老的学生，在教学时一直沿用老先生的教材，而且敬佩朱老与时俱进、笔耕不辍的精神。在本教材的编写过程中，编者也得到老先生教材的极大启发，受益匪浅。因此可

前言

以说，这本双语教材是朱老中文教材的另一种表达方式，在此谨向朱青教授致以最崇高的敬意，并对所有参考书目的原作者表示深切的感谢。

另外，编者在本教材的编写过程中还得到了诸多领导和同仁的帮助和支持，如贵州大学经济学院副院长李本光教授亲自审稿、严格把关，经济学院财政金融系主任蒋雪梅副教授、经济学院经济与贸易系曾海鹰教授对书稿提出了宝贵的意见和建议，在此一并表示衷心的感谢。

本教材的出版得到了北京理工大学出版社相关工作人员的大力支持与帮助，在此表示深深的感谢。

由于编者水平有限，本教材中难免存在疏漏之处，恳请广大读者批评指正。

编　者

目 录

PART ONE
THEORY OF INTERNATIONAL TAXATION

Chapter 1 INTRODUCTION TO INTERNATIONAL TAXATION ······ (3)
1.1　The concept of international taxation ······ (3)
1.2　The developmental trend of international taxation ······ (10)

Chapter 2 JURISDICTIONS OF INCOME TAX ······ (15)
2.1　Introduction to tax jurisdiction and its establishment principles ······ (15)
2.2　The judgment norms on source jurisdiction ······ (17)
2.3　The judgment norms on residence jurisdiction ······ (23)
2.4　The judgment norms on citizen jurisdiction ······ (33)
2.5　The present implementation status of income tax jurisdictions in different countries ······ (35)

PART TWO
PRACTICE OF INTERNATIONAL TAXATION

Chapter 3 OVERVIEW OF INTERNATIONAL DOUBLE TAXATION ······ (41)
3.1　The concept of international double taxation ······ (41)
3.2　The causes of international double taxation ······ (43)

Chapter 4 INTERNATIONAL DOUBLE TAXATION RELIEF ······ (47)
4.1　Ways of international double taxation relief ······ (48)
4.2　Methods of international double taxation relief ······ (49)
4.3　Comparison of different methods of international double taxation relief ······ (74)

Chapter 5 INTRODUCTION TO INTERNATIONAL TAX AVOIDANCE ······ (77)
5.1　The concept of international tax avoidance ······ (77)
5.2　The causes of international tax avoidance ······ (80)

5.3　Tax havens ······ (82)

Chapter 6　GENERAL METHODS OF INTERNATIONAL TAX AVOIDANCE ······ (87)
6.1　Transferring tax avoidance of subject ······ (88)
6.2　Transferring tax avoidance of object ······ (95)

Chapter 7　TAX AVOIDANCE MODE OF TAX HAVENS ······ (115)
7.1　Fictitious business in tax havens ······ (116)
7.2　Fictitious trust property in tax havens ······ (121)

Chapter 8　INTERNATIONAL ANTI-AVOIDANCE METHODS AND MEASURES ······ (126)
8.1　The general methods of international anti-avoidance ······ (127)
8.2　The special legal measures of international anti-avoidance ······ (133)
8.3　Controlled foreign corporation (CFC) rules ······ (141)
8.4　Transfer pricing rules ······ (144)

Chapter 9　INTERNATIONAL TAX TREATIES ······ (156)
9.1　Overview ······ (156)
9.2　Contents of a typical international tax treaty ······ (160)

第1篇　国际税收理论

第1章　国际税收导论 ······ (171)
1.1　国际税收的概念 ······ (171)
1.2　国际税收的发展趋势 ······ (176)

第2章　所得税的税收管辖权 ······ (179)
2.1　税收管辖权及其确立原则 ······ (179)
2.2　收入来源地管辖权判定标准 ······ (181)
2.3　居民管辖权判定标准 ······ (185)
2.4　公民管辖权判定标准 ······ (192)
2.5　各国所得税税收管辖权实施的现状 ······ (193)

第2篇　国际税收实务

第3章　国际重复征税概述 ······ (199)
3.1　国际重复征税的概念 ······ (199)
3.2　国际重复征税产生的原因 ······ (200)

第4章　消除国际重复征税 ······ (204)
4.1　消除国际重复征税的方式 ······ (204)
4.2　消除国际重复征税的方法 ······ (205)
4.3　消除国际重复征税不同方法的比较 ······ (224)

第5章　国际避税 ······ (226)
5.1　国际避税的概念 ······ (226)

5.2　国际避税产生的原因 ……………………………………………………（228）
　5.3　避税港 ………………………………………………………………………（230）

第 6 章　国际避税的一般方法 ……………………………………………………（234）
　6.1　主体转移性避税 ……………………………………………………………（234）
　6.2　客体转移性避税 ……………………………………………………………（240）

第 7 章　避税港避税模式 …………………………………………………………（255）
　7.1　虚构避税港营业 ……………………………………………………………（256）
　7.2　虚构避税港信托财产 ………………………………………………………（260）

第 8 章　国际反避税的方法与措施 ………………………………………………（263）
　8.1　国际反避税的一般方法 ……………………………………………………（264）
　8.2　国际反避税的特别法律措施 ………………………………………………（268）
　8.3　受控外国公司法 ……………………………………………………………（274）
　8.4　转让定价税制 ………………………………………………………………（276）

第 9 章　国际税收协定 ……………………………………………………………（285）
　9.1　概况 …………………………………………………………………………（285）
　9.2　典型国际税收协定的内容 …………………………………………………（288）

参考文献 ……………………………………………………………………………（294）

PART ONE
THEORY OF INTERNATIONAL TAXATION

Chapter 1

INTRODUCTION TO INTERNATIONAL TAXATION

第1讲

 Ideological and political points of the course

1. Taxes are taken from the people and used by the people.
2. Under the background of "One Belt, One Road", our tax system should adapt to the developmental trend of international taxation and integrate into the international societies.

 Learning Objectives

1. Master the concept of international taxation essentially.
2. Distinguish the difference and connection between international taxation, national taxation and foreign taxation.
3. Know the developmental trend of international taxation.

 Course Importing

The European Union is a regional as well as international organization with high integration of policy and economy. In European Union, it has common external tariff and unified currency—the euro, even the EU government has its own independent revenue sources which can be called "own revenue resources". So, is the EU a tax authority which is beyond national sovereignty? Can it levy taxpayers directly from its member states?

1.1 The concept of international taxation

1.1.1 What is international taxation?

Tax is a kind of compulsory levy on the taxpayers within the government's jurisdiction which relies upon its political power. It is a significant way of obtaining revenue for the government which reflects the levy and payment relationship between the country and the taxpayers. It includes not only the relationship between the government and its domestic taxpayers, but also the relationship between the government and its foreign taxpayers. Well, is international taxation also a kind of compulsory levy? Is it a tool of obtaining revenue for the international societies which relies on a sort of supranational politics? The answer is negative. Because there isn't a kind of political power which is superior to independent sovereignty of any other country, it needn't talk about the compulsory levy in the international societies.

Since long time before, some foreign scholars have been engaging in the research on the subject of international taxation. But after the Second World War, theory of international taxation developed rapidly and became an important part of foreign taxation. There must be some premises for its nomination and existence.

1.The conditions of nomination for international taxation

From the point of view of theory, the nomination and existence of international taxation are decided by two conditions on the basis of tax. One is that transnational income exists largely. Another is the fact that countries in the world levy the income tax universally and exercise different tax powers. Only the two conditions exist at the same time, does the problem of sharing tax profit appear. So, it is necessary to coordinate the tax profit between countries and then the tax distribution relationships nominate.

The two conditions which decide the nomination and existence of international taxation also provide judgment standards for the objective existence of international taxation from the point of view of theory and practice.

(1) There is inevitable direct connection between the appearance of transnational income and the nomination of international taxation.

Transnational income is the income owned by a resident taxpayer or a citizen taxpayer of a country, but actually, it derives from another country. It is the material basis of nomination for international taxation.

Under the closed economic environment, national collection only involves commodities produced and circulated within its territory and the income and assets owned by its native taxpayers. But under the open economy conditions, the goods produced in a country can flow into another through international trade. The taxpayers of a country who are engaged in international economic activities like transnational investment will have income or obtain property from abroad, which leads to the formation of transnational income. At this time, within its scope of tax jurisdiction, the government will levy on not only the goods imported from foreign countries and the ones exported from its own country, but also the foreign income or property owned by national taxpayers as well as the ones owned by foreign taxpayers within its territory. For the taxpayer's income stride across borders, the tax relationship is also crossed the border. As a result, the problem of how to share tax benefit between states for the same transnational income appears. Only at this time, does the objective economic condition offer premise condition to the generation of international taxation.

(2) There is substantial connection between the nomination of international taxation and the fact that countries in the world levy income tax universally and exercise different tax powers.

As the transnational income exists, the concerned countries should list it as their object of taxation and exercise their taxation right. The source country, where the transnational income

Chapter 1 INTRODUCTION TO INTERNATIONAL TAXATION

comes from, will levy on the income from source, and the resident or citizenship country where the owner lives who earns the transnational income will also levy on the same income in general. Thus it causes the confliction of tax allocation between countries which leads to the occurrence of tax distribution relationship between countries. Therefore, international taxation is the performance of governments which exercise their tax power on transnational income of transnational taxpayers; also it is the "invasion" and "coordination" of a country to another country's financial interests. Only countries in the world levy income tax universally and exercise different tax jurisdictions, transnational income exists also, could international taxation be nominated.

2. The concept of international taxation

To sum up, the concept of international taxation could be understood from two aspects of narrow and generalized sense.

1) Narrow sense

From the narrow sense, international taxation refers to tax allocation and coordination relationships between two or more governments when they levy on the transnational income of transnational taxpayers separately, based on their respective tax sovereignty.

The concept includes the following three important meaning.

(1) International taxation cannot exist alone, which is separated from national taxation.

National taxation must have its own government revenue collecting office and taxpayers. However, international taxation could impossibly have its own specific ones which are separated from national taxation. It can only depend on national taxation.

The example of European Union can explain this problem well. The "own revenue resources" of EU is in fact obtained from each member state which imposes tax compulsorily on its taxpayers instead of direct taxation on the taxpayers of member states by the EU government. For example, there is an item called the tariff revenue in the "own revenue resources". It is not collected by the EU government itself, instead, it is paid to the EU budget from each member country after they levy tariff on imported products and deduct 10% handling fee from the income. As another example, value-added tax commission is the largest income in "own revenue resources" of European Union, but it is also not levied directly by EU government on the taxpayers of member countries. It is paid to the EU budget by the member states in accordance with uniform diameter value-added tax base according to a certain proportion.

(2) International taxation cannot leave the key factors of transnational taxpayer.

Usually, a "non-transnational" taxpayer bears tax obligations of one country. It involves only the relationship between two parties of levying and paying in one country without causing tax distribution relationship between different countries. So in the concept of international taxation, we must specify that its taxpayer is transnationalone. Otherwise, international tax relation is out of the question.

(3) International taxation is the allocation and coordination relationships between different countries.

When a country levies on transnational income of its transnational taxpayer in its tax jurisdiction, it often involves the financial interest of other countries. Then, tax relationship between different countries is implicated in international taxation, and it is just the essence of international taxation.

Tax relations between different countries mainly perform in two aspects.

①Tax distribution relationships between different countries.

Tax distribution relationships between different countries relate to the problem of tax benefit distributions that are on the same object of taxation, which country can levy and how much the country can levy respectively. When the levy of a country results in another country cannot levy, or when a country levies more taxes which leads to less taxing of another country, tax distribution relationships between two countries will occur. For example, when a transnational income is collected by two governments at the same time, for avoidance of international double taxation on the same income which will increase the tax burden of transnational taxpayer, the residence country of taxpayer can give up its taxation right to foreign income earned by resident, and let the source country exercise taxation right alone; or the residence country gives priority to taxation right to the source country and levies on the difference between the lower tax rate of source country and the higher tax rate of residence country after the foreign income has been collected by the source country. In two of these cases, tax distribution relationship will occur between source country and residence country. Another example is that in order to prevent the import and export countries from levying domestic commodity tax on the same batch of goods in international trade, international societies regulate unified that the goods of international trade will be collected by the import country instead of export country. As a result, the tax benefits of export country will be affected because it gives up its right to levy on export goods and the import and export countries also have a certain degree of tax distribution relationship. As another example, when the multinational corporation is engaged in international tax avoidance, as the multinational corporation usually tries to transfer some profit of the group from a subsidiary which locates in the country with high tax rate to another subsidiary in the country with low tax rate for achievement, the income tax base of the country with high tax rate will be affected inevitably. Certain tax distribution relationship between the two countries will occur of course.

②Tax coordination relationships between different countries.

Taxation is the sovereignty of a country. A sovereign state has the right to decide on what to levy and on what not to levy, it also has the right to decide how much to collect. That is to say, in taxation, a country can go its own way without consideration of other countries' likes and dislikes. However, in an open world economy, countries in the world rely on and depend on each other. Actually, states can not set their own tax system at random and exercise their taxation right arbitrarily. They have to consider the economic relations with other countries on many issues which require some coordination in the tax system, tax policy and other aspects between counties. The coordination involves two aspects.

The first aspect is the cooperative coordination which refers to the relevant countries reaching an agreement by negotiation on their tax base, tax rate, tax rules, etc. According to the agreement, they can determine the tax system and collection methods on commodity and taxpayers of other countries. Like the signed agreements for avoidance of double taxation between countries are the performances of cooperative coordination.

The second aspect is the non-cooperative coordination which refers to a kind of international tax coordination made by a country to keep its tax system consistent with other countries. Driven by the competition pressure of other countries, the government can adjust its tax system unilaterally, meanwhile, the tax system of other countries remain unchanged. The essence is the tax international competition. For example, in the mid-1980s, in order to prevent the capital outflow and tax revenue outflow[①] from happening, western countries have reduced their corporate income tax rates which caused the average corporate income tax rate reducing from 50% to around 23% now. In addition, to attract foreign capital, the developing countries also competed to give foreign investors preferential tax treatment. It is actually a kind of non-cooperative coordination.

2) Broad perspective

From the broad perspective, international taxation refers to some tax problems and tax phenomenon under the condition of opening economy because of two reasons.

The tax problems and tax phenomenon are the research contents of international taxation which mainly include the following aspects.

(1) The issue of tax jurisdiction.

Tax jurisdiction is one of the important contents of international taxation, and it is also one of the basic issues, in theory and practice. So many problems of international taxation such as the occurrence of international double taxation, the coordination of tax distribution relationships between countries, are closely related to tax jurisdiction. At the Same time, from the considerations of equity and efficiency principles, in addition to studying the rationality and contradiction of existing tax jurisdiction, studying the basic theory and practical problems of tax jurisdiction deeply, international taxation tries to establish a kind of more normative and ideal tax jurisdiction.

(2) The issue of international double taxation.

International double taxation is an important issue, in theory and practice, of international taxation which involves the phenomenon of double taxation on the transnational income of transnational taxpayer by two or more countries. Obviously, it is disadvantageous to the development of international economic activities. It affects directly not only the taxpayers' benefits, but also affects the financial interests of relevant states to different degrees. Therefore, it is necessary for international community to coordinate the tax right of different countries for prevention or alleviation of international double taxation. Hence, the research scopes of international taxation focus on mainly the reasons and ways of international double taxation and the best solutions of solving it.

(3) The issue of international tax avoidance and its prevention.

International tax avoidance means that the transnational taxpayer utilizes the difference and loopholes in tax systems between different countries to avoid or relieve his tax burden after appropriate financial arrangements. The effect of international tax avoidance and international double taxation is just opposite. It will not increase the tax burden of taxpayer, but will damage the tax

---

① Tax revenue outflow refers to the multinational corporation transfer the profit which should be realized in a country to another country with lower tax rate by means of transfer pricing which causes the former country income tax revenue loss.

benefit of related nations. So, in the situation where transnational business activity is very common, all the governments take the work of guarding against international tax avoidance as an important task of tax management. Accordingly, international taxation focuses on the ways and methods of international tax avoidance and probes into how to establish the effective measures for the prevention of international tax avoidance in order to protect national sovereignty interests and realize fair tax burden.

(4) The issue of international tax agreements.

Because there is not a supranational international tax law or international tax system in the world, the distribution and coordination relationships between countries can only rely on the signing of bilateral or multilateral tax treaties to deal with and specify. The growth of tax treaties over the past decade has been exponential. There are now over 3 000 bilateral tax treaties in existence. Therefore, on the basis of studying the existing international tax agreements between developed countries, developed and developing countries and developing countries, international taxation tries to sum up the effective measures or methods of solving the problems in international taxation, as well as the standards and specifications of management and coordination for national tax distribution relationships to promote the development and communication of international economic and technical cooperation.

As we all know, there is no independent object of taxation and tax category in international taxation and there is great difference in tax types of different countries. According to the attributes of object of taxation, tax can be classified into commodity tax, property tax and income tax.

Commodity tax includes value-added tax, consumption tax, business tax and tariff, etc; Property tax includes real estate tax, vehicle and vessel tax, etc. The tax objects of turnover tax and specific property tax are some specific commodity or specific property. Because at a certain point of time, the space in which the commodity or property move or exist belongs to one country or another, all the levies are generally not beyond the boundary of a certain country. The issue of levying across nations will not happen and it also will not influence other nations' financial interests. Furthermore, tax on goods and property is generally indirect tax. The tax burden can be passed on to the buyers or consumers of commodity. So, turnover tax and specific property tax are generally not included in the research scope of international taxation.

However, the tax objects of income tax include taxpayer's income and his general property value, and the latter is called general property tax such as enterprise income tax, individual income tax, capital gain tax, gift tax, settlement tax and inheritance tax, etc. These tax objects such as a taxpayer's wages, profit or general property value are abstract which are not connected with a certain specific object directly, but with those owners directly who have the income or property values. The owners include transnational natural person and legal entity. Thus the income or property value belonging to the owners can be transnational which may be collected by many countries. So, a series of international taxation issues occur.

Based on this, the issues the author talks about in this book focus on mainly the income tax and property tax of international taxation.

1.1.2 The differences and connections between international taxation and related concepts

When we talk about international taxation, we often think of the concepts of national tax and foreign tax, etc. Some people even confuse them with each other, which leads to the misunderstanding on international taxation. In fact, there are important differences and connections between them.

1. International taxation and national tax

National tax is a kind of compulsory levy which relies upon the government's political power that reflects the levy and payment relationship between the government and its taxpayers. The taxpayer can be a business or a person. The taxpayer within the scope of a government's political jurisdiction includes not only the native persons, but also the foreigners. So, there exist extraordinary connections and distinctions between international taxation and national tax.

1) The connections

(1) National tax is the foundation of international taxation.

The essential elements of tax system including subject of taxation, tax base, and object of taxation are the foundations for international taxation existence. If the countries have no actual taxable items and tax rates in their domestic tax laws, it is not necessary to discuss the distribution and coordination relationships between different countries when they levy on the same transnational income of the same taxpayer at the same time. Then, international taxation has no its existence soil and foundation.

(2) National tax will be influenced by international taxation.

Under the background of globalization economic development, when any country formulates its essential elements of tax system, it can not ignore the effect of international economy environment. Especially, when a government formulates its tax laws, the contents of its tax law will be influenced by the tax laws of other countries to some degree including some international tax agreements.

2) The difference

(1) Implication.

National tax is a forced collection form based on the state political power, but international taxation is the tax issues and tax relations derived from national tax, which is not a forced collection form meanwhile. There isn't a kind of political power which is superior to independent sovereignty of any other country and there is no an international tax law used to levy on the worldwide income.

(2) Relationship.

National tax involves the equity distribution relationships between country and taxpayer, but international taxation involves the tax equity distribution and coordination relationships between different countries because of the interaction of different countries' tax systems.

(3) Tax categories.

National tax can be classified into different tax categories according to the objects of taxation. As international taxation is not an actual tax form, it has no its single tax categories.

2. International taxation and foreign tax

Foreign tax refers to all the collections that a government levies on foreigners (including foreign enterprises and individuals), which reflects the relationship between the government and the foreign taxpayers based on the state political power within its tax jurisdiction. The relationship is not beyond the government's jurisdiction and enters the international scope. Therefore, foreign tax still belongs to national revenue. It is just the part separated from national tax system and has its independent categories of tax. Meanwhile, international taxation is the international aspects of national tax law. Such laws and regulations can be found in the so-called foreign tax and non-foreign tax.

In China, foreign taxes are the tax categories specifically set for the foreigners, foreign enterprises or enterprises with foreign investment within Chinese territory. The following tax categories like the *Income Tax of People's Republic of China on Enterprises with Foreign Investment and Foreign Enterprises* levied from 1991 (the tax was abolished from 2008)、the *Industrial and Commercial Consolidated Tax* levied before the reform on tax system in 1994 and the *Individual Income Tax* are all the national tax of China.

1.2　The developmental trend of international taxation

International taxation is closely related to economy and its developmental trend is also inseparable from the global economy development. Some economists have pointed out that in the worldwide increasingly integrated trend of national economy, on one hand, the development of international taxation has greatly promoted the development of global economic integration; on the other hand, the transnational flows of commodity, capital, technology, personnel freely make the tax base global which is not fixed on a particular country. It puts forward new requirements for international taxation and brings new challenges. From the direction of international economic development, the future developmental trends of international taxation are as follows.

1.2.1　In the area of commodity tax, the coordination of VAT and consumption tax will gradually substitute for the coordination of customs duty and will become the core of it.

In the historical process of international coordination for commodity tax, the international coordination of customs duty is always the core. However, after the Second World War, through GATT's (General Agreement on Tariffs and Trade) eight rounds negotiation of tariff concession, national tariff rates dropped substantially. From the theory, the integration of international economic requires states to completely cancel import and export duties. But in fact, to make up the loss of income due to tariffs decline, more and more countries levy VAT (value-added tax) and perfect their original consumption tax to make them become the replaced financial resources. On the one hand, it can increase financial income. On the other hand, these domestic taxes can also be used to replace tariff as trade barriers under certain conditions. For example, some European countries levied consumption tax on bananas imported from Latin American countries and some Nordic countries levied consumption tax on wine imported from foreign country with high rates but levied consumption tax on whisky of their own production with low rates. It is actually the utilization of consumption tax as protective tools for their own products. However, in the situations of future international economic relations are closer, the practice of using domestic commodity tax instead of tariff as trade protective tools cannot be accepted by international community. If it happens, the international community should coordinate the commodity taxes of relevant countries like tariff. So, the coordination of VAT and consumption tax will gradually substitute for the coordination of customs duty and will become the core in the area of commodity tax coordination.

1.2.2 In the area of income tax, the tax competition between countries will be more violent. In order to prevent fiscal degradation from happening, it is necessary for international societies to coordinate different countries' capital income tax system.

In the background of free flow of transnational capital, the attribute of chasing profit of capital decides that it must flow to the country with higher after-tax profits. If a country wants to attract the capital of other countries to increase its domestic income tax base, it has to reduce its tax rate applicable to capital gains. It is actually a kind of behavior of harming others to benefit itself. But once other country finds it happens, it will also reduce its domestic income tax rate which results in the so-called "international competition" of income tax. It is a kind of income tax non-cooperative coordination between countries which will make the entire income tax rates drop to an unreasonable level. It will cause great reduction of national finance strength which is called "fiscal degradation".

Once international income tax competition breaks out without the intervention of international community, it is likely to continue and bring a certain loss to all countries. And it is possible that in the near future, the taxes on income and capital will not exist and the governments can only rely on a number of domestic commodity taxes to meet their expenditure demands. The best way to prevent income tax international competition from happening is to coordinate the national income tax rates and tax bases of all countries.

1.2.3 With the development of regional international economy integration, the regional international tax coordination will have broader future. Countries will strengthen their international cooperation for tax collection and management and combat international tax avoidance and tax evasion together.

From the present development trend of world economic, the future global economic integration will start from the regional economic integration. And the development of regional economic integration cannot be inseparable from tax coordination within the scope of region. In fact, there is no regional international economic integration without regional international tax coordination. For example, free trade areas and customs unions require coordinating the tariffs of member countries. The establishment of common market requires coordinating the domestic commodity tax and capital gains tax of members. In 2010, China and ASEAN established the largest free trade area in the world, which covered the largest population. 90% of the products traded between the two sides would be tariff-free. With the future development of regional international economic integration, not only will more countries participate in the activities of regional tax coordination, but the depth and range of regional tax coordination will also expand gradually. On the basis, to stop international tax avoidance and tax evasion and solve the problem of international double taxation, the tax authorities will strengthen their further international cooperation of tax collection and management on the exchange of tax information and the assistance of tax affairs each other.

1.2.4 International taxation will develop from the stage of non-normative to normative

Long time ago, international taxation issues were often settled by a number of unilateral solutions through modification on the domestic tax system or signed some bilateral tax agreements for coordination. It belonged to the non-normative development stage of international taxation. However, with the rapid expansion of international economic exchanges and the transnational income becoming more international, also the income tax is widely used, the above unilateral processing mode and non-normative bilateral tax agreements are unable to meet the needs of development. International community needs urgently a more complete and normative international tax coordination method to guide states to deal with tax distribution relationships between each other. So in 1963, the Organization for Economic Cooperation and Development (OECD) formulated and promulgated the "the Organization for Economic Co-operation and Development Model Tax Convention on Income and on Capital" which was revised in 1977 (hereinafter referred to as the "OECD Model Treaty"); United Nations tax experts group also enacted in 1968 and published in 1979 the "United Nations Model Double Taxation Convention between Developed and Developing Countries" (hereinafter referred to as the "UN Model Treaty"). Although the two models of international tax treaties have no legally binding to every country, in fact they have played an important exemplary role. They have become the rules for coordination of tax distribution relationship. They have made tax distribution relationships between countries more normative and they are the important signs of non-normative stage to normative stage of international taxation development.

1.2.5 With the development of electronic commerce (digital economy), there will be many new issues in the field of international taxation, which need to be studied and solved by governments and the international community

In e-commerce transactions, whether the customer's home country (income source country) should tax on the business income of foreign sellers; In e-commerce transactions, it is sometimes difficult to determine the nature and category of transaction income, which makes it difficult to distinguish taxation rights between relevant countries; Under the condition of electronic commerce, taxpayers' international tax evasion and tax avoidance activities will be more hidden, so the international community should study the measures to stop them. For these new conditions, the international community must come up with an effective solution as soon as possible. The first of the 15 action plans on Base Erosion and Profit Shifting (BEPS) published by the OECD in October,

Chapter 1　INTRODUCTION TO INTERNATIONAL TAXATION

2015 was about the digital economy. Unfortunately, the action plan did not offer a practical solution, only a commitment to produce a report reflecting the research's findings by 2020.

 Key words, phrases and special terms

revenue	财政收入
transnational income	跨国所得
tax distribution relationship	税收分配关系
resident taxpayer	居民纳税人
citizen taxpayer	公民纳税人
transnational investment	跨国投资
tax jurisdiction	税收管辖权
object of taxation	征税对象
source country	来源国
residence country	居住国
tax sovereignty	课税主权
government revenue collecting office	征税机关
European Union	欧洲联盟（欧盟）
value-added tax	增值税
tax base	税基
tax obligation	纳税义务
international double taxation	国际双重征税
tax burden	税负
domestic commodity tax	国内商品税
multinational corporation	跨国公司
international tax avoidance	国际避税
cooperative coordination	合作性协调
income tax	所得税
international tax agreements	国际税收协定
category of tax	税种
taxable items	税目
property tax	财产税
consumption tax	消费税
business tax	营业税
vehicle and vessel tax	车船税
turnover tax	流转税
real estate tax	房产税
specific property tax	个别财产税
general property tax	一般财产税
enterprise income tax	企业所得税
individual income tax	个人所得税

capital gains tax	资本利得税
gift tax	赠与税
settlement tax	遗产税
inheritance tax	继承税
legalentity	法人
national tax	国家税收
foreign tax	涉外税收
essential elements of tax system	税制要素
enterprises with foreign investment	外商投资企业
income tax of People's Republic of China on enterprises with foreign investment and foreign enterprises	外商投资企业和外国企业所得税
industrial and commercial consolidated tax	工商统一税
customs duty	关税
import duty	进口关税
export duty	出口关税
fiscal degradation	财政降格
tax evasion	偷税
free trade areas	自由贸易区
customs unions	关税同盟

Problems of thinking

1. What's the definition of international taxation? What's its characteristic?

2. What's the difference and connection between international taxation and national taxation?

3. How to distinguish international taxation from foreign tax?

4. What's the researching scope of international taxation?

5. What's the developmental trend of international taxation in the future?

Chapter 2

JURISDICTIONS OF INCOME TAX

 Ideological and political points of the course

1. Effectively safeguard the tax jurisdiction of our country, and the national sovereignty is sacrosanct.

2. Tax payers should maintain their tax credit and pay tax in accordance with laws and regulations.

 Learning Objectives

1. Master the concept of tax jurisdiction essentially and know the types of income tax jurisdictions.
2. Distinguish and understand the judgment norms on different tax jurisdictions.
3. Distinguish the obligation to pay tax between resident and non-resident taxpayer.
4. Know the implementation status of income tax jurisdictions in the world.

 Course Importing

In Britain, may a tramp who sleeps often in the park or on the road without the fixed domicile be the fiscal resident of the country?

 2.1 Introduction to tax jurisdiction and its establishment principles

2.1.1 Definition of tax jurisdiction

So many issues in international taxation such as the occurrence of double taxation and the coordination of tax distribution between countries are closely related to tax jurisdiction of relevant countries. Studying on tax jurisdiction is the important premise of solving international taxation problems.

Tax jurisdiction is the sovereignty of a country in tax. It is a kind of management power owned by a government when it exercises its tax sovereignty. It means that the government can decide on whom to levy, what to levy and how much can be levied. Tax jurisdiction is independent and exclusive, which means a state has the complete autonomy on tax when it processes its local tax affairs without being influenced by external interference and control.

2.1.2 The establishment principles of tax jurisdiction

The political power scope of a sovereign state can mainly reach to two aspects. On one hand, from the geographical concept, it includes the state's full space of its territory, territorial sea and air space. On the other hand, from the personal concept, it includes all of the citizens or residents in a country (including the natural person and the legal entity). Because the tax jurisdiction is an important part of national sovereignty, a state has the right to choose the establishment principles of tax jurisdiction from the above two different concepts. Respectively, they are called the principles of dependency and personality.

1. Principle of dependency

The principle of dependency is an establishment principle of tax jurisdiction when a state exercises its tax power according to the taxpayer's income sources place or the place where his economic activity locates.

According to the principle of dependency, a government can only exercise its tax power on the income derived from it or on the economic behavior occurred within its sovereignty. That is to say, the government can only levy on the taxpayer's income which comes from its boundary or the economic activities that the taxpayer is engaged within its territory in accordance with the provisions of its tax law. Meanwhile, the taxpayer's income from abroad will not be levied. On the income tax collection, according to the principle of dependency, the government has the power to levy on all of income earned within the boundary without considering the person who gets the income is the resident or foreigner.

Generally speaking, a state takes the principle of dependency on indirect tax, but for the income tax, it is different. It will take the principle of dependency on the non-resident taxpayers and take the principle of personality on the resident taxpayers.

2. Principle of personality

The principle of personality is another establishment principle of tax jurisdiction when a state exercises its tax power on all of its citizens and residents according to the taxpayer's nationality and domicile.

According to the principle of personality, the government has the power to levy on all the income earned by its domestic citizens and residents without considering the income coming from domestic or abroad. The principle of personality is often applied to direct tax like income tax and settlement tax.

2.1.3 The types of income tax jurisdictions

There are no uniform international rules for establishment and exercise of tax jurisdiction. Every sovereign state has the right to choose its tax jurisdiction based on its political & economic situation and fiscal policy. The income tax jurisdiction can be established in accordance with the principle of dependency and personality. They are the source jurisdiction and residence or citizen jurisdiction. The source jurisdiction and the residence jurisdiction are two basic types.

1. Source jurisdiction

Source jurisdiction is a kind of tax jurisdiction established in accordance with the principle of dependency. It means the government will only exercise its tax power over all the income earned or is considered being earned within its boundary. It is also called the geographical tax jurisdiction.

Income may be taxable under the tax laws of a country because of a nexus between the country and the activities that generate the income. According to international usage, a jurisdictional claim based on such a nexus is called "source jurisdiction". All countries imposing an income tax exercise source jurisdiction; that is, they tax income arising or having its source in their country.

2. Residence jurisdiction

Residence jurisdiction is another kind of tax jurisdiction established in accordance with the principle of personality. It means the government can impose on all the income earned by its residents who are specified in its tax law, including natural person and legal entity.

A country may also impose a tax on income because of a nexus between the country and the person earning the income. A jurisdictional claim over income based on a nexus between the country making that claim and the person subject to tax is called "residence jurisdiction". Persons subject to the residence jurisdiction of a country generally are taxable on their worldwide income, without reference to the source of the income. That is, the person is typically taxable on both domestic-source income and foreign-source income.

3. Citizen jurisdiction

Citizen jurisdiction is also a kind of tax jurisdiction established in accordance with the principle of personality. It means the government can impose on the worldwide income owned by its citizen who has its nationality.

2.2　The judgment norms on source jurisdiction

In the country which exercises source jurisdiction, the government will consider the source place of a taxpayer's income instead of the residence place where the taxpayer lives or his identification. It is the source place of income that determines the tax liability for taxpayer. Therefore, it is called "tax from the source". Obviously, the characteristic of source jurisdiction is that a government imposes only the income coming from domestic but does not impose income from aboard. Because this tax jurisdiction reflects not only the rationality of international economic interest distribution, but also the convenience of tax administrative, it has been recognized worldwide, and has been widely adopted.

The source place of income is the place where the taxpayer gets his income. It is the basis and standard for a government exercises its source jurisdiction to the taxpayer. When a country taxes the income of a person, at first, it must make it clear that the revenue or income actually comes from its territory. Income earned from a certain country refers to that income which derives from the boundary regardless of its payment location. Source place of income and income payment location are two different concepts. They are consistent sometimes and inconsistent sometimes. Some income comes from one country, but its payment location is not in the same country meanwhile. For example, the wages or salaries of the foreigner working in China originate from China but is paid by his employer abroad. The wages of staff sent abroad by Chinese government are paid by China, but actually its origin is abroad. As source place of personal income is not consistent with its payment location sometimes, it is clearly stipulated in every country's tax law that all income gained from the domestic territory; no matter its payment location is at home or abroad, it is derived from the country and will be subject to individual income tax. It shows the implementation of source jurisdiction depending on the determination of income source place. That is how to make reasonable and scientific explanation to the income source place to determine whether the taxpayer and the country have a nexus with regard to income. Ultimately, the country can determine whether the taxpayer's income is derived from its territory or not. If it is, the taxpayer has the domestic tax obligations. If not, the taxpayer hasn't. Not only do investors and transnational taxpayers pay close attention to this problem, but also it is one of the core problems for international tax coordination and specification. However, the determination of income source place has to rely on certain standards. Because there are different income projects such as business income, service income, investment income, and other income, the judgment norms used by different countries on source jurisdiction are also different.

2.2.1 The determination of source place on business income

Business income is the operation profit which is the net income of individual or legal entity which is engaged in productive or non-productive activities. Whether the income is the taxpayer's taxable income depends on mainly whether the operation activities is the taxpayer's main economic activities or not. For example, dividend and interest of a security company which is engaged in securities investment belong to the company's business income, but the dividend and interest of a manufacturing company because of possession of other company's equity and debt do not belong to its business income. Now, the standards for judging source place of business income include the following two norms.

1. Permanent establishment norms (PE norms)

A PE is a fixed place or a fixed base of business through which the business of an enterprise is wholly or partly carried on. Its scope is very wide, including a management agency, a branch, an office, a factory, a workshop, a mine, an oil or gas well, a quarry, a construction site and so on. Countries of civil law system adopt the PE norms to judge whether or not the taxpayers' business income derives from the country.

In general, a PE must have the following three basic conditions.

①A PE must be a place of business and it has no size limitation. Usually it refers to all the housing, venues, equipment or facilities such as machinery equipment, warehouse, booth and so on without consideration whether they belong to the taxpayer himself or are rent.

②A PE must be fixed. It must operate at a specific geographical location and its activities at that location must endure for more than a temporary period (generally for more than 6 months). It does not include any business activities without specific location. However, the temporary interruption or pause of business activities at specific location does not affect the presence of a PE. Therefore, the basic condition for a PE is that the place of business is relatively stable or permanent instead of temporary. It has to show that it is permanent.

③A PE must be a place through which the business of an enterprise is wholly or partly carried on. It is not a place for an enterprise's activities of non-business preparation or auxiliary.

According to the PE norms, if a non-resident company has a PE in a country and achieves business income through the PE, then the source country will be able to conclude the business income coming from the country and the income will be taxable. Conversely, if not, the government can't conclude the business income of the non-resident company is derived from the country and the income will not be taxable. Obviously, in the state which adopts PE norms, whether the business income of the non-resident company is taxable or not mainly depends on whether the company sets up a PE in the country or not.

But there is another problem here: if a non-resident company has a PE in a country but its business income is not derived from the PE, can the government levy on the business income? In this issue, countries in the world adhere to two principles: One is the actual income principle (also known as the attribution principle) which refers to that a country will tax only on the actual business income of the non-resident company through the domestic PE and the business income through other ways except for PE will not be taxable. The other principle is the force of attraction rule (also known as the attraction principle). It means if a non-resident company has a PE in the country, though some of its business activities are not carried on through the PE, as long as the business activities are the same or similar to those activities conducted through the PE, the business income not achieved through the PE will be attributable to its PE and be taxable in the country.

China also adopts the PE norms to judge the source place of business income. At the same time, our country does not exercise the attraction principle for taxation on foreign enterprises. As stipulated in Article 3 (2) of *the Enterprises Income Tax Law of the People's Republic of China* that all of the non-resident companies which establish the institutions or places in China should pay enterprise income tax to China on their income from China and attributable to the institutions or places. And it is stipulated in the Article 3 (3) that all of the non-resident companies which do not establish the institutions or places in China or those that establish the institutions or places in China but their income have no actual connection with the institutions or places should pay enterprise income tax to China on their income originated from China. The Article 4 stipulates that the tax rate of enterprise income tax is 25% and the non-resident company which gets the income stipulated in the Article 3 (3) is applicable to 20%. The above regulations show that if a non-resident company does not set up institutions or places in China and signs contract with the domestic units or individuals directly (like the selling of production), the income it gets can not be considered as the income derived from China. Therefore, Chinese government can not exercise source jurisdiction on the income. For example in 2018, an American Inc which did not establish any institutions in China sold a machine to a Chinese enterprise directly with the selling price was 1,000,000 Yuan. It obtained sales profit of 100,000 Yuan. According to the PE norms, the 100,000 Yuan didn't originate from China. So the American Inc did not need to pay tax to Chinese government. But if the American Inc set up offices in China and sold the machine through the offices, the sales profit of 100,000 Yuan was taxable in China.

2. Trading floor norms

The countries of common law system often adopt the trading floor norms to judge the source place of business income instead of the PE norms. For example, in British law, only the income trading in the UK is the source income. The transactions here include all kinds of trading and manufacturing activities. On confirming of whether the trade activity happens in the UK, it is mainly based on whether or not the trading floor is in the UK. As for manufacturing profit, the place where the manufacturing activity takes place is the source place. Canada has the similar requirements with UK. It regards the habitual place where the contracts are signed as the trading place. It is also stipulated in the tax law of the United States that the profit earned in the country for engaging in a trade or business activity is the source income from the United States. But when it judges the source place of trade profit, it takes the actual sales place as the source place instead of the place where the contracts are signed which is slightly different from Canada and UK. On confirming of the source place where the manufacturing profit comes from, just like the UK, the United States regards the place where the product is made or processed as the source place.

2.2.2 The determination of source place on service income

According to the condition of whether the service income relies on employment, service income can be divided into independent service income and dependent service income. Independent service income refers to the income achieved by an individual of free occupation who is engaged in the performance of professional services or other independent activities. "Professional services" refer to individuals engage in various unmercenary labors independently that includes the services of physicians, lawyers, engineers, architects, dentists, and accountants, as well as independent scientific, literary, artistic, educational and teaching activities. Independent service income is independent and random. Dependent service income is referred to the wages, salaries and other rewards of individuals who are employed by employers.

Now, the standards for judging source place of service income include the following three norms.

1. Place of rendering service norms

It means where the transnational taxpayer renders his service or in which country he works, the income he earns is viewed as the income originated from this country. For independent services, the norms focus mainly on the location where the fixed base locates. If a person has a fixed base in a country like the clinics, offices etc, and achieves income through the fixed base, so the country can determine the income originating from its territory. For dependent services, the norms focus mainly on the location where the employee is employed. The country where the employee is employed is the source place of dependent services.

2. Income payer norms

It means the country, the fixed base or the PE where the taxpayer who pays for the service locates is the source place of income. If a transnational taxpayer's service income is paid by the residents of the country or the PE located in the country, then the country is the source place of this service income.

3. Place of signing contract norms

It means the place of signing contracts is viewed as the source place of employment income.

At present, many countries adopt the place of rendering service norms which means the government can determine the source place of service income according to the location where the service is performed. For example, it is stipulated in Article 5 of *Regulations for Implementation of Individual Income Tax Law of the People's Republic of China* that all the service income from China for the reasons of job, employment or contract performance is viewed as the income derived from China, no matter its location of payment is in China or not and the income shall be taxable. As stipulated in Article 7 of *Regulations for Implementation of Enterprises Income Tax Law of the People's Republic of China* that the place of rendering service is the source place of service income. The regulations of American tax law are similar to Chinese. As long as a person renders service in the United States, the government will regard the service income as the income derived from the country, no matter the nationality of the employer or the employee is the United States of America, as well as the residence or the payment of the employer or the employee is in the United States or not. Meanwhile, some countries adopt the income payer norms to determine the source place of service income. For example, the English court has always insisted that the source place of employment income is the place of paying income. Brazil adopts the income payer norms also. Countries adopt the place of signing contracts norms include Ireland, etc.

2.2.3 The determination of source place on investment income

Investment income refers to the income earned by the taxpayer because he provides his capital, property or right for others to use, mainly including dividend, interest, royalties and rents, etc. Dividend is the investor's income earned because he owns a company's share or other similar equity. Interest is the investor's income earned on basis of his creditor's rights. Royalties are the investor's income because he offered his patent, trademark right, good-will, copyright, marketing right, proprietary technology or other intangible property to others for usage. Rent is the use fee collected by the lesser to the lessee.

Investment income has the characteristics that the payer is relatively stable, while the beneficiary is scattered. Especially in the transnational indirect investment, investors are not necessarily live or perform in the country where the investment project locates. When the beneficiary and payer of investment income, such as the creditor and debtor, the providers and users of franchise are in the same country, it is not difficult to determine the source place of this kind of investment income. That is to say, it comes from this country. But if the right providers and users are not in the same country, that is to say, they are in different countries, how can we determine the source place of this kind of investment income? In some countries, especially in developed and developing countries, they have different views. In order to improve the transfer mobility of capital, developed countries generally advocate that the source place of this kind of income is the place where the right provider locates and the income should be levied independently by the country where the right provider lives. On the contrary, for reducing the loss of foreign exchange, some developing countries view the place of this kind of income as the source place where the right use. They advocate that the implementation of source jurisdiction should be exercised by the countries which pay the dividends, interest and royalties which means it is taxable in the country where the right user lives.

So, international societies normally distribute reasonably the tax sovereignty of the relevant countries where the providers and users live, based on the principle of benefit sharing together. In the UN Model Treaty, it is stipulated that the investment income can be levied by the country where the right provider lives and the country where the right user lives can exercise source jurisdiction also. That is to say, both countries have the right to impose. But when it is imposed by the country where the user lives, it must have a maximum tax amount to leave adequate tax room for the country where the right provider lives. The maximum tax amount is negotiated usually by the Contracting States. In the tax treaty of China and Japan, it is stipulated that the dividend, interest and royalties originates from China but paid to Japanese resident shall be viewed as the income derived from China on the condition that the payee is the actual beneficiary. Chinese government can impose the income but the tax rate shall not be over 10%.

If the dividend, interest and royalties are achieved through the PE, they should be included in the business profit of the PE and be levied on the normal rate of enterprise income tax. If they are not achieved through the PE, the source country will levy generally withholding tax on the gross income with low tax rate. The so-called gross income refers to the income without deducting cost. Withholding tax is a kind of proportional tax whose rate is lower than the rate of enterprise income tax. It is adopted by the relevant countries independently. This method, on one hand, ensures that the relevant countries can share the tax power equally; on the other hand, it takes the deducted cost factors into consideration in determining the rate. So, the tax base is still the net income of investment.

2.2.4 The determination of source place on property income

Property income is the income earned by the taxpayer because he owns, uses, transfers his property (also called capital gains).

As for the real estate, all countries take it for granted that the place where the real estate actually locates is the source place of property income. For example, it is stipulated in Article 7 of *Regulations for Implementation of Enterprises Income Tax Law of the People's Republic of China* that the source place of real estate income is the place where the real estate locates.

But as for chattel, the rules for judging the source place of property income are not the same. Some countries regard the place where the chattel is sold or transferred (the place where the chattel's ownership transferred) as the source place. For example, the United States adopted this rule before 1986. Some countries regard the place where the chattel owner lives as the source place. (For example, at present, the United States takes this rule to determine the source place for transferring or selling stock, bond, commodity and other investment real estate). Some countries regard the place where the transferred chattel actually locates as the source place. China takes the transfer place standard and the transfer residence standard as the norms to determine the source place for chattel transferring. As stipulated in Article 5 of *Regulations for Implementation of Individual Income Tax Law of the People's Republic of China* that the income due to transferring other properties (the real estates except for buildings, land use rights, etc.) is viewed as the income derived from China. It is also stipulated in Article 7 of *Regulations for Implementation of Enterprises Income Tax Law of the People's Republic of China* that the place where the enterprise or institutions transferring the chattel locates is the source place. The source place of transferring income for equity investment asset is the place where the enterprise invested locates.

2.2.5   The determination of source place on inheritance income

For the transnational inheritance income, the determination of source country is different depending on specific circumstances. When the inheritance is a real estate or a tangible chattel, the country where the inheritance locates is the source place and the country where the inheritance locates will exercise the source jurisdiction on the inheritance income. When the inheritance is stock or creditor's right, the place where the company who issues the stock or the debtor lives is the source place and the residence country can exercise the source jurisdiction on the inheritance income.

2.3   The judgment norms on residence jurisdiction

When a state exercises its residence jurisdiction, what it considers is the resident identity of a taxpayer instead of the source place of the income. It is based on whether the taxpayer lives in the country or has the resident identity to determine its jurisdiction and taxation scope. Generally speaking, all the domestic residents (including natural person and legal entity), regardless of the income or gains including how many kinds and regardless of it coming from home or abroad, the residence country has the power to tax on the taxpayer's worldwide income. So we can see that the characteristics of residence jurisdiction are the equal taxation on the resident taxpayer's domestic-source income and foreign-source income.

A "resident" of a country is an individual or a legal entity which is taxable in that country "for reason of his domicile, residence, place of management or any other criterion of a similar nature". In the area of tax, a resident is a person who has a nexus to a country to be liable to tax. For a natural person, this so-called "tax resident" is different from the concept of resident in residential management regulations. Because there are residential management regulations in so many countries, the foreigners must have the residence license issued by the governments for legal residence. Otherwise, it is illegal residence and the person is not the legal resident of this country. But the concept of resident in tax collection and management focuses on the taxpayer's fact of long live in the country which does not belong to the residential management regulations. It means a taxpayer can be the tax resident if he lives in a country for a long time even without the residence license. In order to differ from the concept of resident in residential management regulations, the tax resident is called "the fiscal resident". The following resident concept mentioned in the next chapters refers to the fiscal resident.

The determination of resident identity relies on some kinds of criterion. The norms of judging the resident identity in the world are different.

2.3.1 The judgment norms on resident identity of individuals

For an individual, resident is a counter concept with respect to visitors and travelers. If a person is a resident of a country, it means he has lived in the country for a long time or intended to residence in the country. He is not a transit traveler or is going to stay in the country for a short time. An ideal test of residence is one that individuals can apply to obtain a clear, certain, and fair result. Certainty is highly desirable because the tax consequences for residents and non-residents are very different, and individuals need to know whether they are residents or non-residents. On the specific situation of every country, the determination of resident identity for an individual is reflected generally through the following three norms.

1. Legal norms

Legal norms are also called intention norms. It means if a taxpayer has the subjective desire to live in a country which exercises the residence jurisdiction, he will become the resident of this country. That is to say, the foreign immigrant who has the desire to live in a country for irregular time and obtains the passport, visa and some other residence certificate is the resident of this country. The residence country has the power of taxation on his worldwide income. Persons out of the above scope are non-residents and the residence country can not exercise the residence jurisdiction on them.

 Teaching Case of 2-1

Before 1984, when the American government determined the identity of a foreigner who entered into its territory, that was whether he was a passerby or a resident, the deciding factor was his living desire. After 1984, the American government regarded the foreigner who obtained the permanent residence right which was the so-called "green card" holder as its resident. Even though the resident didn't live in the United States actually, from the January 1st of the following year after his obtaining the "green card", he would become the fiscal resident of the United States. Because the act itself of holding "green card" showed that the person had the long-term living wishes in the United States.

 Teaching Case of 2-2

It is stipulated in Greece tax law that if a person intends to live in Greece, he is the fiscal Greek resident. Britain law also stipulates that an adult's domicile relies on his or her permanent resident

desire. In the 1970s there was a similar case in the UK. There was a gentleman who was born in Canada in 1910. In 1932 he joined the Royal Air Force of the UK and retired from the army in 1959. After that, he had been working in an British private research institution until 1961 and retired thoroughly. After his retirement, his British wife and he continued to live in England. During this period, the gentleman kept retaining his Canadian nationality and passport and often had some financial dealings with Canada. He also hoped that his wife and he could go back to Canada in an old age. He also expressed that if his wife died before him, he would go back to Canada to spend the rest of his life. The court judged that even though the gentleman had lived in Britain for 44 years, he was still not a UK tax resident.

2. Domicile norms

Domicile norms are also called household register norms which mean if a taxpayer has a permanent domicile or a habitual residence in the country which exercises residence jurisdiction, he is the resident of this country and his wholly worldwide income will be taxable to the government. Person without domicile in the country is the non-resident and the government has no power to exercise its residence jurisdiction on him.

This so-called "domicile" is a permanent dwelling. Usually, it refers to a taxpayer's long-term rather than temporary possession of the dwelling. The appearance of the domicile must be obvious, it is generally the location of a person's family (spouse, children) or the place where his principal property is located. According to the concept, all the individuals who have domiciles in a country are the domestic residents of this country and they have to bear the unlimited tax liabilities of the residence country. Otherwise, they will be viewed as the non-residents and the government will not exercise its residence jurisdiction on them such as Japan and Germany.

Domicile is also an important standard in our country for judging the resident identity of individuals. As stipulated in Article 1 of *the Individual Income Tax Law of the People's Republic of China* that for an individual owning domicile in China or lives in China without domicile for more than 183 days, all of his income originated from China and aboard is taxable. Besides, it is stipulated in Article 2 of *Regulations for Implementation of Enterprises Income Tax law of the People's Republic of China* that individual owning domicile in China is the individual who lives in China habitually for the household registration, family or the economic connection. It shows in Chinese tax law, the standard for judging personal residence identity is the "habitual residence". Here "in the Chinese habitual residence" means after the individual finishes his learning, working, visiting relatives, tourism outside of Chinese, he must return to China to live. While, the individual does not have to live in China actually. It means as long as an individual's "habitual residence" is in China, in a certain taxable year, even he does not live in China actually, he is still regarded as having residence in China and he is the Chinese resident and taxpayer this year.

3. Residence norms

This so-called "residence" is a habitual dwelling. Generally, it refers to a temporary dwelling place of a person who keeps staying in a country for a period of time. It is the taxpayer's irregular and temporary dwelling for some purposes like business, education, and making a living. It can be the house owned by the taxpayer and the apartment or hotel rented by the taxpayer. Because the residence is an important sign to determine the tax liability, in some countries, it is also called "the fiscal domicile". Countries take the residence norms include Britain, Germany, Canada, Australia and so on.

Compared with domicile, residence in many countries has not the strict legal definition. Consequently, the understanding and judgment norms with regard to residence in different countries are not the same. But it is generally believed that they have at least two differences:

①Domicile is a personal permanent dwelling, but residence is just the personal temporary dwelling for some reasons.

②Domicile usually involves an intention which means that an individual intends to live in a place permanently. While the residence is usually referred to the real estate for personal long-term effective use which emphasizes the fact of living, that is to say, somebody has lived in someplace for a long time or he has the condition for a long period of residence. It does not emphasize his long time living willing.

 Teaching Case of 2-3

It is stipulated in the Britain tax law that as long as an individual has residence in Britain, no matter how long he lives, if he has ever stayed in Britain within a taxable year, he is regarded as the Britain resident. Also, it is stipulated in the German tax law that only one of the two norms of domicile and habitual residence exists, it can be viewed as the individual's domicile and the taxpayer is the Germany resident. In the stipulation of "habitual residence", an individual who has physical presence in Germany for 3 months is regarded as the person who has the habitual residence in Germany and he is the German resident.

4. Present time norms

Present time norms are also called stayed time norms or residence time norms. It means if an individual's presence or residence in a country is over the stated time, he will be the resident of this country and his worldwide income will be taxable in this country, too. If his present time is shorter than the stated time, he is just the non-resident and the country can not exercise its residence jurisdiction on him. So many countries adopt the present time norms such as Britain, Germany, Japan, France, India, Switzerland, China, etc. The norms emphasizes the fact that in a taxable year whether the individual is present in the country or not and for how long he is present, without considering where he is present. As in 1928, in the trial of a tax case, the British courts stated that a tramp without the fixed domicile and slept often in the park or on the road may be the fiscal resident of the country.

However, when countries adopting present time norms determine the individual's identity, the specific provisions and requirements of present time or period are not the same. As specified in the tax law of Britain, Germany, Canada and China that individuals present in the country for 183 days or more in a taxable year are residents. The present time is different in Japan, Korea and Argentina whose present time is 365 days or more. But even in the countries adopting the same present time norms, there is difference in calculation of present time which is reflected in the following three aspects.

1) The difference in continuous and cumulative calculation of present time

Some countries adopting present time norms stipulate that the only the continuous present time is over the stated time in the tax law, a transnational individual can be viewed as the domestic resident. For example, it is specified in Chinese tax law that an individual who has lived in China continuously for more than 183 days, no matter what his nationality is, he will be regarded as Chinese resident. But some countries stipulate that as long as the cumulative present time is over the stated time in the tax law, a transnational individual can be viewed as the domestic resident. For example, it is specified in Japanese tax law that an individual who has lived in Japan continuously or cumulatively for more than 1 year is the Japanese resident.

2) The difference in calculation of starting point for present time

Some countries determine the individual's resident identity according to the transnational taxpayer's present time in a fiscal year is over the stated time or not. If the wholly present time of an individual exceeds the stated time but it straddles over two different fiscal years, and it is shorter than the stated time in a single fiscal year, the individual can not be considered as the resident of this country. As is specified in Chinese tax law, an individual who has lived in China for more than 183 days is an individual who has lived in China cumulatively for more than 183 days in a fiscal year. For the individual's temporary departure①, the departure days will not be deducted. Other countries determine the individual's resident identity according to the individual's physical present in this country whether is over the stated time or not. As long as an individual's present time is over the stated time, he will be the resident of this country. It is not important with regard to whether the present time is in a single fiscal year or not. That is to say, as long as an individual lives in the country for the stated time in a fiscal year, an accounting year or any continuous 12 months, he is the resident of this country.

3) The difference in regulations between different countries

Of course, the methods of calculating present days must be specified in the tax law when the country adopts the present time norms.In this issue, the regulations are not the same.

Most of the countries in the world (like the United States) stipulate that the individual's present time less than a day is calculated as a day. It means as long as an individual presents in a country for several hours or several minutes, his present time is calculated as a day. Some countries (like the Ireland) stipulate that only the individual presents in the country until midnight, his present time is calculated as a day. Some other countries (like the Britain) calculate present time in hours. Only when the individual's present time added together in the country reaches 24 hours is that he is just present for a day. There are similar regulations in Individual Income Tax Law of the People's Republic of China. When the present time for individuals without domicile in China is calculated, staying in China for more than 24 hours a day shall be counted as the present days in China. The above regulation of calculation method is very important. Because the calcula-

---

①Temporary departure refers to the departure which is not over 30 days for one time or is not over cumulative 90 for many times.

ting of present time for more than a day or less a day maybe change the resident identity of individuals who have no domiciles in China. It maybe influence his tax liability in China, therefore.

In the above three norms, the legal norms (also called intention norms) belong to the subjective category and it is hard to judge accurately. So countries generally do not adopt it separately, but they use it in combination with other norms. For example, individuals present in Brazil for more than 1 year are Brazil residents regardless of their living desires. But for the foreigners who have obtained the long-term resident visa, if they are willing to be Brazil residents, they can be viewed as Brazil residents despite their present time is less than a year. Because the domicile norms have the fixed and permanent characteristics, it is easy to determine the taxpayer's resident identity. However, when we determine a taxpayer's identity in the income tax law, we should much more consider the taxpayer's actual location of economic activity. The domicile, though as a personal legal permanent dwelling, does not necessarily reflect a person's real activity place. In the day of frequent international exchanges for scientific and technological personnel, the phenomenon of individual's living out of domicile is increasingly apparent. Clearly, only by adopting the domicile norms to determine a taxpayer's resident identity, is it defective. Therefore, some countries adopt other auxiliary norms to make up the inadequacy of domicile norms. Compared with domicile norms, it is more reasonable to use residence to determine an individual's resident identify. Because it reflects the contact between the personal and his main economic activity place to a large extent. However, there is deficiency in residence norms. The residence itself is a vague concept in relevant national tax laws due to the lack of some objective and unified identification mark, there is still great flexibility in practical application. It is easy to cause the dispute between the taxpayers and the tax authorities. In contrast, the present time norms are more specific and clear, it is easy for the implementation in practice. But its prescribed length of residence is often inversely proportional to the scope of implementation of residence jurisdiction. Obviously, the above three kinds of norms have their own advantages and disadvantages. Because of this, for better implementation of residence jurisdiction, many countries often adopt two or more norms in practice to determine accurately the resident identity for individuals. Our country adopts both the domicile norms and the present time norms to determine the taxpayer's resident identity. It is stipulated in Article 1 of *the Individual Income Tax Law of the People's Republic of China* that for an individual owning domicile in China or living in China cumulatively without domicile for more than 183 days, all his income originated from China and aboard is taxable.

2.3.2 The judgment norms on resident identity of legal entity

Legalentity is the entity of a civil legal relationship which is different and relative to individual. It generally refers to the social organization established by the relevant state laws and legal procedures, having necessary property and institutions. It is able to enjoy civil rights and bear civil obligation independently and can sue and be sued in the court. Similar to imposing on individuals, when a country that implements residence jurisdiction imposes on legal entities, firstly it also has to determine whether they are the domestic residents or not. At present, the judgment norms on residence of legal entity in the world include the following standards.

Chapter 2 JURISDICTIONS OF INCOME TAX

1. Place-of-incorporation test

Place-of-incorporation test is also called legal test which means all the legal entities established in the country according to the national law are the residents of this country, no matter their head offices, managements or business activities places are inbound or outbound. The incorporation place is also called "legal domicile". One of the obvious advantages of this test is its easy operation (because the company's registration place is unique and easy to be identified). It provides simplicity and certainty to the government and the taxpayer. It also allows a taxpayer to choose its initial place of residence freely. Countries that market themselves as tax havens typically offer convenient and inexpensive arrangements for incorporating under their laws. But it is disadvantageous to the tax avoidance for legal entity by means of changing its incorporation place. In general, a corporation can not freely change its place of incorporation without triggering a tax on the gains that may have accrued on its property, including intangible property that may have a very high market value. It places some limits on the ability of corporations to shift their residence country for tax avoidance purposes, so many countries use the place-of-incorporation test.

Countries adopting the place-of-incorporation test include the United States, Britain, Japan, France, Germany, Belgium, Italy, Norway, New Zealand, Australia, Finland, Sweden, Switzerland, Denmark, India, Thailand, China and so on. For example, it is stipulated in American tax law that any transnational corporation which registers in American state according to any of its state laws, no matter its head office is in American or not, also no matter its owner is American or foreigner, it is American resident corporation and the government of the United States has the power to levy on its worldwide income.

2. Place-of-management test

Place-of-management test means all the legal entities which establish management institutions in the country that implements residence jurisdiction are the residents of this country. As long as the management institution of a legal entity is established in a country, no matter it registers in other country, it is the resident of this country. The management place is sometimes called "Fiscal domicile". But the corporation's management place is easy to transfer and it will not generally trigger a tax on the gains that it may have accrued on properties, it is easily exploited for tax avoidance reasons of legal entity. We assume, for example, that M company (MCo) is a corporation managed in Country A, which uses a place-of-management test. MCo has developed valuable intangible property and intends to license to taxpayers located in Country B. To avoid tax in Country A on the expected royalties, MCo shifts its place of management to Country H, a low-tax country. The large accrued gain on MCo's intangible property is not taxable in Country A because no transfer of that property occurred. MCo then licenses the technology to users in Country B. The royalties received by MCo escape taxation in Country A because MCo is not resident in Country A and that country does not tax foreign royalties earned by foreign corporations. If Country A in the above example used the place-of-incorporation test, MCo could not transfer its residence to Country H without undergoing a corporate reorganization that resulted in the transfer of its assets to a corporation organized in Country H. Such a transfer would triggered a realization of the accrued gain on the intangible property, thereby limiting or even eliminating MCo's opportunity for tax avoidance.

Place-of-management of legal entity can be divided into two concepts, which are the center of management & control and the place of effective management. In practice, some countries adopt the center of management & control test to determine the residence of legal entity such as Australia, Canada, Germany, Ireland, New Zealand, Norway, Singapore, and the UK; Some other countries adopt the place of effective management test to determine the residence of legal entity such as Belgium, Denmark, Portugal, Spain, South Africa, etc. In general, the center of management and control is the highest authority of the corporation which is responsible for the corporation's policy formulation and operation control. These rights include the corporation's financial power, the acquisition and disposition of property, business decision-making power and the power of appointment and removal of senior management personnel. Generally speaking, the place of using the powers should be the residence where the individuals possessing these powers live or the regular place where they meet to use the powers. For the corporation's directors often hold the above important powers, so many countries (such as Australia, Canada, Ireland, New Zealand, the UK, etc.) determine a corporation's center of management and control based on their directors' or main directors' residences or the place where their board of directors meet. In addition, some countries also determine a corporation's center of management and control according to the shareholders' meeting place or the location where the corporation's records storage.

What's the definition of effective management organization? This problem is a little complicated and currently there is no a unified answer to the question. In some countries (such as Denmark, Holland and Spain), it refers to the corporation's day-to-day business management organization which is responsible for the implementation of decision-making and the specific operations management. In some other countries (such as Switzerland), it refers to the corporation's decision-making organization, it is the same concept with the center of management & control.

3. Place-of-head office test

Place-of-head office test is also called household register test which refers to any legal entity who establishes head office in the country that exercises residence jurisdiction is the resident legal entity of this country.

The head office is a corporation's overall management and control organization which is responsible for the corporation's vital decision-making, the corporation's entire business activities and its unified business accounting profit and loss, including various types of headquarters, general factories and companies which are viewed as management and control. Any corporation or enterprise who establishes head office actually in the country that exercises residence jurisdiction is the resident legal entity of this country. Countries adopting place-of-head office test to determine the residence of transnational legal entity include France, Belgium, Japan, China, etc.

4. Place-of-capital controlled test

Place-of-capital controlled test is also called the controlled vote test which means the government uses the resident identities of shareholders who control the voting power of the corporation as the basis to determine a corporation's resident identity. As is stipulated in the tax law of the United States, for a transnational corporation although it is registered abroad, as long as more than 50% of its voting stocks are held by the American shareholders, it can be identified as the American resident corporation and the American government can exercise jurisdiction on it. But if a legal entity is jointly held and controlled by residents of different countries, or its stocks are publicly transacted, it is difficult to adopt the place-of-capital controlled test. The corporation's profit then should be distributed like the partnership and should be taxable by different shareholders in different countries.

From the above several tests and their practices, we know that so many countries adopt two or more tests to determine the resident identity of legal entity. Because each test has its advantages and disadvantages, using a single test is not useful to safeguard national tax equity. Compared with the past, new Chinese Enterprise Income Tax Law has great changes in the judgment on the enterprises' resident identity. The new test is that as long as a corporation meets one of the two tests, place-of-incorporation test or place-of-management test, it is Chinese resident corporation. For example, it is stipulated in Article 2 of *the Enterprises Income Tax Law of the People's Republic of China* that the resident corporation in this law refers to the corporation registered in China or in foreign country but its actual management organization is in China. The regulations are in fact similar to those of the UK, Ireland, Portugal, and Switzerland. According to this judgment norm, if a corporation registered in foreign country establishes its effective management organization in China, the corporation is the Chinese resident corporation. On the contrary, if a corporation registered in China transfers its effective management organization out of China, it is still the Chinese resident corporation.

2.3.3 Tax liabilities of resident and non-resident

For a taxpayer, his tax liability is closely related to the types of tax jurisdiction and the tax administrative system which are exercised by the government, it is also connected with his resident identity in this country. Here, we will analyze the different tax liabilities of resident and non-resident in combination with some national tax laws.

1. Tax liabilities of resident

As is mentioned above, a country which implements residence jurisdiction will levy on its residents' all income derived from home or aboard. From the view of taxpayer, he will pay taxes to the residence country government not only on his income within this country, but also on his foreign income. The tax liability on the worldwide income for a resident taxpayer is called the unlimited tax liability. In a country which implements residence jurisdiction, the taxpayer, no matter whether he is an individual or a legal entity, must fulfill the unlimited tax liability to the government of residence country.

In practice, some countries classify the individuals into long-term residents and short-term residents, and both of them have the unlimited tax liabilities. But the short-term residents bear the conditional unlimited tax liabilities and the long-term residents bear the unconditional unlimited liabilities. For example, it is stipulated in Article 6 of the *Regulations for Implementation of Individual Income Tax Law of the People's Republic of China* that the foreign income of an individual who has presence in China for more than 1 year but less than 6 years (he is a short-term resident) and has no domicile in China is taxable on the part paid by the domestic corporation, enterprise, other organization or individual upon the approval of the competent tax authorities. That is to say, the short-term resident does not have to pay taxes to Chinese government on his foreign income paid by the foreign corporation, enterprise or individual. It shows that the short-term residents have conditional unlimited tax liabilities in China. Also is it stipulated in the Article 6 that for an individual who has presence in China for more than 6 years, from the No.7 year, as long as he lives in China for more than 183 days, his worldwide income is taxable to Chinese government. But if he lives in China less than 183 days, only his income derived from China in this taxable year is taxable to Chinese government. For example, a foreigner came to work in China at the end of October in 2009. From then on, he had been living and working in China. In 2015, the foreigner left China to perform his duty in country of citizenship. He was absent in China for 35 days and then came back to China to continue his living and working. Because the temporary departure specified in Chinese tax law is not over 30 days for one time, his departure in 2015 did not belong to the temporary departure and he was not a Chinese resident in that year. In 2015, only his income derived from China was taxable to Chinese government.

  The unlimited tax liability for a legal entity in some country has its specific characteristics. In some developed countries like the United States, Britain and Canada, a legal entity has to pay taxes on its worldwide income which is the same as an individual. But it also stipulates that for a domestic company, before its dividend or profit derived from a foreign subsidiary and repatriated to the residence country, it needn't pay tax on them to the domestic income tax. After their repatriation, they are taxable in the residence country. Since the corporation's tax liability on its overseas dividend or profit is not generated at the same time when its overseas income generates and it is deferred to the time when the overseas income is repatriated to the residence country, the above regulations are generally called "deferral". Apparently, deferral is a kind of temporary negation of global income taxation principle according to the resident jurisdiction. The implementation of deferral in developed countries is connected with the fact that they admit the independent legal status of the foreign subsidiary. Because, if the residence country where the parent corporation locates taxes on the profit derived from the foreign subsidiary without considering whether the overseas income is repatriated or not, it means tearing up the "veil" of its foreign subsidiary and regarding the foreign subsidiary and domestic parent corporation as a whole to tax. The inevitable result is a negation of independent legal status of the foreign subsidiary. Of course, the implementation of deferral in developed countries is beneficial to their participation of international competition for their domestic companies. Because the developed countries had higher income tax rate before, in the provisions of deferral, when the domestic companies invest in some developing countries with lower income tax rate, as long as the profit of foreign subsidiaries is not repatriated to the residence countries, the foreign investment income of the parent corporations in developed countries do not have to bear the higher tax burden of the residence countries. It is very favorable for the domestic company with lower tax burden to compete with local company in developing countries. In addition, due to the inflation of the residence country where the parent corporation locates, if the parent corporation retains the foreign dividend or profit in aboard for some time and repatriates it, the value of tax paid to the residence country will be greatly reduced. Stanley Surrey, who was the assistant secretary of the United States Treasury and the professor of the law college of American Harvard University once pointed out that if the American corporation retained the profit of its controlled foreign corporation in overseas for 15 years and remitted it back, the profit was not taxable in fact. It is necessary to point out that there is no the regulation of deferral in Chinese tax law.

2. Tax liabilities of non-resident

In a country which implements residence jurisdiction and source jurisdiction, the non-resident taxpayer only has to pay tax on the income earned from this country to the government. The tax liability on income derived from a country for a taxpayer is called limited tax liability. The taxpayer, no matter whether he is an individual or a legal entity, must fulfill his limited tax liability in the non-residence country (the source country or the host country).

2.4 The judgment norms on citizen jurisdiction

2.4.1 The concept of citizen jurisdiction

Citizen jurisdiction is a kind of tax jurisdiction established according to the principle of personality, which means that the government has the power to levy on the worldwide income of its citizens.

When a government exercises its citizen jurisdiction, it considers only thetaxpayer's citizen identity instead of his residence. Based on whether a taxpayer owns the domestic citizenship, the government can determine whether it can impose on the taxpayer's income or not. Its characteristic is that the income derived from home and abroad is equally taxable.

2.4.2 The determination of citizen identity

When a government exercises its citizen jurisdiction, it must first consider the nexus between the taxpayer and the country. Citizens or nationals usually refer to individuals having certain nationalities and owning legal rights and obligations, and sometimes it also include legal entities, partnerships and groups under the law. The determination of an individual's citizenship depends on mainly his nationality. If he has the nationality of a country, he is the citizen of this country. That means the prerequisite for determination of citizenship is the nationality and the nationality norms are adopted by so many countries.

The so-called nationality refers to the title or mark of someone by place of birth or ancestry to indicate his identity. The acquisition of nationality is mainly specified by the domestic laws of a country. When countries determine the original nationality of an individual, they usually adopt two kinds of principles, which are respectively the jus soli and jus sanguinis.

1. Jus soli

The jus soli means that the government takes an individual's place of birth as the judgment norms to determine his original nationality.

According to this principle, all individuals born in the territory can obtain the nationality. It was stipulated in the American law that any individual born in America owned American nationality. The Nationality Law of the People's Republic of China stipulates: "individual who is born in China and one or both of his parents is Chinese citizen has Chinese nationality."

2. Jus sanguinis

The jus sanguinis means that the government takes an individual's descent (the nationality of his parents) as the judgment norms to determine his original nationality.

According to this principle, any individual who has ancestry lineage with domestic citizen can obtain the nationality and enjoy all civil rights of national law, but he also bears all civil obligations.

A country implementing citizen jurisdiction will levy on the worldwide income of its citizen. From the view of taxpayer, he has to bear the unlimited tax liability to his nationality country on all his income.

2.4.3 The treatment of nationality changing and dual-nationality

After an individual obtains his nationality by birth or ancestry, he may change his nationality such as naturalization, loss of nationality and restoration of nationality.

Naturalization refers to acquisition of a country's nationality naturally for the reasons of marriage, adoption, claim, transfer of territory and so on according to a country's domestic laws. It also refers that, in accordance with the nationality law and immigration law, after the application is approved, an individual's original nationality is changed into the nationality of the application or from the stateless to the nationality of the application.

Loss of nationality refers that a nation loses his original nationality due to voluntary exit, obtaining nationality of other country or deprived of citizenship in accordance with the national law.

Restoration of nationality refers to an individual's recovery of his original nationality that has lost it for some reasons after his application for recovery according to the domestic laws.

Because there is difference in the regulations of nationality in different countries and the changing of nationality does exit for some reasons, an individual maybe have two nationalities. That is dual-nationality. For example, a citizen of a country which exercises jus sanguinis bore a child in America that exercises jus soli, and the child has dual-nationality. Another example is that if a woman is married to a foreigner or a child is adopted by a foreigner, they can retain their original nationality and obtain the nationality of the husband or the adopter.

For the problem of dual-nationality, the relevant countries generally settle it through consultation. Most of the countries, including China, advocate the principle of "one person, one nationality". It means that all countries should cancel the transnational individual's nationality after he acquires legally another citizenship and do not give the nationality to the transnational individual who still retains another citizenship. For the transnational individual who changes or loses his nationality, he is the citizen of the country into which his nationality changes and from the day of changing, the new nationality country can levy on his income, meanwhile, his original nationality country has to stop exercising its citizen jurisdiction on him. For the transnational individual who restores nationality from other country, the original nationality country will exercise its citizen jurisdiction from the day of restoration and another country has to stop exercising its citizen jurisdiction at the same time.

2.5 The present implementation status of income tax jurisdictions in different countries

Since tax jurisdictions belong to the state's sovereignty, every country which owns sovereignty has the power to select the type of tax jurisdiction which is suitable for it based on its own country's condition. Almost all countries exercise source jurisdiction according to the principle of dependency, namely levy on the income "from the source". Therefore, the source jurisdiction has got a unified understanding by most of the countries. It requires the transnational taxpayer to bear the limited tax liability to the country where his economic and tax matters occurred. But most of the countries in the world adopt at the same time both the source jurisdiction and the residence jurisdiction according to the principles of dependency and personality, namely they levy the taxpayer's income from the source and focus on the taxpayer's "identity". They require the transnational taxpayer to bear the unlimited or comprehensive tax liability to the source country. Citizen jurisdiction should be equal to resident jurisdiction.

It is worth mentioning that most countries generally agree and follow the principle of priority for source jurisdiction. That is to say, for the same transnational income, the source country has the priority of taxing. It admits that source jurisdiction has priority to resident jurisdiction in tax power. This is because an investor first ought to pay tax to the country where he earns his income. If the source country can not levy on the taxpayer's income priority but the residence country can levy firstly, the source country will not allow the foreign residents to do business and make money within its territory. At the same time, most countries in the world, especially the developed countries, hoping to earn income through technology transfer and international trade from other countries, have to admit that the source country has the priority of taxing. However, the priority is not exclusive. It is demonstrated in two aspects. On one hand, priority is limited. Source country can not levy on all income of non-resident from the source, but only can levy on the income of individuals living in the country for a certain period of time and the PE of non-resident companies. On the other hand, the priority can not completely exclude the tax jurisdiction of residence country. After the imposition of source country priority, the residence country will still exercise its jurisdiction on taxpayers according to different conditions. So, for the taxpayer's transnational income, the source country can levy priority and after that, the residence country can exercise its residence jurisdiction. This approach has been accepted in international tax practice by most countries in the world.

From the view of tax systems in the world, there are mainly three types of implementation of income tax jurisdictions.

1. Exercise source jurisdiction and residence jurisdiction at the same time

Under this situation, a country will exercise its tax power on the following three categories of income, namely, the domestic income of residents, the foreign income of residents and the domestic income of foreigners. At present, China and most of the countries in the world adopt this approach.

2. Exercise single source jurisdiction

Exercise single source jurisdiction means a country will exercise its tax power on the taxpayer's income derived from the country. It includes the domestic income of residents and foreigners excluding the foreign income of residents. At present, the countries and regions which exercise single source jurisdiction include Argentina, Uruguay, Panama, Costa Rica, Kenya, Zambia, Malaysia, and so on. In addition, a number of countries and regions exercise single source jurisdiction in their corporation income tax, but they exercise source jurisdiction and residence jurisdiction at the same time in their individual income tax. Of course, it is from the overall interests that these countries and regions choose to implement the single source jurisdiction. The one exercising single source jurisdiction are mostly the developing countries. They need to introduce foreign capital in their economic development. Therefore, they choose to exercise the single source jurisdiction in the income tax to make the foreign traders use the approach to establish corporations in the local and do not have to pay enterprise income tax in the local which can attract foreign direct investment. In this case, the countries and regions implementing single source jurisdiction have become actually a kind of tax havens.

3. Exercise source jurisdiction, residence jurisdiction and citizen jurisdiction at the same time

This situation occurs mainly in some states which emphasize their scope of tax rights. It exercises citizen jurisdiction except for source and residence jurisdictions in its individual income tax. Taking the United States as a example, it is stipulated in American laws that even if an American citizen lives abroad for a long time and is not American fiscal resident, he has to make tax declaration to American government on his worldwide income.

 Key words, phrases and special terms

tax jurisdiction	税收管辖权
territory	领土
territorial sea	领海
air space	领空
the principle of dependency	属地主义原则
the principle of personality	属人主义原则
resident taxpayer	居民纳税人
domicile	住所
residence	居所
source jurisdiction	收入来源地管辖权
residence jurisdiction	居民管辖权
citizen jurisdiction	公民管辖权
business income	经营所得

service income	劳务所得
investment income	投资所得
dividend	股息
interest	利息
permanent establishment (PE)	常设机构
non-resident company	非居民公司
attribution principle	归属原则
force of attraction rule	引力原则

the Enterprises Income Tax law of the People's Republic of China
《中华人民共和国企业所得税法》

trading floor norms	交易地点标准
independent service income	独立劳务所得
dependent service income	非独立劳务所得

Regulations for Implementation of Individual Income Tax Law of the People's Republic of China
《中华人民共和国个人所得税法实施条例》

property	产权, 财产
royalties	特许权使用费
rent	租金
creditor's right	债权
patent right	专利权
trademark right	商标权
good-will	商誉
copy right	版权
marketing right	经销权
proprietary technology	专有技术
intangible property	无形资产
franchise	特许权
withholding tax	预提税
real estate	不动产
chattel	动产
unlimited tax liability	无限纳税义务
straddle over year	跨年度
State General Administration of Taxation	国家税务总局
place-of-incorporation test	注册地标准
place-of-management test	管理机构所在地标准
place-of-head office test	总机构所在地标准
place-of-capital controlled test	资本控制标准
deferral	推迟课税
parent corporation	母公司
subsidiary	子公司

controlled foreign corporation (CFC)	受控外国子公司
jus soli	出生地主义
jus sanguinis	血统主义
international tax havens	国际避税港

Problems of thinking

1. What's tax jurisdiction? What are the establishment principles of tax jurisdiction?
2. How many types are there in income tax jurisdictions?
3. How to determine a transnational individual's resident identity?
4. What are the judgment norms on resident identity of legal entity?
5. What's unlimited tax liability? Who has the unlimited tax liability?
6. How is the present implementation of income tax jurisdictions in different countries?

PART TWO
PRACTICE OF INTERNATIONAL TAXATION

Chapter 3

OVERVIEW OF INTERNATIONAL DOUBLE TAXATION

 Ideological and political points of the course

In order to reduce the tax burden and avoid double taxation, China has carried out the "replacement of Business Tax with Value-added Tax". We should thoroughly understand the basic spirit of it and the significance of structural tax reduction to reduce the tax burden of enterprises. At present, our country has implemented large-scale tax reduction and reduced burdens on the macro level, helping enterprises to overcome difficulties which is a reflection of the superiority of the socialist system.

 Learning Objectives

1. Master the concept of international double taxation essentially and know it is mainly caused by the overlap of tax jurisdictions between countries.

2. Clearly understand international double taxation is the focus of tax distribution relationships between countries and it is also the important theory and practice problem of international taxation.

 Course Importing

An English teacher from Britain came to China to teach for one year. Was it possible for her to be taxed by both the British and Chinese governments on her income during her one-year stay in China?

 3.1 The concept of international double taxation

International double taxation on income is a most common and outstanding issue in the area of international taxation. Because the solution to this problem involves the tax rights of relevant countries, it has been one of the important research topics of international taxation.

Double taxation refers to the same object of taxation is levied by the same or similar category of tax at the same period more than once. It must be stressed that it is the imposition by the same or similar category of tax. If an object of taxation is levied by different categories of tax, it does not belong to the issue of double taxation we discuss here. For example, the wages of workers in some countries will be levied not only by individual income tax but also by social insurance tax (salary tax). But the attributes of the two categories of tax are different, so if they levy on the same wages, it is not the double taxation. Double taxation can occur within a country or between countries.

3.1.1 Domestic double taxation

As for income tax, domestic double taxation is most likely to happen in federal countries. It can be divided into longitudinal and horizontal classes. Take the United States as an example, the so-called longitudinal domestic double taxation refers to the federal government and state government exercise tax rights on the same income of the same taxpayer at the same time. The horizontal domestic double taxation refers to two or more state governments exercising tax rights on the same income of the same taxpayer at the same time.

3.1.2 International double taxation

International double taxation is similar to the above horizontal domestic double taxation. But the government revenue collecting office is no longer the different states in a country. They are two or more sovereign states. So, international double taxation has been defined as the imposition of comparable income taxes by two or more sovereign countries on the same item of income (including capital gains) of the same or different taxable person for the same taxable period. International double taxation can be divided into juridical double taxation and economic double taxation, which is based on whether the taxpayer is the same person or not.

1. Juridical double taxation

Juridical double taxation refers to the imposition on the same income of the same transnational taxpayer by two or more countries. It emphasizes that the taxpayer and the object of taxation has the same identity. The definition of juridical double taxation is better understood. For instance, a resident of country A obtains income in country B, both of the two countries will levy on the income, which leads to the occurrence of transnational juridical double taxation. In another example, a company of a third country establishes a PE in country A. If it is engaged in business activities in country B through the PE and obtains income, both of the two countries can levy on the business income, which leads to the occurrence of international juridical double taxation. However, for the same taxpayer who participates in international economic activities, his tax burden should not be greater than the tax liability within a country.

2. Economic double taxation

Economic double taxation refers to the imposition on the same income of different transnational taxpayers by two or more countries. It emphasizes that international double taxation includes not only the juridical double taxation, but the double taxation caused by the different identities between the taxpayer and the object of taxation, as well as the different determination criteria and

Chapter 3 OVERVIEW OF INTERNATIONAL DOUBLE TAXATION

calculation methods for the same income. For example, a parent company of country A gets dividend income from its subsidiary which locates in country B. The dividend income is a part of after-tax profit of the subsidiary in country B. For the parent company and the subsidiary are different taxpayers but their objects of taxation are the same, the double taxation on the same profit (the dividend paid by the subsidiary to the parent company) is the economic double taxation. In addition, economic double taxation may also arise when income is taxed to a partnership and to the partners or when it is taxed to a trust and to the beneficiaries of the trust.

3.2 The causes of international double taxation

International double taxation is the focal point of the contradiction of tax distribution relationships between countries. It is an important issue that the community of international taxation must research. The reasons for the occurrence of international double taxation are closely related to the following factors, such as the different tax jurisdictions implemented in different countries, different legal regulations about enterprise's income distribution or expense deduction and different views on the transfer price of associated enterprises.

3.2.1 The overlaps of tax jurisdictions of two or more countries

1. The overlap of the same kind of tax jurisdictions

The overlap of the same kind of tax jurisdictions is mainly caused by the conflicting standards used by relevant countries to determine the source place of income or the identity of resident. Once the same income is determined to come from the nation by two countries at the same time or the same taxpayer is determined to be the domestic resident by two countries at the same time, the source jurisdictions or residence jurisdictions of two countries will overlap. In addition, if a taxpayer has dual nationalities and the two countries exercise citizen jurisdictions, the citizen jurisdictions of two countries will also overlap. In order to illustrate the overlap of the same kind of tax jurisdictions between countries, examples are as follows.

1) Source-source conflicts

Two or more countries assert the right to tax the same income of a taxpayer because they all claim that the income is sourced in their country.

 Teaching Case of 3-1

Two Countries of A and B claim the same business income that is sourced in their country and both of them have the source jurisdiction on the income.

For example, if a company of Country A establishes a PE in Country B, Country B uses the PE norms to determine the business income source and country A uses the trading floor norms. Under this circumstance, if this company sells goods to a company in Country B through the PE but signs the contract in country A, then Country A can claim the business income that is sourced in Country A and assert the right to tax the income according to the trading floor norms, meanwhile, Country B can also claim the same business income that is sourced in country B and assert the right to tax the

43

same income of the PE according to the PE norms.

 Teaching Case of 3-2

Two Countries of A and B claim the same service income that is sourced in their country and their source jurisdictions will overlap on the same service income.

For example, on the issue of determining the source place of service income, if country A uses place of rendering service norms but Country B uses income payer norms, when a resident of country B renders service to a company in Country A but the service income is paid by the branch company established in Country B, the service income of the resident will be claimed source in both of the two countries.

2) Residence-residence conflicts

Two or more countries assert the right to tax the same income of a taxpayer because they claim that the taxpayer is a resident of their country. A taxpayer that is a resident of two countries is commonly referred to as a "dual-resident taxpayer".

 Teaching Case of 3-3

Two countries of A and B determine the same individual as their resident and both of them have residence jurisdiction on the individual, which leads to the overlap of residence jurisdiction.

For example, an individual has a permanent dwelling in country A but was sent to country B for working for a year. Country A determines the individual as its resident according to the domicile norms and country B determines him as its resident in this taxable year also according to the present time norms. So, the residence jurisdictions of the two countries overlap here.

Another example is that two countries of A and B exercise residence jurisdiction and use the present time norms to determine the resident identity, but there is difference between them. It is stipulated in tax law of country A that any individual who has been present in country A for more than 180 days is the resident of country A and any resident who has been absent from country A for more than 180 days is the non-resident of country A. It is stipulated in tax law of country B that any individual who has been present in country B for more than 90 days is the resident of country B, otherwise, he is the non-resident of country B. If a resident of country A leaves country A to do business in country B and has been present in country B for more than 150 days. During that period of time, he obtains some income in country B. According to the present time norms, country B determines him as the resident of this country and exercises residence jurisdiction on the income because his present time in country B has exceeded 90 days. But country A still determines him as the resident of country A, because he has been absent from country A for only 150 days, that is, less than 180 days, and exercises residence jurisdiction on him. For the connotation of present time norms in country A and B are not the same, both of the two countries can determine him as their resident and assert the right to tax his income, which caases the overlap of residence jurisdiction and ultimately leads to the international double taxation.

Chapter 3   OVERVIEW OF INTERNATIONAL DOUBLE TAXATION

 Teaching Case of 3-4

Two countries of A and B determine the same legal entity as their resident, which leads to the overlap of residence jurisdiction. There are mainly the following two cases: The first case is that country A uses the place-of-incorporation test to determine the resident identity of a legal entity and country B uses the place-of-management test or the place-of-head office test. If a company registers in country A and establishes its management or head office in country B, both of the two countries can determine the legal entity as their resident. For example, a transnational corporation registers in America but its actual management office is in Britain. The United States can determine the corporation as its resident according to the place-of-incorporation test. Meanwhile, the Britain can also determine it as its resident according to the place-of-management test. Because the two countries use different judgment norms to determine the resident identity of a legal entity, the overlap of residence jurisdictions will occur and the international double taxation appears. The second case is that two countries of A and B use the place-of-management test to determine the resident identity of a legal entity but some parts of a company's management office are in country A and some parts are in country B such as its board of directors is held in country A and its general manager department is located in country B. At that time, country A and B can determine the corporation as their resident based on the above facts.

3) Citizen-citizen conflicts

Two or more countries assert the right to tax the same income of a taxpayer because they claim the taxpayer is a citizen of their country.

 Teaching Case of 3-5

A taxpayer has the dual-nationality of the United States and Canada. The two countries exercise citizen jurisdiction. So, the worldwide income of this taxpayer is taxable to both the countries.

2. The overlap of different kinds of tax jurisdictions

The overlap of different kinds of tax jurisdictions between countries mainly includes the following three situations:

(1) The overlap of residence jurisdiction and source jurisdiction;

(2) The overlap of citizen jurisdiction and source jurisdiction;

(3) The overlap of citizen jurisdiction and residence jurisdiction.

For most of the countries in the world exercise source jurisdiction and residence jurisdiction at the same time, the overlap of them is the most common. For example, if a resident of Country A is engaged in business activities in Country B and obtains income there, Country A can assert the right to tax the income based on the residence jurisdiction and Country B can also levy on the same income based on the source jurisdiction. So, the tax jurisdictions of two countries overlap on the same income. If the two countries exercise their jurisdiction separately, the same income will inevitably be subject to international double taxation. The overlap of citizen jurisdiction and source jurisdiction is similar to the above situation, it is not necessary to restate.

3.2.2 Different legal regulations about enterprise's income distribution or expense deduction between countries

For instance, an enterprise of country A paid interest to an enterprise of Country B. But Country A will not allow the interest paid to be deducted before income tax and Country B will levy on the interest. At that time, international double taxation will happen.

3.2.3 Different views on the transfer price of associated enterprises

The detailed contents will be introduced in Chapter 8.

Key words, phrases and special terms

overlap	重叠
international double taxation	国际重复征税
juridical double taxation	法律性重复征税
economic double taxation	经济性重复征税
associated enterprises	关联企业

 Problems of thinking

1. What's the difference between juridical double taxation and economic double taxation?
2. What's international double taxation? What causes its happening?
3. How many types of overlaps of tax jurisdictions are there?

Chapter 4

INTERNATIONAL DOUBLE TAXATION RELIEF

Ideological and political points of the course

In the calculation of individual income tax of China, the reform of the tax method for comprehensive income and the appearance of personal special additional deduction have greatly reduced the tax burden of individual income tax payers, especially when the tax reduction effect of middle-income groups is more obvious. The common people's wallet is bigger, their living standard is improved and their sense of happiness is greatly increased. The new individual income tax reform takes into account all aspects of taxpayers' lives and reflects the "fairness" of the socialist system.

Learning Objectives

1. Deepen understand and grasp the ways and methods of international double taxation relief.
2. Master comprehensively the calculation methods of limitation on credit, direct credit and indirect credit.
3. Know the specific operation methods and skills of credit method under tax sparing credit.
4. Graspon the whole the relationships between international tax credit, limitation on credit and tax sparing credit.

Course Importing

When an individual has dual-resident identity and is determined as the domestic resident by two countries according to their domestic laws and both countries can exercise their residence jurisdictions on him, how can the two governments coordinate their tax interests to avoid the taxpayer's double taxation?

International double taxation affects not only the transnational taxpayers' interest directly, but also causes different effects on the involved international economic activities and the relevant national financial interests. In order to establish a reasonable tax distribution relationship between countries and to rationalize taxpayer's burden, so that the taxpayer can make full use of international capital, reasonable use of international resources and develop international economic, how to deal with international double taxation according to the principle of benefit reciprocity also becomes an important theoretical issue in international taxation.

4.1 Ways of international double taxation relief

For how to deal with international double taxation, countries in the world have taken some effective ways. Over the years, the practice shows that we should strive to avoid the international double taxation before it occurs, but after its occurrence, we should strive to relieve it. Generally, countries can use two ways to solve the problem. One way is that a country limits its exercise of tax jurisdiction actively in its domestic tax provisions, which is a unilateral way. The second way is that two or more governments sign tax agreements or treaties to make some provisions be carried out in these countries, which solves international double taxation ultimately. From the view of developmental trend, most countries will gradually adopt or choose the second way to solve the problems of international double taxation. Therefore, the ways of international double taxation relief can be usually classified into three types, which are unilateral, bilateral and multilateral respectively.

1. Unilateral way

In order to encourage domestic residents be engage in international economic activities actively or to invest abroad, most of the countries implementing residence jurisdiction set some limits on their tax jurisdiction in their domestic tax laws unilaterally for solving the double taxation on the foreign income of domestic resident. Under the worldwide application situation, unilateral way can be generally divided into two methods, which are respectively exemption method and credit method. The specific contents will be elaborated in the Chapter 4 section 2.

2. Bilateral way

For taking the benefits of residence country, source country and transnational taxpayer into account, countries of residence and source will sign the bilateral tax agreements through negotiations between the two governments to solve the international double taxation and coordinate tax distribution relationships between the sovereign states. The practice of signing bilateral tax agreements is an effective way to solve international double taxation. Since 1960s, the signing of bilateral tax agreements have become a significant characteristic of international economic relations. Bilateral way to coordinate tax distribution relationships between countries has become popular in the world.

3. Multilateral way

Multilateral way refers that two or more sovereign states sign multilateral tax treaties for international double taxation relief through negotiations to coordinate tax distribution relationships between countries. For example, the multilateral tax treaties of Nordic countries signed by Denmark,

Finland, Iceland, Norway and Sweden and entered into force on December 29, 1983 belong to the multilateral way. Because the international political and economic relations between countries are complex and there is disparity of economic structures and tax system structures between countries, few countries use the multilateral way. But with the development of the world economy, as well as the speeding up of regional economic integration, the countries which use multilateral way to solve international double taxation will be more and more.

4.2 Methods of international double taxation relief

No international consensus has been reached on the appropriate method for granting relief from international double taxation. According to the reasons of international double taxation, methods of international double taxation relief can be divided into the following two categories.

4.2.1 Methods of international double taxation relief for the overlap of the same kind of tax jurisdictions

The overlap of the same kind of tax jurisdictions between countries is caused mainly by the conflicting judgment norms of source country and the identity of resident (or citizen). In order to prevent international double taxation from happening due to the overlap of the same kind of tax jurisdictions, it is necessary for the international community to constrain the tax jurisdictions of different countries in the case of conflicting judgment standards for avoidance of double taxation on the same income or on the same resident (citizen) according to their own tax laws respectively. At present, the international communities have established relatively mature standards in this area which are mainly formed by the relevant provisions in the OECD Model Treaty and the UN Model Treaty.

1. International standards of constraining source jurisdiction

According to the different kinds of income, international standards of constraining source jurisdiction are basically the following contents.

1) Business income

Now, countries in the world usually use the PE norms and the trading floor norms to judge source place of business income. But both of the OECD Model Treaty and the UN Model Treaty advocate for using the PE norms to determine whether a government has the right of taxation on the business income derived from it. That is to say, if an enterprise obtains business income through its PE which is in another country, the business income should be taxable in another country. While, the trading floor norms cannot be the basis of taxing on the business income of non-residents.

For example, a British resident company sells a batch of goods to a Chinese company according to the contract. The British company establishes a PE in China. It sells the goods through the PE but signs the contract in Britain. According to the PE norms, the sales profit of the goods should be taxable by Chinese government in spite that the sales profit is sourced in the UK according to the British judicial precedent. Of course, if the British company has no PE in China, Chinese government can not levy on the sales profit. Then, the British government can exercise its source jurisdiction on the sales profit.

2) Service income

Both of the OECD Model Treaty and the UN Model Treaty divide personal service activities into independent and dependent personal service activities. The former refers to the personal independent activities such as independent scientific, literary, artistic, educational and teaching activities, as well as independent activities of physicians, lawyers, engineers, architects, dentists and accountants. The latter refers to various service activities based on employment.

No international consensus has been reached on the issue of whether the independent personal service income should be levied by the source country or by the residence country. The OECD Model Treaty views the independent personal service income as a kind of business income and advocates that it should be taxed by the residence country. Unless the individual has a "fixed base" in another country where he engages in the independent service activities, any country other than the residence country can not levy on the independent personal service income. Even if a resident of a country has a fixed base in another country, the country (the non-residence country) can only levy on the income which is attributable to the fixed base. The UN Model Treaty relaxes the conditions of taxing on the independent personal service income for the non-residence country. In addition to the "fixed base" condition in the OECD Model Treaty, it is also stipulated in the UN Model Treaty that if a resident of a country stays in another country for accumulation more than 183 days (including 183 days) because of rendering independence service activities, or the remuneration of a resident in a country while rendering service in another country is paid by the resident of another country or the remuneration is burdened by a PE or a fixed base which is located in another country, and the amount of the remuneration in a fiscal year is over the amount negotiated by the Contracting States, another country can also levy on the individual's service income sourced in the country.

For the issue of whether the dependent personal service income should be levied by the source country or by the residence country, the OECD Model Treaty and the UN Model Treaty have the same regulation. That is, a resident's wages, salaries and other rewards of a Contracting State for employment are generally taxed by his residence country unless his employment is actually exercised in the other Contracting State.[①] If the employment of a resident of a Contracting State is actually exercised in the other Contracting State, his wages, salaries and other rewards are taxable to the other Contracting State under certain conditions.

3) Investment income

For the dividends and interest of the investment income, international societies generally take the practice of sharing the rights of taxation by the countries of payer and beneficiary. Because if both countries levy on the dividends and interest respectively according to their own stipulated tax rate, it will lead to a double taxation on the same income. But if it allows imposing tax credit, the country of beneficiary may have no tax to levy after the payment to the country of payer. Therefore, in order to prevent the double taxation on the same dividend and interest and also make the countries of payer and beneficiary share the rights of taxation, the OECD Model Treaty and the UN

[①] According to the OECD Model Treaty notes, the employment is actually exercised in the other Contracting State refers to the resident is physically present in the other contracting state.

Model Treaty proposed that dividend and interest should be levied firstly by the country of payer with a lower tax rate to ensure the country of beneficiary can still levy on some income after its implement of tax credit on the foreign income. As for the specific tax rate of payment country, the OECD Model Treaty has also made clear regulations: For the paid dividend, when the beneficiary directly holds at least 25% of the capital of the paying company, the tax rate shall not be over 5% and in other cases, the tax rate shall not be over 15%. For the paid interest, the tax rate shall not be over 10%. The withholding tax rate of dividends in every country is generally 25% to 35%. There is no specific limited tax rate in the UN Model Treaty and it only requires the relevant countries to determine the tax rate of payment country through negotiations.

Compared with dividends and interest, there is no uniform international standards for royalties. The OECD Model Treaty advocates that royalties shall be taxable by the residence country of beneficiary (i.e., the owner of the franchise) exclusively unless the beneficiary has a PE or a fixed base in the country where the franchise is used. And the rights or properties of royalties have practical links with the PE or the fixed base. Only in this case, shall the royalties be attributable to the PE or the fixed base and be taxable by the country where the franchise is used. But the UN Model Treaty advocates that the country where the royalties occurred shall have greater taxing power. Except for the condition that the beneficiary of the royalties has a PE or a fixed base in the country where the royalties occurred, the UN Model Treaty stipulates that the country where the royalties occurred can levy on the royalties paid to the beneficiary of another country with some limited tax rates and the limited tax rate can be negotiated by the relevant countries. China is mainly the franchise using country, in order to safeguard Chinese tax equity, it generally refers to the UN Model Treaty to sign tax agreements. For the royalties paid to the overseas companies by Chinese enterprises and institutions, withholding tax shall be collected with a limited tax rate of 10%.

4) Property income

From the view of civil law, real estates refer to the land and the attachments to the ground, including all kinds of buildings and various types of plants growing in the land. The characteristic of real estates is that they can not be separated or moved from the land. Once they are separated or moved from the land, their attributes will be changed and their values will be greatly reduced. Besides, the fixed ancillary equipment of buildings also belongs to real estates. Immovable property in tax model treaty includes not only the real estates in civil law, but also includes attachments to the real estates, livestock and equipment used in agriculture and forestry, power applicable for land and property according to general laws, immovable property usufruct[1] and so on, which does not include ships and aircraft. For the real estates income and the real estates transferring income, the taxing power stipulated in the OECD Model Treaty and the UN Model Treaty is consistent with the tax laws in every country, which means they shall be taxable by the country where the real estates locate.

Chattel refers to property except for real estate, such as machinery and equipment, vehicles, animal, all kinds of daily necessities of life and so on. The characteristic of chattel is that it can be

---

[1] Usufruct refers to the right of using and reaping profit of others' items.

moved freely and its value is not affected by moving. For the transferring income of chattel, the OECD and UN Model Treaties stipulate that the income shall be taxable by the transfer's residence country except for the following conditions:

(1) If a resident of a country transfers his chattel of his PE or his fixed base which is in another country, the transferring income shall be taxable by the country where his PE or his fixed base locates.

(2) The transferring income of ships, aircraft and vessel engaged in international transportation or inland waterway or the chattel transferring income of attachments to the above ships, aircraft and vessel shall be taxable by the country where its effective management office locates.

It is also stipulated in the OECD and UN Model Treaties that the right to tax gains from the disposition of shares of a company is reserved to the source country when the assets of the company consist primarily of immovable property.

2. International standards of constraining residence jurisdiction

1) International standards of constraining residence jurisdiction for individuals

When an individual has dual-resident identity and is determined as the domestic resident by two countries according to their domestic laws and both of the two countries can exercise their residence jurisdictions on him, the OECD and UN Model Treaties are required to determine the individual's resident identity in the habitual order of permanent home, center of vital interests, habitual dwelling, citizenship and negotiation by both countries.

2) International standards of constraining residence jurisdiction for legal entities

As for legal entities, according to the spirits of the OECD and UN Model Treaties, if the same legal cntity is determined by two countries as their resident company, place-of-management test should be used to determine which country has the power to exercise its residence jurisdiction. According to the international standards, if the place-of-incorporation test is in conflict with the place-of-management test when judging the resident identity of a legal entity, the place-of-incorporation test should be subordinate to the place-of-management test. Of course, for those countries using the place-of-incorporation test to judge the identity of legal entity, the above regulation is hard to accept. So some tax agreements also stipulate that if a legal entity is determined as the resident company by two countries respectively, it should not be the resident company of any country.

4.2.2 Methods of international double taxation relief for the overlap of different kinds of tax jurisdictions

As mentioned before, there are mainly three types of overlaps of different kinds of tax jurisdictions. Among them, the most important and common type is the residence-source overlap between two countries. In international tax practice, a lot of issues are also about how to solve the international double taxation caused by residence-source overlap. Under the current situation, the solving methods can be generally summarized as: the country exercising residence jurisdiction admits the source country's priority taxing status over the residence country's taxing right. In the process of exercising its domestic taxing power, the residence country will use some methods to reduce or avoid international double taxation. It is the importance of source jurisdiction and the prio-

Chapter 4 INTERNATIONAL DOUBLE TAXATION RELIEF

rity taxing status of source country that determines.

The methods allowed using for double taxation relief by national tax laws and international tax agreements are respectively the deduction method, low taxation method, exemption method and credit method. A country can use only one of these methods, or it may use some combination of methods.

1. Deduction method

The deduction, ethod refers that the residence country allows its taxpayers to claim a deduction for taxes, including income taxes, paid to a foreign government with respect to foreign-source income. It means that countries use the deduction method to tax their residents on their worldwide income and allow those taxpayers to take a deduction for foreign taxes paid in the computation of their taxable income. In effect, foreign taxes—income taxes and other types of taxes—are treated as current expenses of doing business or earning income in the foreign jurisdiction. The deduction method is the least generous method of granting relief from international double taxation.

To illustrate the deduction method, we give a simple example.

Simulated demonstration of 4-1

[*Background*]: *A resident of country A earns* 100,000 *Yuan from country A and* 20,000 *Yuan from country B in a taxable year. The income tax rate of country A and country B is respectively* 40% *and* 50%. *Now, calculate the final domestic tax of the resident to country A.*

[*Calculation*]:

Total income of the resident: 100,000+20,000 = 120,000 (*Yuan*).

Tax paid to country B: 20,000×50% = 10,000 (*Yuan*).

Taxable income of country A: 120,000−10,000 = 110,000 (*Yuan*).

Tax before deduction to country A: 120,000×40% = 48,000 (*Yuan*).

The final domestic tax after deduction to country A: 110,000×40% = 44,000 (*Yuan*).

Total calculation: (100,000+20,000−20,000×50%) ×40% = (120,000−10,000) ×40% = 110,000×40% = 44,000 (*Yuan*).

[*Comments*]: *country A adopting the deduction method, the resident can pay less tax at the most of* 4,000 *Yuan* [10,000×40% *or* (48,000−44,000)] *to the government of it but still bears at least* 6,000 *Yuan* [(44,000+10,000−48,000) *or* (10,000−10,000×40%)] *of double taxation of income tax. So, deduction method can't completely solve the international double taxation, it can only mitigate or moderate the contradiction of international double taxation to a certain extent.*

Simulated demonstration of 4-2

[*Background*]: *Assume a resident company of country A earns* 1,000,000 *Yuan in a taxable year.* 700,000 *Yuan is from country A* (*the residence country*) *and* 300,000 *Yuan is from country B* (*the non-residence country*). *The corporation income tax rate of country A and country B is respectively* 40% *and* 30%. *If country A adopts deduction method, analyze the final domestic tax of the company to country A.*

[Calculation]:

Tax paid to country B: (300,000×30%) = 90,000 (Yuan).

Taxable income from country B: (300,000−90,000) = 210,000 (Yuan).

Taxable income from country A: 700,000 (Yuan).

Total income at home and abroad: 700,000+210,000=910,000 (Yuan).

The final domestic tax after deduction to country A: [910,000×40% or (700,000+300,000−300,000×30%) ×40%] = 364,000 (Yuan).

[Comments]: In the above demonstration, if the company bears only the tax burden of country A, there is no double taxation and the tax amount payable is 400,000 Yuan (1,000,000×40%); If country A does not adopt deduction method, the company's total tax payable at home and abroad is 490,000 Yuan (1,000,000×40%+300,000×30%). But if country A adopts deduction method, the total tax amount payable of the company is actually 454,000 Yuan (364,000+90,000). Obviously, deduction method can alleviate but can not completely avoid international double taxation.

From the above analysis, we can see that deduction method can not completely solve the problem of international double taxation. The direct effect of the deduction method is that the foreign-source income of residents earning foreign-source income and paying foreign income taxes on that income is taxable at a higher combined tax rate than the rate applied to the domestic-source income. As a result, the deduction method creates a bias in favor of domestic investment over foreign investment whenever the foreign investment is likely to attract a foreign income tax. Therefore, both the OECD and UN Model Treaties do not advocate using the deduction method to solve international double taxation in tax agreements between countries. But the deduction method has not disappeared. Several countries that have adopted the credit method retain the deduction method as an optional form of relief and as a way of dealing with foreign taxes that are not creditable for one reason or another. In addition, some countries use the deduction method for taxes paid with respect to income derived from foreign indirect investments. In the past, the deduction method also existed in Chinese tax law. As is stipulated in Article 28 of *Detailed Rules for the Implementation of Income Tax law of the People's Republic of China on Enterprises with Foreign Investment and Foreign Enterprises* that "the income tax already paid abroad on the profits (dividends), interest, rents, royalties and other income which happens outside China but is actually related to the institutions and places established in China by the foreign enterprises, except for regulations stipulated by the state, can be deducted as expense".[①]

2. Low taxation method

The low taxation method refers that the government of residence country establishes a separate collection standards of low tax rate on the foreign-source income of its residents but taxes the domestic income at the normal tax rate to reduce double taxation. The low taxation method can reduce double taxation to a certain extent, which means that it can alleviate the contradiction of actual double taxation, but it can not fundamentally solve the problem.

[①] The new enterprise income tax law has changed to use the credit method to solve the problem of international double taxation for the foreign-source income.

Chapter 4 INTERNATIONAL DOUBLE TAXATION RELIEF

 Simulated demonstration of 4-3

[Background]: *A resident of country A earns 800,000 Yuan from country A and 200,000 Yuan from country B in a taxable year. The income tax rate of country A and country B is respectively 35% and 40%. But country A uses low rate of 10% to tax on the foreign-source income of its resident. If country A adopts low taxation method, calculate the final domestic tax of the resident to country A.*

[Calculation]:

Tax should be paid to country A: (800,000+200,000) ×35% = 350,000 (Yuan).

Tax paid to country B: 200,000×40% = 80,000 (Yuan).

Tax actually collected by country A: 800,000×35%+200,000×10% = 300,000 (Yuan).

The total tax of the resident: 300,000+80,000 = 380,000 (Yuan).

Tax given up by country A: 350,000−300,000 = 50,000 (Yuan).

[Comments]: *If international double taxation exists, the total tax of the resident is 430,000 Yuan (350,000+80,000), but country A adopting the low taxation method, the total tax is reduced to 380,000 Yuan that the taxpayer can pay less 50,000 Yuan.*

From the above demonstration, we can see that low taxation method just refers to the residence country taxes on the foreign-source income which has been taxed abroad at low tax rate, but the foreign-source income is not entirely tax free by the residence country. So, just like the deduction method, it can only mitigate but can't completely solve the international double taxation. Therefore, both the OECD and UN Model Treaties do not advocate using the low taxation method to avoid international double taxation. At present, only a handful of countries use this method to relieve international double taxation in their domestic tax laws. For example, it is stipulated in the income tax law of Belgium that the income obtained from foreign branches of the domestic company has a reduction of 75% of the company income tax.

3. Exemption method

The exemption Method refers that the residence country provides its taxpayers with an exemption for foreign-source income. With the exemption method, the country of residence taxes its residents on their domestic-source income and exempts them from domestic tax on their foreign-source income. In effect, jurisdiction to tax rests exclusively with the country of source. The exemption method completely eliminates residence-source international double taxation caused by residence-source overlap because only onejurisdiction, the source country, is imposing tax.

Very few countries and regions adopt the exemption method with respect to all foreign-source income earned by their residents. In effect, these countries and regions tax only income from domestic sources. For this reason, they are often said to tax on a territorial basis rather than a worldwide basis. For most countries using the exemption method, however, the exemption of foreign-source income is limited to certain types of income, most commonly, the business income and dividend from foreign affiliates. Further, the exemption method is often restricted to income that has been subject to tax or subject to a minimum rate of tax by the foreign country.

In practical application, according to the income tax system implemented in every country, it needs to be negotiated whether or not to adopt the proportional tax rate or progressive tax rate and whether or not to realize the exemption method by way of bilateral tax agreements. The exemption method can be divided into full exemption and exemption with progression.

(1) Full exemption refers that the government of residence country exempts its resident's all foreign-source income from domestic tax and only taxes on the domestic-source income of the resident. Also, it does not take the foreign-source income into account in determining the rate of tax applicable to the taxpayer's domestic-source income. Because the method of full exemption causes much financial losses to the government of residence country, few countries, including only France, Australia and some Latin American countries, adopt this method.

(2) Exemption with progression refers that the government of residence country exempts its resident's foreign-source income from domestic tax and only taxes on the domestic-source income of the resident. But when it determines the tax rate applicable to the taxpayer's domestic-source income, the country has the right to put the foreign-source income and the domestic-source income together to consider the tax rate. This method mainly applies to the countries adopting progressive income tax system and it is realized by way of signing bilateral tax agreements.

To illustrate the exemption method, an example is as follows.

Simulated demonstration of 4-4

[Background]: A resident of country A earns 100,000 Yuan from country A, 50,000 Yuan from country B and 50,000 Yuan from country C in a taxable year. A's individual income tax rate is 4 grades of full progressive tax rate, namely: the yearly taxable income is 50,000 Yuan or less (including 50,000), the applicable tax rate is 5%; the part of income over 50,000 Yuan but not over 150,000 Yuan is applicable to the tax rate of 10%; the part of income over 150,000 Yuan but not over 300,000 Yuan is applicable to the tax rate of 15%; the part of income over 300,000 Yuan is applicable to the tax rate of 20%. The individual income tax rate of country B and country C is respectively 15% and 20%. If country A adopts exemption method, calculate the final tax of the resident.

[Calculation]:

Under the full exemption:

Tax should be paid to country A: 100,000×10% = 10,000 (Yuan).

Under the exemption with progression:

Country A will not tax on the foreign-source income of 100,000 Yuan (=50,000+50,000) and only tax on the 100,000 Yuan from country A. But the applicable tax rate for the 100,000 Yuan is not 10% based on the domestic-source income. Instead, it will levy at the rate of 15% based on the whole income of foreign-source and domestic-source. So, the final tax of the resident is as follows:

Tax should be paid to country A: 100,000×15% = 15,000 (Yuan).

Tax paid to country B: 50,000×15% = 7 500 (Yuan).

Tax paid to country C: 50,000×20% = 10,000 (Yuan).

The final tax of the resident: 15,000+7 500+10,000 = 32 500 (Yuan).

[Comments]: If country A adopts the exemption with progression, it can collect more 5,000 Yuan (=15,000-10,000).

Chapter 4 INTERNATIONAL DOUBLE TAXATION RELIEF

 Simulated demonstration of 4-5

[**Background**]: *In the simulated demonstration of 4-4, If country A adopts 4 grades of progressive tax rate in excess of specific amount (the tax rate schedule and other conditions are the same as the above demonstration), then, under the full exemption and the exemption with progression, how to calculate the final tax of the resident?*

[**Calculation**]:

Under the full exemption: Tax should be paid to country A: $(100,000-50,000) \times 10\% + 50,000 \times 5\% = 7,500$ (Yuan).

Under the exemption with progression:

Tax should be paid to country A: $(200,000-150,000) \times 15\% + (150,000-100,000) \times 10\% = 12,500$ (Yuan).

Tax paid to country B: $50,000 \times 15\% = 7,500$ (Yuan).

Tax paid to country C: $50,000 \times 20\% = 10,000$ (Yuan).

The final tax of the resident: $12,500 + 7,500 + 10,000 = 30,000$ (Yuan).

[**Comments**]: *If country A adopts the exemption with progression, it can collect more 5,000 Yuan ($=12,500-7,500$).*

The reasons why some countries implement the exemption method are closely related with their national conditions and economic policy. Countries adopting exemption method are mostly developed countries which have a lot of surplus capital relatively. To find a way out for the capital, they adopt a series of tax policies to encourage the domestic capital to output. One of the important content of these tax incentives is to exempt transnational income or earnings brought by the output of capital. So, an exemption system encourages resident taxpayers to invest abroad in countries with lower tax rates, especially in tax havens, and it encourages them to divert domestic-source income to such countries. For example, a taxpayer residing in an exemption country, who earns interest on funds in that country and has to pay interest tax to that country, has a strong incentive to move the funds to a foreign country that imposes low or no taxes on interest income. Therefore, in order to avoid being contrary to the principle of tax neutrality, countries implementing exemption method often have strictly limited conditions on the foreign-source income: the foreign-source income that could be exempted has to be committed to imposing taxes and under conditions that are roughly comparable to its own rates and conditions. For the foreign-source income derived from international tax havens which have no income tax system or tax at very low rates, there is generally no exemption. Several countries use the exemption method for active business income earned through a foreign branch or permanent establishment. Several countries also exempt certain dividends received from foreign corporations in which resident corporations have a minimum ownership interest, usually 5 or 10 percent. This exemption for dividends is often referred to as a participation exemption.

Of course, the exemption method is relatively simple for the tax authorities to administer and is effective in eliminating international double taxation. So, both the OECD and UN Model Treaties take it as one of the recommended methods of international double taxation avoidance.

4. Credit method

The credit method refers that the residence country provides its taxpayers with a credit against taxes otherwise payable for income taxes paid to a foreign country. For some instances, the credit method extends to income taxes which are paid to foreignlocal government. This method is also called the foreign tax credit method, which means when agovernment imposes taxes on foreign-source income of a resident, it allows the resident to reduce his domestic taxes payable by the amount of the foreign tax paid by the resident taxpayer on the foreign-source income and the actual taxes collected by the government is the difference between tax payable to the residence country and foreign taxes that have already been paid. Obviously, credit method can effectively eliminate international double taxation. Recognition of the priority but not exclusive status of source jurisdiction is its prerequisite. That is to say, for the same income of a transnational taxpayer, both the governments of source country and residence country can levy on it. However, the government of source country can exercise its tax jurisdiction before the residence country when the income occurs. Then, the government of residence country can levy on the income after its repatriation to the residence country and take the credit method to solve the international double taxation. Because of the importance and complexity of credit method, we will carry out a detailed introduction from several aspects.

1) Limitation on credit

As noted earlier, credit method is a kind of method which allows the resident to reduce his domestic taxes payablc by the amount of the foreign tax paid by the resident taxpayer on the foreign-source income. But the income tax rates of source country and residence country are different. With the credit method, foreign-source income is subject to domestic tax whenever the foreign tax rate is less than the domestic tax rate. The net domestic tax in such circumstances is an amount equal to the difference between the two tax rates multiplied by the foreign-source income. If the tax rates of source country and residence country are the same, the resident can credit all his foreign tax paid to the source country against his domestic tax on the foreign-source income and residence country needn't levy on the foreign-source income, too. Now, there is a problem, that is whether the credit country can pay tax refund when its taxpayer pays a foreign income tax at an effective rate that is higher than the domestic effective tax rate? If it does so, it is called full credit. On the contrary, if the credit amount of tax payable to the residence country can not exceed the tax payable equal to the tax rate of the residence country multiplied by the foreign-source income. (i.e. limitation on credit), it is called ordinary credit. The following simulated demonstration is to illustrate the difference between them.

Simulated demonstration of 4-6

[**Background**]: *A company had its head office in country A and set up branches in 3 countries. The tax it paid in a taxable year was shown in Table 4-1.*

Chapter 4 INTERNATIONAL DOUBLE TAXATION RELIEF

Table 4-1 Taxation situation of branchs companies

company	income /yuan	foreign tax rate/%	foreign tax /yuan	domestic tax rate/%	domestic tax /yuan	tax difference /yuan
Head office in country A	1,000,000	—	—	35	350,000	—
Branch in country B	1,000,000	30	300,000	35	350,000	+50,000
Branch in country C	1,000,000	35	350,000	35	350,000	0
Branch in country D	1,000,000	40	400,000	35	350,000	−50,000
Total	4,000,000	—	1,050,000	—	1,400,000	—

[**Calculation**]: *From the above table, we know that the branch in country B should pay the tax difference of 50,000 Yuan to country A (350,000−300,000). The tax paid by the branch in country C could be credited in country A. The tax paid by the branch in country D had an excess credit of 50,000 Yuan (400,000−350,000) which was not deductible.*

[**Comments**]: *In this case, if there is no limitation on credit and allows the foreign tax which is paid to the country with high tax rate to be credited fully, it allows the foreign government with high tax rate to poach revenue from domestic government, which means that the domestic government has to pay the tax difference to the foreign government on behalf of taxpayer. The practice of transferring tax burden of taxpayers from countries with high tax rates to low tax rates is obviously unfair. So, in order to protect the tax interest of residence country, it is necessary to provide limitation on credit for the foreign-source income which has been taxed by the source country.*

In practice, every country adopts ordinary credit to protect domestic interest of tax. Because, if it adopts full credit, the resident of country with low tax rate will invest to the country with high tax rate. The government of country with low tax rate will not get any tax from the resident and the tax from the domestic income will be also damaged. What is more, if the resident of country with low tax rate only has foreign-source income and has not any domestic-source income, under the full credit, the government of residence country has to pay him tax refund from tax that other residents have paid (i.e. tax rebate). Every country is unwilling to accept the above two cases, so the credit country provides its taxpayers with credit within the limitation. There are also such provisions in Chinese law of tax. It is stipulated in Article 21 of *the Enterprises Income Tax Law of the People's Republic of China* that the tax which is paid overseas of enterprise from foreign-source income can be credited from current tax payable in China and the limitation on credit can not exceed the tax payable equal to the tax rate of China multiplied by the foreign-source income.

Limitation on credit refers to the maximum deduction that the government of residence allows its resident taxpayer to credit his foreign tax paid abroad. It is usually limited to the amount of the domestic tax payable on the foreign-source income. Within the limitation, the foreign tax paid by the international taxpayer can be credited fully. If the foreign tax paid exceeds the limitation on credit, the maximum deduction for the foreign tax paid is only the limitation. It needs to be pointed out that the limitation on credit is the maximum deduction for the foreign tax paid, but it might not equal to the actual creditable amount of taxpayer. The actual creditable amount is the lesser of foreign tax paid and the limitation on credit. For example, a resident taxpayer pays foreign tax of

100,000 Yuan on his foreign-source income in the source country and the domestic tax payable on the foreign-source income is 150,000 Yuan (the limitation on credit). The actual creditable amount is 100,000 Yuan. In this case, the limitation on credit of the taxpayer is greater than the actual creditable amount. The difference between them is called the balance of limitation. On the contrary, if the taxpayer pays foreign tax of 200,000 Yuan and the limitation on credit in his residence country is 150,000 Yuan, the actual creditable amount is 150,000 Yuan. Under this circumstance, the taxpayer has an excess credit of 50,000 Yuan that can not offset taxes imposed on domestic income. The difference that the foreign tax is greater than the domestic limitation on credit is called by us the excess credit. In the above example, the excess credit is 50,000 Yuan. Many countries allow foreign income taxes that cannot be credited in the current year (excess credit) to be carried forward and credited against domestic taxes in the future and the balance of limitation in the future can be used to offset the excess credit in previous years. But the carry-forward period differs from country to country. It is 7 years in Canada, 5 years in the United States, 3 years in Japan and 5 years in China.

Assume, that R is a resident in Country A, which imposes tax at a rate of 30 percent. In year 1, R earns foreign income of 100 and pays foreign tax of 50. The tax is allowed as a credit against the Country A tax of 30. To the extent that the foreign tax exceeds the Country A tax 20, the foreign tax is not deductible, and R has an excess credit of 20. In year 2, R earns foreign income of 100 and pays foreign tax of 25. R is allowed a credit of 30—the current foreign tax of 25 plus 5 of the excess credit carried forward from year 1. R has an excess credit of 15 for use in the future.

On tax policy grounds, the credit method is generally recognized to be the best method for eliminating international double taxation. The credit method, however, is not free from difficulties. Most importantly, the operation of credit method can be complex from both the government and taxpayer sides. One of the difficultproblems that must be resolved are how to calculate the limitations on credit. On a source-by-source or item-by-item basis? On a country-by-country basis? Or on an overall basis, with various special rules applicable to certain types of income? Or some combination of these methods? Detailed, technical, and highly complicated legislative provisions are needed to resolve these and other matters if the credit method is to operate effectively. The compliance and administrative burdens imposed on taxpayers and tax authorities as a result of these complex rules are probably both necessary and justifiable with respect to income earned in countries of tax havens. Otherwise, domestic tax could be avoided by diverting domestic-source income to tax havens.

Countries use a variety of types of limitations. So in practice, the limitation on credit can be classified into three types. They are respectively the overall (or worldwide) limitation, the country-by-country (or pre-country) limitation and the item-by-item limitation.

(1) Under an overall limitation.

Under an overall (or worldwide) limitation, all foreign taxes are aggregated; in other words, the credit is limited to the lesser of the aggregate of foreign taxes paid and the domestic tax payable on the total amount of the taxpayer's foreign-source income. This method permits the average of high foreign taxes paid to some countries with low foreign taxes paid to other countries.

Chapter 4 INTERNATIONAL DOUBLE TAXATION RELIEF

The calculation formula is as follows:

The overall limitation = tax payable on the total amount of foreign-source and domestic-source income × (foreign taxable income ÷ total taxable income)

In the above formula, tax payable on the total amount of foreign-source and domestic-source income is the income tax payable to the government of residence equal to domestic tax rate multiplied by the foreign-source and domestic-source income. If the residence country adopts proportional tax rate, the above calculation formula can be simplified as:

The overall limitation = total taxable income of foreign-source × domestic tax rate of residence country

However, it must be pointed out that, if the residence country adopts progressive tax rate, the above calculation formula cannot be simplified.

 Simulated demonstration of 4-7

[*Background*]: *The content is the same with simulated demonstration of 4-6.*

[*Calculation*]: *Reference to table 4-1, The overall limitation for the head office in Country A:*
4,000,000 × 35% × (3,000,000/4,000,000) = 1,400,000 × (3,000,000/4,000,000) = 1,050,000 (*Yuan*).

Or 3,000,000 × 35% = 1,050,000 (*Yuan*).

Because the total foreign taxes of the head office (the total taxes paid by three branches) is 1,050,000 Yuan, which is equal to the above overall limitation, all of the foreign taxes that have already been paid can be credited fully, that is, the actual creditable amount is 1,050,000 Yuan and the final taxes collected by Country A is 350,000 Yuan (1,400,000 − 1 050,000). But under a country-by-country limitation, the branch in country B should pay the tax difference of 50,000 Yuan to country A (350,000 − 300,000) and the tax paid by the branch in country D had an excess credit of 50,000 Yuan (400,000 − 350,000) which cannot be deductible. Thus, the actual taxes imposed by Country A is 400,000 (350,000 + 50,000) Yuan. We can see that this method permits the average of high foreign taxes paid to some countries (such as Country D) with low foreign taxes paid to other countries (such as Country B). So, the difference of 50,000 Yuan and the excess credit of 50,000 Yuan are averaged and all the foreign taxes paid can be credited fully. For the head office, under the overall limitations, it can credit more 50,000 Yuan than the country-by-country limitation.

[*Comments*]: *From the above calculation and credit effect, the overall limitation does provide convenience for calculation of creditable foreign taxes on foreign-source income of domestic resident taxpayers. Moreover, the method is simple relatively and overcomes the disadvantages of tedious calculation of country-by-country limitation. So, this method was adopted since 1970s by most countries in the world. For example, the United States adopted country-by-country limitation before 1975. But in order to simplify collection procedures, it has been implementing overall limitation since 1975.*

From the above analysis, we can see when the income tax paid by an international taxpayer to a foreign country exceeds his limitation on credit in the residence country and the income tax paid to another foreign country is lower than his limitation, the overall limitation is advantageous for the transnational taxpayer. Because he can use the credit balance of a country to make up for the excess credit in another country. The result is a part of or all the excess foreign income taxes can be credited in current year. The advantages of this method cannot be enjoyed by other credit methods. However, in above case, this method will affect the interests of a sovereign state, for it will reduce the revenue of residence country. But, if a transnational taxpayer has gains in a foreign country and losses in another foreign country, this method will write off parts of his total foreign income which will make the molecule and denominator in the formula reduce the same amount (the losses) at the same time, resulting in the reduction of limitation. It is detrimental to the transnational taxpayer and is beneficial to the government of residence country. Aiming at the defect of the method, some countries have adopted another credit method, namely, the country-by-country limitation.

(2) Under an country-by-country limitation.

Under a country-by-country limitation, the credit is limited to the lesser of the taxes paid to each foreign country and the domestic tax payable on the taxpayer's income from each country. This method prevents the average of high and low foreign taxes paid to various countries, but it permits the average of high and low rates of foreign tax paid to a particular country on different types of income.

The calculation formula is as follows:

The country-by-country limitation = tax payable on the total amount of foreign-source and domestic-source income × (taxable income of a foreign country ÷ total taxable income)

Also, if the residence country adopts proportional tax rate, the above calculation formula can be simplified as:

The country-by-country limitation = taxable income of a foreign country × domestic tax rate of residence country

According to the above calculation formula, we can calculate the taxpayer's per-country limitation and compare them with the foreign tax paid to each foreign country to determine the actual creditable amount of the taxpayer.

 Simulated demonstration of 4-8

[**Background**]: The content is the same with simulated demonstration of 4-6.

[**Calculation**]: Reference to table 4-1, if Country A adopts country-by-country limitation, the per-country limitation for the head office in Country A is:

Limitation of branch in Country B = 4,000,000 × 35% × (1,000,000/4,000,000) = 350,000 (Yuan).

Or 1,000,000 × 35% = 350,000 (Yuan).

The actual creditable amount: because the foreign tax paid in Country B is 300,000 Yuan which is less than the limitation of branch in Country B, the actual creditable amount is 300,000 Yuan.

Limitation of branch in Country C: 1,000,000 × 35% = 350,000 (Yuan).

The actual creditable amount: because the foreign tax paid in Country C is 350,000 Yuan equal to the limitation of branch in Country C, the actual creditable amount is 350,000 Yuan.

Limitation of branch in Country D: 1,000,000 × 35% = 350,000 (Yuan).

Chapter 4 INTERNATIONAL DOUBLE TAXATION RELIEF

The actual creditable amount: *because the foreign tax paid in Country D is* 400,000 *Yuan which is more than the limitation of branch in Country D and the excess credit cannot be deductible, the actual creditable amount is* 350,000 *Yuan.*

The total limitation for the head office in Country A: 300,000 + 350,000 + 350,000 = 1,000,000 (*Yuan*).

Tax payable to Country A of the head office after credit: 4,000,000×35%−1,000,000=450,000 (*Yuan*).

[**Comments**]: *From the above calculation we can see, if a taxpayer has foreign-source income from different foreign countries, the formula of per-country limitation is applicable to the situation that foreign income tax rate is higher than the domestic income tax rate. When the foreign income tax rate is less than or equal to the domestic income tax rate, we just need to add the foreign taxes paid in different foreign countries together to determine the actual creditable amount.*

The country-by-country limitation can avoid the disadvantages of using credit balance of a country to make up for excess credit in another country which is beneficial to the government of residence country. However, if a transnational taxpayer has gains in a foreign country and losses in another foreign country, this method is beneficial to the transnational taxpayer and the limitation is reasonable. Because it can avoid the disadvantages of overall limitation in the same situation which will make gains and losses offset each other and make the molecule and denominator in the formula reduce the same amount at the same time, resulting in the reduction of limitation.

Generally speaking, the per-country limitation can take account of the economic interests of the government and taxpayers rationally. It determines the limitation on credit and actual creditable amount of each country according to their actual situations which is more close to the reality. So in credit countries, most of them adopt this method. For example, the UK, Germany and Finland have implemented per-country limitation. The United States is one of the earliest countries which implemented this method, but from 1970s, except for some specified items of income, it began to implement overall limitation for other income. However, due to some defects of overall limitation which will urge taxpayers to find a country or region with less or no tax to invest, it is tantamount to stimulate taxpayers to invest in countries with low tax instead of residence country. Obviously, it is opposite to American capital-output neutrality principle. At present, some American scholars advocate abolition of overall limitation and re-using country-by-country limitation.

Therefore, effect of overall limitation and per-country limitation is not the same under different situations. Two methods have their advantages and disadvantages which are complementary. However, these advantages and disadvantages are relative to the interests of residence country and international taxpayers. Any sovereign state has right to choose which credit method is adopted in their tax system. It is stipulated in Chinese enterprise income tax law that we adopt country-by-country limitation.

(3) Under an item-by-item limitation.

Under an item-by-item limitation, the credit is limited to the lesser of the foreign tax paid on each particular item of income and the domestic tax payable on that item of income. This method prevents averaging and is probably the best method from a theoretical perspective, although few countries use it in practice. In this context, an "item" of income is some defined as category of income, such as interest income or shipping income. In principle, a country might define an item of income as any category of income subject to a special tax regime in a foreign country. For example, if Country B taxed business profits at 50 percent and interest income at 10 percent, Country A might treat business income and interest income arising in Country B as separated items of income for purposes of imposing a limitation on the credit for taxes paid by its residents to Country B.

Before 1970s, most countries adopted country-by-country limitation, but after that, overall limitation gradually displaced it. It is worth noticing that some countries use low income tax rates on dividends, interest, royalties and other investment income and some countries take low tax preferential policy on agriculture, forestry, fishery and mining income. Thus, in order to prevent transnational taxpayers from using the balance of limitation in a foreign country with low tax rate to offset the excess credit in another country with high tax rates, some countries clearly stipulate to use separate calculation method of limitation on credit on separate item of foreign-source income, while they have adopted overall limitation.

The calculation formula is as follows:

The item-by-item limitation = tax payable on the total amount of foreign-source and domestic-source income × (taxable income of an item in a foreign country ÷ total taxable income)

Of course, if the residence country adopts proportional tax rate, the above calculation formula can be simplified. As a supplement to overall limitation, item-by-item limitation can make up for the lack of overall limitation. In fact, the above problem exists not only in overall limitation, but also in country-by-country limitation.

The calculation method of limitation on credit for Chinese enterprises and individuals is mainly country-by-country limitation. It is stipulated in Chinese relevant tax laws that if the enterprise can provide foreign duty paid certificate comprehensively, we can use the per-country limitation instead of item-by-item limitation to calculate its foreign tax credit. It is the same with the individuals, but there is some difference between them that we adopt per-country and item-by-item limitation together for individuals in China.

The three methods for limiting the foreign tax credit are not mutually exclusive. For example, a country could use an overall limitation as the basic limitation but the item-by-item limitation for certain types of incomes such as interest income and shipping income. The United States uses this type of hybrid method. Its separate limitations for different types of incomes are often referred to as "the separate baskets approach".

2) Direct credit and indirect credit

Because foreign tax credit method involves a wide range of different income of companies, enterprises, individuals who have different economic relationships and has different processing modes, the calculation is more complicated. In practical application, credit method can be divided into direct credit and indirect credit.

(1) Direct credit.

Direct credit refers that the taxpayer of residence country uses the foreign taxes paid by him directly to credit his domestic taxes payable. The foreign taxes paid directly by residents can be the

Chapter 4 INTERNATIONAL DOUBLE TAXATION RELIEF

taxes on individual residents' business income because of their economic activities, can be the taxes paid by the foreign branches of the head office in residence country (the head office and its branch belong to the same legal entity in law) and also can be the withholding taxes on investment income of parent company from its foreign subsidiary such as dividends and interest. Obviously, credit method is applicable for transnational taxpayers of the same economic entities. Its basic characteristic is that the foreign tax allowable as a credit must be the income tax paid directly by transnational taxpayers to the non-residence country and the income tax paid indirectly cannot be creditable. So, this method is applicable for the credit of individual income tax, enterprise income tax between head office and branch and withholding tax between parent company and its foreign subsidiary.

Under direct credit, the calculation formula of tax payable to residence country is as follows:

Tax payable to residence country = (taxable income of residence country + taxable income of source country) ×tax rate of residence country − actual creditable amount

= total taxable income of resident×tax rate of residence country − actual creditable amount

 Simulated demonstration of 4-9

[**Background**]: *Assume that ACo, the resident corporation of Country A, earns 100 million Yuan in a taxable year. Among them, 80,000,000 Yuan is from Country A and 20,000,000 Yuan is from its branch in Country B (the source country). Now, calculate the amount of tax payable to Country A of ACo under direct credit.*

[**Calculation** 1]:

If the applicable tax rate in Country A and B is 30 percent, the amount of allowance as a credit against the tax payable in Country A is the total foreign income tax paid to Country B by its branch.

Country A tax before credit on its worldwide income = 100 million×30% = 30,000,000 (Yuan).

Foreign tax paid by branch in Country B = 20,000,000×30% = 6,000,000 (Yuan).

The actual creditable amount = 6,000,000 (Yuan).

Country A tax after credit = 30,000,000 − 6,000,000 = 24,000,000 (Yuan).

Total tax = 24,000,000 + 6,000,000 = 30,000,000 (Yuan).

[**Comments** 1]:

In the above situation, when the tax rate of residence and source country is the same, the head office in residence country can use all of the foreign tax paid by its foreign branch to credit its tax payable. The total tax of the head office is still 30,000,000 Yuan and does change because of having foreign income.

[**Calculation** 2]:

If the applicable tax rate in Country A and Country B is respectively 30 percent and 20 percent, the amount of allowance as a credit against the tax payable in Country A is only the actual foreign tax paid by the branch to Country B. After the credit, the head office has to pay additional tax on income from Country B at the rate of difference of two countries.

Country A tax before credit on its worldwide income: 100 million×30% = 30,000,000 (Yuan).

Foreign tax paid by branch in Country B: 20,000,000×20% = 4,000,000 (Yuan).

Limitation on credit of branch: 20,000,000×30% = 6,000,000 (Yuan).

The actual creditable amount: 4,000,000 (Yuan).

Country A tax after credit: 30,000,000−4,000,000 = 26,000,000 (Yuan).

Total tax: 26,000,000+4,000,000 = 30,000,000 (Yuan).

[Comments 2]:

In the above situation, when the tax rate of residence country is higher than the rate of source country, the total tax on the income from Country A and B after credit is equal to the tax payable to Country A on the worldwide income of the head office.

[Calculation 3]:

If the applicable tax rate in Country A and Country B is respectively 30 percent and 40 percent, the amount of allowable as a credit against the tax payable in Country A is the amount of tax on foreign income of branch at the rate of Country A, not the actual tax paid by the branch to Country B.

Country A tax before credit on its worldwide income: 100 million×30% = 30,000,000 (Yuan).

Foreign tax paid by branch in Country B: 20,000,000×40% = 8,000,000 (Yuan).

Limitation on credit of branch: 20,000,000×30% = 6,000,000 (Yuan).

The actual creditable amount: 6,000,000 (Yuan).

Country A tax after credit: 30,000,000−6,000,000 = 24,000,000 (Yuan).

Total tax: 24,000,000+8,000,000 = 32,000,000 (Yuan).

[Comments 3]:

In the above situation, when the tax rate of source country is higher than the rate of residence country, because of the limitation on credit rules in residence country, parts of the foreign tax paid by the taxpayer isn't creditable in the residence country. So, the actual tax burden of taxpayer is higher than that of the above two situations (the ACo has to pay more tax of 2,000,000 Yuan).

(2) Indirect credit.

Many credit countries provide what is often referred to as an "indirect" foreign tax credit. The indirect credit is a credit granted to a domestic corporation for the foreign income taxes paid by a foreign affiliated company. It is granted at the time when the domestic corporation receives a dividend distribution from its foreign affiliate. The amount allowable as a credit is the amount of the underlying foreign tax paid by the foreign affiliate on the income out of which the dividend was paid. That is to say, the basic characteristic of indirect credit is that only parts of foreign taxes paid can be credited indirectly against tax payable of residence country.

Indirect credit occurs in the following situation. A parent company has a subsidiary in a foreign country. The subsidiary pays corporate income tax to the local government and distributes its after-tax profits to the parent company as a dividend according to the parent company's equity proportion. For the dividend received by the parent company is paid out of the after-tax profits of the subsidiary, this part of dividend is subject to underlying foreign tax for certain. Moreover, the parent company and its subsidiary are different legal entities, so, the underlying tax paid by the subsidiary but burdened by the parent company is just an indirect payment by the parent company instead of a direct payment. In this way, if the parent company uses the foreign tax to credit its tax payable in the residence country, it belongs to indirect credit. It is necessary to point it out that indirect credit between parent company and its subsidiary is applicable only for enterprise income tax of subsidiary in foreign country. If the dividend received by parent company is subject to withholding tax by source country, the withholding tax also is creditable against parent company's tax payable to residence country, subject to any applicable limitation rule. The credit for withholding tax is a direct foreign tax credit, not an indirect credit, because the parent company itself is treated as the payer of the withholding tax. Moreover, the dividend received by the parent company is only parts of the subsidiary's after-tax profits, we cannot exactly or directly know how much enterprise income taxes is imposed on this part of dividend in source country, as well as how much the "gross-up amount" is, (i.e. the pre-tax income), they must be calculated. So, when the government of residence country taxes on the dividends received by the parent company from its foreign subsidiary in summary, it will regard the gross-up amount of profits as the income received from the subsidiary and merge it into the parent company's total income for taxing. The amount allowable as a credit is just some parts of income tax allocated to the dividend.

Ordinarily, a foreign tax credit is allowable only for foreign income taxes that a resident taxpayer directly pays. In effect, the indirect credit ignores the separated corporate existence of the domestic and foreign corporations for the limited purpose of allowing the credit. To claim a credit for taxes paid by a foreign affiliate, the domestic corporation must own at least a minimum percentage, usually 10 percent, of the capital of the foreign corporation.

Under indirect credit, tax payable to residence country by parent company is calculated in two steps.

The first step, calculate the parent company's gross-up amount of income from its foreign subsidiary.

The parent company's gross-up amount of income from its foreign subsidiary = dividends received by parent company + underlying foreign income tax paid by subsidiary on the income out of which the dividend was paid

Also, if the foreign subsidiary adopts proportional income tax rate, the above calculation formula can be simplified as:

The parent company's gross-up amount of income from its foreign subsidiary = dividends received by parent company ÷ (1−income tax rate of subsidiary)

The second step, calculate the foreign tax paid indirectly by the parent company.

Foreign tax paid on the dividends by the parent company = foreign income tax paid by the subsidiary × (dividends received by parent company ÷ after-tax profits of subsidiary)

Also, if the foreign subsidiary adopts proportional income tax rate, the above calculation formula can be simplified as:

Foreign tax paid on the dividends by the parent company = dividends received by parent company ÷ (1−income tax rate of subsidiary) × income tax rate of subsidiary

Finally, we have to compare the foreign tax paid indirectly by the parent company with the limitation on credit (the calculation method is the same as under direct credit). If the former is less than the later, it can be fully credited against tax payable in residence country, otherwise, the amount allowable as a credit is only the limitation.

The basic operation of indirect credit is illustrated in the following examples.

 Simulated demonstration of 4-10

[Background]: *Assume that a parent company, the resident corporation of Country A, sets up a subsidiary in Country B (the subsidiary isn't the parent company's wholly-owned subsidiary). The corporation tax rate of Country A and B is respectively 35% and 30%. The subsidiary's income for a taxable year is 10,000,000 Yuan and Country B levies tax of 3,000,000 (10,000,000×30%) Yuan on that income. The subsidiary distributes 1,000,000 Yuan from its after-tax profits of 7,000,000 (10,000,000-3,000,000) Yuan to the parent company as a dividend. (Assume that the parent company has no income from Country A).*

[Calculation]:

The parent company's gross-up amount of income from its foreign subsidiary: 1,000,000 + 3,000,000×[1,000,000÷(10,000,000-3,000,000)] = 1,428,571 (Yuan).

Or

The parent company's gross-up amount of income from its foreign subsidiary: 1,000,000÷(1-30%) = 1,428,571 (Yuan).

Foreign income tax paid on the dividends by the parent company: 3,000,000×(1,000,000÷[10,000,000-3,000,000]) = 428,571 (Yuan).

Or

Foreign income tax paid on the dividends by the parent company: 1,000,000÷(1-30%) × 30% = 428,571 (Yuan).

Limitation on credit of subsidiary: 1,428,571×35% = 500,000 (Yuan).

The actual creditable amount: 428,571 (Yuan).

Country A tax after credit: 500,000-428,571 = 71 429 (Yuan).

[Comments]: *From the above calculation we can see, the income tax of 71,429 Yuan paid by the parent company to Country A is actually the additional tax collected by Country A after credit. In general situation, the subsidiary's income is subject to not only corporate income tax by source country, but also withholding tax when the dividend is distributed to the parent company. Therefore, the residence country will combine direct credit with indirect credit for taxing.*

 Simulated demonstration of 4-11

[Background]: *Assume the content is the same with simulated demonstration of 4-10. Withholding tax rate of Country B is 10%. When the subsidiary distributes 1,000,000 Yuan to parent company as a dividend, it is subject to withholding tax of 100,000 Yuan.*

[Calculation]: *Taxes paid and credit are illustrated below.*

Foreign taxes paid directly and indirectly by the parent company: 100,000+428,571 = 528,571

(Yuan).

Limitation on credit of subsidiary: 1,428,571×35%≈500,000 (Yuan).

The actual creditable amount: 500,000 (Yuan).

Country A tax after credit: 500,000−500,000=0 (Yuan).

[**Comments**]: From the above calculation we can see, the parent company doesn't pay any tax to Country A. In another word, Country A doesn't collect any tax from the parent company.

 Simulated demonstration of 4-12

[**Background**]: Assume that a parent company, resident of Country A, sets up a subsidiary in Country B and has its 50% of stocks (the subsidiary isn't the parent company's wholly-owned subsidiary). In a taxable year, the parent company earns 10,000,000 Yuan from Country A and the subsidiary earns 5,000,000 Yuan from Country B. The corporation tax rate of Country A and B is respectively 40% and 35%. Moreover, Country B allows the subsidiary to retain 10% of after-tax profits (i.e. undistributed profits) and the dividend distributed to the parent company is subject to withholding tax at a rate of 10%.

[**Calculation**]: Taxes paid and credit are illustrated below.

Taxes paid by the subsidiary:

Corporate income tax paid to Country B: 5,000,000×35%=1,750,000 (Yuan).

After-tax profit: 5,000,000−1,750,000=3,250,000 (Yuan).

The retained after-tax profit: 3,250,000×10%=325,000 (Yuan).

Distributable dividends: 3,250,000−325,000=2,925,000 (Yuan).

Dividend paid to the parent company: 2,925,000×50%=1,462,500 (Yuan).

Withholding tax on the dividend paid: 1,462,500×10%=146,250 (Yuan).

Taxes paid by the parent company:

The parent company's gross-up amount of income from its foreign subsidiary: 1,462,500+1,750,000×(1,462,500÷3,250,000) = 2,250,000 (Yuan).

Or

The parent company's gross-up amount of income from its foreign subsidiary: 1,462,500÷(1−35%) = 2,250,000 (Yuan).

Foreign income tax paid on the dividends by the parent company: 1,750,000×(1,462,500÷3,250,000) = 787,500 (Yuan).

Or

Foreign income tax paid on the dividends by the parent company: 1,462,500÷(1−35%)×35% =787,500 (Yuan).

Limitation on credit of subsidiary: 2,250,000×40%=900,000 (Yuan).

Foreign taxes paid directly and indirectly by the parent company: 146,250+787,500=933,750 (Yuan).

The actual creditable amount: 900,000 (Yuan).

Country A tax after credit: (10,000,000 + 2,250,000) × 40% − 900,000 = 4,000,000 (Yuan).

[Comments]: *In the above calculation, we have to calculate the results according to the above two important formulas instead of the percentage of holding stocks.*

To avoid double taxation between parent company and its multilateral foreign affiliated companies, indirect credit is applicable not only to the dividend received by the parent company from its foreign subsidiary, but also applicable to the dividend from its foreign grandson company, great-grandson company and other multilateral foreign affiliated companies. But the specific calculation steps are more complex.

3) Allocation of expenses

Whether a country uses an exemption method or a credit method for providing relief from international double taxation, it should have rules for allocating a proper portion of the expenses incurred by its taxpayers between their foreign-source gross income and their domestic-source gross income. Most countries recognize the need for such rules when they are taxing non-residents on their domestic-source income. They routinely deny such non-residents a deduction for expenses unless those expenses are properly related to the earning of the domestic income subject to tax. Few countries seem to be aware of the comparable need to apportion properly the expenses of their domestic taxpayers between domestic-source and foreign-source income.

For countries that exempt foreign-source income, expenses incurred by the taxpayer to earn the income should not be deductible. For example, a taxpayer should not be allowed to deduct its interest expense on borrowed funds used to earn exempt foreign-source income. A country that allows such expenses to be deductible provides its taxpayers with an incentive to earn exempt foreign-source income rather than taxable domestic-source income. In effect, the country is providing an exemption not only for foreign-source income but also for a portion of domestic-source income.

Most countries lack specific rules for attributing expenses to foreign-source income. Two approaches that might be used for that purpose are tracing and apportionment.

A tracing approach involves a factual inquiry into the connection between the expenses and the foreign-source income. Apportionment, on the other hand, involves the allocation of expenses by formula, either on the basis of the proportion of the taxpayer's foreign assets to its total assets or the proportion of its foreign gross income to its total gross income. Unlike tracing, apportionment is based on an assumption that the relevant expenses were incurred to support all of the taxpayer's assets or income-earning activities equally.

Countries that implement the credit method should allow resident taxpayers to deduct expenses incurred to earn foreign-source income because those taxpayers are taxable on their worldwide income. As explained above, however, the foreign tax credit is invariably limited to the amount of a country's tax otherwise imposed on foreign-source taxable income. For this purpose, the amount of a taxpayer's foreign-source taxable income must be computed properly or the limitation on the credit will be improperly inflated. To compute foreign-source income properly, the taxpayer should be required to deduct from foreign-source gross income the expenses incurred to earn that income.

The need for expense allocation rules can be illustrated with a simple example.

Chapter 4 INTERNATIONAL DOUBLE TAXATION RELIEF

Simulated demonstration of 4-13

[**Background**]: Assume that a resident corporation borrows 1,000 Yuan with interest at 8 percent annually and uses the loan proceeds to finance the business activities of a foreign branch. The foreign branch produces gross income of 280 Yuan. After deducting the interest payment of 80 Yuan, the branch's net income is 200 Yuan. The net income of 200 Yuan is subject to foreign tax of 50 percent, resulting in a tax of 100 Yuan. If the corporation's domestic-source income is 2,000 Yuan, the corporation's total net income is 2,200 Yuan. Assuming that the domestic tax rate is 40 percent, the tax payable, prior to subtracting the allowable credit, is 880 Yuan (40% of 2,200 Yuan). Subject to the limitation rules, the corporation is entitled to a credit for the foreign taxes paid. The credit is limited, however, to the lesser of 100 Yuan and 80 Yuan (880×200/2,200). The 80 Yuan in this calculation represents the amount of domestic tax otherwise imposed on the taxpayer's foreign-source taxable income, as shown in Table 4-2.

Table 4-2 Tax Situation of a resident company unit: Yuan

Gross foreign income	280
Interest expense	80
Net foreign income	200
Foreign tax (50% rate)	100
Net domestic income	2,000
Total income (200+2,000)	2,200
Tax of 40%	880
Credit for foreign tax	80
Total tax	800

[**Comments**]: In the above example, the interest of 80 Yuan was applied or allocated totally against the foreign-source income. If it had been applied against domestic-source income, because the limitation was 112 Yuan (880×280/2,200), only 112 Yuan of the foreign taxes of 140 Yuan (280×50%) would be creditable against the domestic tax which was more than 80 Yuan. Assuming that the interest is properly attributable to the foreign-source income, it should be so attributed in computing the limitation on the credit because the domestic tax system otherwise would be given a credit for foreign taxes in excess of the domestic taxes on the foreign-source net income. It is crucial, therefore, in protecting the domestic tax base, for interest and other expenses to be attributed properly to domestic-source and foreign-source income.

An appropriated amount of expenses should be also attributed to foreign-source income for purposes of computing the limitation on the indirect credit. In addition, the indirect credit raises the issue of the timing of the deduction of expenses incurred by a resident parent corporation to earn foreign-source income through a foreign affiliate. Residence-country tax on foreign-source income earned through a foreign affiliate is generally postponed until the resident parent corporation receives a dividend (or other taxable distribution). Interest and other expenses incurred by the resident taxpayer to earn that deferred income should not be deductible, at least theoretically, until the income to which they are related is subject to taxation. These payments should become deductible when the resident taxpayer receives a taxable distribution of the related income from its foreign affiliate. Few countries currently attempt to deal with this timing issue.

4) Tax sparing credit

Tax sparing credit is a credit granted by the residence country for foreign taxes that for some reason were not actually paid to the source country but that would have been paid under the country's normal tax rules. The usual reason for the tax not being paid is that the source country has provided a tax holiday or other tax incentive to foreign investors as an encouragement to invest or conduct business in the country. In the absence of tax sparing credit, the actual beneficiary of a tax incentive provided by a source country to attract foreign investment may be the residence country rather than the foreign investor. This result occurs whenever the reduction in source-country tax is replaced by an increase in residence-country tax. For the residence country, tax sparing credit is not a way of avoiding international double taxation, but a preferential tax measure granted by the residence country to its taxpayer who is engaged in international economic activities.

Simulated demonstration of 4-14

[Background]: Assume Country A, a developing country whose normal corporate tax rate is 30 percent, offers foreign corporations a 10-year tax holiday if they establish a manufacturing enterprise in Country A. BCo, a resident corporation of Country B, establishes a manufacturing plan in Country A. Country B imposes corporate tax at a rate of 40 percent and uses a foreign tax credit system.

[Calculation]: At Table 4-3, BCo earns income of 1,000 in Country A in the first year. In the absence of the tax holiday, Country A would impose a tax of 300 (1,000×30%) on BCo. Country B would impose on BCo a tax of 100, determined by subtracting from the tax of 400 (1,000×40%) otherwise payable a foreign tax credit of 300. So, the total tax liability of BCo is 400 (300+100); The tax holiday eliminates Country B's tax of 300. BCo's tax liability in Country B becomes 400 minus the allowable credit, which is zero because BCo did not actually pay any tax to Country A. The total tax liability of BCo is still 400 (0+400). Thus, the tax revenue of 300 forgone by Country A in granting the tax holiday to BCo goes to the benefit of Country B and not BCo.

If Country B were willing to give a tax sparing credit to BCo for the taxes forgone by Country A, then BCo would get the benefit of the tax holiday. Its income in Country A would be 1,000, and it would pay no tax to Country A. It would have an initial tax obligation of 400 in Country B but would be allowed to reduce that amount by the 300 of tax forgone by Country A, for a total tax liability of 100.

Table 4-3 Tax situation of foreign company in countries A and B unit: Yuan

Country A	
Income from Country A	1,000
Country A tax before holiday	300
Tax holiday credit	300
Country A tax	0

Chapter 4 INTERNATIONAL DOUBLE TAXATION RELIEF

续表

Country B	
Income from Country A	1,000
Country B tax	400
Tax sparing credit	300
Total Country B tax	100

[**Comments**]: *The shifting of the benefit of an incentive from the foreign investor to its home country's treasury in the absence of tax sparing is illustrated by the above example. That is to say, the tax forgone by developing country will become the tax revenue of investor's home country most of which are developed countries. It reduces revenue of developing country and increases revenue of developed country. So, tax sparing is primarily a feature of tax treaties between developing and developed countries. Some developing countries traditionally have refused to enter into a tax treaty with a developed country unless they obtain a tax sparing credit. Many developed countries extend some form of tax sparing to developing countries by way of treaty as a matter of course. Some developed countries have voluntarily granted tax sparing in their treaties with developing countries as a way of encouraging investment in those countries. But other developed countries have granted the tax sparing credit only reluctantly.*

The United States is adamantly opposed to tax sparing and has not granted it in any of its tax treaties. Consequently, for many years it concluded very few tax treaties with developing countries. The US position is that the grant of a credit for phantom taxes—taxes not actually paid—is inconsistent with the efficiency and fairness goals of its foreign tax credit and encourages developing countries to engage in beggar-my-neighbor bidding wars with their tax incentive programs. This position has been characterized as "arrogant" "imperialistic" and "patronizing", but it is a defensible assessment of the effects of tax sparing. In recent years, the hard-line view of many developing countries has softened, and the list of US tax treaties with developing countries is growing rapidly.

The merits of tax sparing credit cannot be divorced from the merits of the tax incentives that they encourage. Although tax incentives have some enthusiastic supporters in the political arena, they are impossible to justify on the basis of tax policy principles. Certain targeted incentives aimed at achieving some identified goal may be justified, but those incentives are so narrowly drawn to prevent abuse that they trend to generate little political support. The general conclusion to be drawn from the voluminous tax literature dealing with tax incentives is that the costs of tax incentives are typically large, the benefits are always uncertain, and only rarely do the potential benefits justify the likely costs.

Another problem with tax sparing is the potential for abusive tax avoidance. For example, generous tax sparing credit in a particular treaty often encourages residents of third countries to establish conduit entities in the country granting tax sparing. Tax sparing also puts pressure on the enforcement of a country's transfer pricing rules because taxpayers have an incentive to shift profits to the source country.

In 1998, the Organization for Eooperation and Development(OECD) published a report, Tax Sparing: A Reconsideration, which suggests that the case for tax sparing is not persuasive. It recommends that tax sparing be restricted to countries whose economic development is at a considerably lower level than that of OECD member countries. It also sets out some best practices for the design of tax sparing provisions to ensure that the provisions are limited to genuine business investments and are not susceptible to abuse.

4.3 Comparison of different methods of international double taxation relief

The methods allowed using for double taxation relief by national tax laws and international tax agreements includs the deduction method, exemption method, credit method and so on. Each of them has its advantages and disadvantages. Which method is more appropriate depends on every country's tax system structure and tax policy. The most fundamental point is that whether both the residence country's and source country's tax jurisdictions are considered and protected together, as well as whether transnational taxpayer's international double taxation is solved in the main.

1. Comparison of the deduction and exemption methods

Difference between deduction and exemption methods is that the exemption method recognizes the exclusive status of source jurisdiction, while the deduction method just admits limited the prioritized status of sourcejurisdiction. Exemption method exempts its taxpayers from domestic tax on their foreign-source income, but deduction method only allows taxpayers to claim a deduction for taxes paid to a foreign government with respect to foreign-source income. So, the taxpayers' tax burden of deduction method is higher than exemption method. That is to say, exemption method completely eliminates international double taxation, but deduction method is only an appropriate care and it is harmful to international investment and international trade.

2. Comparison of the credit and deduction methods

Recognition of the prioritized status of source jurisdiction is the credit method's prerequisite and the residence country provides its taxpayers with a credit against taxes otherwise payable for income taxes paid to a foreign country within limitation, while the deduction method just admits limited the prioritized status of source jurisdiction and only allows taxpayers to claim a partial deduction for taxes on foreign-source income. Obviously, credit method can effectively eliminate international double taxation but deduction method cannot. Of course, both of them are in common with full consideration of exercising residence country's residence jurisdiction.

3. Comparison of the exemption and credit methods

Exemption method gives up completely tax jurisdiction on taxpayer's foreign-source income, but credit method still exercises residence jurisdiction and just allows taxpayer to credit taxes paid to foreign government. In practice, exemption method can be divided into full exemption and exemption with progression. For the full exemption, the government of residence country recognizes completely the exclusive status of source jurisdiction and gives up its residence jurisdiction. For the

Chapter 4　INTERNATIONAL DOUBLE TAXATION RELIEF

exemption with progression, it is different. Although looked at a superficial glance, it also recognizes the exclusive status of source jurisdiction and gives up the residence jurisdiction, because of its unique calculation method and effect, when the government of residence country exempts its resident's foreign-source income from domestic tax and only taxes on the domestic-source income, it can obtain some parts of revenue for choosing higher tax rate on domestic-source income, which is in fact a protection to residence country's tax right. Under the same situation, its effect is the same as or maybe even better than credit method. Besides, both of them are in common with recognition of exclusive status of source jurisdiction and effect of solving international double taxation.

Key words, phrases and special terms

limitation on credit	抵免限额
direct credit	直接抵免
indirect credit	间接抵免
credit method	抵免法
tax sparing credit	税收饶让抵免
exemption method	免税法
Contracting State	缔约国
withholding tax	预提税
immovable property	不动产
immovable property usufruct	不动产用益权
permanent home	永久性住所
center of vital interests	重要利益中心
habitual dwelling	习惯性居住地
deduction method	扣除法
low taxation method	低税法
tax amount payable	应纳税额
Detailed Rules for the Implementation of Income Tax Law of the People's Republic of China on Enterprises with Foreign Investment and Foreign Enterprises	《中华人民共和国外商投资企业和外国企业所得税法实施细则》
proportional tax rate	比例税率
progressive tax rate	累进税率
full exemption	全额免税法
exemption with progression	累进免税法
individual income tax	个人所得税
progressive taxrate in excess of specific amount	超额累进税率
participation exemption	参股免税
tax payable	应纳税额
full credit	全额抵免
ordinary credit	普通抵免
tax refund	退税

balance of limitation　　　　　　　　　　抵免限额余额
excess credit　　　　　　　　　　　　　　超限抵免额
overall（or worldwide）limitation　　　　综合抵免限额
country-by-country（or per-country）limitation　　分国抵免限额
item-by-item limitation　　　　　　　　　分项抵免限额
actual creditable amount　　　　　　　　 实际抵免额
duty paid certificate　　　　　　　　　　完税凭证
pay additional tax　　　　　　　　　　　 补税
foreign affiliated company　　　　　　　 外国关联公司
underlying foreign tax　　　　　　　　　 子公司所在国税款
gross-up amount　　　　　　　　　　　　　股息还原含税额
tracing approach　　　　　　　　　　　　 追溯法
apportionment approach　　　　　　　　　 分摊法
tax holiday　　　　　　　　　　　　　　　免税期

Problems of thinking

1. What are ways of international double taxation relief?

2. What are methods of international double taxation relief?

3. What's the limitation on credit? How to compute it? Explain its rationality.

4. What's direct credit? What's indirect credit?

5. Under credit method, how does the parent company pay domestic taxes to its residence country?

6. What's the tax sparing? What's its usefulness?

Chapter 5
INTRODUCTION TO INTERNATIONAL TAX AVOIDANCE

Ideological and political points of the course

Customs duties are involved in foreign countries, and the imposition of customs duties on goods is bound to raise the operating costs of taxpayers and directly affect the development of international trade. It is not only an economic relationship, but also a political relationship. Considering Chinese economy and the fact that China has taken the active performance to fulfill its role as a major country, we recognize Chinese significant contribution to the people of the world, especially its assistance to developing countries.

Learning Objectives

1. Grasp comprehensively the difference and connections between tax avoidance, tax evasion and tax saving.
2. Master the concept of international tax avoidance essentially and know the causes of its nomination.
3. Know the concept of tax havens and its types.
4. Master the characteristics of tax havens.

Course Importing

Tax havens have different names in different countries: it is called "tax havens" in English country, "fiscal havens" in French and "fiscal oasis" in Germany. Often, tax haven countries and regions often describe themselves as "financial center". What is their nature?

5.1 The concept of international tax avoidance

As we know, everything has two aspects which are positive and negative. And international taxation is no exception. As the opposite side of international double taxation, international tax avoidance is also a popular and interesting social economic phenomenon and it is the inevitable outcome of the development of commodity economy. International double taxation will damage the transnational taxpayer's economic interests, which is not conducive to the development of international economic activities; and international tax avoidance can relieve transnational taxpayer's tax burden, but it will affect the tax benefits of relevant states and distort tax distribution relationships between countries. Therefore, governments and international community should not only take measures to avoid the international double taxation, but also take measures to prevent transnational taxpayer's international tax avoidance.

1. The meaning of tax avoidance

to understand what tax avoidance, It is natural firstly is to find out what international tax avoidance is. Tax avoidance is always an important problem in tax collection and management work of all countries, which is different from tax saving, tax evasion and tax dodging, but also has some commons with them. Is tax avoidance legal or illegal? To answer this question, we have to analyze and compare it comprehensively with tax saving, tax evasion and tax dodging.

1) Tax saving

Tax saving is also called tax planning which is well-known to every household in western countries but little-known in China. Tax planning refers that the taxpayers make advanced planning andarrangements for their business activities, as well as optimization choice of tax programmers to reduce their tax burden as much as possible and obtain proper tax benefits in a lawful fashion, according to the government's guidance of tax policy.

Characteristics of tax planning are legitimacy, planning and purpose. In addition, under the historical conditions of social production, tax planning also reflects the requirements of comprehension and profession. Especially since 1950s, the professional trend of tax planning is very obvious. Faced up to the social production, the expanding international market day by day and complicated tax systems in the world, many enterprises and companies are hiring tax consulting, tax lawyers, auditors, accountants, international financial consultant and other senior professional personnel to engage in tax planning activities, in order to save tax payments. At the same time, there are so many accountants, lawyers and tax offices opening up and developing consulting business with respect to tax planning which results in the emerging of tax agency as the tertiary industry with the time. Therefore, tax saving is a legal activity which should not be opposed and should be protected in tax.

2) Tax evasion and tax dodging

Tax evasion refers that the taxpayer pays no or less tax by illegal means, usually involving fraudulent nondisclosure of willful deceit. For the basic meaning of tax evasion, people have reached a certain consensus, namely, tax evasion is a kind of illegal activity to reduce taxpayer's tax liability by illegal means. However, it is not explained clearly whether the taxpayer uses the illegal means intentionally or not. In fact, tax evasion may include unconscious violations and intentionally illegal activity. The former mainly refers that the taxpayers violate the provisions of tax law because of ignorance or inadvertence and simply paying no or less tax, that is the tax dodging. For example, because the taxpayers are not familiar with provisions of tax laws and accounting systems or be negligent, they fail to declare some taxable items, less calculate the quantity of taxable products, miscount sales amount or operating profit, misuse tax category, tax items, tax rates and other reasons, plus the lack of collection personnel's business level which leads to tax dodging. Meanwhile, tax evasion refers that the taxpayer pays no or less tax by illegal means intentionally, usually involving fraudulent nondisclosure of willful deceit. But sometimes it is not easy to prove that the taxpayer pay no or less tax intentionally. Therefore, they can be referred to as tax evasion together.

To sum up, the basic characteristics of tax evasion is illegal and fraudulent, so it could be called tax fraud. Compared with tax saving, the difference between tax evasion and tax saving is very obvious. The former is illegal and the latter is permitted by laws. The former is the fraud to tax liability confirmed; the latter is the preceding planning and arrangements to business, investment and financial transactions before the tax obligation engenders.

3) Tax avoidance

Tax avoidance is a controversial concept. It is generally believed that tax avoidance is the deferral, avoidance or reduction of tax by lawful means. Samuelson, the contemporary renowned economist, pointed out in his analysis of United States federal tax systems that legal tax avoidance is more important than tax evasion. The reason is that there are so many "loopholes" in regulations enacted by parliaments which allow large income is not taxed or taxed with lower rate. The above contents show that no matter from either the motivation or the final results, there is no obvious dividing line between tax avoidance and tax evasion. Both of them are taxpayers' intentional activities to reduce their tax burden. But they are different concepts after all. Generally, there exists the following difference between them.

(1) Tax evasion refers that the taxpayer avoids tax payments by a variety of means after his tax obligation has occurred, meanwhile, tax avoidance is the avoidance or reduction of tax payable.

(2) Tax evasion goes against tax laws directly which is illegal. But tax avoidance uses loopholes in tax law which doesn't infringe tax law directly. So its form is legal.

(3) Tax evasion is not only in violation of tax law, but also often uses some criminal means such as making false accounting books or forging documents, so it should be punished by law (criminal detention or imprisonment). tax avoidance is a legal behavior and doesn't go against tax law, so it shouldn't be punished by law.

The main difference between tax avoidance and tax saving is that the former is against the national tax policy guidance and intent though it is legal. The latter is legal completely and consistent with tax policy guidance or encouragement.

To prevent tax avoidance, the government can take two measures: One is to improve the tax law and stop the loopholes in it to make the taxpayer have no chance to avoid tax; the other is to introduce the concept of "power shopping" or "law shopping" to tax laws. It means in one aspect, the taxpayer has the right to choose the way of minimizing his tax obligations to run business. In another aspect, for the transaction that the taxpayer arranges with consideration for tax avoidance entirely, the government can disregard it and deem the taxpayer abusing his right given by the government. The tax authority may, according to the principle of genuine business objective, disregard the taxpayer's arrangement for tax avoidance and adjust its consequences.

2. The meaning of international tax avoidance

International tax avoidance is the extension and development of tax avoidance in international scope. It means that the transnational taxpayer utilizes the difference and loopholes in tax laws of different countries to avoid or reduce his tax liability by all kinds of overt and legal ways. The two key points to grasp the concept of international tax avoidance are as follows.

1) The difference of international tax avoidance from national tax avoidance

National tax avoidance refers that the taxpayer uses the loopholes in domestic tax laws for avoiding tax without transnational business activity. Tax liability avoided is only the domestic tax obligation in residence country. But international tax avoidance refers that the transnational taxpayer utilizes the difference between tax systems of different countries and loopholes in foreign or international tax laws to avoid tax. It requires that the taxpayer to be engaged in some transnational activities, immigrates himself, or transfers his own capital or property out of the residence country and makes it flow between countries. The tax obligations avoided through international tax avoidance are not limited to the obligation in the residence country, but also includes the obligation in the source country. The purpose of the taxpayer is not only reduction of tax burden in a country, but the reduction of the global tax burden.

2) The difference of international tax avoidance from international tax evasion

International taxevasion refers that the taxpayer uses illegal ways to escape his tax liability which has already engendered in the transnational business activities. Just like the national tax evasion, it is a kind of illegal behavior. But the way used by taxpayer in international tax avoidance is usually overt and legal which isn't against the national tax laws. So, it does not belong to illegal behavior in general. Due to the fact that the attribute of international tax avoidance and international tax evasion is different, the treatment is different, too. For international tax evasion, the relevant countries will punish the taxpayer just like the domestic tax evasion. But for international tax avoidance, the relevant country can only improve the national foreign tax laws or amend the tax treaties it signs with other countries and stop the loopholes in it to make the taxpayer have no chance to avoid tax. Of course, it can't punish the taxpayer severely like international tax evasion.

5.2　The causes of international tax avoidance

The initial causes of tax avoidance are taxpayers' resisting government's heavy tax burden and keeping their interests. After various tax evasions and severely punished by law, they want to seek more effective methods to avoid tax burden. The causes of international tax avoidance are the same. After the Second World War, international tax avoidance nominates widely and has been developing rapidly in the world. The causes are nothing more than the intrinsic motivation and external conditions, namely, the causes of international tax avoidance include two aspects of subjective and objective.

1. From the subjective point of view

The transnational taxpayer's pursuit of maximum profits is the intrinsic motivation of interna-

Chapter 5 INTRODUCTION TO INTERNATIONAL TAX AVOIDANCE

tional tax avoidance. Profit maximization is the common goals of all taxpayers who are engaged in production, business and investment activities. It is the same as transnational taxpayers. There are so many ways of reducing tax liability such as hidden illegal tax evasion and overt tax avoidance. However, if the transnational taxpayer adopts tax evasion to reduce his tax burden, he will be punished severely by the relevant country. Thus, his reputation is gone and his money is lost. Finally, the loss outweighs the gain. Therefore, many multinational taxpayers wouldn't take this way with great risks to reduce their tax burden, but they are willing to use the way of tax avoidance to achieve their goals. Because tax avoidance is not illegal and won't be cracked down by law, meanwhile, it can bring extra profit to taxpayers, thus, the most effective and less risky way of reducing tax burden is no more than tax avoidance.

2. From the objective point of view

The differences of tax systems between countries (regions) and loopholes in tax laws are the external conditions of international tax avoidance. People often say that the internal cause is the power, the external cause is the condition, and only the combination of internal and external causes can lead to the result. All in all, the objective causes of international tax avoidance are mainly the following several aspects.

(1) Different tax jurisdictions between countries (regions) and different judgment norms on resident identity and source place of income between countries (regions) provide a tax jurisdiction vacuum for transnational taxpayers which make it possible that the taxpayers can avoid any tax liabilities of any countries and regions.

In history, there was a famous Langbo case for tax avoidance which used the tax jurisdiction vacuum. Langbo, a British inventor of a turbine blade, transferred his invention to a company of Qatar and got technology transfer fee of $47,500. Because the beneficiary of technology transfer fee, Langbo, was not the resident of Qatar, he didn't have to pay taxes to Qatar government and avoided the tax liability. At the same time, Langbo sold his house in Britain and moved to China Hong Kong. Because he had no domicile in Britain, he avoided the tax liability to Britain government. Hong Kong only exercises source jurisdiction and does not impose taxes on the income from areas outside Hong Kong. In this way, Langbo had got a lot of technology transfer fee, but because it was in the tax jurisdiction vacuum of different countries (regions), he didn't have to pay any taxes to any countries.

(2) Different tax rates. Tax rate is the core of tax law which directly decides the tax burden of taxpayers. If the tax rates of all countries and regions in the world are the same and there is no place for international tax avoidance, taxpayers can not avoid taxes through transnational flows of personnel or property. But in practice, great difference between tax rates of different countries exists. Some high, some low, and some countries even do not levy income tax. It provides taxpayers with chances to transfer income from countries with high tax rate to countries with low tax rate for tax avoidance. Especially, the wide existence of tax havens is one of the important prerequisite of international tax avoidance.

(3) Wide existence of international tax treaties. In order to prevent international double taxation, there are a large number of international tax treaties in the world. However, some provisions

of tax treaties can easily be used by transnational taxpayers for international tax avoidance. For example, nowadays, many countries impose much higher withholding tax on dividends, interest, royalties paid to foreign residents by domestic residents. But if a country enters into a tax treaty with another country, the rate of withholding tax on dividend, interest paid to the foreign residents of contracting states will be greatly reduced. Then, if a resident company of a third country wants to get the benefits of withholding tax from the tax treaty, he can just establish an intermediary affiliated company in one of the contracting states for convenient using the tax treaty to reduce its tax liability of withholding tax. This is the issue of treaty shopping which will be discussed below. It is an important way to multinational corporations for international tax avoidance. The wide existence of international tax treaties provides convenience to international tax avoidance.

(4) The loopholes in foreign tax law. The loopholes in foreign tax law of a country can also provide favorable conditions to the taxpayer for international tax avoidance. Typical example of this aspect is the deferral of domestic tax provision in some developed countries. Deferral of domestic tax refers to the practice of subjecting the profits derived from foreign investment through foreign corporations to taxation only when the profits are repatriated to the residence country of the investor. In fact, the reason why developed countries exercise deferral of domestic tax is to promote the development of domestic resident company's overseas subsidiaries and enhance their competition ability with local companies. But this provision is later used by many multi-national corporations for international tax avoidance. They set up their own subsidiaries in low-tax country or international tax havens, transfer profits to the subsidiaries through a variety of means and keep the profits distributed in overseas subsidiaries for long time. Due to the deferral of domestic tax, the multinational corporations avoid heavier tax of residence country successfully by this method.

In addition, there are some objective non-tax reasons for the nomination of transnational tax avoidance. For example, the degree of relaxed or strict foreign exchange control and the difference between company laws, immigration laws, bank secrecy acts and inflation will affect greatly the transnational taxpayer's international tax avoidance behavior, that is, it may lead to the transfer of taxpayers or tax objects from one country to another.

 5.3　Tax havens

In the social economic life, quite a number of countries and regions implement tax policy with zero tax or low tax for certain economic purpose and formulate preferential tax regimes which provide legitimate convenient conditions to multinational investor for international tax avoidance. These countries and regions have very strong attraction for foreign investors which are so-called "international tax havens".
To reduce the tax burden, multinational investors often use them for international tax avoidance.

5.3.1　The concept of tax havens

When people talk about tax havens, they also often call them free port, peace port or safe port. Under this situation, the so-called "port" often refers to a country or a region which is be-

Chapter 5 INTRODUCTION TO INTERNATIONAL TAX AVOIDANCE

yond its initial narrow sense of "port" or "harbor".

Tax havens, also known as international tax havens, refer to those countries or regions which subject income (or some forms of income) or entities (or certain entities) to low or no taxation. In essence, tax havens refer to those places where foreigners can obtain income or own assets and don't have to pay high taxes, its existence is an important prerequisite to transnational taxpayers for international tax avoidance.

Although people have been very familiar with "tax havens", so far, there is not a universally accepted definition about it. According to the OECD report, a tax haven is a country with no nominal taxes on income from mobile business activities which also meet at least one of the following three additional conditions:

(1) it does not exchange tax information effectively with other countries.

(2) it provides tax benefits to taxpayers in a non-transparent fashion.

(3) it does not require non-residents to engage in substantial business activities in the tax haven in order to qualify for tax benefits. So, some countries rely on a list of countries without any definition of what is a tax haven.

The general definition of a tax haven is invariably based on a comparison of the taxes levied in the foreign country and in the residence country. If the foreign country actually levies taxes at approximately the same rate as the residence country, the foreign country should not be considered as a tax haven because it can not be used to defer or avoid substantial amounts of residence country taxes. The comparison of domestic and foreign tax rates can be based on: nominal tax rates, average effective tax rates or the actual foreign tax paid by a particular CFC (controlled foreign company).

The use of nominal tax rates to identify a tax haven is problematic because it ignores the generous deductions, exemptions, credits, or allowances that may be afforded by a foreign country. The only advantage of using nominal tax rates is that they are easy to determine. The average effective tax rate of a country is a somewhat better indicator of its status as a tax haven. Effective tax rates, however, are often difficult to determine, and they would have to be determined annually for every country where a CFC of a resident corporation is resident. Moreover, just because a country with high effective tax rates does not mean that a particular CFC resident in that country may not be subject to low foreign taxes. A few countries, such as Finland, Germany, and Spain, use the effective tax rate approach in defining a tax haven. For example, under the German CFC rules, a CFC is considered to be resident in a low-tax country if the effective tax rate in the country is less than 25 percent. In Finland and Portugal, the CFC rules apply to CFCs resident in countries that levy tax at effective rates that are less than 60 percent of the Finnish and Portuguese taxes respectively. Most countries, however, focus on the actual foreign tax paid by a CFC. For example, in France and Norway, the CFC rules apply if the actual foreign tax paid by the CFC on the relevant income is less than two-thirds of the French or Norwegian tax that the CFC would have paid if it had been resident in France or Norway. The comparison of the actual foreign tax paid by a CFC and the domestic tax that the CFC would have paid as a resident is the theoretically correct approach because it focuses on the situation of each particular CFC. This approach imposes the onerous compliance burden on taxpayers of computing the amount of their domestic tax.

As a result of the difficulties of defining a tax haven, most countries have supplemented their tax haven definition with a list of either tax haven countries or non-tax haven countries. The list may be included in domestic legislation, or it may be issued by the tax authorities. Such a list is intended to provide taxpayers and tax officials with concrete guidance. The legal significance of the lists varies widely. In some cases, the fact that a country appears on the list is determinative of its status as a tax haven or a non-tax haven. In other cases, the list is used merely to establish a rebut-table presumption that a country is a tax haven.

5.3.2 Types of tax havens

Generally, tax havens can be divided into the following types.

(1) Countries or regions without any income tax. Among them, some countries and regions not only do not levy income tax, but also do not impose any property tax. This type of tax haven is usually referred to as a "pure tax haven" or "typical tax haven". At present, this type of pure tax haven includes mainly Bahamas, Bermuda, Cayman Islands, Nauru, Vanuatu, Turks and Caicos Islands and Tonga.

(2) Countries or regions with low income tax. This type of tax haven includes Switzerland, Ireland, Liechtenstein, the Channel Islands, British Virgin Islands and Solomon Islands.

(3) Countries or regions with only source jurisdiction for income tax. Such countries and regions impose income tax (generally, tax rate is low), but the taxpayer's overseas income is free of tax. So under some conditions, it provides a convenience for multinational corporation's tax avoidance. In the past, many Latin American countries belonged to this type of tax haven such as Panama and Costa Rica. China Hong Kong also belongs to this type of tax haven.

(4) Countries or regions which impose normal tax on domestic companies but offer some special tax preferences to some special companies. This type of tax haven includes Luxembourg and Barbados.

(5) Countries or regions having numerous tax treaties with other countries. According to the international tax treaty, the contracting state has to offer each other some tax preferences to the resident of another contracting state, most of which is the withholding tax preferences. If a country has extensive international tax treaties with other countries, it might be used by the resident of a third country for international tax avoidance by means of abusing international tax treaties. So, many people insist that these countries or regions which have a large number of international tax treaties with other countries should also be viewed as tax havens, such as Holland.

5.3.3 Characteristics of tax heavens

Looking at all types of tax havens, We will fird that it generally have tax and non-tax characteristics.

1. Tax characteristics

1) Unique "low tax" structures

A low tax burden is a basic characteristic of tax haven. Not only the tax burden in GDP is

Chapter 5 INTRODUCTION TO INTERNATIONAL TAX AVOIDANCE

low, but also the tax burden of direct tax is not high. Objects of direct tax are generally property, capital, profit or income and its tax burden is hard to shift. But the low tax burden of direct tax can attract external resources like magnet.

2) The tax structure with income tax being the mainpart

Except a few consumption goods, countries and regions in tax havens generally do not impose turnover tax and their import and export duty for commodity is also very loose.

2. Non-tax characteristics

Except for no tax or low tax, tax havens have some other advantages which appeal to transnational investors greatly. These advantages are in fact the non-tax characteristics of tax havens and only with these characteristics will tax havens really become transnational investors' "tax avoidance havens".

1) Stable politics and society

As a tax haven, political and social stability is the prerequisite; otherwise it can not attract multinational corporations to invest there. At present, some famous tax havens in the world are small countries or semi-autonomous regions with stable politics. Many countries and regions even have no army and it is generally believed that this has laid the foundation for the stable politics of these countries and regions (minimal possibility of coups and civil war). In contrast, because of continued war, many multinational corporations withdrew from Lebanon, the past famous Asian tax haven lost the tax haven status.

2) Convenient transportation and communication

Convenient transportation and communication are "hardware" of tax havens. Now, most of the countries and regions in tax havens have paid great attention to this condition. From the distribution of tax havens in the world, it is not difficult to see that tax havens are mainly distributed in three regions which are the Atlantic and the Caribbean near the North and South America, Europe, the Far East and Oceania. Usually, the important tax havens are closed either to the United States or to Western Europe, Southeast Asia and Australia. They are much closed to the main capital exporting country in geographical location which creates convenient conditions for attracting multinational corporation's investment. In addition, tax havens generally have developed traffic between primary investment countries. Bermuda is only 1,247 kilometers from New York of the United States. There is a flight from Bermuda to New York every 2 hours and the flight time is less than 2 hours. Flight time from Cayman Islands to Miami of the United States is only 1 hour and there are several flights every day. Flight time from Jersey and Guernsey to London is only 1 hour.

3) Strict bank secrecy systems

The main purpose of transnational group company of using tax haven is to transfer profits from its associated company in high tax country to its base company in tax havens artificially. Not surprisingly, it will damage the tax benefits of high tax country, so high tax country will be very concerned about the problem of domestic company's shifting profits abroad. In this case, if the tax haven had no strict bank secrecy systems for customer's deposits, multinational corporation's shifting profits to tax havens will be exposed and high tax country's anti-avoidance measures are relatively easy to obtain results. In order to attract company for tax avoidance, tax haven countries or regions generally have paid great attention to the issues of bank secrecy systems. Some of them have made the bank secrecy act and the secret disclosure of bank staff will be severely punished.

4) No restriction on remitting funds outside of the country

If a multinational corporation wants to use tax haven for tax avoidance, it has to transfer its funds between the base company in tax haven which requires the government of tax haven has no restrictions on remitting funds outside of the country. At present, main tax havens in the world basically meet the requirement of the multinational corporation. There are two main conditions: One situation is that there is no foreign exchange control and most of the tax havens are in the case such as the Cayman Islands, Panama, Switzerland, Luxemburg, Liechtenstein and china Hong Kong. Another situation is that although the tax haven has foreign exchange control, it does not apply to non-resident company such as Bermuda, Netherlands Antilles and Bahamas.

Key words, phrases and special terms

tax avoidance	避税
tax evasion	偷税
tax saving	节税
tax dodging	漏税
tax planning	税收筹划
tertiary industry	第三产业
tax fraud	税收欺诈
loophole	漏洞
technology transfer fee	技术转让费
foreign exchange control	外汇管制
Ccontrolled foreign compang (CFC)	受控外国公司
capital exporting country	资本输出国
group corporation	集团公司

Problems of thinking

1. What's the difference between tax avoidance and tax evasion?

2. What's international tax avoidance? What are the subjective and objective causes of it?

3. What's tax haven? How many types are there with respect to tax havens? What are the characteristics?

4. What conditions should have for a country to become a tax haven?

Chapter 6

GENERAL METHODS OF INTERNATIONAL TAX AVOIDANCE

Ideological and political points of the course

Income tax is a tax levied on income. Those with income pay tax and those without income do not. The collection of corporate income tax is not to reduce the owner's equity of enterprises, but to promote enterprises to strengthen their management activities and improve their profit-making ability which is more conducive to adjusting industrial structure and promoting economic development. Therefore, taxpayers should actively pay taxes. The tax evasion incidents of some movie stars make us realize the importance of paying taxes according to the law. In addition, the preferential policies of corporate income tax also reflect the strong support of the state to small and micro enterprises, high-tech enterprises, software enterprises and so on.

Learning Objectives

1. Grasp comprehensively the general methods of international tax avoidance.
2. Master the tax subject's and object's common methods of transferring tax avoidance.
3. Know the main contents of non-transferring tax avoidance of tax subject and object.

Course Importing

A common business model of a multinational company in a high tax residence country (or a nationality country) is to engage in business activities in the form of a branch in the early days of foreign operation. And when the branch begins to obtain profit, it will be promptly transformed into a subsidiary. What do you think of this phenomenon?

Under the unified domestic law in a country having tax sovereignty, a certain tax subject's burden on a tax object is established. However, if the tax subject and tax object transfer in space to a different country with different tax sovereignty, due to their different domestic laws and different tax treaties they following in dealing with the international tax relationships between other countries, tax burden will inevitably vary greatly. Therefore, when the multinational taxpayer consciously uses it to reduce the international tax burden, international transfer of tax subject and object will become the main methods of international tax avoidance. International transfer here contains two aspects of meanings which are across territory and across tax border. In practice, the transfer of tax subject (hereinafrer refrred to as "Subject") and object (hereinafter referred to as "object") can be performed separately or combined.

6.1 Transferring tax avoidance of subject

Transfer of subject is also known as the flow of person. In international taxation, subject is referred to transnational taxpayers, which includes individuals and multinational legal entities. Transfer of subject contains very extensive content, which is not limited to international transferring of individuals and legal entities, but also includes individual's changing his identity of taxpayer in a country (from the resident to non-resident) and trying to avoid being any resident of any country. Generally speaking, the main purpose of transferring subject is to avoid resident or citizen jurisdiction of high tax country and to reduce the tax burden.

6.1.1 Methods of transferring tax avoidance of subject

For transferring tax avoidance of transnational taxpayer, they usually adopt different methods with consideration of the judgment norms of whether they are the legal norms or the household register norms which are implemented by relevant countries on tax jurisdiction. In addition, they can also adopt other disguised methods.

1. In countries applying legal norms

1) Changing nationality of transnational individual

In countries applying legal norms, transnational taxpayers' unlimited tax liabilities are decided by their identities of nationality or citizenship which are like the invisible rope and connect them closely with the citizen jurisdictions of countries of citizenship. Wherever they go, they can never go out of the tax border of the countries of citizenship. Obviously, in factors causing unlimited tax liability, nationality has the most rigidity. If a transnational taxpayer wants to transfer or avoid his tax burden in country of citizenship with high tax and get rid of the restraint from citizen jurisdiction, the only way is to give up his original nationality and acquire the nationality of another country. Because the changing of nationality is restrictive by the nationality law and immigration law of relevant country, of course, with complicated procedures, and it is guarded by the country exercising citizen jurisdiction, the attempt to change nationality for tax avoidance is hard to work.

2) Changing nationality of transnational legal entity

In countries applying legal norms, the "nationality" of transnational legal entity is obtained by registering legally in the country. Therefore, if a transnational legal entity wants to avoid its tax burden in country of citizenship and change its nationality, as long as it revokes the registration in the country of citizenship and registers in another country, it can avoid its unlimited tax liability under the citizen jurisdiction. However, for an individual or a legal entity, no matter how it transfers or avoids the country of citizenship, it does not necessarily mean that this will eliminate all of

Chapter 6 GENERAL METHODS OF INTERNATIONAL TAX AVOIDANCE

the unlimited tax liability. Because the country implementing citizen jurisdiction often exercises residence jurisdiction at the same time. If some continuous factors and activities of a taxpayer in a country will still fall into the scope of residence jurisdiction, the unlimited tax liability of the taxpayer can not be avoided.

2. In countries applying the household register norms

In countries applying the household register norms, domicile, residence and present time constitute the related factors of unlimited tax liability. If a transnational taxpayer resident in country of high tax wants to transfer or avoid his residence country for tax avoidance, he has to eliminate these related factors by all kinds of ways.

1) Domicile or residence transferring or avoidance of transnational individuals

In a country applying the household register norms, the transferring or avoidance of residence country for a transnational individual is far less difficult than in a country applying legal norms. He has many choices, because the judgment norms on resident are varied.

(1) The genuine migration of domicile.

If a transnational individual resident in a country with high tax, who has a large number of income and properties at home and abroad, wants to reduce his tax burden of unlimited tax liability in residence country, he can directly move to a country with low tax. This is an expatriate behavior which can effectively stop the unlimited tax liability in the original residence country. For the phenomenon purely to avoid the high tax burden and genuinely move abroad, it is referred to as "tax exile" in the international arena. The so-called "tax exile" refers to the phenomenon that the taxpayer gives up his identity of resident in order to avoid paying taxes and perennially constantly moves from one country to another country. This approach is used mainly by two types of individuals: One type is the retired taxpayers, who moved to low tax countries or specific low tax areas from their original high tax countries in order to obtain the benefits in terms of tax on pension, settlement or property such as migration to tax havens, free trade zone, economic development zone, special zone, etc. Another type is the taxpayers who live in a country but work in another country for tax avoidance such as living in Japan and working in Singapore. From the general speaking, the way of genuine migration of domicile for tax avoidance will not involve many legal problems. As long as the taxpayer has certain permitting transferring procedures. So, it is difficult to determine the main purpose of the taxpayer is to avoid tax or not. But the avoidance of gift tax and settlement tax will involve some technical and legal problems. For example: transfer property or gift heritage to tax havens or free port, then achieve the gift and legacy in the name of the company established in tax havens or free port.

(2) The temporary migration of domicile.

It refers that the transnational individual resident in high tax country moves abroad for one or two years for a particular purpose of tax avoidance, and moves back to the residence country after he achieves the purpose. So, it is also called the false move.

 Teaching Case of 6-1

Before the 1971 December, Canada didn't tax on capital gains before it amended its tax sys-

tems. If a Dutch wanted to sell his large stocks in a Holland company and avoided the Holland capital gains tax, he could move to Canada and sell his shares there. Because there were not special provisions with respect to limitations on the practice in tax treaties between Holland and Canada, this type of income could be taxed only by the residence country. But the residence country of the taxpayer was then Canada instead of Holland; therefore, he could avoid all of the capital gains tax in Holland.

(3) Shorten the present time and temporary departure.

Because the judgment norms on determination of residence are closely related to the present time, a transnational individual can use the present time less than six months or a year to avoid residence. To the judgment norms of continuous presence in a country for six months or a year, the taxpayer can depart temporarily and re-enter which makes the present time be less than the continuous stated time for tax avoidance.

Although the provision to determine the residence is so strict in many countries that the transnational taxpayer's intention of presence in a country for long-term and avoidance of residence is hard to be successful, in a year or a longer period of time, the transnational taxpayer still has the opportunity to avoid his tax liability in a country. For example, through the travel between different countries, or presence in different hotels only for a short period of time, sometimes even living on a boat or in a private yacht, a taxpayer can avoid being controlled by residence jurisdiction because of having residence in any country. In the relevant literatures abroad, the people who run around here and there for avoidance of residence jurisdiction are often called "tax refugees". However, for an individual using the above mentioned ways to avoid tax, he must make himself become, at least nominally or formally, a "real" immigration to avoid giving the government an impression of false or partial migration. For the tax avoidance immigrants, many countries have corresponding anti-avoidance measures. For example, the Holland government clearly stipulates that any individual, who has given up residence in Holland and moves abroad, but hasn't a foreign domicile in a year and returns to Holland, shall be recognized as a citizen of Holland and all of income he earns during this period of time is taxable to Holland. The specific provisions of other countries are not the same as Holland, but their basic spirits are the same. So, the transnational taxpayer must try to prevent providing this evidence of incomplete migration to the government. Otherwise, he has to take the risk of double taxation.

(4) Being a temporary taxpayer.

When an individual is sent abroad to engage in some temporary work, he can often enjoy certain preferential tax treatment. The countries often determine the contents of preferential tax according to the features of temporary and non-residential of the individuals sent. Some countries determine the temporary and non-residential based on the present time of the individuals, and some countries adopt the fixed domicile norms. They provide so many preferential taxes for temporary entry and non-resident, in which the exemption projects account for a large proportion.

 Teaching Case of 6-2

The government of the United States stipulates that any income earned by an alien living in the

Chapter 6 GENERAL METHODS OF INTERNATIONAL TAX AVOIDANCE

United States for not more than three months is exempt from income tax. The provisions of Pakistan stipulate that any individual who lives in Pakistan less than nine months is exempt from income tax. A number of countries recognize the individuals without having their official identities of resident or citizen as "the temporary immigrants" and these individuals are free of tax before they are recognized as the "complete" residents or citizens. For example, the USA implements green card system for its residents. Any individual without the green card is considered as "the temporary immigrant" and the individual hasn't any tax liability to the government of the USA. Therefore, foreigners into the United States as "the temporary immigrants" do not have to pay taxes on the income they obtained in the United States.

In addition, for attracting more foreign experts to come to work, a number of countries provide preferential tax to them as the extra compensation for their work abroad. But these tax incentives can easily be used as a method of international tax avoidance.

 Teaching Case of 6-3

Belgium is a high tax country, but it regards the managers sent to work in the PE established in Belgium by foreign companies, who have been living in Belgium for five years to eight years, as "non-residents". Also, it regards individuals working in Belgium with the identities of foreign scientists, who live in Belgium permanently, as "non-residents". For these managers and scientists, only their salaries will be taxed to Belgium. Except the general deduction, they can enjoy special preferential deduction of 30% from their salaries taxable, which can be up to 1,500,000 BEF. Moreover, in any taxable year, if these taxpayers' half work time is in abroad, then, they will obtain free tax of 50% on their taxable income.

(5) Partial migration.

It refers that the multinational individual does not completely give up and get rid of all the factors related to domicile or residence and still keeps some social or economic attachment or contact with his original residence country. For example, a taxpayer moves out, but his family does not move; or transfers part of property that constitutes the ID but still has labor activities and maintains the bank account in the residence country. On the one hand, due to the difference of tax systems between different countries and the lack of enough coordination with tax authorities, the partial migration will provide the taxpayer with opportunity to avoid tax, which can use the fuzzy dividing line between judgment norms on domicile and tax treatments to non-residents for tax avoidance. But on the other hand, because the taxpayer still maintains connections with the residence country, partial migration may also bring the taxpayer the risk of international double taxation.

2) Residence transferring or avoidance of legal entities

(1) False emigration and transfer.

In countries applying the household register norms such as most European countries, residence is the crucial feature to determine whether a company is a resident company or a non-resident company. But an important standard to judge the residence is the place of effective control and management which is based on facts. For example, we can see such case in the UK: A company registered in Britain can be a resident company of another country, while a company registered in other countries may be a British resident company. Therefore, the most important core of changing residence for tax avoidance is to eliminate all actual characteristics of being the place of effective control and management in the residence and source countries, making the residence of company "nihility".

Teaching Case of 6-4

Svel French Steel Co., Ltd used the following ways and methods to avoid having residence in Britain and being the British taxpayer. The British shareholders of the company were not allowed to participate in the management activities. The shares of them were separated from the control and management power. They only had the right to participate and receive dividends. The company selected the non-UK residents to do management work, such as managers and members of the board of directors. The company didn't have meeting of the board of directors and shareholders meeting in Britain. All meetings, materials and reports related to the company were not carried out in British territory, and records or files were kept outside of the UK. No using English telegraph, telecommunications and other relevant ways to issue instructions or commands. For the special need of dealing with emergencies or incidental transactions, the company set up a separate service company in the UK and paid corporation tax in accordance with the approved profit margin to avoid attracting special attention of the British government. All the facts proved that the ways and methods were very correct and effective. According to the report, during the 10 years from 1973 to 1985, the company successfully avoided tax payable of 781 370, 000 dollars to the British government.

In addition, the practice of false emigration of administrative office can also be used, namely, changing the head office into a branch through changing registration or changing the company's management system from the original general manager system to directors system, or on the contrary, at the same time, setting up the new board of directors or the general manager office in the corresponding low tax country.

(2) The genuine migration of residence.

It refers that a transnational legal entity transfers genuinely its administrative office or effective management center from the high tax residence country to a low tax country. It is the most thorough way for the transnational legal entity to get out of the tax jurisdiction of residence country with high tax, but it is difficult to be carried out and will generally harass people and waste money from the financial point of view. If a company really wants to move abroad, there are many things that can not be taken away. Although something can be taken away, because of the costs of dismounting, transportation and downtime losses are too high and not worthwhile, it will be sold in the local. Therefore, the numerous taxes on capital gains derived from selling assets by the company are inevitable and will be collected by the local tax authorities according to the approved tax rate, unless the company has a large number of financial losses to offset the capital gains. The factor effectively restrains the fiscal transfer of residence companies in country with high tax. Likewise, it is this factor that promotes the company to forge financial losses to offset capital gains in the process of migration for tax avoidance. But overall, the genuine migration of residence for a legal entity is not

Chapter 6 GENERAL METHODS OF INTERNATIONAL TAX AVOIDANCE

easy to use for tax avoidance. There are both advantages and disadvantages.

6.1.2 Method of non-transferring tax avoidance of subject——treaty shopping

In the process of seeking international tax avoidance, transnational taxpayers do not necessarily need to transfer themselves, they can also use other methods. It means that seemingly, transnational taxpayers do not migrate between tax borders and stay at home. At the same time, they incite others to create some forms of media in another country, usually taking the form of trust, to transfer partial income or property which causes the legal phenomenon of separating income or properties from their original owners. The aim is to avoid paying income tax, inheritance tax and gift tax to the residence country of the final owners on their income or property. This method is called "dummy trust assets" which is one of the typical activities of tax avoidance.

 Teaching Case of 6-5

For avoiding domestic income tax, a company of New Zealand had ever transferred its annual profit of 70% to a trust company in Bahamas. The Bahamas is a famous tax haven in the world whose tax rate is 35% to 50% lower than that of New Zealand. Therefore, the company can effectively avoid annually 3,000,000 to 4,700,000 dollars of taxes.

1. The objective conditions of treaty shopping

At present, many countries adopt the way of signing bilateral tax treaties to resolve the international double taxation and adjust the allocation relations of tax benefits between countries. In order to eliminate international double taxation, the Contracting States must make the corresponding constraints and concessions which forms the preferential terms for the residents of both Contracting States, such as reducing withholding tax rates of source country on the investment income of residents or exempting on certain items of income. But only residents and nationals (in some cases) of a Contracting State are entitled to benefits under an income tax treaty. However, because most of the countries in the world adopt the policy of allowing capital flowing out of the boundary in different degrees, it enables transnational individuals and legal entities to set up new entities in another country freely for business purposes. The above objective conditions have opened up a new field for transnational taxpayers to avoid taxes which enable the residents of third countries to obtain the treaty benefits not otherwise available by all sorts of tricks. This practice is referred to by tax specialists as treaty shopping.

A common practice is that taxpayers who are not residents or nationals of a Contracting State have frequently sought to obtain the benefits of a tax treaty by organizing a corporation or other legal entity in one of the Contracting States to serve as a conduit for income earned in the other Contracting State. Obviously, treaty shopping will reduce the normal tax revenue of relevant Contracting States which is a kind of special transferring tax avoidance of subjects in disguise. It should be noted that although a taxpayer may engage in treaty shopping to obtain any special treaty benefit not otherwise available, most treaty shopping has involved attempts of taxpayers to obtain reduced withholding rates on dividends, interest, and royalties.

2. The common ways of treaty shopping

The main feature of ways of treaty shopping is setting up the intermediary which can be classified into the following three ways.

(1) Setting up a direct conduit company.

This is a classic form of treaty shopping which involves the use of unrelated financial intermediaries located in a treaty country to make investments for taxpayers who are not themselves eligible for treaty benefits.

Teaching Case of 6-6

For example, We assume that T company is a resident of Country TH, a tax haven jurisdiction that does not have a tax treaty with Country A. Country A does have a tax treaty with Country B under which Country A reduces its normal withholding tax rate from 30 percent to zero on interest paid to residents of Country B. TCo invests 1 million dollars with BCo, an independent financial intermediary that is resident in Country B. BCo uses the 1 million dollars to purchase a bond issued by an unrelated Country A manufacturer. The manufacturer pays BCo 100,000 dollars in interest on the bond. BCo claims that the 100,000 dollars is exempt from Country A's withholding tax under the treaty with Country B. BCo pays T Co 100,000 dollars, minus some commission, as a return on T Co's original investment. This example utilizes what is commonly referred to as a back-to-back loan to minimize taxes. BCo, the financial intermediary, avoids tax in Country A under the tax treaty with Country B and avoids paying significant tax in Country B because the 100,000 dollars of gross income received from Country A is offset by the deduction of the amount paid to T.

The BCo, established in Country B, is like a conduit sticking out from the Non-Contracting State to draw the income of low tax state, so it is vividly called the direct Conduit Company.

(2) Setting up a stepping-stone conduit company.

Another classic form of treaty shopping involves the use of a controlled corporation organized in a treaty country.

Teaching Case of 6-7

For example, We assume that T Co, in the above example, organizes a wholly-owned affiliate, C Company (CCo), in Country C. T Co subscribes 2 million for shares of CCo, and CCo uses that money to purchase shares of stock of various companies in Country A listed on the stock exchange of Country A. CCo receives dividends of 400,000 dollars on the shares. Country A has a tax treaty with Country C that reduces the Country A withholding tax on dividends paid to Country C residents from 30 percent to 15 percent. As a resident of Country C, CCo claims the benefit of the treaty to reduce its tax otherwise payable on the 400,000 dollars of dividends. CCo is exempt from tax in Country C because that country does not tax foreign dividends under its domestic tax law.

During the process of T Co's obtaining income from Country C, CCo is like a stepping stone for crossing a river, so it is vividly called the stepping-stone conduit company.

Chapter 6 GENERAL METHODS OF INTERNATIONAL TAX AVOIDANCE

(3) Setting up a low equity holding company by using the bilateral relations directly.

Because it is clearly defined in the tax treaty of some countries that the necessary condition of enjoying the tax preference for a resident company in a Contracting State on its payment of dividends, interest or royalties to another resident company in another Contracting State is that the shares of the company controlled by the same foreign investor can not exceed a certain proportion (such as 25%). Thus, the foreign investor can set up a foreign low equity holding company meticulously to achieve tax benefits.

For example, one so-called "one-fifth structure" arrangement is a typical example which is often used by some countries signing tax treaty with Germany. According to the German usual practice of signing tax treaty, if the beneficiary of dividends of a German company is a foreign company and the foreign company holds at least 25% of shares of the German company which distributes dividends, the German company can not enjoy the tax benefits on its dividends paid to the foreign company under the tax treaty. Under this situation, a foreign company owning shares of a German company can set up five subsidiaries first in its residence country according to the domestic laws, and then arrange them to hold respectively the shares of the German company to obtain the tax treaty benefits. Of course, each subsidiary has the German company's shares of less than 25% which makes each of them enjoy benefits from the tax treaty with Germany.

At the same time, in the international tax avoidance, some legal entities always want to avoid taxes by means of establishing their offices and branches in overseas, but in fact, quite a number of overseas offices and branches have a lot of inconvenience in administrative management with high cost and low efficiency. Therefore, it is better to find a resident bank in the overseas business transit country or other places to help deal with the business. Then the company can use the bilateral tax treaties signed by the residence country of the bank between the countries of debit and credit to obtain the tax benefits.

  Teaching Case of 6-8

A taxpayer signs a trust agreement with a bank who will receive interest for the taxpayer. When the residence country of the trustee bank has a bilateral tax treaty with the residence country of interest payers, the paid interest will have withholding tax preference. Thus, the taxpayer can enjoy the tax benefits.

For instance, Japan and the United States signed a mutually beneficial tax treaty which stipulated that the interest received by the Japanese banks from residents of the United States could obtain reduction of 50% of tax burden. Therefore, when a Chinese company loans to an American company, the Chinese company may entrust a Japanese bank to collect interest on the loans from the American company to obtain tax benefits of less paying.

 ## 6.2 Transferring tax avoidance of object

Object transfer has the feature of passivity which follows the taxpayers' business arrangements and transactions. Without business activities of subjects, the object transfer is impossible.

6.2.1 Methods of transferring tax avoidance of object

Transferring tax avoidance of object usually involves the object passes across borders, moves between different departments of a same entity or between two entities. Methods of transferring tax avoidance of object are varied which involve different countries and taxpayers.

1. Avoid being a PE

In determining whether tax on non-residents' business income, some European countries have been using the concept of PE. That is to say, a business organization of PE will be taxed by the countries, otherwise, it would not be taxed. Therefore, for a taxpayer, avoiding being a PE means avoiding the limited tax liability in the non-residence country. Especially, when the tax rate of the non-residence country is higher than that of the residence country, this point is very important.

Under Article 5 of the OECD and UN Model Treaties, a PE generally is "a fixed place of business through which the business of an enterprise is wholly or partly carried on". This definition is related to the physical attachment factors of a country. For example, both of the OECD and UN Model Treaties provide the following list of examples of business premises that often constitute a PE: a place of management, a branch, an office, a factory, a workshop, a mine, an oil or gas well, a quarry, or any other place of extraction of natural resources. But in some cases, it is much difficult to find out the physical attachment factors. Therefore, the two model treaties introduce the second decision factor. That is, the definition of a PE in the OECD Model Treaty includes certain dependent agents of an enterprise that act on behalf of the enterprise and have, and habitually exercise, an authority to conclude contracts on behalf of the enterprise. Most tax treaties treat such agents as PEs of their principals. The agency rule in the UN Model Treaty is more expansive, extending to dependent agents that maintain a stock of goods from which they make deliveries on behalf of their principals. Some tax treaties follow the UN Model Treaty on this point. Some commentators argue that the definition of a PE should also be expanded to include most dependent agents carrying on substantial business on behalf of an enterprise whether or not they have the authority to conclude contracts. These commentators argue that the power to conclude contracts has little commercial significance because modern methods of communication permit nearly instantaneous contact between agents and their foreign principals. The second decision factor is intertwined with the physical factors listed above, which makes it very difficult to avoiding being a PE for a non-resident. But it is not to say that there is no possibility. Because there are some duty-free exceptions for business income in the tax laws and tax treaties, they provide an opportunity for tax avoidance.

The advantage provided by the above mentioned contents to the transnational taxpayer is they can avoid taxes through engaging in one or more free tax activities. Also, they can use the service company for tax avoidance. If the transnational taxpayer's company is established in a tax haven or other countries which have tax treaties or agreements, the effect will be more obvious.

 **Teaching Case of 6-9**

In 1973, the Spanish Leader textiles clothing Limited Company (Leader Company for short) established an office in Rotterdam of Holland whose role was to collect the textile and clothing infor-

Chapter 6 GENERAL METHODS OF INTERNATIONAL TAX AVOIDANCE

mation of Nordic countries for the company. According to the bilateral tax treaties signed between the governments of Spanish and Holland, the office specially used for collecting information was not the PE, which did not bear the tax liability. However, in only a year, the Leader Company earned 21,200,000 dollars through two transactions by using the information provided by the Holland office. Although the office in Rotterdam bore all the relevant negotiations and consultations with respect to contract signing and order quantity, because the office did not sign the contract and order on behalf of the Lead Company, the Holland tax authorities had no way to tax on the income.

In recent years, business activities without setting up PE have become more and more. Because of the improvement of technical level and shortening of production cycle, quite a few enterprises can achieve their business activities in the government's tax exemption period and obtain considerable income. The short-term operating mode brings a lot of trouble to the tax departments of various countries.

Teaching Case of 6-10

Some overseas construction contract firms of Korea have assumed a large number of construction projects in the Middle East and Latin American countries. Due to the provisions of the Middle East and Latin American countries that the income of the non-resident companies within half a year is exempt from tax, so the Korean overseas construction contract firms often manage to complete the project within six months for tax avoidance.

Teaching Case of 6-11

In the 1970s, Japan built many maritime mobile factories and workshops. In the 1980s, they flowed to Asia, Africa and South America for operation. As long as they reached one place, they bought the local raw materials for processing and sold the finished products in local. The whole production cycle was only one or two months. After the sale, they sailed away and did not have to pay any taxes to the local government. Only the taxes they avoided reached to millions of dollars. Japan has never published the Data. It is estimated that from the 1970s to the end of 1980s, the Japanese maritime mobile factories and workshops have avoided taxes of billions of dollars of different countries. For example, a Japanese company came to China to purchase peanut in 1981. The company sent out a maritime mobile workshop to China port and stayed there for 27 days. During that period of time, they processed peanut into peanut butter, crushed the skin of peanut into plate and sold them to China. At last, 64% of the Chinese income of selling peanut was returned to Japan for buying the plates. Moreover, the Japanese income of selling peanut plates was not taxed at all. The direct reason for this phenomenon is that China and most other countries have made rules of present time for non-resident company which was used legally by the Japanese companies to avoid taxes.

2. Transfer income and expenses by using of the PE

Under the situation of being a PE, a company can arrange skillfully the transactions between the head office and the PE, the PE and the PE, to avoid tax. If a multinational legal entity, who is an investor, decides to invest abroad in the form of PE and the PE is the head office of the legal entity. How to distribute the overall business income (Lncluding profits and losses) between the head office and the overseas PE? In practice, this kind of problem is mainly reflected in the profit distribution between the head office and the branches.

In tax treaties between countries, there is generally the profit attribution principle which means the country where the PE locates has the power to tax on the income attributable to the PE. There are two common methods in the world with respect to this: one is called the direct method. From a legal perspective, the PE is not an independent legal entity. But the under the direct method, a PE is regarded as an independent enterprise and is deemed to carry out transactions with the head office or other PEs according to the independent accounting principles or the Arm's length principle. The characteristic of the direct method is the independent accounting of the profits of the PE. The other is called the indirect method. With consideration of the legal fact, it regards the head office and the foreign PE as an entity which generates the common profits or losses in the world. So, according to certain rules and formulas, it allocates the business income or losses between the head office and the foreign PE.

The direct method and the indirect method often have different results in practice. The direct method seeks objective criteria such as the Arm's length principle under the market conditions and uses the cost-plus method or similar methods to determine the "normal" profit margin of the PE. So it requires the PE to preserve the complete and independent account books to reflect the actual income and expenses. Meanwhile, the indirect method usually uses some formulas to calculate and distribute an enterprise's all business results. The formula should take some important variables into account that reflect the enterprise's overall financial situation, such as the total income, turnover, capital structure, investment ratio and the proportion of employees. According to the different characteristics of business operation, the indirect method can select some suitable variables as an objective basis for calculation of the distribution of profit and losses. For example, for the processing industry, it can select certain cost ratios, such as the cost of production or the amount of wages to distribute profits. For the banking industry, the operation funds ratio or loans ratio can be used as the distribution basis. And for the insurance industry, the sum insured is used to distribute profits.

Seen from the conditions required and distribution form of the direct method and the indirect method, there is a wide possibility of international tax avoidance. Because in the tax laws and tax treaties of different countries, it is difficult to find the reference terms with respect to the "normal" business activities. The industrial and commercial activity is varied with many forms. Generally, there is no "normal state". When the tax authorities determine the "normal rate of return" of the relevant activity or the PE, they are usually based on their own experience and the final profit margin is usually consulted by the taxpayers and the tax authorities. All of this provides the opportunity for the transnational taxpayer to use tax avoidance techniques. The common ways of transferring income and expenses by using of the PE for transnational taxpayers are as follows.

(1) Transfer business property by using the PE.

There are two important problems to be solved with respect to transfer business property between the head office and the PE or between the PEs. One is that whether the company shifting out

Chapter 6 GENERAL METHODS OF INTERNATIONAL TAX AVOIDANCE

the business property obtains a capital gain and bears the tax liability for reflecting it in its accounting book. How to estimate this capital gain? The other problem is that the calculation of the value of the property transferred into the other company for determination of the basis of its future depreciation. This calculation has two kinds of methods: One is based on the book value of the property, namely, that using the original cost of the property, minus the depreciation expenses charged by the shifting company. The other is based on the replacement cost, namely, calculating the property according to the market price when it is transferred into the company. Therefore, a multinational company can usually use the difference of estimation or calculation of the business property by the countries of transferor and transferee or the difference between tax rates to transfer the property between the head office and the PE or between the PEs for reducing its current or future tax liability as much as possible.

(2) Transfer interest, royalties and other similar expenses by using the PE.

These expenses can be between the company and the third party or between the head office and its PE. They are strictly distinguished in the tax laws and tax treaties of many countries: If the expense paid by a taxpayer to the third party is considered as the genuine payment, it can be deducted as expense from tax. But the expense between the head office and its PE or between different PEs is regarded as the false payment. It is not deductible from tax for the payer and it is not the profit of the payee. However, in practice, it is sometimes difficult to accurately grasp these provisions in principle. There is so much ambiguity in items of deductible and not deductible. If a transnational taxpayer uses them cleverly, he can achieve the purpose of reducing tax burden.

(3) Transfer administrative expenses by using the PE.

Although the PE located abroad has some important decision autonomy, the main management work of a multinational corporation is often carried on in the residence country of the head office which results in a problem of how to distribute the administrative expenses of the head office between the PE and the head office. In the country adopting the direct method to determine the profits of a PE, the tax authority needs to know whether the head office manages the PE and to what extent it actually manages the PE. If the PE really benefits from the management activity, it will bear the relevant administrative expenses of the head office and deduct it from its profits. Then, whether the expenses paid to the head office by a PE include the profit in addition to make up for the cost? If the PE and the head office are really two independent entities and their economic functions are not the same, such a profit mark-up is acceptable. Because, if an independent third party provides this kind of service, the charges must include the profit higher than the actual cost. However, the PE and the head office are actually one legal entity and the PE is just regarded as an independent and separate entity. To pay the management service of the head office, how much money taken from its profit by a PE is reasonable? In fact, it is difficult to find a unified answer, only depending on the national tax laws and tax treaties. Some tax treaties make it very clear on this point such as the tax treaty between Switzerland and Holland. It stipulates that a fixed ratio of profits of the PE is created by the management activity of the head office, namely, that 10%~20% of net profit of the PE is attributable to the head office. But, according to the opinions in the OECD Model Treaty, it should not consider the so-called theoretical management profit when the country determines the amount of taxable income of the PE.

It is because of the tremendous flexibility of distributing administrative expenses and the difference of tax systems between countries that the transnational taxpayer can use them to reduce his tax burden. For example, try to distribute more expenses to the PE located in the high tax country, therefore, reduce the total profits and tax burden of the head office.

(4) Transfer service expenses by using the PE.

In practice, the PE often provides some ancillary services to its head office which can be technical or management. On the contrary, the head office may provide similar services to its PE. In addition, the PE can advertise products produced by the head office, but it does not produce and operate these products. Is it charged for this kind of service? Whether the profit factor like commission should be included in charge? There are different views and understanding about it. Under the direct method, the expense it should pay to the head office is considered as its profits. But except the actual expense, is the commission concluded in the expense? Obviously, the commission should be included in the service income between independent enterprises, but the PE and its head office are actually one legal entity. It is usually hard to calculate accurately the symbolic percentage of commission and find out the commission to rewrite it in the accounts of the PE. So, according to the OECD Model Treaty, the commission of this kind of service should not be included in the profits of a PE. On the contrary, if the head office provides services to a PE, the commission paid by the PE can not be allowed to list on its accounts in calculating its profits.

The transnational corporations can use these provisions to transfer parts of its service activities from a high tax country to the PE located in a low tax country, which means parts of profit are transferred to the low tax country.

(5) Transfer tax burden by using the losses strategy of the PE.

Although the multinational corporations usually gather their profits together with the current profits and losses of their foreign PE to declare taxes to the residence or nationality country, the losses in a high tax country and the losses in a low tax county have different results. Due to the different countries' provisions of treating the losses vary greatly, declaration of a PE's losses in a most favorable country at a most favorable time provides great leeway for transnational taxpayer's tax avoidance.

3. Transfer income and expenses by using the transfer prices between the related corporations

When a multinational corporation engages in the foreign investment or other business activities, in addition to the PE, a more common form adopted by it is to set up an independent legal subsidiary. Through joint ventures, equity participation and other forms, the multinational corporation can obtain the control power of the subsidiary and the subsidiary will become a member of the group. Because of the special economic interests and connection between the parent company and its subsidiary and between subsidiaries, it has formed the so-called related corporations in international taxation. With the expansion of economic exchanges between the countries, many cross-border transactions are actually taken place between the complex related corporations within the group. The group corporation can use this special relationship to avoid or evade taxes by using the

Chapter 6 GENERAL METHODS OF INTERNATIONAL TAX AVOIDANCE

transfer prices to influence the allocation of income and expenses of the related corporations. It has affected the tax distribution between countries and has become a significant issue to which the national tax authorities pay close attention. As one of the most important ways of transferring tax avoidance of object, transfer pricing involves wide ranges with complicated contents. Here is a simple example of preliminary description.

Simulated demonstration of 6-1

[*Background*]: M Group has three subsidiaries of ACo, BCo and CCo, organized respectively in Country X, Y and Z. The corporation income tax rate of three countries is respectively 50%, 40% and 25%. ACo produces and assembles television parts for BCo.

[*Calculation*]: ACo produced a batch of parts at a cost of 1 million dollars plus a profit of 300,000 dollars, it should be directly sold to BCo for 1,300,000 dollars. After BCo's assembly, the finished products should be put into market for the total price of 1,600,000 dollars. But in fact, ACo did not sell this batch of parts to BCo directly, but sold it to CCo at the cost of 1 million dollars. CCo then resold it to BCo at a high price of 1,500,000 dollars. After BCo's assembly, the finished products were still put into market for the total price of 1,600,000 dollars. In this way, the profits, taxes payable and tax burdens of the subsidiaries and the M Group will be changed greatly. The specific changes are shown in Table 6-1 and Table 6-2.

Table 6-1 Before transfer pricing

Item	profits / dollars	Tax payable / dollars	Tax burden / %
ACo	300,000	150,000	50
BCo	300,000	120,000	40
CCo	0	0	0
M Group Company	600,000	270,000	45

Table 6-2 After transfer pricing

Item	profits / dollars	Tax payable / dollars	Tax burden / %
ACo	0	0	0
BCo	100,000	40,000	40
CCo	500,000	125,000	25
M Group Company	600,000	165,000	27.5

Obviously, after the transfer pricing, the M Group paid less taxes of 105,000 dollars (270,000 - 165,000) and its overall reduction of tax burden was 38.89% [(45% - 27.5%)/45%].

[*Comments*]: From here we can see that the multinational corporation has close relationship with the transfer pricing. The multinational corporation can make use of transfer pricing and the differences of the national tax burden between countries for distorted allocation of international income and expenses to transfer profits from high tax countries to low tax countries for reduction of its global tax burden.

To sum up, a transfer price is a price set by a taxpayer when selling to, buying from, or sharing resources with a related person. For example, if ACo manufactures goods in Country A and sells them to its foreign affiliate, BCo, organized in Country B, the price at which that sale takes place is called a transfer price. A transfer price is usually contrasted with a market price, which is the price set in the marketplace for transfers of goods and services between unrelated persons.

1) The common forms of transfer pricing

Multinational companies use transfer prices for sales and other transfers of goods and services within their corporate group. These inter-company prices are the most important category of transfer prices. Transfer prices are also used by individuals dealing with corporations or other entities under their control and by individuals dealing with close family members. In practice, transfer pricing has a variety of forms. We can classify and analyze it from the following five aspects.

(1) The purchase and sale of goods.

In the internalt ransactions of multinational company, purchase and sale of goods play an extremely important role which involves the tangible goods trade such as raw materials, fuel, low value consumables, spare parts, semi-finished products, finished products, etc. The price of internal transactions has the opposite impact on the two sides of purchase and sale.

①Control the import and export prices of raw materials and spare parts to influence the product cost of related corporations. For example, in order to reduce the subsidiary's product cost and obtain higher profits, the parent company can supply raw materials to its subsidiaries at a low price, or the subsidiaries sell spare parts to the parent company at high price. On the contrary, if the parent company sells raw materials to its subsidiaries at high price, or the subsidiaries sells spare parts to the parent company at low price, the product cost of subsidiaries will be increased which will reduce their profits. This phenomenon is called in China the "high in and low out" which is one of the important reasons causing some foreign-funded enterprises' losses.

②The parent company uses the international marketing network and controls the subsidiary's sale to depress or improve the purchase price of subsidiary's products. Conversely, when uses the sales organizations within the subsidiary system to sell products of parent company, the group company can improve or depress commission paid by the parent company to its subsidiary to influence the subsidiary's sale income, thus affecting the tax payable of the subsidiary.

③In the purchase and sale of goods, the group company can use the transportation system controlled by the parent company to charge higher or lower freight, cost of loading and unloading and insurance premium to influence the sales cost of subsidiaries.

④Company makes artificial bad debts and loss compensations in the parent company and its subsidiary to increase the subsidiary's expenses.

⑤When the internal transactions in the group company take the form of materials for processing, the group company can depress the processing fees paid to the subsidiary to reduce the income of the subsidiary for tax avoidance.

(2) Loan business.

Controlling of loan interest rates to affect the subsidiary's product cost is also a form of transfer pricing. For example, the parent company uses the financial institutions of the system to provide

Chapter 6 GENERAL METHODS OF INTERNATIONAL TAX AVOIDANCE

preferential loans to its subsidiary without or with low interest which can reduce the product cost of the subsidiary. On the contrary, it can also increase the subsidiary's product cost with high interest.

With respect to the capital circulation in the form of credit within the group company, some transactions avoid taxes by the way of advanced payment of interest, some others use the interest balance to achieve the purpose of tax avoidance. The former case takes place when a company expects that it will earn huge profits this year and pay more taxes. The company will borrow a large loan from the related corporation before the end of the financial year. The borrowing condition is that the overall interest of the loan has to be paid in advance. Thus, the interest will be included in the current tax deduction and the amount of profits will be reduced. After the end of the fiscal year, the company will repay the loan. The latter case takes place when a profitable company borrows a huge loan at market rate and re-loans it to the related corporation at a symbolic low interest rate. In the later years, the company can adjust it to the market rate. The larger difference between the interest rates of borrowing and lending will cause to offset the current profits by losses and delay the current tax liability.

(3) Rendering of service.

Service scope is so wide that providing services of design, repair, advertising, research and consulting between related corporations involves fees and service charges standard. Even the management activities of the head office are also regarded as a kind of service and the management costs will be shared to each branch according to a certain proportion. By controlling the level of service fees, the multinational corporation can control the costs and profits of different members of the group company. For example, by over charges excessive management fees to the subsidiary, the parent company can shift its administrative fees (such as the manager's annuity of the parent company) to the subsidiary's management costs and reduce the profits of the subsidiary.

(4) Usage and transfer of intangible assets.

By the way of controlling royalties through the usage and transfer of intangible assets such as patent, proprietary technology, trademark, copyright and goodwill, the parent company can affect the costs and profits of subsidiaries. This kind of payment sometimes affects the changes of group company's capital structure, sometimes affects the allocation of income and cost. Take the patent for example, the parent company may charge lower royalties to its wholly-owned subsidiary and higher royalties to the subsidiary with minority stakes.

(5) Purchase and lease of fixed assets.

In the case of fixed assets investment, the purchase price of fixed assets affects not only the company's equity share, but also the amortization of depreciation. For example, the price of equipment provided by the parent company to the subsidiary will directly affect the product cost allocated. Increasing of the original value of fixed assets means increasing the depreciation which will inevitably increase the production costs of subsidiaries, on the contrary, it will reduce the costs.

2) The motivation of transfer pricing

By controlling transfer prices, the multinational corporations can make its overseas subsidiaries or branches obey its global strategic goal to achieve the maximum profit which is their basic purpose of using transfer prices. If we analyze it further, in the context of multinational corporation's activities of transfer pricing, we can find its tax and non-tax motivations.

(1) The tax motivation.

The tax motivation of transfer pricing is mainly to reduce the tax burden and is most close to corporation tax. Because members of transnational group corporations locate in different countries, the group company often uses the differences of tax rates and tax rules in different countries to make the entity in high tax country depress the sales price, fees and expenses allocation standard to the related entity in low tax country. On the contrary, the entity in low tax country can increase the sales price, fees and expenses allocation standard to the related entity in high tax country. By this means, the group company can transfer some profits which should be realized and taxed in high tax country to the low tax country. Therefore, parts of reduction of tax revenue in high tax country change into the tax revenue of low tax country and other parts directly increase the entire group company's after-tax income. In two countries with great difference in tax rates, the transfer pricing of related corporation often shows very significant tax motivation.

①Lighten tax burden of corporation tax.

Most countries in the world impose corporation tax on business profits of companies. Therefore, the reduction of tax burden of corporation tax is in the first place of the transfer pricing tax motivation. We use a simple example to illustrate it.

Teaching Case of 6-12

M Group Company has three subsidiaries of ACo, BCo and CCo, organized respectively in Country X, Y and Z. The corporation income tax rate of three countries is respectively 50%, 40% and 20%. ACo produces and assembles video parts for BCo. ACo produced a batch of parts at a cost of 2 million dollars and should directly sell them to BCo for 2,400,000 dollars. After BCo's assembly, the finished products should be put into market for the total price of 3,000,000 dollars. In this way, ACo's tax burden should be 200,000 dollars ([2,400,000-2,000,000]×50%). BCo's tax burden should be 240,000 dollars ([3,000,000-2,400,000]×40%). And the overall tax burden of the group company should be 440,000 dollars (200,000+240,000). But for reduction of tax, ACo did not sell this batch of parts to BCo directly, but sold it to CCo at low price of 2,100,000 dollars. CCo then resold it to BCo at a high price of 2,800,000 dollars. After BCo's assembly, the finished products were still put into market for the total price of 3,000,000 dollars. Then, tax burden of each company is shown in Table 6-3 and Table 6-4.

Table 6-3 Before transfer pricing

Item	profits/dollars	Tax payable/dollars	Tax burden/%
ACo	400,000	200,000	50
BCo	600,000	240,000	40
CCo	0	0	0
M Group Company	1,000,000	440,000	44

Chapter 6 GENERAL METHODS OF INTERNATIONAL TAX AVOIDANCE

Table 6-4 After transfer pricing

Item	profits/dollars	Tax payable/dollars	Tax burden/%
ACo	100,000	50,000	50
BCo	200,000	80,000	40
CCo	700,000	140,000	20
M Group Company	1,000,000	270,000	27

Obviously, after the transfer pricing, the group company paid less taxes of 170,000 dollars (440,000-270,000) and its overall tax burden was 270,000 dollars. X country's Treasury has 150,000 dollars losses (200,000-50,000), Y country's Treasury has 160,000 dollars losses (240,000-80,000) and Z country's Treasury has increased income of 140,000 dollars (0+140,000). Therefore, in this kind of transfer pricing, the group company and the low tax country benefit from it but the high tax country suffers losses. The former benefit of 310,000 dollars (170,000+140,000) is equal to the latter losses (150,000+160,000). So, in the case of great difference of tax rates in different countries, transfer pricing can be used as an effective way for tax avoidance.

②Avoid withholding tax.

Every country often imposes higher withholding tax on the domestic negative income of foreign companies or individuals (such as dividends, interest, rents, royalties, etc). The tax burden can not be ignored in the absence of tax treaty between the two countries. But by using transfer pricing, the tax burden of withholding tax can be reduced to some extent.

Teaching Case of 6-13

ACo of Country X is the parent company of BCo of Country Y. BCo should pay dividends of 1 million dollars to ACo from its current profits. Y's withholding tax rate is 20% and BCo should pay withholding tax of 200,000 dollars to Country Y. In order to avoid the withholding tax, instead of paying dividends directly to ACo, BCo sold a batch of parts worth of 3 million dollars to ACo at only a price of 2 million dollars to substitute for the payment of dividends.

③Increase the foreign tax credit.

When the country where the parent company locates implements the foreign tax credit method and the full credit, the usage of transfer pricing can increase the current foreign tax credit.

(2) The non-tax motivation.

In addition to considerations from tax, we can see more non-tax motivations in transfer pricing. In the countries with the similar tax rates, transfer pricing is largely due to other management motivations. Even in countries with great different tax rates, we can also find many important non-tax motivations behind transfer pricing.

①Enter and control the market.

If the entering into a foreign market is a company's target, the company can sell its products to the foreign affiliate at a low price through transfer pricing. Then the foreign affiliate can sell the products at an unmatched price by local competitors. Even if the country where the foreign affiliate locates has anti-dumping regulations on imported finished products, there will not be great impact.

The company can sell parts and semi-finished products to its foreign affiliate at a low price. The assembly or the final processing will be finished by the foreign affiliate and the finished products will be sold at the price of dumping if they were directly imported. Because the final processing of the products is completed in the country where the foreign affiliate locates, it belongs to the domestic production rather than the dumping.

②Adjust profits and change the image of subsidiaries in the local.

When a parent company wants to make its new set subsidiary have a high reputation in the competition, easily issue stocks and bonds in the local or obtain credit to expand the operation scale and occupy more market shares, it often provides raw materials, components, and services at a low price but repurchases the products at a high price, which can make the subsidiary show a higher profit rate. On the contrary, if the parent company wants to hide a subsidiary's profitability, it can increase the selling price to the subsidiary and depress the repurchase price. Because when a subsidiary operates well and profitably, a lot of expected problems may happen. For example, workers of the subsidiary may make demands of wages growth or enjoying more shares of the profits; the host country may have more political pressure to confiscate the high profits of foreign companies; new competitors, attracted by the high profits, may join in the industry and intensify the competition. Therefore, through increasing the transfer prices to appropriately cool the subsidiaries profitability is a kind of management strategy of the parent company. This point has a very obvious performance in the joint venture company.

③Transfer funds and obtain more subsidies and tax rebates.

On the consideration of balancing the international payments, some countries implement strict foreign exchange control which limit the local subsidiaries on remitting profits in dividends. However, by using the higher prices at which the foreign parent company ships goods or renders services to the subsidiary can pull up funds indirectly from the country. In addition, some subsidiaries can not obtain capitals in the local because of limiting by the local investment laws. The foreign parent company can finance its foreign affiliate by transfer pricing. And in order to encourage exports, some countries usually provide subsidies or tax rebates to the exported goods based on their value. Therefore, the higher the price of exported goods, the more subsidies or tax rebates the company can obtain.

④Avoid foreign exchange risk.

In international business activities, foreign exchange risk is everywhere. The ups and downs of exchange rate will directly affect the multinational corporation's earnings. In order to avoid the risk of exchange rate fluctuation or obtain the interests of exchange rate differential, the multinational corporation often uses transfer pricing to make the subsidiary advance or delay the payment of profits or transfer losses to a specific related corporation. In addition, low-cost transfers can be used to make more products enter into a country with strict foreign exchange control or quota control of the value of imported goods. For example, a subsidiary can buy products from its foreign parent company at half price, so that it can get the demanded products more than double.

⑤Accelerate the cost recovery and profit repatriation.

To accelerate the cost recovery and profit repatriation from subsidiaries, the parent company can increase the selling prices and service charges to subsidiaries, meanwhile, depressing the fees

Chapter 6 GENERAL METHODS OF INTERNATIONAL TAX AVOIDANCE

of subsidiaries to the parent company; to accelerate the investment recovery in the joint venture and to get more income, the parent company can also improve the supply price and charging standards to the joint venture, meanwhile, depressing the repurchase price. This kind of circumstance often appears when the country where the subsidiary locates has political instability and dim investment prospects.

⑥Get more benefits from the joint venture.

A subsidiary of joint venture will inevitably involve the local partners of the host country. So, the foreign parent company has incentives to implement transfer pricing. For example, when each of the joint venture parties has 50% of the shares, and no matter how well the joint venture is operated, the foreign parent company can at most have half of the after-tax profits. However, the local partner has the right to share the profits of this subsidiary, but has no right to share the foreign parent company's profits. The foreign parent company just grasps this point and gets profits in advance by the high transfer prices before the subsidiary's final profits are formed. In this way, the parent company not only takes half of the profits it should have, but also takes parts of the profits that belong to local partners of the subsidiary in passing.

Only to understand this truth, can we understand a lot of puzzled phenomena in the foreign economic cooperation: in the situation of lower tax rates and many tax preferences provided in some special economic zones in China, why there are still quite a lot of multinational corporations whose parent companies locate in high tax countries shift profits outwards from the joint ventures in China by transfer pricing; in a long-time state of losses, why the foreign investors of the joint venture are still willing to continue the operation. An important reason is that the transfer pricing plays a magical role. In the case of foreign investors' transfer pricing, many joint ventures have false losses and actual earnings which cause Chinese tax revenue outflows.

To sum up, the correct attitude on transfer pricing of a government can be summarized as the following two aspects. On the one hand, the government can not deny its rationality and legitimacy and implement severe punitive measures against the taxpayer's any transfer pricing behaviors because it has tax avoidance function or it can objectively produce the effect of tax avoidance. On the other hand, the government can not let it alone and ignore its adverse effects on domestic tax revenue because it plays an important role in the internal management of multinational corporations.

4. Making use of tax havens for transferring tax avoidance of object

If a transnational taxpayer in high tax country wants to obtain more benefits from the transfer of the object, he usually considers making use of tax havens. By way of setting up various kinds of Letter-box Companies, making up different business activities and trust assets and using transfer pricing, the transnational taxpayer can transfer objects such as capital, goods and services into tax havens. In the process of the transnational taxpayer's achievement of tax avoidance, the related corporations and business activities in tax havens will play a function of "separation" and "isolation". That is to say, a part of the taxpayer's income is separated from the high tax country, which is isolated from implementation of its residence jurisdiction. Because the object flows to a tax haven has fallen into another legal entity. The profits derived from the transferred object can be accumulated in the tax haven with no or low tax and when the transnational taxpayer needs, it can be invested to new items. This is the so-called the tax haven's accumulation function and the role of capital turntable. Because the tax havens not only attract the objects to flow into but also the frequent destinations of subjects transferring, it forms the special tax avoidance mode which will be further discussed in chapter 7.

6.2.2 Methods of non-transferring tax avoidance of object

Non-transferring tax avoidance of object refers that the object does not move across borders or tax borders in the form. But arranged by a multinational taxpayer carefully, it can still play a role in transferring tax avoidance of object. It belongs to a special form of object transferring.

1. Using the provision of deferral

In the aspect of non-transferring tax avoidance of object, one of the most effective methods adopted by the transnational taxpayer is to set up an entity in a low tax country or in a tax haven (usually has the qualification of a legal entity, such as a subsidiary) to accumulate income and property which is based on the provision of deferral of some countries. Deferral of domestic tax refers to the practice of subjecting the profits derived from foreign investment through foreign corporations to taxation only when the profits are repatriated to the residence country of the investor. In fact, the reason why developed countries exercise deferral of domestic tax is to promote the development of domestic resident company's overseas subsidiaries and enhance their competition ability with local companies. But this provision is later used by many multinational corporations for international tax avoidance. They set up their own subsidiaries in low-tax country or tax havens, transfer profits to the subsidiaries through a variety of means and keep the profits distributed in overseas subsidiaries for a long time. Due to the deferral of domestic tax, the multinational corporations avoid heavier tax of residence country successfully by this method.

Teaching Case of 6-14

ACo, resident corporation of Japan, intends to set up a subsidiary in a tax haven and owns the subsidiary's 40% of its shares. The other 60% of shares is owned respectively by BCo, resident corporation of Japan, a Korea company and a Singapore company with 20% of each. According to the provisions of Japanese tax law, for any company located in tax havens, as long as its shares of more than 50% are owned by the Japanese residents, the company is regarded as a Japanese base company. Even if its after-tax profit is not remitted as dividends back to Japan, it has to declare taxes to Japanese government. Therefore, if the BCo transfers its shares to a non-resident company, the subsidiary can enjoy the tax preferences of deferral.

From the residence country with high tax, the abuse of deferral is a kind of tax avoidance which delays the taxpayer's liability in the residence country (or the nationality country). The prerequisite for the use of deferral is that the transnational taxpayer has to set up a subsidiary in a suitable low tax country or a tax haven (often, it is a wholly-owned subsidiary) and then by means of other objects' transferring, the profits can be formed and accumulated in the subsidiary. The profits may not be remitted to the parent company at all, or they may be delayed for a period of time and remitted back in the form of dividends. For the transnational taxpayers in the residence

Chapter 6 GENERAL METHODS OF INTERNATIONAL TAX AVOIDANCE

(nationality) country with high tax, the deferral means to get an interest-free loan which can increase the group company's liquidity.

2. Avoiding tax by irrational retained profits

The multinational corporation can avoid tax by irrational retained profits. Of course, this situation may occur in domestic companies. Usually, governments allow companies to retain a certain profit after tax. The rational retained profits provide important internal sources of funds for the development of companies. However, if the retained profit exceeds the rational limits (i.e. the government's prescriptive normal need), it is easy to be regarded as irrational retained profit. By means of irrational retained profits, the multinational corporation tends to frozen temporarily a part of dividend that should be distributed to shareholders and accumulate it in the form of accumulation fund. Then the parts of profits may be transformed into the appreciation amount of the stock value held by the shareholders, the multinational corporation can achieve the purpose of tax avoidance.

 Simulated demonstration of 6-2

[*Background*]: In 2019, a multinational corporation had global sales income of 10 million dollars, sales cost of 5 million dollars, approved deduction of 500 thousand dollars and allowable foreign credit of 500 thousand dollars on the foreign source income (Equal to the foreign taxes actually paid). The corporation income tax rate of the residence country was 34% and it was stipulated that the retained profit could not be less than 20% of the after-tax profit.

[*Calculation*]:
The sales profit: 1,000−500=500 (ten thousand dollars).
The income taxable: 500−50=450 (ten thousand dollars).
The corporation income tax payable: 450×34%=153 (ten thousand dollars).
The corporation income tax actually paid: 153−50=103 (ten thousand dollars).
Profit after tax: 450−(103+50) = 297 (ten thousand dollars).
The dividend distributable according to the provisions: 297 × 80% = 237.6 (ten thousand dollars).

That is to say, the 2,376,000 dollars should be distributed to the shareholders as dividends according to the proportion of equity and pay withholding tax (when dividends were remitted outside of the residence country). Then each of the shareholders should pay individual income tax in their residence country according to their domestic tax laws on the dividend they received.

[*Operation*]: For the purpose of tax avoidance, the corporation might lower the proportion of dividend distribution intentionally, even not distribute dividends. Assume that the corporation decided to distribute dividends of 594,000 dollars (= 2,970,000×20%), that meant almost only a very small part of the profit was distributed as dividend to the shareholders and the corporation only paid few withholding tax on the profit. The individual income tax paid by each of the shareholders would be also reduced accordingly, so the purpose of reducing tax burden of shareholders was achieved.

[*Comments*]: The less distribution of the dividend does not mean the losses of shareholders equity, and instead, it can be transformed into the stock value held by the shareholders. When the after-year production and benefits increase because of it, dividend per share increases, too. So, the stock prices may also rise. When the shareholders need money, they can sell their stocks to obtain the high income. In general, the capital gains tax on sale of stock is much less than the individual income tax. Or when the after-year tax rate of the shareholders' residence country is reduced, the corporation distributes the profit to reduce the shareholders tax burden.

3. Selecting carefully the foreign modes of business operation

1) The choice of a branch or a subsidiary

As we mentioned before, when a multinational corporation decides to invest and engage in business activities in foreign countries, it can choose one of the two modes: a PE or a subsidiary. But most of the operation PE take the form of branches, such as the branch company, branch bank or branch office. In fact, a foreign corporation engaging in substantial business activities in a country is typically taxable in that country on the income derived through those activities or through any corporate assets used in connection with those activities. That corporate presence in a country is generally referred to as a "branch". In tax parlance, a branch is often discussed as if it were an entity with a separate existence. It is convenient, for example, to discuss how a branch is taxed, to compute its income and maintain books of account for it. In all of these situations, nevertheless, the term "branch" is being used metaphorically. In contrast to a subsidiary, a branch is not a legal entity and cannot take actions on its own. The property and activities of a branch are actually the property and activities of the corporation of which it is a part. For tax avoidance, the choice of a branch or a subsidiary depends on a number of financial and non-financial conditions.

In practice, branches and subsidiaries have their own pros and cons.

From the tax perspective, the branch has the following advantages: it needn't pay the capital registered tax and stamp tax; it needn't pay the withholding tax on the interest, royalties and the dividend; it has the chance to use the exemption method which is one of the methods for international double taxation relief. Moreover, in the early days of a new investment and business activities, the foreign branch often has losses. As a convention, the residence country where the head office of a transnational taxpayer locates generally allows the foreign branches to use these losses to offset the total profits of the head office. This approach can also be used to deal with the profits or losses due to currency exchange. It is the main advantage of branches.

The disadvantages of a branch are as follows: Because it has no independent legal status in the host country, therefore, it is ineligible for the tax incentives such as a tax holiday and other investment incentives, which are provided by the local government for the subsidiary; if a branch changes into a subsidiary in the future, it is likely to bear the capital gains tax and the change may have prior approval of taxation and foreign exchange control authorities; once a branch obtains profits, the head office has to pay taxes on the profits to its residence country (or the nationality country) in the same taxable year. If the tax rate of the source country is lower than that of the residence country (or the national country), the branch is unable to obtain the benefits of deferral.

On the contrary, a subsidiary is opposite to a branch. The advantages and disadvantages of a branch are just the disadvantages and advantages of a subsidiary. A transnational taxpayer usually weighs the advantages and disadvantages repeatedly and then makes the most advantageous selec-

Chapter 6 GENERAL METHODS OF INTERNATIONAL TAX AVOIDANCE

tion for him. A common choice of a transnational taxpayer in a high tax residence country (or a nationality country) is to engage in business activities in the form of a branch in the early days of foreign operation. Therefore, the early losses can be used to offset the profits of the head office in time and reduce the tax payable to the residence country (or the nationality country). And when the branch begins to obtain profit, it will be promptly transformed into a subsidiary to enjoy the benefits of deferral. In accordance with this form of tax avoidance, some countries formulate corresponding measures to prevent the transnational taxpayer from double-dip benefits.

Teaching Case of 6-15

A multinational corporation of country M wanted to set up an asparagus planting and processing enterprises in China and sent an economic adviser to China to investigate the investment policy. In the choice of Chinese-foreign cooperative enterprise or Chinese-foreign joint venture, the adviser consulted the relevant departments of China about the foreign tax policy and suggested that the project should adopt the form of Chinese-foreign cooperative enterprises. Moreover, he thought the enterprise should be invested by the subsidiary set up in Country H by the multinational corporation.

His suggestion was based on the following consideration: Asparagus is a kind of roots plant. If the seeds were sown in a new planting area, the time for asparagus reaching the first harvest would be 4 years or 5 years which would make the enterprise suffer greater losses in the initial stage. If the enterprise took the form of Chinese-foreign joint venture, it would be viewed as a subsidiary of Country M and H, and the losses could only be made up in the Chinese-foreign joint venture. But if the enterprise took the form of Chinese-foreign Cooperative enterprise, it would be viewed as a branch of Country M and H, and the losses could be made up in the head office of Country M. It could not only reduce the enterprise's pressure at the beginning of the establishment, but also can reduce the tax burden of the head office.

2) The choice of a partnership or a company

When a transnational individual chooses the mode of operation, he often faces the problem of choosing a partnership or a company. In the provisions of tax laws of many countries, the business profit of a partnership does not subject to corporate income tax, but to individual income tax according to the investment proportion. From the aspect of avoiding corporate income tax, the partnership has great attraction for the transnational individual.

Teaching Case of 6-16

A man of Country A planned to operate a tropical fruit shop in Country B. The expected annual profit was 40,000 dollars. If the shop was a partnership and the individual income tax rate was 40%, the man could obtain net profits of 24,000 dollars after tax. If the shop was a company and the corporate income tax rate was 30%, the man could obtain net profits of 28,000 dollars after tax. If all of the profits were distributed to the man as dividends, the man had to pay individual income tax of 11,200 dollars (=28,000×40%). Therefore, the net profits after tax he obtained were only 16,800 dollars. Compared to the former, he paid more income tax of 7,200 dollars. From the reduction of tax burden, the taxpayer would take the form of a partnership instead of a company.

However, it only considers the issue from the perspective of relieving double taxation. In fact, there are many factors that affect the management decision and the partnership is not necessarily a best management form. A partner has unlimited liability; the partnership share cannot be freely transferred; a partnership is not free to issue shares to expand its operation scale; once profit produced, it is reflected directly in the partner's current tax liability; in most of the countries, a partnership has no independent legal status which will prevent it from enjoying the treatment of tax treaties and all kinds of tax preferences provided to a company. In contrast, a company can overcome these shortcomings. Therefore, in the investment and business decision-making, tax is an important but is not the only determining factor.

4. Using the tax preferences and selecting the low tax point of investments

Affected by the different political systems, economic development levels, the overall economic development strategies, industrial policies and other factors, there must be lots of differences between the tax systems of various countries which make the tax burdens of different taxpayers and different tax objects difficult to be balanced and consistent. It provides the transnational taxpayers with the opportunity to choose, and enables them to adopt cleverly the appropriate investment forms with low tax or to obtain some items of low tax, which are referred to as the low tax points of investment.

1) Making full use of tax preferences

The low tax points are in tax preferences everywhere. For different economic or political purposes, many countries implement some tax preferences. Especially, the tax incentives for investment such as accelerated depreciation, investment credit, differential tax rate, tax loss carry-forward and the tax holiday are popular in both the developing countries and the developed countries. These tax preferences are to guide the taxpayer for the investment activities in the specified direction. However, they may lead to the expansion of tax loopholes.

For example, for the development of some domestic poor areas, acceleration of some new industry and expanding of exports, a country may reduce tax rate in these areas consciously or provide some tax holidays to attract investors and achieve the country's expected plans. Transnational taxpayers can use these low tax points legally to reduce their tax burdens in non-residence countries.

 Teaching Case of 6-17

A glass company wants to update a set of water supply device. The one with a circular or water-saving function is 1,000,000 dollars. The one with the ordinary function is 800,000 dollars. If the company buys the former one, it will spend more money. But it is stipulated in the tax law that the water-saving device can enjoy a investment credit of 40%. In addition to saving water consumption, the company can save water charges of 20,000 dollars every year. After comparison, the company decides to buy the device with water-saving function.

2) Looking for low tax points from tax approach

When interest is paid by a resident corporation to a non-resident, the interest is deductible by the payer in computing income unless there are special rules to the contrary. Often, the interest

Chapter 6 GENERAL METHODS OF INTERNATIONAL TAX AVOIDANCE

is either not taxable to the non-resident or is subject to a reduced rate of withholding tax pursuant to an applicable tax treaty. If the non-resident lender is also a shareholder of the resident corporation, the residence country's corporate tax base may be seriously eroded by the payment of interest rather than dividends. Unlike interest, dividends paid by a resident corporation are generally not deductible. Accordingly, income earned by a resident corporation and distributed to its shareholders is subject to two levels of tax—corporate tax when the income is earned by the corporation and shareholder tax when the income is distributed to the shareholders as a dividend. If the shareholder is a non-resident, the shareholder tax is usually imposed as a withholding tax. In contrast, income earned by a resident corporation and distributed in the form of interest to a non-resident lender, who is also a shareholder of the corporation, is subject to only one level of tax. Because the interest is deductible by the corporation, usually the only source-country tax is the withholding tax on the interest payment to the non-resident. The advantage of paying interest to non-residents compared to paying dividends constitutes an inherent bias in favor of debt financing of resident corporations by non-resident investors. The phenomenon is called "thin capitalization".

Simulated demonstration of 6-3

[**Background**]: A new set-up enterprise earned income of 10,000,000 Yuan in 2020. The approved deduction was 500,000 Yuan and the allowable foreign credit was 100,000 Yuan. The enterprise income tax rate of the residence country was 40%. Now, calculate the amount of tax payable of the enterprise to the residence country in 2020.

[**Calculation**]:

The income taxable: 1,000−50=950 (ten thousand Yuan).

The enterprise income tax payable: 950×40% = 380 (ten thousand Yuan).

The enterprise income tax actually paid: 380−10=370 (ten thousand Yuan).

[**Operation**]: For reduction of the tax burden, under the condition that the shareholders did not pay the required capital fully, the enterprise borrowed money from its overseas shareholders and paid interest of 1,500,000 Yuan. Assume the withholding tax rate of the residence country was 20%, now, calculate the amount of tax payable of the enterprise to the residence country in 2020.

The income taxable: 1,000− (50+150) = 800 (ten thousand Yuan).

The enterprise income tax payable: 800×40% = 320 (ten thousand Yuan).

The enterprise income tax actually paid: 320−10=310 (ten thousand Yuan).

The withholding tax on interest: 150×20% = 30 (ten thousand Yuan).

[**Comments**]: From the example we can see that when the enterprise had abnormal loan, it could pay less tax of 300,000 Yuan (370−[310+30]).

[**Conclusion**]: As the example illustrates, financing a resident corporation with debt is considerably more effective in reducing the source country tax than financing with equity. The major reason is that interest is deductible, whereas dividends are not deductible. In addition, a resident corporation can repay a loan at any time without triggering tax, whereas a corporation may not be able to repay equity investments (redeem shares or reduce capital) without triggering a taxable dividend.

Key words, phrases and special terms

tax border	税境
tax exile	税收流亡
free trade zone	自由贸易区
customs frontier	关境
the board of directors	董事会
shareholders meeting	股东大会
profit margin	利润率
treaty shopping	滥用税收协定
conduit company	导管公司、中介公司
back-to-back loan	倒手贷款
holding company	控股公司
arm's length principle	公平交易原则
transfer pricing	转让定价
related corporation	关联公司
foreign affiliate	外国关联公司
insurance premium	保险费
materials for processing	来料加工
letter-box company	信箱公司
base company	基地公司
accumulation fund	公积金
stamp tax	印花税
tax holiday	免税期
Chinese-foreign joint venture	中外合资经营企业
Chinese-foreign cooperative enterprise	中外合作经营企业
accelerated depreciation	加速折旧
thin capitalization	资本弱化

 Problems of thinking

1. What are the general methods of international tax avoidance for transnational taxpayers?

2. What are the subject's common methods of transferring tax avoidance? What are the object's common methods of transferring tax avoidance?

3. What is the treaty shopping? What are the common ways of treaty shopping?

4. What are the common forms of transfer pricing?

5. What are the tax and non-tax motivations of transfer pricing?

6. What is tax deferral? What is the significance to the taxpayer?

7. What are the advantages and disadvantages of branches and subsidiaries?

8. How important is the transfer pricing to the business of multinational corporations?

Chapter 7
TAX AVOIDANCE MODE OF TAX HAVENS

 Ideological and political points of the course

After Hong Kong China's return to the motherland, with political stability and economic prosperity, Chinese enterprises should make better use of Hong Kong China's status as an "international financial center"and strengthen their confidence in the path, theory, system and culture of socialism with Chinese characteristics while doing greater and better international trade business.

 Learning Objectives

1.Focus on understanding and mastering the two tax avoidance modes of tax havens.
2.Master the specific ways of fictitious business and fictitious trust property in tax havens for avoiding tax.
3.Evaluate correctly the function of tax havens.

 Course Importing

As an "international financial center", how can China Hong Kong play an active role to help Chinese enterprises in their process of "going global"?

Tax havens are noticeable phenomena of contemporary world economy. The policies implemented by tax havens have great influence on the flow of international capital, investment distribution, multinational corporation's distribution of income and expenses and the revenue of relevant countries. The proliferation and increased use of tax havens in the last 50 years have been staggering. Many developments have contributed to the growth of tax havens and their use, including:

(1) The elimination of exchange controls and the liberalization of cross-border trade and investment.

(2) Improved communications, transportation and financial services.

(3) The adoption by tax havens of flexible commercial regimes and strict bank secrecy and confidentiality requirements.

(4) Aggressive marketing.

Long-established tax havens have become very sophisticated in marketing their services to every geographical region of the world and to every conceivable tax planning need. Newer tax havens have arisen to try and get a piece of the action.

For a transnational taxpayer engaging in transnational business, how to use tax havens is usually an important part of his international tax planning. The use of tax havens almost involves in all aspects of transferring tax avoidance of subject and object. It is a comprehensive tax avoidance mode which centralizes international migration, disguised transfer, treaty shopping, transfer pricing and other means of tax avoidance. The transnational taxpayers' basic tax avoidance mode of tax havens can be classified into two types: fictitious business and fictitious trust property in tax havens.

7.1　Fictitious business in tax havens

A common way for transnational taxpayers to use tax havens for tax avoidance is to make up business in tax havens. Some companies established in tax havens have little or no real business activities in tax havens. The basic way of fictitious business in tax havens is to make up transfer transactions of selling goods, technology and providing service in tax havens that originally should be carried on through the head office or the parent company to other countries or regions. Thus, parts or all of income will be held up in tax havens. Then, through loans and investment, the income can be remitted to the residence country and avoid the tax burden in high tax countries.

The companies which play an intermediary role in the fictitious business are various controlled companies which are based on tax havens, which include generally the letter-box company and all kinds of professional companies such as holding company, investment company, financing company, rental company, shipping company, insurance company, patent company, trading company and other service company, etc. Many of them belong to the foreign base company.

Foreign base company refers to the company established in tax havens as the base of avoiding tax which is engaged in transferring and accumulation of business or investment profits with the third country. For example, a company of country A wants to invest in country C. First, it can set up a foreign base company in country B, a tax haven, and then invests in country C through the base company. This is a typical foreign base company engaged in "the third country business". In real life, there is a typical foreign base company. For example, a company wants to invest in the home country, but it sets up first a foreign base company in country B, a tax haven, and then invests in the home country through the base company. The following contents focus on the establishment of various controlled companies and their avoidance characteristics.

1. The letter-box company

The letter-box company refers to those various "file" companies who only complete the necessary registration procedure in the country and have a legal organization form. Such company only exists in the file and only has a letter box and a managing director. The company's activities of business, manufacturing, management are actually carried on elsewhere. These companies are generally

Chapter 7 TAX AVOIDANCE MODE OF TAX HAVENS

set up in tax havens and they are the typical tax havens companies, also, they are the most important forms of the foreign base companies.

 Teaching Case of 7-1

The Norfolk Island of Australia was once a tax haven. In 1972, there were 1,450 registered companies on the island almost equal to the number of its residents, namely, every resident has a company. So many companies gathered in such a small place. How could the actual business activities be carried out? Another example is Bermuda, whose land area is only 53.3 square kilometers and a population of only 60,000. If it really wants to set up the business enterprises, only the American investments of ten billion dollars cannot be held there. Obviously, the real investments in Bermuda are just the "accounts" of companies.

2. The holding company

The holding company refers to a company which controls large shares or has significant voting rights in one or more subsidiaries. The holding proportion can be 100% high or 50% below. Its income is mainly the dividends and the capital gains of selling shares. Establishment of a holding company in tax havens is one of the ways of tax avoidance, because the tax havens may not tax or only impose little tax on dividend and capital gains. In fact, many tax havens offer special preferential tax treatment to holding companies, such as Holland, Netherlands Antilles, Luxemburg, Singapore and Switzerland.

 Simulated demonstration of 7-1

[***Background***]: *A parent company in a high tax country has subsidiaries in several low tax countries and it wants to use the subsidiaries profits to set up other subsidiaries in some other countries. But if the present subsidiaries pay dividends to the parent company, the parent company's residence country will levy high taxes on the dividends. Therefore, the parent company should try to avoid paying high income tax to set up subsidiaries in foreign countries; otherwise, it would have to pay a high price.*

[***Operation***]: *Assume that the parent company's residence country has not anti-avoidance provisions in its tax law with respect to the tax havens and then everything will be easy: the parent company only needs to establish a subsidiary in a tax haven to control the shares of the foreign subsidiaries.*

[***Comments***]: *As the stock right has been transferred to the subsidiary in a tax haven, the parent company needn't pay income tax to the residence country on the dividends.*

3. The investment company

The investment company is a company specialized in securities investment. These securities include stocks, corporate bonds or other securities which only account for little or very little proportion of a company's shares and have no any important voting rights in the enterprise's management decision-making. This is the difference between investment companies and holding companies. But their aim is to eliminate or reduce the tax burden of dividend, interest, rent, transportation, insurance, royalties and business income and the burden of capital gains for selling property. Moreover, in tax treaties of some countries, provisions of levying no or less tax on investment income subject to withholding tax also provide favorable conditions for investment companies.

There are three different ways of setting up an investment company. The first one is that a group company establishes a financing company in a tax haven; the second one is that individuals set up an investment company in a tax haven; the third one is so-called the "offshore investment funds".

An offshore investment fund is a kind of mutual investment funds established by the companies and individuals in high tax country. In another word, it refers to the foreign investment company set up by companies and individuals. It is very mobile, flexible and complex. Such offshore investment funds allow resident taxpayers to defer domestic tax on their passive investment income. Offshore funds may also permit taxpayers to convert what would be ordinary income into capital gains on the disposition of the shares of the fund. Such funds are generally established in tax havens like Bahamas, the Netherlands Antilles and China Hong Kong. For example, the Holland Lauren fund is established in Kuraso of the Netherlands Antilles to avoid the withholding tax to Holland on the financial interest of dividend distributed by the funds to its members.

4. The financing company

The financing company is an agency which acts as the lending intermediary in a group company or provides funds to the third party. In order not to pay or pay less interest income tax, to obtain the permission of tax deduction for a group company's paying interest to a high tax country, or to use the favorable tax treaties of not or less paying withholding tax on interest to the payment country, transnational taxpayers can usually set up financing companies in tax havens. Therefore, when a group company invests in securities or purchases real estates, the temporary capital it needs is often provided by the financing company established in tax havens.

Teaching Case of 7-2

The American companies often set up financing subsidiaries in Netherlands Antilles. This is because the United States and Netherlands Antilles signed a tax treaty. It stipulates that the interest paid by the companies in Netherlands Antilles to American bondholders exempts from withholding tax. Netherlands Antilles has no income tax. In this case, the American companies can put a large number of interests to the financing company's account to obtain the benefits of low or no tax. Also, the German companies often establish financing companies in Luxemburg and tax havens like Panama, Liberia, Singapore, and China Hong Kong are often used to establish financing companies to avoid tax.

5. The rental company

The rental company is an organization specialized in the activities of rental, leasing trade and hire purchase. Many countries offer special tax preferences for transnational taxpayers such as accelerated depreciation and tax credits for investment to encourage enterprises to obtain or own in-

Chapter 7 TAX AVOIDANCE MODE OF TAX HAVENS

dustrial equipments or properties. According to the general provisions, these tax benefits will be achieved by those who own the properties instead of those who will soon sell these properties. So, when a taxpayer uses the credit capital to purchase a batch of equipments and immediately transfers them to another taxpayer, whether the transfer contract is a sales contract or a lease contract is very important. If it is a lease contract rather than a sales contract, the transferor is entitled to the tax preferences. Therefore, transnational taxpayers can take advantage of these provisions to set up rental companies in tax havens to avoid taxes by renting, leasing trade and hire purchase pricing.

Teaching Case of 7-3

A parent company of Country A set up subsidiaries in Country C and Country B, and Country B was a tax haven. The parent company bought a batch of equipments using borrowed money, and then leased them to the subsidiary in Country B at the possibly low price. The subsidiary in Country B subleased them to the subsidiary in Country C at the possibly high price. In this process, as the legal owner of the leased property, the parent company in Country A can extract depreciation on leased equipments. As the economic owner of the leased property, the subsidiary in Country B can also extract depreciation on the rented equipments. Except the lease pricing and depreciation, the rental company can also enjoy the benefits of encouraging investment of tax authorities to achieve the purpose of tax avoidance.

6. The shipping company

Another way of tax avoidance for transnational taxpayers is to set up an international shipping company in tax havens, including international shipping companies and airline companies. Because the ownership and management right of these companies can be in different countries, their head offices can be located in a third country (usually in tax havens), and their ships or aircrafts can be re-registered elsewhere, which makes them escape from the jurisdictions of high tax countries, they can avoid or reduce the income tax and capital gains tax.

Teaching Case of 7-4

At the end of the Second World War, the United States, Britain, Holland and Sweden were all the world's leading shipbuilding countries. At that time, industrial enterprises were under the strong pressure from trade union and the provisions of work and living conditions limited their profitability. So, the shipping companies began to register in Panama and Liberia. These countries were not only tax havens, but also provided conditions to the companies to avoid the laws and limitation to the business activities of trade union from their home countries. For example, Liberia is a small country in southwest of West Africa. It has a population of only 1,700,000 and produces rubber. Due to the low tax policy, it attracts so many foreign companies to establish a lot of plantations there and its rubber field is the first in Africa. In addition, the country uses the geographical advantage of close to the Atlantic to impose low tax on foreign ships. Therefore, the total tonnage of international ships flying the flag of Liberia is at the forefront of the world which is so-called the "flags of convenience".

From the point of view of reducing tax, transnational taxpayers can also use the large losses of shipping companies or aircraft companies located in high tax countries or the lease, rental and sublease of transportation such as ships and aircrafts to avoid income tax. There are many international shipping companies or aircraft companies in tax havens such as Panama, Liberia, Bahamas, Bermuda, Cayman Islands, China Hong Kong and Netherlands Antilles. Tax havens such as Greece and Cyprus are also good places where the international taxpayers are willing to establish shipping companies for tax avoidance.

7. The insurance company

The insurance company is a kind of organization which provides insurance and reinsurance of business activities to the members of the group company, including itself, and is completely controlled by the group company.

Usually, in the business activities of enterprises, there is a great deal of insurance expenses every year. But sometimes the insurance company is not willing to accept a transnational group company's required insurance project. So, it is necessary for the transnational group company to set up its own controlled insurance company which will take the risk insurance of the group company's business activities. In this regard, tax havens can provide much convenience for the insurance company. So during the past ten or twenty years, many international group companies have set up their own controlled insurance companies in tax havens. Compared with the insurance premium paid to an independent insurance company, there is so much benefit to establish the company's own controlled insurance company in tax havens. On the one hand, the insurance premium can be reduced. On the other hand, it can also undertake parts of or all of losses that can not be assumed by a third party insurance company. In addition, the controlled insurance companies are often viewed as a center of accumulating profits which can adjust the parent company's operation costs. For example, a controlled insurance company can provide normal insurance to the parent company's assets like other independent insurance company but the premium rate it claims is lower or higher than that of other independent insurance companies which increases or decreases the operation costs of the parent company. Tax havens like Bahamas, Bermuda, Cayman Islands, China Hong Kong, Netherlands Antilles and Panama have become the "paradise" of controlled insurance companies. Among them, Bermuda has become a tax haven where the insurance and reinsurance companies most concentrate in the world.

8. The patent company

The patent company is a company specialized in the acquirement and usage of patent, trademark, copyright, trademark or other industrial property rights or the use of franchise. Because there are preferential provisions such as exemption or reduction with respect to withholding tax on the payment of royalties in some countries' tax treaties (such as low tax countries or tax havens), to pay low or no withholding tax, transnational taxpayers can establish a patent company in those countries to engage in the activities of acquirement and usage of patents or the use of franchise. And the best "paradise" for these activities is the tax haven.

Teaching Case of 7-5

(ACo) has a proprietary technology of high value and is going to transfer it to a user in a Middle East country by license trade. The Middle East country does not impose withholding tax on the royalties paid to foreign companies. In order to avoid paying tax on the transferring income of proprietary technology in the residence country, ACo can establish a patent company in a tax haven and let it sign a contract of assignment with the user in the Middle East country which creates a false impression that the transfer does not occur in ACo's home country and avoids the domestic income tax.

9. The trading company

The trading company refers to the company engaging in exchanging of goods and services which only issues invoices to the purchase, sales and other business activities of the Group Company. Transnational taxpayers often establish a trading company in tax havens to make up false business and transfer the profits in high tax countries to the trading company in tax havens. However, transnational taxpayers do not regard tax havens with tax treaties as their best choice of setting up the trading company. This is because their purchase and sales transactions often involve in or out of tax havens, the provisions of exchanging tax information specified in tax treaties often bring troubles to them. So, considering from the angle of security, transnational taxpayers tend to choose those tax havens without tax treaties as good places to build trading companies such as Bahamas, Bermuda, China Hong Kong and Panama.

10. The service company

The service company refers to the company engaging in partial management, cartel agreement organization, offshore investment funds management or other similar services. Multinational corporations often establish service companies in tax havens for expenses allocation. That is to say, by means of paying service charges to the service companies in tax havens, Multinational corporations can transfer the profits in high tax countries to the service companies in tax havens and avoid the income tax of high tax countries. And the senior managers can also work in the service companies in tax havens to avoid their individual income tax.

To sum up, many of the companies established by transnational taxpayers in tax havens for tax avoidance belong to the foreign base company. The tax avoidance activities through the foreign base company, especially the letter-box company, can form an income accumulation center between the source country and the gainer of income. Through the accumulation of dividends, interest, royalties, or income from real estates and securities, the taxpayers can reinvest and avoid tax with less or no tax.

7.2　Fictitious trust property in tax havens

At present in many countries, in addition to income tax, the tax burden of settlement tax, inheritance tax, gift tax, capital transfer tax and general property tax on transnational individuals can not be ignored. The rate of gift tax and settlement tax is generally about 50%, some even as high as 70% to 90%. Transnational individuals can use tax havens by ways of subject's non-transferring or object's transferring to avoid taxes. Fictitious trust property in tax havens is a common way.

Trust refers that an individual (the consignor) entrusts his assets or rights (trust property) to another individual (the consignee) and the consignee manages and uses the trust property in accordance with the requirements of the consignor to be in favor of the beneficiary. The beneficiary may be a third party designated by the consignor or the consignor himself.

Trust is a legal relationship instead of a legal entity like a company, whose existence is usually limited to a certain time. But in tax havens, due to trust existence and no trust laws, the trust can in fact continue indefinitely, as in the Channel Islands. Trust has many benefits such as providing conditions to inherit properties, keeping secret for properties, facilitating of investment, engaging in business risk activities and avoiding or reduction of tax burdens of property and income. So, many countries and regions of tax haven allow foreigners to set up trust in their territory. At the same time, transnational taxpayers are willing to use trust to engage in the activities of tax avoidance. Methods of fictitious trust property in tax havens are mainly the following ones.

1. Establishment of personal holding trust company

A personal holding trust company is company whose passive investment income to total income is more than 60% and more than 50% of its shares are held by 5 or less than 5 persons. The holders of this company are easy to be replaced by the multinational individual's relatives; therefore, it is actually controlled by one person. In this way, transnational taxpayers can use the special conditions in tax havens of imposing no tax on income and inheritance to avoid taxes.

Teaching Case of 7-6

A transnational taxpayer of Country A with high tax sets up a personal holding trust company in Country B, a tax haven. He entrusts properties of Country A or properties far away from Country B to the company in tax haven and let it manage them. Then, he makes this part of properties and their business income and all of the properties and business income accumulated in Country A or elsewhere reflect in the company, and gradually transfers them to Country B. So, he can first avoid all of or most of the income tax on the business income derived from the properties. Then, the company uses the transferred trust capital to purchase stocks in the local and obtains profits from the passive investment. It can also enjoy tax benefits of paying no capital gains tax. Moreover, after the death of the transnational taxpayer of Country A, the company can transfer the properties or the trust funds to the designated beneficiaries (such as his relatives, friends, etc.) according to the consignor's designated ways before his death. Thus, he can avoid all of or most of the huge inheritance tax.

2. Establishment of controlled trust company

Transnational taxpayers can not only use the establishment of trust properties in tax havens to engage in passive investment activities for tax avoidance, but also can use the establishment of trust properties in tax havens to engage in active investment activities to cover the shareholders' equities in the company for tax avoidance. For example, a transnational taxpayer of Country A with high tax can set up a controlled trust company and a controlled holding company in Country B, a tax haven. He can be engaged in investment activities through the controlled holding company and entrust it to the controlled trust company. In this way, the holding company's equity belongs to the trust company lawfully and the trust company will manage the holding company. But the real beneficiary of these financial interests is the transnational taxpayer of consignor, at the same time, the beneficiary himself in Country A with high tax. This is a typical way of fictitious trust properties in tax havens.

 Teaching Case of 7-7

For avoidance of domestic income tax, Runge Bridge Company of New Zealand transferred 70% of its annual profits to Bahamas in the form of trust. Bahamas is a tax haven with lower tax rate of 35% to 50% than New Zealand. Therefore, the company can effectively avoid 3,000,000 to 4,700,000 dollars of tax payments annually.

3. Signature of a trust contract

In international economic activities, many companies want to set up their own offices and branches in overseas to achieve tax avoidance. But in fact, quite a number of overseas offices and branches have a lot of inconvenience in administrative management with high cost and low efficiency. Therefore, it is better to find a resident company in the overseas country of transit or other places to help to deal with the business and use the tax treaty between the residence country of the company with other countries to provide convenience to both sides.

 Simulated demonstration of 7-2

[*Background*]: Japan and the United States signed a mutually beneficial bilateral tax treaty which stipulated that Japanese banks could pay less interest tax of 50% on the deposits from American residents (The United States specified that the interest tax rate was 20% and Japanese banks could pay only 10%). A Chinese company had loan relations with an American company, the Chinese company was the loan provider and the American company was the loan demand.

[*Operation*]: The Chinese company could entrust a Japanese bank to collect interest from the American company on behalf of the Chinese company.

[*Comments*]: The above approach could make the Chinese company enjoy the benefits of paying 50% of less tax.

To sum up, tax havens have positive and negative effects at the same time.

Firstly, international tax havens can provide the benefits of paying less tax and obtaining more profits for investors which leads to the capital flows continuously from the high tax countries to international tax havens. The foreign active investments can speed up the centralization and accumulation of funds in tax haven countries and regions, promote the expansion of production scale and speed up further socialization. The foreign passive investments can also increase the foreign exchange funds of governments or enterprises in these tax havens countries. The foreign enterprises' registration, land and the office rental can also increase income of these countries and regions. Foreigners settled in tax havens to avoid high tax can also bring a number of foreign exchanges. All of the activities of international investors will promote the finance of tax havens internationalization and produce a financial market easily to raise foreign investments. Secondly, international tax havens can attract the inflows of foreign advanced technology and equipment which promotes the technology revolution of these countries and regions. Finally, for the density of foreigners in international tax havens, the construction of foreign factories, the establishment of companies and the settlement of foreign immigrants, it is necessary to increase a number of workers, staff and service personnel, which increases the employment rate in these countries and regions.

Of course, when we talk about the positive effects of international tax havens, we cannot ignore its negative effects.

Firstly, although the foreign companies set up a variety of companies or institutions in international tax havens, a considerable part of them is fictional with an objective of tax avoidance. Such companies have fewer investments on tangible assets and will not bring the advanced equipment and technology with practical significance to the international tax havens. They are often some companies with only a sign, and as long as something happens or a better tax haven exists, they will immediately transfer. Therefore, it lacks the stability. Secondly, even for various banks and financial companies with genuine business activities, they are often engaged in passive investments. Once the investment business declines, profit falls or the local or international capital market fluctuates, the companies will soon transfer their funds to other countries to seek more profits which will cause great influence to the formed financial systems in tax havens. Thirdly, most of the international tax havens are developing countries and regions with low level of culture and technology, the foreign companies prefer to hire immigrants from their own countries or from other developed countries as clerk, which cannot solve well the employment problem of international tax havens. Finally, and most importantly, tax preferences of international tax havens to attract foreign investments are often partly offset by the anti-avoidance measures taken unilaterally by the capital output countries, and sometimes they cannot work at all.

Key words, phrases and special terms

holding company	控股公司
investment company	投资公司
financing company	金融公司
rental company	租赁公司
shipping company	航运公司
insurance company	保险公司
patent company	专利公司
trading company	贸易公司
foreign base company	外国基地公司
offshore investment funds	离岸投资基金
hire purchase	租购
service charges	劳务费
consignor	委托人
consignee	受托人
beneficiary	受益人
personal holding trust company	个人持股信托公司

Chapter 7　TAX AVOIDANCE MODE OF TAX HAVENS

Problems of thinking

1. How do the transnational taxpayers use tax havens to engage in activities of tax avoidance?
2. How to use the trust properties in tax havens to avoid tax?
3. How to evaluate international tax havens?

Chapter 8

INTERNATIONAL ANTI-AVOIDANCE METHODS AND MEASURES

 Ideological and political points of the course

Corporate Income Tax Law 4 the People's Republic of China and *Individual Income Tax Law 4 the People's Republic of China* both have strengthened anti-avoidance provisions for transnational taxpayers, which is of great significance to safeguard our tax sovereignty.

 Learning Objectives

1. Fully understand and grasp the significance of international anti-avoidance.
2. Understand various international anti-avoidance measures.
3. Master the contents of CFC Rules and transfer pricing rules.

Course Importing

According to the media reports, in 1995 one of the world famous multinational companies in the United States sets up a wholly foreign owned enterprise in Beijing, and then after two capital increase, its registered capital reached 20 million dollars. But for a long time, the enterprise had been losing money and its average profit margin was only −18%. Meanwhile, the industry's average profit margin in Beijing was about 12%. How to deal with the tax avoidance problems of enterprises with foreign investment in China?

In recent years, activities of international tax avoidance vary greatly and keep unabated, and various tax havens encourage the momentum. Intertwined with international tax evasion, it will inevitably lead to distortions of competition and abnormal flows of international capital, which causes an adverse effect on many countries' fiscal revenue. Income and wealth is redistributed and shifted to those who carried out tax avoidance and tax evasion successfully. These persons pay less tax than they should pay, while those law-abiding taxpayers actually pay every penny. Worse still, in order to ensure the predetermined budget, the government has to raise tax rates or levy new taxes, which increases the burden on those honest taxpayers. Obviously, this is unfair. Therefore, it is a

Chapter 8 INTERNATIONAL ANTI-AVOIDANCE METHODS AND MEASURES

totally worthwhile event to reduce effectively the international tax avoidance and tax evasion. So, most countries have anti-avoidance rules to deal with certain types of international tax avoidance. In the long-term practice, some developed countries have gradually formed a set of anti-avoidance measures worthy of reference. The key is to use legal measures in legislation and enforcement of laws. Of course, expanding and strengthening bilateral cooperation among governments, deliberation and exploration of multilateral anti-avoidance cooperation in greater international scope are very important.

8.1　The general methods of international anti-avoidance

Due to different national conditions, there will be inevitably different anti-avoidance measures. This section focuses on the introduction to the general methods of international anti-avoidance and describes the general situation of it. The specific measures will be discussed in the following sections.

8.1.1　Strengthening unilateral legislative measures for anti-avoidance

Tax legislation with high quality will lay the foundation for its own implementation. Complete provisions, precise wording and clear explanation are important symbols of it and the "armor" of tax laws from decayed. Perfecting tax laws, plugging the loopholes and strengthening the protection capability of tax law is an important aspect of tax authorities to win the anti-avoidance struggle. Therefore, the legislation is the base of anti-avoidance. At the same time, in order to strengthen effectively the tax authorities' status in the struggle for anti-avoidance and anti-evasion, tax legislation should make favorable provisions for tax authorities to work. The unilateral anti-avoidance measures are roughly the following several types.

1. Issuing anti-avoidance provisions

Anti-avoidance provisions in tax laws of the countries can be usually classified into four categories.

1) The general anti-avoidance provisions

The general anti-avoidance provisions mainly concentrate on the description of the object of taxation. There are two methods of description of tax objects: one is from the civil law and another is from the broad and general economic concept. Take income tax for an example, the former is a regulation system which can be used as an independent legal form to define the business cost deductible; the latter defines clearly that the deductible cost is all of the cost incurred in the normal course of business which is a comprehensive total income concept such as the clause of "taxable income is any kind of income from the enterprise" or the similar statements.

Obviously, in the former method, although the legal term is strict accuracy, the expression of tax objects from the legal concept will bind the anti-avoidance ability of tax authorities and make them entangled in legal wording. The latter method uses the economic concept rather than the legal concept to express tax objects, which enhances the response ability of tax authorities and increases the practice opportunities of tax authorities to take actions against international tax avoidance. Extensive economic regulations in tax law can reflect more flexibility and adaptability than the rigid wording in civil law. However, because this method is not specifying enough, there is some uncertainty in the implementation. It needs the match of other anti-avoidance provisions to work better.

2) The special anti-avoidance provisions

In practice, the taxpayers use up-to-date legal means and explanations to avoid falling into the scope of tax law by preventing the existence of tax base. In view of this situation, the special anti-avoidance provisions stipulate clear and specific tax objects, namely, specifying certain activities or income as tax objects in law and leave no chance to taxpayers for seeking loopholes in the interpretation of the law. Many provisions of tax laws in the USA, France, Belgium and Britain are drawn up in this way.

3) Special and general anti-avoidance provisions

It refers to specify some transactions and tax obligations in provisions of tax laws and stipulate the general provisions at the same time. For example, in the section 367th of *American Internal Revenue Code*, the exchange of share to property and other exchange are specified in the provisions. At the same time, the taxpayers must prove to the tax authorities that the main purpose of this exchange is not to avoid federal income tax. The advantage of this method is that when the legislature takes legislative measures, it grants tax authorities wide discretion at the same time, which can prevent some astute taxpayers from using loopholes in tax laws.

4) The comprehensive anti-avoidance provisions

It is a kind of provision applicable for different types of tax avoidance to the similar or comparable tax avoidance behavior. For example, the regulations on transfer pricing of associated company in the section 482nd of *American Internal Revenue Code*, the clause 57th of French tax code and the clause 24th of Belgian tax law and the provisions on business activities in tax havens in Subpart F rules of *American Internal Revenue Code* belong to this kind of anti-avoidance provisions.

2. Strengthening the obligation of tax

The measures of strengthening the obligation of tax usually include three aspects.

1) Stipulated in tax laws that the taxpayers have extended obligation to provide tax information

Generally, the tax authority of a taxpayer's residence country (or nationality country) can not directly obtain the foreign activity information of the resident (or citizen) and can't go abroad for investigation, because it is beyond its jurisdiction. To solve the problem, tax law of most countries generally requires that the resident (or citizen) taxpayer has the obligation to provide tax information about his foreign business activities to the residence country (or nationality country). The information provider can be a resident taxpayer, a third party having business relationship with the taxpayer or a non-resident taxpayer.

Of course, this obligation goes against the protection of taxpayer's commercial secrets which may cause damage to the person concerned. According to the reporting obligation specified in tax laws, taxpayers must open a part of business secrets to the tax authority, but the confidentiality ob-

Chapter 8 INTERNATIONAL ANTI-AVOIDANCE METHODS AND MEASURES

ligation of revenue officials is far from watertight.

2) Stipulated in tax laws that the taxpayers have obligation to obtain the consent of the government for some transactions in advance

In anti-avoidance provisions, the most stringent legislation is that taxpayers must obtain prior consent of the tax authority for some transactions; otherwise, it is illegal and should be punished. It includes not only the resident taxpayers, sometimes including foreigners cooperating with such transactions.

 Teaching Case of 8-1

It is stipulated in British income tax and corporate tax that if a resident legal entity transfers its British domicile abroad or its domestic properties to a foreign legal entity controlled by it, it has to obtain the prior consent of the ministry of finance. Otherwise, it will be punished as follows: First, it has to continue to perform unlimited tax liability to the British government as before; second, it should be punished and imposed sanctions. There is a similar provision in American tax laws. For example, when an American multinational taxpayer engages in certain transactions, he has an obligation to provide evidences to the tax authorities in advance to prove his main purpose is not for tax avoidance or tax evasion.

3) Stipulated in tax laws that the taxpayers have obligation to provide proof on international tax avoidance cases afterwards

According to the general principles of procedural law, the plaintiff in the lawsuit bears the burden of persuasion. In other words, the plaintiff must provide sufficient evidence that the court can judge the defendant guilty in the lawsuit. However, when the international tax evasion and tax avoidance cases occur, it is a heavy burden for the tax authorities of relevant countries to provide evidences. In order to get rid of the passive situation, some countries begin to abandon the traditional principles of procedural law, and instead, they stipulate in their tax laws that the taxpayers have obligation to provide proof to the tax authorities afterwards. Generally, it requires the taxpayer at least to provide evidences for the following two cases: the foreign facts involved in the case: the normal business across the border of tax. There were such provisions in Belgium income tax laws and France tax code. Unless the taxpayer can provide contrary evidences, some of his payment, especially, the payment to international tax havens will be viewed as fiction and cannot be deducted from his taxable profits. This approach is called the inversion of persuasion burden. In some countries, although the burden of persuasion is not defined clearly in tax laws, it also stipulates that the taxpayers have the obligation to coordinate with the tax authorities' adjustment and provide the required information.

8.1.2 Strengthening unilateral tax administration

The above unilateral legislative measures for anti-avoidance can work by strengthening the following aspects of tax administration.

1. Collection of relevant information

Based on the actual situation, the tax authorities in the world often use the power granted by laws to design all kinds of reports with different purposes for taxpayers to fill in to get required information for anti-avoidance. In this respect, the USA did the most. Some of the forms designed by the Treasury Department of United States are listed below.

①The forms of 957th and 958th for the officers, directors or shareholders in the foreign holding companies. (The form of 957th requires the nature of business and all types of stocks to be described in details, and the shareholders must be registered. The form of 958th requires details described the total income and deductible items.)

②The form of 2592nd for the CFC.

③The form of 3520th for establishment or transferring of some foreign trust.

④The form of 4683rd for declaration on foreign bank accounts, securities accounts and other financial accounts.

⑤The form of 4790th for currency or monetary securities desingned by.

In addition, from the need of international tax avoidance, tax authorities in the world also pay attention to strengthen the contacts and cooperation with other government departments (such as customs, foreign exchange control bureau) to grasp more comprehensive information.

2. Strengthening of tax investigation and tax audit

Strengthening of tax personnel training is the effective measures of ensuring effective tax investigation. For against the basic tax avoidance means used by multinational corporation, the American Internal Revenue Bureau has opened special courses for the tax inspectors, teaching them a large number of technical methods of how to find out tax evasion and tax avoidance, including talking to the senior staffs outgoing or in-service, especially, talking to the fired staffs, talking to the company's leaders and checking the activities of directors in their travel stopover (mainly the tax havens).

In addition to tax investigation, the tax authorities must carry on the tax audit. Rather than waiting for a reluctant foreign government to check up on their taxpayers, a tax department often prefers to audit those taxpayers itself, including hiring private international accounting firm to audit information provided by transnational taxpayers. This audit often focuses on several major methods of international tax avoidance and tax evasion and the audited object is generally the private enterprise or large multinational corporation with more problems. Under international custom, however, the tax authorities of one country cannot visit another country for the purpose of auditing a taxpayer's records unless invited to do so by the foreign government. Some governments consider it inappropriate to make such a visit without also obtaining the concurrence of the taxpayer. Several countries have addressed this problem by conducting joint audit programs under which a particular taxpayer (and its affiliates) is audited by the tax authorities of both countries. The practice of many countries shows that the additional tax collected through tax investigation and tax audit is far more than the cost spent by the tax departments.

Teaching Case of 8-2

The American "net value method" refers that the tax authorities use the transnational taxpayer's net income listed in the balance sheet at the beginning of a year to compare with the estimated in-

Chapter 8 INTERNATIONAL ANTI-AVOIDANCE METHODS AND MEASURES

crease or decrease in value of net income listed in the balance sheet at the end of the year to calculate the rough taxable income during this period of time after deducting certain living expenses and other expenses, and to check whether the taxpayer conceals the taxable income or not. Another example is the American "bank deposit method" which means that the tax authorities compare the transnational taxpayer's actual income and expenditures with the estimated amount with reference to his bank account to check whether there is under-reporting income or not.

3. Getting the bank's cooperation

Almost all countries have laws to allow banks to keep secrets for clients; some countries (regions) even give criminal sanctions to bank staffs who disclose customer secrets. But some countries break the blockade by means of specifying in their lawful regulations that the domestic banks must fulfill the obligation. For example, the American tax authorities use the court decision to check the bank account. When a client of a domestic bank is suspected of tax fraud, the bank will obey the court order conscientiously. But the foreign banks will be put in a quandary. Most of the national tax authorities can just strive for the foreign banks' cooperation actively to fight against international tax avoidance. This kind of cooperation can be achieved at least through efforts of both sides. First, the cooperation between tax authorities and foreign banks can be realized by signing the treaty against organized crime between countries. Second, all facts and information obtained by the tax authorities must be strictly confidential.

 Teaching Case of 8-3

Swiss banks have a very strict secrecy system, but the American Internal Revenue Bureau still enjoys special treatment through the bilateral tax treaties signed by the two countries and achieves the Swiss banks' cooperation. In certain circumstances (or cases) such as the trick of forging relevant financial documents, the treaty allows the American Internal Revenue Bureau to check the Swiss bank accounts. Except for that, Swiss do not generally allow national tax authorities to touch Swiss bank accounts. Through the cooperation, the American Internal Revenue Bureau has found some major international cases for tax evasion and dodging and it has given them a severe blow.

8.1.3 Carrying out international cooperation actively

To prevent international tax avoidance and evasion, if we only rely on a country's unilateral measures, the effect is limited. Therefore, to strengthen the cooperation in the field of tax between the governments concerned is very important. At present, the anti-avoidance measures in tax treaties or agreements between countries include mainly two aspects: one is to establish the information exchange system; the other is to carry out the administrative cooperation in tax collection. They will be discussed respectively in the following contents.

1. The exchange of information

The tax authorities of a country often experience extreme difficulty in obtaining information concerning the foreign activities of residents, let alone verify the information. For example, many countries, including all tax haven countries, have strict bank secrecy laws. Tax haven countries rarely have tax treaties with developed countries that provide for the exchange of information concerning tax matters. During the 1980s, the United States entered into several exchange of information agreements with tax haven countries, but these agreements targeted at uncovering funds laundered by drug traffickers and are not effective in uncovering more ordinary cases of tax avoidance or evasion. More recently, in response to the OECD project on harmful tax competition, a number of tax haven countries have entered into more meaningful exchange of information agreements with OECD countries. Even when tax havens are not involved, gathering information and auditing the reported income of a resident taxpayer from foreign sources presents special difficulties. Many countries address the information-gathering problem by including an exchange of information provision in their tax treaties.

Article 26 (Exchange of Information) of the OECD and UN Model Treaties provides an exchange of "such information as necessary for carrying out the provisions of this Convention or of the domestic laws of the Contracting States concerning taxes covered by the Convention". The UN Model Treaty makes it clear that information may be exchanged not only to enforce the tax laws of the Contracting States but to combat tax avoidance. An exchange of information may take place under the OECD and UN Model Treaties as a result of a specific request from a treaty partner, through an arrangement for an automatic exchange of information, or by the initiative of a Contracting State acting spontaneously. Actual treaties may provide for a more or less expansive exchange of information. For example, some tax treaties provide an exchange of information with respect to all domestic taxes. In contrast, other tax treaties provide an exchange of information only to the necessary extent for carrying out the provisions of the treaty itself.

Of course, information obtained by the tax department of a Contracting State under an exchange of information article must be kept confidential, although release of the information in court proceedings generally is allowed. A Contracting State is not obligated under the exchange of information article to carry out administrative procedures on behalf of its treaty partner that is contrary to its own laws or practices, or that would result in the disclosure of trade secrets of similar information. An escape clause generally allows a Contracting State not to provide requested information if its disclosure would be "contrary to public policy". For countries having strict bank secrecy laws, the exchange of information article may be close to meaningless because those countries are not authorized under their domestic laws to obtain much useful information about the financial activities of taxpayers.

Teaching Case of 8-4

A Japanese has been living in China for 6 years. According to Individual Income Tax Law of the People's Repubilc of China, the Japanese is Chinese resident and should pay taxes to Chinese government on all his income obtained from the inside and outside of China. In order to deal with the Japanese tax matters properly, Chinese government must verify his income to Japanese government or Japanese tax authorities. According to the bilateral tax treaties concluded between China and Japan, the Japanese government and its tax authorities have the responsibility for providing information to Chinese government about the Japanese income. In terms of the contents of exchanging information,

Chapter 8 INTERNATIONAL ANTI-AVOIDANCE METHODS AND MEASURES

there are mainly three aspects. The frist one is the exchange of required information for implementing the tax treaties such as the taxpayer's income in the residence country and the source country, transfer pricing between the affiliated enterprises, the relationship between the payer and the beneficiary of interest and royalties and the branch's or subsidiary's opening, business, close, market price or commercial activities, etc. The second one is the exchange of domestic tax laws such as the detailed rules for implementation of the tax laws and the unilateral legal measures taken by the country to prevent international tax evasion and avoidance. Through the information exchange and coordination, the contracting states will not conflict with the requirements of the tax treaties when they exercise their domestic laws. The cast one is the exchange of information for preventing tax fraud and tax evasion.

2. Administrative cooperation

The main contents of administrative cooperation include a contracting state performs certain tax behavior on behalf of another contracting state such as delivering the notice of tax payment on behalf or implementing certain security measures to the relevant taxpayer and his property before the tax liability is firmed. Under this circumstance, the administrative cooperation can effectively prevent tax avoidance and evasion.

For the need of reciprocity and preventing international tax evasion or tax avoidance, some countries have reached certain tax arrangements in their tax administrative assistance treaties. For example, the Convention on Mutual Administrative Assistance in Tax Matters, a multinational model treaty prepared by the OECD and the Council of Europe, provides for extensive cooperation on collection of assessed taxes. The convention, having also provides mutual assistance in the service of legal documents that relate to a tax covered by it, The convention has been signed by the requisite number of countries to bring it into effect it. The Protocol to the Canada-United States Tax Convention signed in 1995 provides a new mechanism that allows for taxes owing to one country to be collected by the other country as if they were taxes owned to the other country. This bold initiative is long overdue. It will prevent taxpayers from avoiding their obligation to pay their assessed taxes in one country by changing their residence to the other country.

8.2 The special legal measures of international anti-avoidance

There is not a universal international tax law in the world, various anti-avoidance measures in international tax tend to reflect the characteristics of relevant countries respectively. However, because of their rationality and practicability, some methods and measures have been referenced and used by more and more countries and they are gradually evolved into the international practice of broad significance.

8.2.1 Restricting emigration for tax avoidance

One of the ways of international tax avoidance for the transnational taxpayer is to move from a high tax country to a low tax country or to a tax haven for getting rid of the resident identity of the high tax country and exempting from the unlimited obligation to the government of it. In order to prevent the domestic residents from moving abroad for tax avoidance, some countries (mainly the developed countries) take some legislative measures to restrict emigration of individuals or legal entities for the purpose of tax avoidance.

1. Measures of restricting emigration of individuals

In many countries, citizens' emigrations are the freedom of individuals, just like their traveling abroad, and the government generally does not interfere with them. So, even if it finds that the citizens have the attempt of emigration for tax avoidance, the government can not limit their departures and can only take some restrictive measures on the economy to reduce the loss of tax revenue of the government to the lowest degree. Some developed countries adopt the approach in legislation of extending conditionally the residents' unlimited tax liabilities to the government.

 Teaching Case of 8-5

It was stipulated in the German foreign tax law published in 1972 *that all the former German citizens, who moved to tax havens and had been German residents or citizens for* 5 *years during their* 10 *years of presenting in Germany before their emigration, also meeting with one of the three conditions, were regarded as maintaining substantial economic connections with Germany and the tax authorities would deem them as the domestic residents in the next* 10 *years and impose them on all their income from Germany and abroad. These conditions were as follows.*

①*The taxpayers did not pay income tax in the immigration country or in spite of paying income tax, the applicable tax rate was less than the* 2/3 *of German tax rate.*

②*The taxpayers maintained substantial economic connections with the German company after their emigration. The specific criteria was obtaining income of more than* 25% *from the limited partnership as partners, or owning* 25% *or more shares of a German company.*

③*The taxpayers had net income from Germany after their emigration which accounted for more than* 30% *of their worldwide income, or up to* 120,000 *German Mark in a taxable year.*

To avoid the unlimited tax liabilities, some of the residents in high tax countries cut off completely their contact with the original residence country and really moved to other country, but also some of them just took the means of false emigration. Under this situation, some countries have taken tough restrictions.

 Teaching Case of 8-6

In 1950s *and* 1960s, *Sweden was one of countries with the most heavy personal tax burden in the world. In order to prevent individuals from avoiding the unlimited tax liabilities to Sweden by means of emigration, it was stipulated in the Municipal Tax Law implemented in* 1966 *that a Swedish citizen was still recognized as the Swedish resident in* 3 *years after he moved to other countries and still had the unlimited tax liabilities to Sweden, unless he was able to prove that he had no longer any substantial connections with Sweden and the burden of persuasion was borne by the taxpayer. Another example is that in* 1999, *Italy announced an anti-avoidance provision that from that taxa-*

Chapter 8   INTERNATIONAL ANTI-AVOIDANCE METHODS AND MEASURES

ble year, any Italian resident who moved to a tax haven country, would be regarded as the Italian resident and still had the unlimited tax liabilities to Italian government even if his name had been removed from the municipal register office. At the same time, the Italian Ministry of Finance announced a list of tax havens including 59 countries and regions such as Switzerland, Liechtenstein and Andorra. In addition, the American income tax law also provides that if an American citizen gives up his citizenship for tax avoidance, he must have the unlimited tax liabilities to American government for 10 years like the American citizen. Finland, Norway and Spain also have similar provisions. Australia, Canada and France even impose "emigration tax" on the emigration person, namely, imposing on his capital gains that are not realized.

Besides, in order to prevent the individual from using the ways of temporary emigration or shorting present time to escape his resident identity, many countries stipulate that for the individual's temporary departure, the departure days will not be deducted from his present time in the country. For example, it is stipulated in Chinese tax law that for an individual who lives in China for more than 1 year, all his income originated in China and abroad is taxable. The temporary departure less than 30 days or the cumulative total departure less than 90 days will not be deducted from his living days in China.

2. Measures of restricting emigration of legal entities

Due to the different norms on determining the identity of a legal entity in different countries, measures of restricting emigration of legal entities are also different. If a country adopts the place-of-incorporation test to determine the resident identity of a legal entity and the resident company wants to emigrate abroad, it has to cancel its domestic registration and re-register in other country. In order to prevent the resident companies from moving to low tax countries for tax avoidance, many countries (such as the United States, Britain, Ireland and Canada) stipulate that if the domestic resident companies register in other countries or transfer their head offices, effective management organizations abroad which no longer belong to the domestic resident companies, the companies must be regarded as being liquidated and their assets will be viewed as the capital gains after sales which are subject to income tax in their original residence countries. That is to say, the government will tax on gains from transferring property abroad. Namely, when appreciated property—property with an accrued gain—is transferred to a related non-resident, some countries deem the property to have been sold for its fair market value so that the accrued gain is subject to tax. Otherwise, domestic tax on the gain might be avoided entirely. Further, some countries impose tax on accrued gains when a taxpayer ceases to be resident. These provisions may be quite complex. Because the emigrating taxpayer has not actually disposed of the property, the taxpayer may not have the necessary funds to pay the tax on the accrued gains. Therefore, there may be special rules allowing the postponement of payment of the tax if the taxpayer provides security for the ultimate payment.

8.2.2   Restricting changing the company's organization forms for tax avoidance

One of the multinational corporation's ways of international tax avoidance is to change the organization form of its foreign affiliates timely—when the foreign branch starts making a profit, it reorganizes it to a subsidiary. In order to prevent the multinational corporation from using this way to avoid tax, some countries have taken a number of preventive measures in laws.

 Teaching Case of 8-7

The American tax law stipulates that if a foreign branch is changed into a foreign subsidiary, the profit of the parent company offset by the past losses of the branch has to be calculated again clearly and the part of profit offset by the losses of the foreign branch has to pay an overdue tax. Britain uses the method of restricting the domestic resident company to transfer business to the non-resident company for stopping the domestic company to reorganize its foreign branch into a subsidiary. Such as the English tax law clearly stipulates that unless approved by the ministry of Finance, it is illegal for a British company to transfer part of its trade or business to a foreign non-resident company. Because the foreign branch is a part of the British company and does not have a foreign resident identity, this provision does not limit a British company to carry out part of its business through a foreign branch. But if the foreign branch is reorganized to a subsidiary, the subsidiary has the foreign resident identity. Because of the above provision, the British company's business can not carry out its business through the foreign subsidiary.

Objectively, it restricts changing the British company's organization forms for tax avoidance.

8.2.3 Restricting treaty shopping

The main purpose of the resident in a third party country to abuse the tax treaty between the other two countries is to avoid withholding tax of relevant countries. At present, except Austria, Finland and a few countries, most countries take the behavior of treaty shopping as a kind of improper behavior and advocate for stopping it. In order to prevent their tax treaties from being used by the resident in a third party country for tax avoidance, some countries have begun to take measures of preventing the treaty shopping. These measures include the following aspects.

1. Formulating domestic regulations to prevent treaty shopping

At present, the country which takes this approach is Switzerland. As is mentioned above, Switzerland is a country with widespread tax treaties and its corporate income tax is so low that it is unusual in the developed countries. According to the tax treaties it signed, the Contracting State will impose low withholding tax on dividends, interest and royalties paid to the Swiss residents, also, Switzerland will levy very low withholding tax on dividends and interest paid to the residents of Contracting State. Furthermore, Switzerland will not levy withholding tax on royalties. Because of these advantages, Switzerland used to be selected by the taxpayers in a third party country as the base of setting up intermediate holding company, financing company or licensing company and used to enjoy withholding tax preference in tax treaties concluded between Switzerland and other countries. Switzerland and the United States signed tax treaties so earlier that the treaty shopping was serious. Under the pressure, the Swiss parliament promulgated the law for Preventing the Abuse of Tax Treaty Law in December of 1962 and decided unilaterally to limit strictly the compa-

Chapter 8 INTERNATIONAL ANTI-AVOIDANCE METHODS AND MEASURES

ny owned or controlled by the residents in a third party country to apply to tax treaty. The law for Preventing the Abuse of Tax Treaty Law stipulated that unless the special conditions were met, the tax preference in tax treaties signed by Switzerland and other countries did not apply to dividends, interest and royalties. After that, the situation of Swiss treaty shopping has been improved.

2. Adding anti-treaty shopping clause in bilateral tax treaties

In order to prevent treaty shopping made by the residents in a third party country, a country can add some preventive clauses in its tax treaty. For example, the United States insists on the inclusion of a limitation on benefits article in its tax treaties to prevent treaty shopping. There are following specific methods. In practice, many countries generally select to use a variety of methods and are rarely confined to one method.

1) The elimination method

That indicates that the tax preference in tax treaty does not apply to certain taxpayers.

 Teaching Case of 8-8

The provision of tax treaty signed by the United States and Luxemburg in 1962 stipulated that the holding company registered in Luxemburg was not applicable for the treaty. So, the resident in a third party country can not use the intermediate holding company established in Luxemburg to enjoy withholding tax preference of the United States. Again, the provisions in some tax treaties signed by Canada stipulate that if the companies registered in Barbados, Cyprus, Israel, Ivory Coast, Jamaica and Sri Lanka can enjoy special tax incentives in the local, they can not enjoy the tax benefits provided by Canada according to the tax treaties. Except the United States and Canada, Australia, Austria, Belgium, Cyprus, Denmark, France, Germany, Luxemburg, Holland, Spain, Sweden and Britain also use elimination method. In general, the restricted companies limited by elimination method are those companies who are easy to act as an intermediary. When using this method, the tax department does not need to check whether the restricted company is an intermediate company established by the foreign investors for tax avoidance. As long as the company cannot eliminate the restricted nature, it can not enjoy the benefits of tax treaty.

2) The method of genuine business objective

That indicates that the tax preference in tax treaty does not apply to taxpayers without genuine business objective but just seeking the tax incentives.

 Teaching Case of 8-9

The provision of the tax treaty between Britain, Holland and Netherlands Antilles stipulates that if the transaction of debt and franchise is carried out just because the taxpayer wants to use the tax treaty without genuine business objective, the withholding tax preference prescribed in the treaty on interest and royalties is not applicable for the taxpayer. Also, the tax treaty between Britain and Switzerland stipulates that if the ownership is just to get the tax benefits in the treaty without genuine business objective, the dividend from the shares cannot enjoy the tax preference. Except Britain, other countries like Australia, Denmark, Holland, Sweden, Switzerland and the United States also use the

method of genuine business objective. Some of the Chinese tax treaties also adopt this method to prevent treaty shopping.

3) The method of tax liability

That indicates that if the income of an intermediate company is not taxable in the country where the company registers, it can not enjoy the tax preference.

 Teaching Case of 8-10

Tax treaties between Belgium, France, Germany, Italy and Switzerland stipulate that interest, royalties and capital gains derived from other Contracting States of a Swiss resident company controlled by non-residents can enjoy the tax preference of the treaties only under the condition that the company has paid state income tax in the local. Besides, Belgium and the UK, Canada and Malaysia, Canada and Singapore, Denmark and Switzerland, Denmark and the UK, Germany and the UK, Holland and New Zealand, Spain and Germany also have relvant provisions about method of tax liability in tax treaties.

4) The beneficiary method

That indicates that the ultimate beneficiary of tax preference provided by the tax treaty must be the real resident of the Contracting State and the resident of a third party country can not benefit from the treaty by setting up a resident company in the Contracting State.

 Teaching Case of 8-11

Tax treaties or tax protocols signed by the USA after 1980 have the Article of defined beneficiary, including treaties between the United States and Australia, Barbados, Cyprus, France, Italy, Canada, Jamaica and New Zealand. Tax treaty memo between the United States and China has similar provisions. For example, the provision of tax treaty between the United States and Cyprus stipulates that the American tax preference is only granted to the following companies.

①More than 75% of the company's share is owned by the Cyprus resident individuals.

②Most of the company's stocks are listed in Cyprus stock market.

③The company's income is not paid a great deal to the residents of a third country instead of the United States and Cyprus.

Except for the United States, other countries like Canada, Denmark, France, Italy, Holland and the UK also use the beneficiary method.

5) The channel method

That indicates that if a resident of the Contracting State pays a large number of income in the form of interest, dividends or royalties to a resident of a third country, the income can not enjoy the withholding tax preference provided in the treaty.

 Teaching Case of 8-12

Case of avoiding withholding tax on equity transfer income of an American company through

Chapter 8 INTERNATIONAL ANTI-AVOIDANCE METHODS AND MEASURES

attempting to use the tax treaty between China and Barbados is as follows.

In May of 2006, the American Company registered the D Company (DCo) in Barbados. In June, DCo invested 33,800,000 dollars to buy a Chinese B Company (BCo) which engaged in the production and sale of liquefied natural gas (A Company, namely ACo) from Chinese BCo in Xinjiang. In July, DCo signed a share transfer agreement with BCo and transferred 24.99% shares of ACo it hold to BCo, the transfer price was 45,968,000 dollars. So far, only within a year, DCo obtained property transfer income of 12,170,000 dollars from the buying and selling of ACo's equity.

In this case, it was obvious that the American Company wanted to use the Article 13 about "property income" of tax treaty between China and Barbados to avoid withholding tax. Before February 2010, the Article 13 of the tax treaty stipulated that Chinese government would not impose withholding tax on the income (transfer income of property) of transferring Chinese resident company's shares by Barbados residents. In the end, the American Company did not achieve the purpose of tax avoidance, because it could not provide the certificate of resident identity of Barbados. Moreover, Chinese used the tax information exchange mechanism which finally proved that DCo was not the resident of Barbados. (According to the Barbados tax law, only the company whose management and control center was in Barbados was the resident company. But DCo just registered in Barbados and three of its directors were all Americans and lived in the United States, so DCo' management and control center was not in Barbados.) Therefore, DCo was not entitled to the preferential treatment of the treaty.

6) The prohibit method

That indicates the country will not sign tax treaties with the country or region which is considered as international tax havens to prevent multinational corporations from setting up intermediate companies in tax havens for their international tax avoidance activities. Including Australia, Austria, Belgium, Denmark, France, Germany, Italy, Luxemburg, Holland, Singapore, Spain, Sweden, Switzerland, Britain and the United States, implement the prohibit method and do not sign tax treaties with tax havens.

8.2.4 Thin capitalization rules

In response to the bias infavor of debt compared with equity, several countries have adopted thin capitalization rules to prevent non-resident shareholders of resident corporations from using excessive debt capital to extract corporate profits in the form of deductible interest rather than as nondeductible dividends. Under these rules, the deduction for interest paid by a resident corporation to a non-resident shareholder is denied to the extent that the corporation is financed excessively by debt. The term "thin capitalization" is apt because the rules apply only when a corporation's equity capital is small in relation to its debt.

Some countries have adopted statutory thin capitalization rules; some rely on administrative guidelines or practices. Still others try to deal with the problem of thin capitalization by general anti-avoidance rules. The statutory thin capitalization rules of the various countries differ considerably. Typically, they share most of the following structural features.

① Non-resident lenders. The thin capitalization rules generally apply only to nonresident lenders who own a significant percentage of the shares of the resident corporation. The level of share ownership varies from 15 percent of the shares to control of the resident corporation.

②Domestic entities. The thin capitalization rules of most countries apply only to resident corporations. The stripping of profits through the payment of excessive interest to related persons may also arise, however, with respect to resident partnerships and trusts and branches of nonresident corporations.

③Determination of excessive interest. Generally, the thin capitalization rules apply only to certain excessive interest paid to non-resident shareholders of a resident corporation. Excessive interest is ordinarily determined with reference to the debt: equity ratio of the domestic corporation. In other words, it is only interest on debt that is artificially large in relation to equity—in effect, debt that is disguised equity—that is not deductible.

Debt/equity ratio for purpose of thin capitalization rules can be established following the below methods.

①A fixed debt/equity ratio.

②with reference to the average debt/equity ratio for all resident corporations or all resident corporations which engage in a particular industrial or commercial sector.

Most countries seem to use a fixed debt/equity ratio of 2∶1 or 3∶1, sometimes with a higher ratio for financial institutions. In China for example, this standard is 5∶1 for financial enterprises and 2∶1 for other enterprises. The calculation of debt and equity as components of the ratio necessitates many subsidiary tax policy decisions. For example, should all debt held by non-residents be taken into account, or just debt held by substantial non-resident shareholders? Should equity include contributed surplus or only share capital and retained earnings? Should hybrid securities such as preferred shares be classified as debt or equity?

An alternative approach, recommended by the OECD, attempts to characterize debt and equity with reference to all the facts and circumstances, including the debt/equity ratio of the resident corporation. This approach is consistent with the arm's length principle used for transfer pricing generally and avoids the inflexibility and arbitrariness of applying a fixed debt/equity ratio. However, it is more difficult to administer and less certain to apply. Yet another approach, represented by the earnings-stripping rule of the United States, determines what excessive interest is with reference to the relationship between the interest and the corporation's income. A corporation generally is not entitled to deduct interest paid to certain non-residents or resident tax-exempt shareholders to the extent that the interest exceeds 50 percent of its income. The US earning-stripping rule contains a safe harbor provision under which corporations that have a debt/equity ratio of no greater than 1.5∶1 are not subject to the rule.

To sum up, the effect of the application of the thin capitalization rules is generally that excessive interest is not deductible. In some countries, this excessive interest is treated as a dividend. In other countries, the excessive interest can be carried forward and deducted in subsequent years.

Chapter 8 INTERNATIONAL ANTI-AVOIDANCE METHODS AND MEASURES

8.3 Controlled foreign corporation (CFC) rules

Most countries tax residents on their worldwide income with a credit for any foreign taxes imposed on foreign-source income. Absent remedial legislation, however, domestic tax on foreign-source income can be deferred or postponed easily by establishing a foreign corporation or trust to receive the income. Because the foreign corporation or trust is generally considered to be a separate taxable entity, the controlling shareholders of the corporation or the beneficiaries of the trust are not taxable until distributions from the corporation or trust are received. This deferral benefit is greatest when the foreign tax on the income of the foreign corporation or trust is low or nil. The problem of deferral is likely to be the most serious, therefore, when a controlled foreign corporation or foreign trust has been established in a tax haven. This problem is most pronounced with respect to passive investment income, because such income can easily be diverted to or accumulated in an offshore entity located in a tax haven. For example, we assume that a corporation resident in Country A earns interest income from marketable securities of 1 000 yuan and that the tax rate in Country A is 40 percent. If the corporation establishes a wholly-owned subsidiary in a tax haven that does not impose tax, it will defer tax of 400 yuan by transferring the securities to the subsidiary. The interest may not be subject to Country A's withholding tax either the interest is not sourced in Country A or the interest is exempt from the withholding tax. Even if the interest is subject to Country A's withholding tax, the corporation will achieve a deferral of Country A tax to the extent of the difference between the corporation tax rate and the withholding tax rate.

Many countries have adopted detailed statutory rules to prevent or restrict the use of CFC to defer or avoid domestic tax. Under those rules, a CFC is not itself subject to residence country tax. Instead, the resident shareholders of the CFC are taxed currently on their proportionate share of some or all of the CFC's income. The amount of that income must be determined in accordance with domestic tax rules and in domestic currency. The United States adopted the CFC rules in 1962, taking the lead. Those rules are popularly referred to as the Sub-part F rules—a reference to the statutory section where they appear. The Sub-part F rules are based on analogous US rules, the foreign personal holding company rules, which were adopted in 1937 to combat certain uses of foreign tax havens by individuals. The adoption of the Sub-part F rules in 1962 was very controversial. As was finally enacted, the rules represented a compromise between the original proposal to eliminate deferral for all income of CFC and the position of US-based multinational corporations that deferral should be eliminated only with respect to passive investment income. The basic compromise was to tax currently most types of passive income and certain types of active business income that could be diverted easily to a tax haven. Amendments since 1962 have tightened up the rules and plugged some of the loopholes. Since the United States adopted Sub-part F in 1962, many other capital exporting countries have enacted CFC rules to protect their tax base.

The basic structure of CFC legislation reflects two competing policies. On the one hand, there is a desire to prevent tax avoidance and to advance the traditional goals of fairness and economic efficiency. On the other hand, countries generally do not want to interfere unreasonably in the ability of resident corporations to compete in foreign markets against corporations resident in other countries. Although the specific features of CFC rules vary considerably, several fundamental structural aspects of the rules are the same in most countries. These major structural aspects of the taxation of controlled foreign corporations are set out below.

8.3.1 Definition of controlled foreign corporation

With a few exceptions, countries restrict the scope of what is generally referred to as CFC legislation to income derived by entities. The entities are as follows.

①Non-residents.

②Corporations or similar entities taxed separately from their owners.

③Entities controlled by domestic shareholders or in which domestic shareholders have a substantial interest.

Entities such as partnerships that are taxable on a conduit or flow-through basis are not within the scope of the CFC rules because the resident shareholders of a foreign partnership are subject to residence-country tax on their share of the partnership's income.

Most CFC legislation applies only to foreign corporations that are controlled by certain domestic shareholders. Control generally means the ownership of more than 50 percent of the outstanding voting shares. Some countries extend the concept of control to include ownership of shares having a value equal to more than 50 percent of the total value of the outstanding shares. A few countries have rules that presume residents to control a foreign corporation even if they own less than 50 percent of the voting shares. For example, the Australian and New Zealand rules deem a resident to control a foreign corporation if the resident owns 40 percent or more of the voting shares of the foreign corporation and no non-resident person has voting control of the corporation. A few countries—France, Portugal, and Denmark—apply their CFC rules to foreign corporations in which residents have a substantial ownership interest. Portugal and Denmark use a 25 percent ownership threshold, whereas France uses a 10 percent rule.

Control also includes indirect control. The CFC rules can not be avoided by having the shares of a tax haven corporation owned by another CFC. For example, if a resident owns 60 percent of the voting shares of a foreign corporation which in turn owns more than 50 percent of the voting shares of a second foreign corporation, the second foreign corporation is considered to be a controlled foreign corporation of the resident. Most countries also have constructive ownership rules to prevent taxpayers from avoiding the CFC rules by fragmenting the ownership of the shares among related persons. For example, if one resident corporation owns 40 percent and another resident corporation owns 20 percent of the voting shares of a foreign corporation, the foreign corporation will be a CFC of both resident corporations if they are related because, for example, they are both wholly-owned subsidiaries of another resident corporation. In some countries, control must be concentrated in a small number of resident shareholders. For example, Australia, Canada, and New Zealand require that five or fewer residents control a foreign corporation. In other countries, even foreign corporations that are widely held by resident shareholders are considered to be controlled foreign corporations.

Chapter 8 INTERNATIONAL ANTI-AVOIDANCE METHODS AND MEASURES

8.3.2 Definition of attributable income

Attributable income refers to certain types of income which should be distributed to the shareholders by a CFC and no longer enjoys the preference of deferral of the residence country. Though it is not paid to the shareholders of the residence country, it is still attributable to the taxable income of the domestic shareholders for declaration. This type of income is also referred to as tainted income which usually consists of passive investment income and base company income.

Passive income includes dividends, interest, rents, royalties, and capital gains. All the countries with CFC rules consider passive income to be tainted income, although they may define passive income differently. Because various types of passive income are easily converted into other types of income through the use of new financial instruments, the definition of passive income must be quite broad to be effective in blocking tax avoidance. Perhaps the most difficult problem in defining passive income for purposes of the CFC rules is identifying situations in which income of a type usually considered to be passive income should be excluded from the CFC rules because it arises from an active business. For example, interest income earned by a genuine financial institution from the ordinary operation of its banking business is generally considered to be active income that is exempt under the CFC rules of many countries. Rents and royalties may similarly be derived from an active business. For example, income derived from a rental car business is not properly subject to tax under a tax regime focusing on tax haven abuses. The distinction between active and passive or inactive income is quite amorphous. For example, in the hands of good tax planners, many forms of offshore leasing might be structured in a way that has the appearance of an active business, although leasing income is easily deflected to a tax haven. If a country's CFC rules do not apply to offshore leasing income, the country's domestic tax base may be eroded. It is also difficult to distinguish between interest earned by a financial institution from retail banking, which should qualify as active income, and investment income earned by the financial institution, which should not qualify as active income.

The term "base company income" is used to refer to any income, other than passive income, that is considered to be tainted income for purposes of CFC rules. The definition of base company income is often quite complex and the scope of the definition for purposes of the CFC rules of various countries is far from uniform. An important component of base company income is income derived by a CFC from selling property or rendering services outside the country in which the CFC is established or to related parties. Under these situations, the use of a CFC to earn such income may be for the principal purpose of avoiding domestic tax rather than for legitimate reasons of international competitiveness.

To sum up, any income of a CFC that is attributable to its domestic shareholders must be computed and taxed in accordance with domestic tax rules and in domestic currency.

8.3.3 Domestic taxpayers applicable for CFC rules

Domestic taxpayers applicable for CFC rules refer to those taxpayers restricted or cracked down by CFC rules. It is they who attempt to use the provision of deferral to avoid domestic taxes on income from CFC. The CFC rules intend to prevent the taxpayers from using the way of deferral for international tax avoidance.

In most countries, the provisions for the taxation of CFC apply to both individual and corporate shareholders; in a few countries, they apply only to resident corporations. The objects cracked down by CFC rules must be the domestic resident shareholders holding stakes in CFC and in most countries, resident shareholders of a CFC are not taxable on their prorate share of the undistributed income of the foreign corporation unless they meet a minimum share ownership requirement (usually 10 percent). The reason for this exemption for shareholders with small portfolio investments is that they may not have sufficient influence over the foreign corporation to require it to distribute its income or to get access to the necessary information to compute their prorate share of the foreign corporation's income.

In the late of 1990s, many countries strengthened the legislation to CFC which mainly expanded the scope of cracking down from the controlled foreign companies to the controlled foreign partnerships.

8.4 Transfer pricing rules

The use of transfer pricing to transfer profits is one of the most common ways for related corporations (especially the multinational corporation) to carry out their tax avoidance activities which seriously affects the national tax rights. Therefore, most countries have transfer pricing rules to prevent related taxpayers from carrying out transactions at artificially high or low prices in order to move income and expenses to various jurisdictions. It is arguable whether these rules are properly classified as international anti-avoidance rules or whether they are just part of a country's basic tax system. However, establishments of transfer pricing rules usually need national coordination, even through the intergovernmental negotiations to reach an agreement, namely, through the tax treaty to implement.

8.4.1 The judgment norms on related corporations

第 8 讲

Transfer pricing rules aim at the transaction prices of multinational related corporations. The correct use of transfer pricing rules for anti-avoidance depends on firstly the accurate judgment, whether the transaction parties are related corporations or not. If they are not, the transfer pricing rules are not applicable for them at all. If they are, the tax authorities shall have the right to review their transaction price. If the price is unreasonable, that is far from the normal market price or reasonable price obviously, the tax authorities can adjust the unreasonable transfer price based on the transfer pricing rules.

In general, related persons should be defined to include two or more persons that are owned or controlled, directly or indirectly, by the same interest. A good indicator of such a relationship is the ability to set transfer prices that differ from market prices. In practice, the related relationship between corporations is mainly reflected in three aspects, namely, management, control and capital. Both the OECD Model Treaty and the UN Model Treaty stipulate that any corporation which

Chapter 8 INTERNATIONAL ANTI-AVOIDANCE METHODS AND MEASURES

meets one of the following two conditions is viewed as having multinational related relationship.

①A company of a contracting state participates directly or indirectly in the management, control or capital of another company of another contracting state.

②The same person participates directly or indirectly in the management, control or capital of the companies of a contracting state and another contracting state.

Here, participation in the management refers to control a company's operation and management rights, and namely, if a company has significant control rights with respect to the operation, buying and selling, financing and so on of another company, the two companies have related relationships. Here, participation in the control refers that a company has the right to appoint the director or senior managers of another company, or has the right to make the basic or major business decisions for another company. And participation in the capital refers to own certain share capital and control certain stock rights of a company. For a stock company, anyone who holds enough shares can control its management and own its decision-making rights. But the percentage of controlling interest is quite amorphous. In the situation that a company's equity is dispersed, the owning of 5% or less than 5% of the company's shares may control the company instead of owning more than 50% of its equity. So in practice, determination of related relationship between companies from the view of participation in the capital depends on the uniform controlling interest ratio made by the tax authorities. At present, countries with transfer pricing rules generally have such provisions, but the ratio is not the same in the world. For example, it is 50% in the United States, Switzerland, New Zealand, Singapore and Korea; it is 30% in Norway; it is 25% in Germany and Spain; In Portugal, it is even 10%. Furthermore, the shareholding ratio generally refers to holding a company's shares directly and indirectly. The indirect shareholding ratio is calculated by multiplication method. For example, ACo holds 60% shares of BCo, BCo owns 40% shares of CCo, then ACo holds indirectly 24% shares of CCo (60%×40%).

Chinahas similar provisions of the judgment norms on related corporations. As is stipulated in Article 109 of *Regulations for Implementation of Enterprises Income Tax Law of the People's Republic of China* that the related parties refer to those companies, organizations or individuals who have one of the following related relationships with the company.

①There are direct or indirect relationship in the capital, management, purchase and sale.

②The compang is directly or indirectly controlled by a third party.

③There are other related interests.

On June 29, 2016, State taxation Administration of the People's Republic of China issued the Notice on Improving Related Declaration and Management of Corresponding Data, which explained in details the controlling ratio in a company's capital (including direct control and indirect control). If a company held another company's shares directly or indirectly of more than 25% in total (including 25%), or both companies were held directly or indirectly by a third party with 25% or more of the shares, they had the related relationships. In addition, the document also stipulated that if a company held indirectly another company's shares through a middle company, as long as the company held the middle company's shares of more than 25%, the shareholding ratio of the company to another company was calculated in accordance with the ratio of the middle company to another company.

8.4.2　Methods of transfer pricing adjustment

In a well-designed income tax system, the tax authorities should have the power to adjust, in appropriate cases, the transfer prices set by related persons. This power should include the power to allocate gross income, deductions, credits, and other allowances among related persons so that the country collects its fair share of tax revenue from economic activities conducted within its borders. An appropriate transfer price, according to international custom, is one that meets the so-called the arm's length principle. This principle is met if a taxpayer sets his transfer prices in his dealings with related persons so that those prices are the same as the prices used in comparable dealings with unrelated persons. There are usually the following methods with respect to the specific transfer pricing adjustment.

1. Traditional methods

1) Comparable uncontrolled price method

The comparable uncontrolled price (CUP) method establishes an arm's length price with reference to sales of similar products made between unrelated persons under similar circumstances. It is the preferred method if such comparable sales exist. This method is widely used for pricing oil, iron ore, wheat, and other goods sold on public commodity markets. It is also useful for pricing manufactured goods that do not depend substantially for their value on special know-how or brand names. It is not well adapted for pricing many intermediate goods, such as custom-made automobile parts, which are not generally sold to unrelated parties. Nor is it suitable for setting the price on sales of goods that are highly dependent for their value on the trade name of the producer. The operation of this method is illustrated by the following example.

Simulated demonstration of 8-1

[*Background*]: *The parent company of Country A set a subsidiary in Country B. The corporation income tax rates of Country A and B were respectively* 50% *and* 20%. *Then, the parent company sold a batch of products to the subsidiary at the transfer price of* 1,200,000 *dollars. After inspection, the tax authorities of Country A found that the price of the same amount of equivalent products in the market was* 1,700,000 *dollars.*

[*Operation*]: *The tax authorities of Country A may adjust the transfer prices according to the CUP method and collect additional tax of* 250,000 (500,000 × 50%) *dollars on the parent company's additional income of* 500,000 *dollars* (1,700,000 − 1,200,000).

[*Comments*]: *The CUP method is suitable for the transactions like tangible assets dealing, loan, rendering of service, lease of property and transfer of intangible assets between transnational related companies, which is the most reasonable and scientific method of adjusting transfer pricing. This method requires the controlled transaction (the related transaction) and the uncontrolled transaction (the unrelated transaction) having strict comparability, otherwise, the price used in the uncontrolled transaction has no reference value.*

2) Resale price method

The resale price (RP) method sets the arm's length price for the sale of goods between related parties by subtracting an appropriate markup from the price at which the goods are ultimately sold to unrelated parties. The paradigm case for its application is the sale by the taxpayer of his manufactured goods to a related party acting as a distributor, followed by a resale to unrelated customers without any further processing of the goods. The appropriate markup is the gross profit, expressed as a percentage of the resale price, which distributors typically earn from similar transactions with unrelated parties. According to the RP method, the calculation formula of the arm's length price is as follows.

$$\text{arm's length price} = \text{resale price} \times (1 - \text{reasonable gross margin})$$

Teaching Case of 8-13

The parent company of Country A sold a batch of products to its subsidiary of Country B at the transfer price of 10,000 dollars. The subsidiary resold the products at the market price of 15,000 dollars in the local. The gross margin of unrelated company of Country B was 20% for selling equivalent products. Under this circumstance, the tax authorities of Country A would adjust the sales price of the parent company to 12,000 dollars in accordance with the RP method. The calculation formula of arm's length price was as $15,000 \times (1-20\%) = 12,000$ dollars.

Simulated demonstration of 8-2

[Background]: In a taxable year, the M company (MCo) engaging in car manufacturing of Country A set up a subsidiary in Country B. The corporation income tax rates of Country A and B are respectively 34% and 17%. The manufacturing cost of MCo for every car is 100,000 dollars and MCo has never sold their products in the market of Country A. Now, MCo sold a car to the subsidiary at the price of 120,000 dollars and the subsidiary resold the car in the local at the price of 190,000 dollars.

[Calculation]:

The profit of MCo: 120,000 - 100,000 = 20,000 (dollars);

The profit of the subsidiary: 190,000 - 120,000 = 70,000 (dollars).

However, the internal price of Group Company does not conform to the arm's length principle. According to the survey of the local tax authorities of Country B, the gross margin of local unrelated company for selling similar products was 20%.

According to the RP method, the sales price of MCo to the subsidiary should be adjusted to 152,000 dollars [$190,000 \times (1-20\%)$].

After the adjustment, the profit of MCo was 52,000 dollars (152,000 - 100,000). The profit of the subsidiary was 38,000 dollars (190,000 - 152,000).

Now, let's compare the profits and taxes of the parent company and the subsidiary before and after the adjustment. It is shown in Table 8-1 and Table 8-2.

Table 8-1   Before adjustment

company	profits/dollars	tax payment/dollars	tax burden/%
parent company (MCo)	20,000	6,800	34
subsidiary	70,000	11,900	17
group company	90,000	18,700	—

Table 8-2   After adjustment

company	profits/dollars	tax payment/dollars	tax burden/%
parent company (MCo)	52,000	17,680	34
subsidiary	38,000	6,460	17
group company	90,000	24,140	—

[Comments]: *RP method is generally applicable for distribution of multinational related company's sales income of industrial production and it is calculated through the difference between the purchase price and sale price. The key is the determination of resale price and gross margin.*

3) Cost plus method

The cost plus method uses the manufacturing and other costs of the related seller as the starting point in establishing the arm's length price. An appropriate amount of profit is added to these costs by multiplying the seller's costs and an appropriate profit percentage. This percentage is determined by reference to the gross profit percentage earned by the seller in transactions with unrelated parties or by comparable unrelated parties in transactions with unrelated parties. A paradigm case for the application of the cost plus method is a sale by a taxpayer of goods it has manufactured to a related party, with the related party affixing its brand name to the goods and selling them to unrelated customers.

Teaching Case of 8-14

A company (ACo) of Country X provided a batch of special parts to the related B company (BCo) of Country Y at the sales price of 10,000 dollars equal to the production cost. Due to the lack of equivalent products on the market, the tax authorities of Country X decided to audit and adjust the transfer pricing of this related transaction in accordance with the cost plus method. According to the tax authorities' information, the local reasonable cost to margins was 20%. Therefore, the sales price of this batch of products after the adjustment should be 12,000 dollars [10,000× (1+20%)]. In this situation, the tax authorities of Country X would calculate ACo's sales income at the price of 12,000 dollars and adjust its taxable income.

The cost plus method is the extension of CUP method which is generally applicable to the situation when there is neither CUP nor RP for some industrial products sales income and royalties of multinational related corporations due to lack of comparable objects. For example, when the related corporations transfer their intangible assets such as patent, proprietary technology and trademark, they will receive some royalties in conformity with the arm's length principle. While, intangible assets have many kinds and have large difference between technology, performance, cost and target benefit, they generally often lack of comparable market price of equivalent products or resale price as the basis of distribution. It is difficult to unify the charge basis. Therefore, we must use more the cost plus method.

4) Cost method

The cost method is based on the actual costs as the standard of distribution. This is a completely different distribution standard which does not include profit and reflects the business relationships between the transnational related corporations instead of the general trade relations. So, the cost method is usually applicable to the expenses or income distribution of multinational related corporations with respect to the affiliated business and a part of non-trade business. Non-trade businesses include loan, service and property leasing, whose income is respectively the interest income, service income and rental income. The cost method requires the company which distributes the cost or expenses to record the cost or expenses related to the transaction in the books of account correctly and take it as the basis of distribution. At the same time, the transaction must be relevant to the production and operation of the company which pays the cost or expenses and makes the company benefited.

Simulated demonstration of 8-3

[*Background*]: M company (MCo) engaging in automobile manufacturing of Country A set up a subsidiary in Country B. In 2019, Mc paid in advance the following expenses for the subsidiary.

①The expense of 50,000 dollars for training technical and accounting personnel of the subsidiary.

②The expense of 7,000 dollars for advertisement.

③The expense of 1,000 dollars for transportation and insurance on purchasing equipments.

④The expense of 8,000 dollars for investigating the international market of raw materials purchasing and products sales.

⑤The expense of 3,000 dollars for hiring senior accountants to audit the subsidiary's accounting statements.

⑥The annual interest expense of 2,000 dollars for loaning from an unrelated bank outside of the related group corporation and lending it to the subsidiary.

⑦The legal expense of 15,000 dollars for the contract disputes between the subsidiary and other foreign company.

[*Operation*]: According to the cost method, all of the above expenses paid by Mc for the subsidiary can be distributed to the subsidiary by the actual amount recorded in the books.

[*Comments*]: The cost method requires the company distributing costs or expenses to record accurately the costs and expenses related to the transaction and take it as the basis of distribution.

2. Additional methods

1) Profit-split method (PSM)

Under the profit-split method, the worldwide taxable income of related parties engaging in a common line of business is computed. The taxable income is then allocated among the related parties in proportion to the contribution they are considered to have made in earning the income. This method typically is employed when none of the traditional methods can be applied. A distinctive feature of the method is that it applies to aggregate profits from a series of transactions and not to individual transactions. The traditional methods, in contrast, are all based on individual transactions. The following example illustrates the application of the profit-split method.

 Teaching Case of 8-15

P company (PCo) and S company (SCo) are related companies engaging in the production and sale of pharmaceuticals. PCo engages in extensive research operations and uses patent processes to manufacture the pharmaceutical products, which it sells to SCo. SCo repackages the products for retail sale, attaches its valuable trade name, and resells them through an extensive marketing operation. PCo does not make sales to unrelated parties, and there are no comparable sales of equivalent products to other unrelated parties. The repackaged products sold by SCo are not comparable to products sold by unrelated parties.

Under these conditions, some countries might use a profit-split method to establish an appropriate transfer price for the pharmaceuticals. We assume that PCo has costs of 300 dollars, SCo has costs of 100 dollars, and the sales proceeds from aggregate sales by SCo to unrelated customers is 600 dollars. Under these facts, the group corporation has net profits of 200 dollars [600-(300+100)]. If PCo's contribution to the enterprise accounts for approximately 75 percent of the total net profits, then a 75/25 split of the profits might be appropriate. Thus PCo would have profits of 150 dollars and SCo would have profits of 50 dollars under the profit-split method.

There are many possible variations of the profit-split method. One variation is to combine it with one or more traditional methods. The traditional methods might be used to allocate average profits from routine activities and the profit-split method might be reserved for dividing entrepreneurial profits from the exploitation of valuable intangible property.

 Teaching Case of 8-16

We assume in the above example that PCo engages in routine production activities and SCo engages in routine sales activities. PCo has gross costs of production of 300 dollars, and unrelated companies engaging in comparable manufacturing activities earn a return of 20 percent of costs. Under these facts, PCo would have profits of 60 dollars (20% of 300) allocated to it under the cost plus method. SCo has gross sales revenue of 600 dollars, and unrelated companies engaging in similar activities have a gross profit margin of 10 percent. Under the resale price method, SCo would have profits allocated to it of 60 dollars (10% of 600). The remaining profits of 80 dollars [200-(60+60)] would be allocated under the profit-split method. We assuming the same 75/25 split is applied, then PCo has profits of 60 dollars (75% of 80) under the profit-split method, for total profits of 120 dollars (60+60). SCo has profits of 20 dollars (25% of 80) under the profit-split method, for total profits of 80 dollars (20+60).

For the profit-split method to operate fairly and effectively, some fair and effective method must be applied to determine the appropriate profit split. One approach recommended by the

Chapter 8 INTERNATIONAL ANTI-AVOIDANCE METHODS AND MEASURES

OECD is to look at the way that profits are split between uncontrolled persons who engage in comparable activities. Unfortunately, such information is typically unavailable. Because the profit-split method is most likely to be applied when valuable intangible property is involved, a profit split based on the relative contributions of the related parties to the development of that intangible property might be appropriate.

2) Transaction net margin method (TNMM)

The transaction net margin method is sometimes referred to as the comparable profit method (CPM), which is a method that may be used under certain circumstances in determining transfer prices for sales of tangible and intangible property. Under TNMM, the taxpayer must establish, for itself or a related party (the tested party), an arm's length range of profits (TNMM range) on a set of transactions. If the tested party's reported profits on those transactions fall within that range, then its transfer prices will be accepted by the tax authorities. If its profits fall outside that range, the tax authorities may adjust transfer prices so that the profits fall within the range, typically at the midpoint.

In very general terms, the profits of a tested party are determined under TNMM by determining the ratio of profits to some economic indicator for an unrelated person and then applying that ratio to calculate the profits of the tested party. We assume, for example, that the unrelated person has taxable income of 80 dollars and invested capital of 800 dollars and invested capital is the economic indicator being used in applying TNMM. The ratio of taxable income to invested capital for the unrelated person is 80 : 800, or 10 percent. If the tested party has invested capital of 500 dollars, then under a simplified version of TNMM, its arm's length profits will be 50 dollars (500×10%).

To refine the application of TNMM, the taxpayer or the government would be required to make a TNMM calculation for more than one unrelated person. The more such calculations are made, the more reliable the results are likely to be. The arm's length profits of the tested party would be an amount falling within the range of profits determined under the several calculations. Statistical techniques might be applied to select the point within that range that would be deemed to be the tested party's arm's length profits. To apply TNMM, the taxpayer must determine a range of profits that unrelated persons would be expected to earn from engaging in comparable transactions. The taxpayer can establish this range in a variety of ways. One way is to determine the rate of return on capital employed by two or more unrelated parties engaging in activities that are broadly similar to the activities of the taxpayer. This rate of return on capital for each unrelated person is then multiplied by the amount of capital of the taxpayer. The second way is for the taxpayer to determine the ratio of operating profits to gross sales receipts for two or more comparable related persons and then apply these ratios to its own sales. The third way is to determine the ratio of gross profit to operating expenses for two or more related persons and then apply these ratios to its own operating expenses. Other economic indicators might be also used in establishing a range of profits.

 Teaching Case of 8-17

We assume, for example, that T company (TCo), the tested party, engages in business activities similar in complexity and character to the activities of A company (ACo) and B company

(BCo), which are corporations unrelated to TCo and to one another. ACo and BCo have ratios of operating profits to gross receipts of 0.2 and 0.3, respectively. TCo has gross receipts of 200,000 dollars. Under TNMM, TCo's arm's length range of profits would be from 40,000 dollars (200,000× 0.2) to 60,000 dollars (200,000×0.3). We assuming the various conditions for application of TNMM are met, TCo's arm's length profits would be deemed to be in the range of 40,000 dollars to 60,000 dollars.

Once the TNMM range has been established, it is necessary to select some amount within that range for the arm's length profits of the tested party. In general, the tax authorities accept the transfer prices shown on the taxpayer's books of account if the profits determined by using those prices fall within the TNMM range. If the taxpayer's reported profits fall outside the range, then the tax authorities treat the midpoint of the range as the arm's length profits. If data for more than two unrelated persons were used to establish the TNMM range, then a weighted average of the resulting profit numbers would be used to establish the midpoint of the range.

8.4.3　Double taxation in transfer pricing adjustment

When an enterprise is engaging in cross-border transactions in two or more countries through affiliated companies and all those countries have the power to adjust the transfer prices of the affiliated companies, the enterprise may be subject to double taxation.

 Teaching Case of 8-18

We assume that D company (DCo) manufactures goods in Country D at a cost of 60 dollars and sells them to an affiliate, E company (ECo). ECo then sells the goods at retail in Country E for 150 dollars. DCo is taxable in Country D on its manufacturing profit and ECo is taxable in Country E on its sales profit. The combined group (DCo and ECo) has a net profit of 90 dollars (150-60). We assume that Country D concludes that the proper transfer price on the sale from DCo to ECo is 130 dollars, whereas Country E concludes that the proper price on that sale is 65 Dollars. double taxation will result because the combined group will have total income of 90 dollars but will be taxable on income of 155 dollars, as the following table 8-3 shows.

Table 8-3　Double taxation resulting from government adjustment of transfer pricing

Project	Country D	Country E
(1) Sales price on transfer from DCo to ECo	130 dollars	65 dollars
(2) DCo's cost of manufacturing	60 dollars	60 dollars
(3) Income of DCo	70 dollars	5 dollars
(4) Retail sales price in Country E	150 dollars	150 dollars
(5) Income of ECo [line (4) -line (1)]	20 dollars	85 dollars
(6) Total Income of DCo and ECo [line (3) +line (5)]	90 dollars	90 dollars
(7) Total income taxable by Country D (line (3), 1st column) and Country E (line (5), 2nd column) = 70 +85 = 155 (dollars)		

Chapter 8 INTERNATIONAL ANTI-AVOIDANCE METHODS AND MEASURES

In order to prevent the economic double taxation on income, after a country adjusts a domestic company's transfer prices and increases its taxable profits, the country where the domestic company's overseas affiliated company locates should decrease its taxable profits simultaneously and adjust its taxes correspondingly. If a country imposes withholding tax on a company's profits remitted abroad, in order to avoid international double taxation, the country where the affiliated company locates should also allow the affiliated company to use the withholding tax paid to credit its domestic taxes. But all of this need the relevant countries reach an agreement and coordinate with each other.

In accordance with Article 9 (2) and 25 of the OECD Model Treaty, most countries entering into tax treaties have committed themselves considering making adjustments to the transfer prices used to compute taxable income of their taxpayers if those prices have been adjusted by a treaty partner in accordance with the arm's length principle. We assume, for example, that A company (ACo) manufactures goods at a cost of 20 dollars and sells them to its foreign affiliate, B company (BCo), at 40 dollars. BCo resells the goods to unrelated persons for 60 dollars. ACo is taxable in Country A, and BCo is taxable in Country B. Country A determines that the proper price for the sale to BCo should be 50 dollars and increases ACo's taxable income by 10 dollars. If Country B concurs with Country A's determination of the proper transfer price, it should allow BCo to increase its costs by 10 dollars and thereby reduce its taxable income by 10 dollars. A modification to a transfer price used by one taxpayer to take account of a modification made to the transfer price used by an affiliated taxpayer is referred to as a "correlative adjustment".

8.4.4 Advance pricing agreement

In recent years, some countries have sought to reach agreement with their taxpayers on the methodologies to be used in setting transfer prices before a transfer pricing dispute has actually arisen. A major objective of the advance approval system is to reduce the high costs that taxpayers and the tax authorities typically incur in litigating disputes over transfer prices. A taxpayer wanting prospective approval of its pricing methodology with respect to one or more transactions typically submits a request to the tax authorities for an "advance pricing agreement" (APA). The taxpayer must give details about the pricing methodology that it intends to apply to the transactions covered by the APA and must explain why that methodology would produce an appropriate result. In some instances, two or more governments may use the dispute-resolution mechanism in their tax treaties to agree jointly on the pricing methodology to be used by a taxpayer. In 1999, the OECD issued guidelines for countries in developing joint APA.

1. The concept of APA

APA refers to the agreement concluded by the taxpayer and the tax authority with respect to the pricing principles and calculation methods of possible related transactions in the future year which are applied by the taxpayer to the tax authority first and the tax authority approves after examination and verification. Its main purpose is to solve the transfer pricing issue in the future. APA can be divided into three categories: single APA (agreement between taxpayers and the tax authority), double APA (agreement between two tax authorities and taxpayers) and multilateral

APA (agreement involving many tax authorities). It is a major subject in international tax management which occurs along with the continuous strengthening of transfer pricing rules in many countries and the increasing contradiction between tax authorities and enterprises.

2. Advantages and disadvantages of APA

APA can bring interest to related parties. For example, the taxpayer can exactly know in advance what reaction the tax authority would make to his transfer pricing in his operation business; it can supply a very good circumstance in which the taxpayer and the tax authority can cooperate each other to determine which kind of transfer pricing method can be used in the taxpayer's transfer pricing activities; it can relieve largely the taxpayer's burden of keeping original documents and makes the taxpayer avoid so much endless appeal procedure.

Though APA can bring some interest to taxpayers, its complicate application procedures and the request for strict information disclosure, as well as the high cost of application make taxpayers hesitate to apply for it. According to a survey of the United States in 1996, in the American multinational corporations surveyed, only 10% of them had signed or were ready to sign APA. Many companies reluctant to sign APA worried that the required contents in the application materials were too detailed and they might be easy to leak the company's secrets. In addition, the application cost of APA was too high and it took too much time and energy.

Although APA has some disadvantages, with accumulating the experience and using more flexible methods, we believe that it will have a wide prospect in the future.

To sum up, international communities have acted and adopted a series of countermeasures for tax avoidance activities of multinational taxpayers. It should be pointed out that the above anti-avoidance measures can play a defensive role from different aspects, however, they can not completely eliminate international tax avoidance, sometimes with little success. The reasons mainly lie in the following aspects: the first is that international tax avoidance causes different financial losses in different countries. Some countries or areas maybe benefit from it, so their anti-avoidance attitudes are not consistent; the second is that international cooperation against tax avoidance mainly takes the bilateral form and there is no any country in the world has signed bilateral tax treaties with all of the countries, which makes it possible for a transnational taxpayer to go around the Contracting States to avoid taxes. Even for the multilateral tax treaties, they are generally limited to a certain international or regional organizations, so there are still loopholes; the third is that there is a gap between the principles and application of some anti-avoidance provisions which makes it difficult to implement in practice. Therefore, how to prevent international tax avoidance, improve tax collection relationship, deal with tax distribution relationship between countries and promote the development of international economy is still an important subject in the world to be researched and solved urgently.

 Key words, phrases and special terms

procedural law　　　　　　　　　　　　　诉讼法
burden of persuasion　　　　　　　　　　举证责任
administrative cooperation　　　　　　　　征管合作

Chapter 8 INTERNATIONAL ANTI-AVOIDANCE METHODS AND MEASURES

thin capitalization rules	资本弱化条例
share capital	股本
retained earnings	留存收益
preferred shares	优先股
the arm's length principle	公平交易原则
the earnings-stripping rule	收益剥离原则
marketable security	有价证券
a wholly-owned subsidiary	全资子公司
constructive ownership rules	推定拥有条例
tainted income	受污所得
Transfer pricing rules	转让定价税制
comparable uncontrolled price method (CUPM)	可比非受控价格法
resale price method (RPM)	再销售价格法
cost plus method (CPM)	成本加成法
cost method (CM)	成本法
profit-split method (PSM)	利润分割法
transaction net margin method (TNMM)	交易净利润法
advance pricing agreement (APA)	预约定价协议

Problems of thinking

1. How to prevent international tax avoidance by means of enactment and perfection of tax laws?

2. How can we restrict treaty shopping?

3. Why do the countries have thin capitalization rules? What is the main content of thin capitalization rules?

4. What is the main content of CFC rules in developed countries?

5. What are the contents of transfer pricing rules?

6. What are the judgment norms on related corporations?

7. What are the methods of transfer pricing adjustment?

8. What is APA? What is the major objective of APA?

9. What interest can APA bring to taxpayers and tax authorities?

Chapter 9
INTERNATIONAL TAX TREATIES

 Ideological and political points of the course

As a responsible major country, China has actively complied with international tax treaties on the basis of safeguarding national sovereignty and made a significant contribution to the development of the world economy.

 Learning Objectives

1. Understand the legal nature and objective of international tax treaties.
2. Master the chief difference between the OECD Model Treaty and the UN Model Treaty.
3. Know the main contents of a typical international tax treaty.

 Course Importing

Since the reform and opening up, China has attached great importance to international tax treaties. Since reform and opening up, China has attached great importance to international tax treaties. From January 1981 to June 2022, China has officially signed 109 treaties to avoid double taxation, of which 105 have entered into force. How to view the influence of OECD Model Treaty and UN Model Treaty on Chinese signing of international tax treaties?

International tax treaties represent an important aspect of the international tax rules of most countries. Over 2,000 bilateral income tax treaties are currently in effect, and the number is growing. The overwhelming majority of these treaties are based in large part on the OECD Model Treaty. The UN Model Treaty is substantially similar to the OECD Model Treaty but includes some provisions that are not included in the OECD Model Treaty. Both of these models are discussed below.

 **9.1 Overview**

International tax treaties generally refer to agreements signed between countries to avoid double taxationon income and capital and to prevent tax evasion.

Chapter 9 INTERNATIONAL TAX TREATIES

9.1.1 Legal nature and effect of international tax treaties

Treaties are agreements between sovereign nations. Article 2 of the Vienna Convention on the Law of Treaties provides that a treaty is an international agreement (in one or more instruments, whatever called) concluded between states and governed by international law. International tax treaties confer rights and impose obligations on the Contracting States. In most countries they do not confer rights on citizens or residents of the two states unless the provisions of the treaty are enacted into law in the same way as domestic legislation.

The relationship between international tax treaties and domestic tax legislation is a complex one in many countries. The basic principle is that the treaty should prevail in the event of a conflict between the provisions of domestic law and a treaty. In some countries—France is an example—this principle has constitutional status. In many countries, the government clearly has the authority under domestic law to override the provisions of a tax treaty. For example, legislative supremacy is a fundamental rule of law in many parliamentary democracies. The courts in many countries may require that the legislature explicitly indicate its intention to override a treaty before giving effect to a conflicting domestic law. Courts may also strain to find some ground for reconciling an apparent conflict between a treaty and domestic legislation. China holds the same view with most countries with respect to the relationship between the domestic tax law and international tax treaties. For example, it is stipulated in Article 58 of the Enterprises Income Tax Law of the People's Republic of China that if the provisions of tax treaties issued by Chinese government with other foreign governments are different from the provisions of this law, the provisions of tax treaties shall be applied first. Obviously, China is a country advocating that international tax treaties take precedence over domestic tax laws.

In general, international tax treaties apply to all income taxes imposed by the Contracting States, including taxes imposed by provincial (state), local, and other sub-national governments. In some federal states, however, the central government is constrained by constitutional mandate or established tradition from entering into tax treaties that limit the taxing powers of their sub-national governments. Accordingly, the tax treaties of such federal states apply only to national taxes. This is the situation for both Canada and the United States. Under such circumstances, a sub-national government may impose taxes in a manner that would not be permitted for its central government. For example, some state governments in the United States (California is the best known example) imposed tax on multinational enterprises on a unitary basis (combined reporting and formula apportionment) despite the US government's treaty commitment to follow the arm's length principle.

Most of international tax treaties do not impose new taxes. Rather, they limit the taxes otherwise imposed by a state. In effect, international tax treaties are primarily relieving in nature. France and several African countries following the French practice are notable exceptions in this regard because taxes may be imposed pursuant to treaty provisions even though not imposed under domestic law.

It should be pointed out that, whether it is "the OECD Model Treaty" or "the UN Model

Treaty", they are not legally binding on all countries. The function of these Model Treaties is to indicate a direction for the future tax treaties signed by the relevant countries. Its purpose is to provide a convenient condition for countries to negotiate tax treaties instead of spending long time in discussing all issues of every clause from the beginning in details. But in the signing of bilateral tax treaties, we should be flexible and add some special provisions applicable for domestic situations instead of copying completely the clauses of the Model Treaties.

9.1.2 Objectives of International Tax Treaties

The objective of international tax treaties, broadly stated, is to facilitate cross-border trade and investment by eliminating the tax impediments to these cross-border flows. This broad objective is supplemented by several more specific, operational objectives.

The most important operational objective of international tax treaties is the elimination of double taxation. Most of the substantive provisions of the typical bilateral tax treaty are directed at the achievement of this goal. For example, international tax treaties contain tie-breaker rules to make a taxpayer who is otherwise resident in both countries a resident in only one of the countries. They also limit or eliminate the source country tax on certain types of income and require residence countries to provide relief for source country taxes either by way of a foreign tax credit or an exemption for the foreign source income. In the early post-World War Ⅱ period, the focus of international tax treaties was almost exclusively on solving the problem of double taxation. At that time, the burgeoning multinational enterprises were facing risks of substantial double taxation, few countries provided unilateral relief for double taxation, and treaty networks were just being developed. Treaty solutions to most of the major double tax problems were worked out in the 1950s and early 1960s, however, and they are now routinely accepted by states when they enter into tax treaties. The major one exception is the double tax problem arising from inconsistent applications by countries of the arm's length principle for establishing transfer prices in transactions between related persons.

The historical emphasis on the elimination of double taxation should not obscure the fact that most international tax treaties have another equally important operational objective—the prevention of fiscal evasion. This objective counterbalances the elimination of double taxation. Just as double taxation imposes an inappropriate barrier to international commerce, the tolerance of fiscal evasion offers an inappropriate incentive to such commerce. Although the elimination of fiscal evasion is an explicit objective of most tax treaties, few provisions in those treaties are designed to achieve it. Even the meaning of the term "fiscal evasion" in the typical international tax treaty is unclear. Some countries, such as Switzerland, define the term narrowly to include only criminal tax evasion. Most Contracting States define the term more broadly to include many types of tax avoidance as well as criminal tax evasion.

In additional to the two principle operational objectives of international tax treaties, there are several ancillary objectives. One ancillary objective is the elimination of discrimination against foreign nationals and non-residents. A second ancillary objective is the exchange of information between the contracting states. Finally, most Contracting States provide a mechanism in their treaties

Chapter 9 INTERNATIONAL TAX TREATIES

for resolving disputes arising from the interaction of their tax systems.

9.1.3 International model tax treaties

There are two influential international model tax treaties—the OECD Model Treaty and UN Model Treaty. In addition, most countries have their own model tax treaties, which are often not published but are provided to other countries for the purpose of negotiating tax treaties. The UN Model Treaty and the various country model tax treaties draw heavily on the OECD Model Treaty.

The OECD Model Treaty has a long history, beginning with early diplomatic treaties of the 19th century. The limited objective of these treaties was to ensure that diplomats of one country working in another would not be discriminated. These diplomatic treaties were extended to cover income taxation once income taxation became significant in the early part of the 20th century. After the First World War, the League of Nations commenced work on the development of a model treaty dealing exclusively with income tax issues. This work culminated in model conventions in 1943 and 1946. These conventions were not unanimously accepted, and the work of creating an acceptable model treaty was taken over by the OECD. As of 2022, the OECD has more than 30 members, consisting of many of the major industrialized countries. The OECD Model Treaty was first published, in draft form, in 1963. It was revised in 1977 and again in 1992, at which time it was converted to a loose-leaf format in order to facilitate more frequent revisions. Revisions were made in 1994, 1995, 1997, 2000, and 2002. The Committee on Fiscal Affairs, which consists of senior tax officials from the member countries, has responsibility for the OECD Model Treaty as well as other aspects of international tax cooperation, operated through the permanent secretariat and several working parties. The staffs of the permanent secretariat dealing with matters of taxation are now part of the Centre for Tax Policy and Administration, which was created in early 2001. The working parties consist of delegates from the member countries. Working party No.1 is responsible for the OECD Model Treaty, and it examines issues related to the treaty on an ongoing basis. A detailed commentary (The OECD Commentary), organized on an article-by-article basis, accompanies the OECD Model Treaty. The commentary has become increasingly important with respect to the interpretation and the application of tax treaties, including some treaties between countries that are not members of the OECD. To take account of the positions of some nonmember states, the OECD opened up the commentary in 1999 to major non-member countries, including Argentina, Brazil, China, Israel, Russia, and South Africa.

The OECD Model Treaty favors capital exporting countries over capital importing countries. Often it eliminates or mitigates double taxation by requiring the source country to give up some or all of its tax on certain categories of income earned by residents of the other treaty country. Almost by definition, developing countries are net capital importers. In addition, most developing countries use the exemption method for granting double taxation relief to their domestic corporations. Consequently, developing countries entering into a tax treaty with a developed country would not benefit from the trade-off of source jurisdiction for residence jurisdiction contained in the OECD Model Treaty. In recognition of the shortcomings of the OECD Model Treaty, developing countries devised their own model treaty under the auspices of the United Nations.

The UN Model Treaty was first published by the United Nations in 1980 and revised, although not substantial change, in 2001. It was drafted by the United Nations Group of Experts on Tax Treaties between Developed and Developing Countries, established in 1967 by the Economic and Social Council of the United Nations. The members of the expert group are tax specialists and tax administrators appointed by their governments but who serve in an individual capacity. Fifteen members are appointed from developing countries and countries with economies in transition, and ten are appointed by developed countries. The UN Model Treaty follows the pattern set by the OECD Model Treaty, and many of its provisions are identical, or nearly so, to those in the OECD Model Treaty. In general, therefore, it makes sense not to view the UN Model Treaty as an entirely separate model treaty bur rather as making limited, but important, modifications to the OECD Model Treaty.

The chief difference between the two models is that the UN Model Treaty imposes fewer restrictions on the tax jurisdiction of the source country. For example, the UN Model Treaty does not contain specific limitations on the withholding tax rates on dividends, interest, and royalties imposed by the source country; instead, the withholding rate levels are left to bilateral negotiations between the Contracting States. And the UN Model Treaty also allocates somewhat greater power to the source country to tax the business income of non-residents by making it easier for a taxpayer to have a PE in that country.

9.2 Contents of a typical international tax treaty

This section describes some of the major provisions of a typical bilateral tax treaty based on the OECD and UN Model Treaties.

9.2.1 Coverage, scope, and legal effect

The two countries that enter into a bilateral income tax treaty are called the "Contracting States". Under Article 1 (Personal Scope) of the typical tax treaty, the provisions of the treaty apply to persons who are "residents of one or both of the Contracting States". Article 4 (Resident) specifies who is a "resident" of a Contracting State for purposes of the treaty by reference to the domestic laws of that Contracting State. A "person" is defined in Article 3 (General Definitions) to include "an individual, a company and any other body of persons". The OECD Commentary indicates that a charitable foundation is a "person" within the meaning of Article 3. Indeed, any legal entity that is recognized under the laws of a Contacting State is likely to be treated as a "person" for tax treaty purposes. Although a partnership is probably a "person" for purposes of a typical treaty, it may not be a resident of one of the Contracting States if the partners rather than the partnership are liable to tax there.

The typical tax treaty expressly lists the national taxes and sometimes the sub-national taxes of the Contracting States to which the treaty applies. Each country's personal income tax and corporate income tax are invariably listed. Most treaties also provide that the treaty applies to amendments of the listed taxes and to subsequently imposed taxes that are identical to or are substantially similar to the listed taxes. Some treaties list certain income and capital taxes that are not to be covered by the treaty. For example, many tax treaties exclude wage taxes earmarked for government pensions from their scope.

Although new tax treaty partners contemplate that their relationship will last indefinitely, they almost always provide the termination of the treaty at the request of either party. Under Article 30 (Termination) of the OECD Model Treaty and Article 29 of the UN Model Treaty, a Contracting State may unilaterally terminate a treaty at the beginning of the upcoming calendar year by giving notice of termination to its treaty partner at least six months before the end of the year. A recent trend is for treaty partners to agree to allow a new treaty to remain in effect for at least five years after the initial exchange of instruments of ratification. Of course the Contracting States may terminate a treaty at any time by mutual consent.

9.2.2　Business Income

The taxation of business income is governed by Article 3, 5, and 7 of the OECD and UN Model Treaties. Article 7 (Business Profits) provides that "an enterprise of a Contracting State" generally is exempt from tax on its profits derived from business carried on in the other Contracting State unless those profits are attributable to its permanent establishment located in that other Contracting State. If an enterprise of a Contracting State has a PE in the other Contracting State, then it is taxable only on the taxable income attributable to the PE. Article 7 (2) of the OECD and UN Model Treaties provides that the profits of a PE should be determined under the arm's length principle. Article 7 (1) of the UN Model Treaty employs a limited force-of-attraction principle in determining the income attributable to a PE. Under that principle, if an enterprise has a PE in a Contracting State, it is taxable not only on the income earned through that PE but also on income derived in that state from the sale of products similar to those sold through the PE or from business activities similar to those activities conducted through the PE. The approach taken in the UN Model Treaty introduces some uncertainty for companies seeking to minimize their taxes in the source country. The advantage of the rule from the government's perspective is that it simplifies administration and reduces opportunities for tax avoidance.

Under Article 5 of the OECD and UN Model Treaties, a PE generally is "a fixed place of business through which the business of an enterprise is wholly or partly carried on". This language is used in essentially identical form in almost all tax treaties. The OECD and UN Model Treaties provide the following list of examples of business premises that often constitute a PE: a place of management, a branch, an office, a factory, a workshop, a mine, an oil or gas well, a quarry, or any other place of extraction of natural resources. For an enterprise to have a "fixed place of business" in a Contracting State, it must operate at a specific geographical location and its activities at that location must endure for more than a temporary period (generally for more than 6 months). The place where equipment, such as an oil pumping machine, is used can constitute a place of business even if that machine is unattended by human agents of the enterprise. For a place of business to be "fixed", it is enough that it has a specific geographical location. For example, a marketplace can be the fixed place of business of an enterprise if the enterprise operates a movable stall within that marketplace on a regular basis. It is immaterial whether an enterprise rents or owns its premises in determining whether the premises constitute a PE.

In the UN Commentary on Article 5, it is suggested that fishing vessels might constitute a PE if the enterprise uses those vessels for commercial fishing within the territorial waters of a Contracting State. That issue, however, remains controversial. Many difficult issues arise in determining whether an enterprise has a PE in a Contracting State as a result of engaging in electronic commerce in that state. The definition of a PE in the OECD Model Treaty includes certain dependent agents of an enterprise that act on behalf of the enterprise and have, and habitually exercise, an authority to conclude contracts on behalf of the enterprise. Most tax treaties treat such agents as PE of their principals. The agency rule in the UN Model Treaty is more expansive, extending to dependent agents that maintain a stock of goods from which they make deliveries on behalf of their principals. Some tax treaties follow the UN Model Treaty on this point. Some commentators argue that the definition of a PE should be also expanded to include most dependent agents carrying on substantial business on behalf of an enterprise whether or not they have the authority to conclude contracts. These commentators argue that the power to conclude contracts has little commercial significance because modern methods of communication permit nearly instantaneous contact between agents and their foreign principals.

In addition, the UN Model Treaty provides that an enterprise engaged in the sale of insurance in a Contracting State shall be deemed to have a PE in that state if it collects premiums in that state or ensures risks located in that state. This rule does not apply, however, if the insurance activities are conducted by an independent agent.

Most treaties provide that a building site, drilling operation, or other temporary project location constitutes a PE if the project continues for some minimum period. In the OECD Model Treaty, the minimum period is one year. The UN Model Treaty uses a minimum period of six months and defines the activities covered by the provision broadly enough to include an assembly site and supervisory activities conducted in connection with a building or assembly site. Developing countries typically adopt a six-month period or an even shorter minimum period in their tax treaties. For example, the minimum period in the India-United states treaty is four months. A few treaties between developed countries extend the minimum period beyond one year. The Japan-United States treaty, for example, has a twenty-four month period.

The UN Model Treaty provides that an enterprise has a PE in a Contracting State if it performs personal services in that state through employees or other personnel for a period of six months in any 12-month period. This provision is intended primarily to guarantee that management and consultancy activities may be taxable in the source country if those activities continue for an extended period. The OECD Model Treaty has no comparable provision.

The OECD and UN Model Treaties generally provide that a facility used primarily for the purchase of goods for export, for the storage or display of goods, or for storage of goods for processing by another enterprise will not constitute a PE of that enterprise. The OECD Model Treaty allows a facility to be used for the delivery of goods without it being a PE. The UN Model Treaty does not provide for that exception in order to permit the source country to tax income derived from the operation of a warehouse. Certain facilities are also excluded from the definition of a PE under both models if they are maintained for activities "of a preparatory or auxiliary character".

A subsidiary does not constitute a PE of its parent company simply because the parent controls it. Similarly, a parent company is not a PE of its subsidiary. These important rules have encouraged most multinational enterprises to operate outside their home country through affiliated companies rather than through foreign branches or PE whenever their activities in a foreign country are likely to be substantial. When a multinational enterprise anticipates only minor contacts with the foreign country, it typically avoids having a PE in that country by operating through independent distributors.

The taxation of business income derived from the operation of ships or aircraft is subject to even greater limitations under Article 8 (Shipping, Inland Waterways Transport and Air Transport) of the OECD and UN Model Treaties. The OECD Model Treaty and alternative A of Article 8 of the UN Model Treaty assign the exclusive right to tax such income to the country where the shipping or aircraft operation is effectively managed, even if the shipping or aircraft enterprise has a PE in the source country. Many treaties assign the exclusive right to tax to the country of residence of the enterprise. Many treaties allow the source country to tax income derived from the purely domestic operation of ships and aircraft. Alternative B of Article 8 of the UN Model Treaty permits the source country to tax income derived from shipping and aircraft activities if such activities are "more than casual".

Rental income derived from movable property is considered to be business profits under the OECD Model Treaty. Therefore, such income is subject to tax by a country only if the taxpayer has a PE in the country and the rent is attributable to the PE. Article 12 of the UN Model Treaty which permits taxation of royalties in the source country includes income from equipment rental in the definition of royalties. The UN Model Treaty also treats income derived from tapes as royalty income.

Rent derived from immovable property is taxable by the source country in accordance with Article 6 of the OECD and UN Model Treaties. For example, income derived from renting an apartment building would be taxable in the Contracting State where the building locates.

9.2.3 Employment and personal services income

Under Article 14 (Independent Personal Services) of the UN Model Treaty, a resident of a Contracting State who performs "professional services or other activities of an independent nature" in the other Contracting State is not taxable in that state unless he or she has a "fixed base" in the State that is regularly available. This provision was included in the OECD Model Treaty until it was removed in 2000. As a result of this change in the OECD Model Treaty, individuals and companies engaging in the performance of independent personal services in a Contracting State are taxable in that state only if they have a PE therein and their income is attributable to the PE. The term "professional services" includes the services of physicians, lawyers, engineers, architects, dentists, and accountants, as well as independent scientific, literary, artistic, educational, and teaching activities. Under the UN Model Treaty, professionals and other persons performing independent services generally may be taxable whether or not they have a fixed base if they are present in the country for more than 183 days of the taxable year or if their compensation is deductible in the source country.

Income from employment performed in a country may be taxable in the country under Article 15 (Dependent Personal Services) of the OECD Model Treaty whether or not the employee has a fixed base in the country. Such income is exempt from tax in the source country, however, if an employee is paid by a foreign employer, the salary is not deductible by the employer in the source country, and the employee is present in the source country for not more than 183 days in any 12-month period.

The generous exemptions from source taxation for professionals and employees generally do not apply to entertainers and athletes (and their retinues). Nor do they apply to non-residents receiving fees for services as a corporate director of a resident corporation. With certain exceptions, individuals performing employment services on behalf of a Contracting State are taxable only by that state. Of course, some government servants who are working in a foreign country as members of their government's diplomatic missions are exempt from tax under special agreements or under the rules of international law. A tax treaty would not affect such exemptions.

Under Article 18 (Pensions) of the OECD Model Treaty, individuals receiving pensions on account of past employment generally are taxable only by the Contracting State of which they are a resident. The UN Model Treaty offers some scope for taxation at source. Government pensions generally are taxable by the Contracting State making the pension payment unless the individual receiving the pension is both a resident and a national of the other Contracting State.

Students and certain business apprentices or trainees who visit a Contracting State for educational or training purposes are generally not taxable in that Contracting State on the foreign payments they receive for maintenance, education, or training under Article 20 (Students) of the OECD and UN Model Treaties. Some tax treaties also provide reciprocal exemptions for visiting professors and teachers.

9.2.4 Income and gains from immovable property

Every country seeks to retain the right to tax income derived from the sale of real property, from the extraction of natural resources located within its geographical borders, and from domestic agriculture and the like. Reflecting this consensus view, Article 6 (Income from Immovable Property) of the OECD and UN Model Treaties reserves for the source country the right to tax income derived from "immovable property". The definition of the term "immovable property" generally is left to the country in which the property is situated, although the term is specifically understood to include income from agriculture, forestry, mineral deposits, and other natural resources. The Article 13 (Capital Gains) makes clear that gains from the disposition of immovable property are also taxable in the source country.

Because the source country is entitled to tax both the income derived from immovable property and gains from the disposition of such property, it does not generally matter for purposes of tax treaties whether a gain from the disposition of immovable property is characterized as income or capital gain. This characterization issue is left to domestic law.

Several countries specifically provide in their tax treaties that the right to tax gains from the disposition of shares of a company is reserved to the source country when the assets of the company consist primarily of immovable property. Article 13 (4) of the UN Model Treaty also contains such a provision. That provision is intended to prevent a taxpayer from avoiding source taxation on gains derived from immovable property by transferring the property to a controlled corporation and then disposing of the shares of the corporation in a transaction that otherwise would be exempt from source taxation under the tax treaty. This rule also applies in the UN Model Treaty and some actual treaties to dispositions of interests in partnerships and trusts. To prevent easy avoidance of the rule, a country should have rules in its domestic law and its treaties under which a disposition of an interest in a company, partnership, or trust is taxable if the value of the interest is derived primarily from immovable property.

9.2.5 Reduced withholding rates on certain investment income

A major objective of most tax treaties is to provide reduced rates of withholding tax levied by the source country on dividends, interest, and royalties paid to residents of the other Contracting State. The goal of these reduced rates is to provide for some sharing of tax revenue between the source country and the residence country.

In accordance with their own perceptions of their national interests, the OECD Model Treaty strongly recommends, that the Contracting States by mutual agreements limit the rates of tax in the source country, shown in Table 9-1.

Table 9-1   Maximum Withholding Rates Endorsed by OECD Model Treaty

Dividends paid to Related Corporations	Dividends paid to Other Persons	Interest	Royalties
5%	15%	10%	0%

Source: OECD Model Treaty (2000), Article 10 (Dividends), Article 11 (Interest), and Article 12 (Royalties).

The maximum withholding rates proposed in the OECD Model Treaty, especially the 0% rate on royalties, are unacceptable to most developing countries. To reflect the interests of the developing countries, the UN Model Treaty does not propose any specific limits on withholding rates. It does contemplate, however, that some limits on withholding rates will be negotiated by the Contracting States. Most tax treaties with developing countries allow maximum withholding rates substantially in excess of the maximum rates proposed in the OECD Model Treaty. It is uncommon, for example, for developing countries to agree to a maximum withholding rate on royalties lower than 15 percent.

Many tax treaties provide for a more complicated set of maximum withholding rates than the rather simple pattern proposed in the OECD Model Treaty. It is commonplace, for example, for a tax treaty to impose separate limitations on the rates applicable to industrial royalties, royalties paid with respect to copyrights of literary works, and royalties paid for the films. Many recent tax treaties provide special rules for the taxation of payments made with respect to computer software. The

OECD Commentary provides some detailed recommendations on how such payments should be taxed, although many countries have indicated an unwillingness to follow the commentary in at least some respects.

9.2.6　Other types of income

Many tax treaties reserve the right to tax income, other than those types of income discussed above, to the country of residence of the taxpayer deriving the income. Article 13 (Capital Gains) of the OECD and UN Model Treaties generally provides that the taxation of capital gains, other than gains attributable to a PE or gains from the alienation of immovable property, is reserved to the residence country. The residual rule contained in Article 21 (Other Income) of the OECD Model Treaty similarly provides that the taxation of items of income not dealt with in other articles of the treaty is given exclusively to the country of residence. Article 21 (Other Income) of the UN Model Treaty reserves to the source state the right to tax unmentioned income items. The Article 21 has become of particular importance in recent years due to the many forms of income derived from new financial instruments. A tax treaty following the OECD Model Treaty precludes taxation at source of income items that may resemble various traditional types of income but which have been modified by contractual arrangements to constitute a type of income that is not mentioned in the treaty.

Some treaties have provisions governing the taxation of alimony and child support payments made by a resident of one Contracting State to a resident of the other Contracting State. The common rule is for the country of residence of the payee to have the right to tax alimony and for the country of residence of the payer to have the right to tax child support.

9.2.7　Fair dealing and cooperation

Several provisions in the typical tax treaty are designed to promote fair dealing and cooperation between the Contracting States. To reduce the risk that the residents and nationals of one Contracting State will be treated unfairly by the other Contracting State, most treaties include a provision in which each Contracting State agrees not to discriminate unfairly against the residents and nationals of the other Contracting State. Although non-discrimination is a worthy objective, it is not easily attained.

Contracting States also attempt to facilitate fair dealing and cooperation by establishing a mechanism in their treaties for resolving disputes that arise from the interaction of their tax systems or from the operation of the treaty itself. Virtually all tax treaties provide some cooperation between the Contracting States in the administration of their tax systems. Article 26 (Exchange of Information) of the OECD and UN Model Treaties provide an exchange of "such information as is necessary for carrying out the provisions of this Convention or of the domestic laws of the Contracting States concerning taxes covered by the Convention". Neither the OECD Model Treaty nor the UN Model Treaty currently provides mutual assistance in the collection or enforcement of taxes, although it would not be surprising if they did so in the near future.

Chapter 9 INTERNATIONAL TAX TREATIES

 Key words, phrases and special terms

tie-breaker rules	加比规则
the OECD Model Treaty	《经合发范本》
the UN Model Treaty	《联合国范本》
the League of Nations	国际联盟
the Economic and Social Council of the United Nations	联合国经社理事会
visiting professors	访问学者

 Problems of thinking

1. What's the relationship between the international tax treaty and the domestic tax law?

2. What's the chief difference between the OECD Model Treaty and the UN Model Treaty?

3. What are the main contents of a typical international tax treaty?

结语

第1篇 国际税收理论

第1章

国际税收导论

📝 时政观点

1. 税收取之于民，用之于民。
2. 在"一带一路"的背景下，我国税收制度要适应国际税收发展趋势、融入国际社会。

🖱 学习目标

1. 重点掌握国际税收的概念。
2. 辨别国际税收与国家税收、涉外税收的区别和联系。
3. 了解国际税收的发展趋势。

🔍 课程导入

欧盟是一个政治、经济领域一体化程度很高的地区性国际组织，其内部有共同的对外关税，也有统一的货币——欧元，甚至欧盟政府还有自己独立的财源——即所谓的"自有财源"。那么，欧盟是一个超越国家主权之上的征税主体吗？它可以向成员国纳税人直接征税吗？

1.1 国际税收的概念

1.1.1 什么是国际税收

税收是一国政府凭借手中的政治权力，对其管辖范围内的纳税人进行的一种强制征收款项，是国家取得财政收入的重要手段，体现的是国家和纳税人之间的征纳关系。这种征纳关系既包括本国政府与本国纳税人之间的关系，也包括本国政府与外国纳税人之间的关系。那么，国际税收是否同样也是一种强制课征形式？它是不是国际社会凭借一种超国家的政治权力取得收入的工具？回答是否定的。因为在完全独立的主权国家之上并不存在这种超国家的政治权力，因而国际范围内的强制课征也就无从谈起。

对于国际税收这门学科的研究，在国外很早就有人进行。但是，国际税收理论迅速发展并成为税收学的一个重要组成部分，则是在第二次世界大战之后。其产生和存在于一定的前提条件下。

1. 国际税收产生的条件

从理论上讲，国际税收的产生和存在，是在税收存在的基础上，由两个前提条件共同决定的：一个是跨国所得的大量存在；另一个是世界各国普遍征收所得税并行使不同的征税权力。只有同时具备这两个条件，才能出现国家之间分享税收的问题，也才有必要进行国家间的税收协调，从而产生国家间的税收分配关系。

决定国际税收产生和存在的这两个前提条件也为国际税收存在的客观必然性提供了理论上和实践上的评价标准。

(1) 跨国所得的出现同国际税收的产生有着直接的必然联系。

跨国所得，是指来源于一国但为另一国居民或公民纳税人所拥有的所得，跨国所得是国际税收产生的物质基础。

在封闭经济的环境下，各国征收只能涉及本国境内生产和流通的商品和本国纳税人在本国境内取得的收入和拥有的财产。而在开放经济的条件下，一国生产的商品会通过国际贸易流入他国，从事跨国投资等国际经济活动的一国纳税人会从境外取得收入或拥有境外财产，都会形成跨国所得。这时，各国在本国税收管辖权范围之内课税就不仅要涉及外国进口商品和本国出口商品，还要涉及本国纳税人的境外所得或财产以及外国纳税人在本国境内取得的所得或拥有的财产。由于纳税人的收入跨越了国境，征纳关系也就随之跨越了国境，并由此产生了国家之间对同一笔跨国所得如何分享税收利益的问题。至此，客观经济状况为国际税收的产生提供了前提条件。

(2) 各国普遍征收所得税并行使不同的征收权力同国际税收的产生有着本质的联系。

由于跨国所得的存在，有关国家都要将它列为各自的征税对象而行使征税权。跨国所得的来源国要从源征税，而跨国所得拥有者的居住国或国籍国一般也要对之征税，从而造成了国家之间在税收分配上的矛盾，也就需要国家间协调税收分配关系。因此，国际税收是各国政府对跨国纳税人的跨国所得行使征税权的表现，是一个国家对另一个国家财权利益的"侵犯"和"协调"。世界各国只有广泛征收所得税并行使不同的税收管辖权，且跨国所得存在，国际税收才会产生。

2. 国际税收的概念

综上所述，国际税收的概念可从狭义和广义两个层面来理解。

1) 狭义层面

从狭义层面来说，国际税收是指两个或两个以上的国家政府，各自基于其课税主权，在对跨国纳税人的跨国所得分别课税时所形成的国与国之间的税收分配和协调关系。

这一概念包括以下三点重要含义。

(1) 国际税收不能脱离国家税收而单独存在。

税收的存在，必须有征税机关与纳税人的存在，但是，国际税收不可能有独立于国家税收的特定的征税机关与纳税人，它只能依附于国家税收。

欧洲的税收就很能说明这个问题。欧盟的"自有财源"，其实来源于各成员国政府对其纳税人的强制课征，并非由欧盟政府对各成员国内的纳税人直接征收。例如，"自有财源"中有一项叫作关税收入，但它并不是由欧盟政府自己课征，而是由各成员国将自己对进口产品课征的关税收入扣除10%的手续费后上缴给欧盟预算的。又如，增值税提成是欧盟"自有财源"中最大的一项收入，但它也不是由欧盟政府向成员国的纳税人直接征收，而是由各成员国根据统一口径的增值税税基按一定比例向欧盟预先缴纳。

(2) 国际税收不能离开跨国纳税人这个关键因素。

通常，一个"非跨国"纳税人只承担一个国家的纳税义务，仅仅涉及一个国家的征纳双方当事人之间的关系，并不会由此引起这个国家和其他国家间的税收分配关系。因此，在国际税收概念中，必须特别指明其纳税人是跨国纳税人；否则，国际税收关系就无从谈起。

(3) 国际税收是不同国家间的税收分配和协调关系。

当一国对其管辖的跨国纳税人的跨国所得进行征税时，往往会涉及他国的财权利益，此时，国际税收问题所隐含的是国与国之间的税收关系，而这种国家之间的税收关系正是国际税收的本质所在。

国家之间的税收关系主要表现在两个方面。

①国与国之间的税收分配关系。

国与国之间的税收分配关系涉及对同一课税对象由哪国征税或各征多少税的税收利益分配问题。当一国征税而导致另一国不能征税，或者当一国多征税而造成另一国少征税时，两国之间便会发生税收分配关系。例如，当一笔跨国所得同时要被两个国家的政府征税时，为了避免对同一笔所得的国际重复征税而增加跨国纳税人的税收负担，纳税人的居住国可以放弃对本国居民国外所得的征税权，而是由所得的来源国单独行使征税权；或者居住国让来源国优先行使征税权，然后再在来源国征税的基础上对这笔国外所得按来源国税率低于居住国税率的差额部分进行补征。在这两种情况下，居住国和来源国之间都会发生一定的税收分配关系。又如，为了防止出口国和进口国对同一批国际贸易商品都课征国内商品税，国际社会目前规定：对国际贸易商品统一由进口国课税，出口国不征税。这样一来，出口国由于放弃了自己对出口商品的征收权，其税收利益就会受到一定影响，进出口国之间因而也要发生一定的税收分配关系。再如，在跨国公司从事国际避税的情况下，由于跨国公司通常要把公司集团的一部分利润由高税国子公司转移到低税国子公司去实现，所以高税国的所得税税基必然要受到影响，两国之间也必然会发生一定的税收分配关系。

②国与国之间的税收协调关系。

税收是一国的主权，一个主权国家有权决定对什么征收、对什么不征收，也有权决定征税额的多少。也就是说，在征税问题上，一国完全可以自行其是，而不必顾及他国的好恶。然而，在开放的世界经济体系中，国与国之间互相依赖、互相依存，各国实际上并不能随意制定自己的税收制度并随意行使自己的征税权，在许多问题上必须考虑本国与其他国家之间的经济关系。这就要求国与国之间在税收制度和税收政策等方面要进行一定的协调。这种协调包含两方面的内容。

第一，合作性协调，即有关国家通过谈判就各自的税基、税率、征税规则等达成协议，并根据协议内容确定对对方国家的商品或纳税人进行征税的制度和办法。例如，国与国之间签订的避免双重征税的税收协定就是这种合作性协调的表现。

第二，非合作性协调，即一个国家在其他国家竞争压力的驱使下，在其他国家税收制度既定不变的情况下，单方面调整自己的税收制度，使本国的税制尽量与他国保持一致而形成的一种税收国际协调，其实质是税收的国际竞争。例如，在20世纪80年代中期，西方国家为了防止资本外流和税收外流①,纷纷降低本国的公司所得税税率,公司所得税税率平均由50%降低到目前的23%左右。另外,发展中国家为了吸引外资也竞相给予外国投资者优惠的税收待遇,这实际上也是一种非合作性的税收协调。

2) 广义层面

从广义层面来说,国际税收是指在开放的经济条件下因纳税人的经济活动扩大到境外以及国与国之间税收法规存在差异或相互冲突而带来的一些税收问题和税收现象。

这些税收问题和税收现象即是国际税收的研究内容,主要包括以下几个方面。

(1) 税收管辖权问题。

税收管辖权问题是国际税收的重要内容之一,也是国际税收的一个基本理论与实务问题。国际税收的种种问题,诸如国际重复征税的发生、国家间税收分配关系的协调等,都与税收管辖权密切相关。同时,从公平与效率原则考虑,国际税收除了研究现存的税收管辖权的合理性与矛盾性,深入研究税收管辖权的基本理论和实际问题外,更力图探讨如何建立一种更加规范和理想的税收管辖权。

(2) 国际重复征税问题。

国际重复征税问题是国际税收的重要理论与实务问题,涉及跨国纳税人的跨国所得被两个及两个以上的国家征税的现象。这显然是不利于国际经济活动的发展的。它不仅直接影响纳税人的切身利益,而且对有关国家的财权利益有不同程度的影响。因此,国际社会有必要对各国的征税权加以协调,以防止或者缓解国际重复征税问题。在此,国际税收主要研究国际重复征税问题产生的原因、方式等,探讨解决国际重复征税问题的最佳办法。

(3) 国际避税及其防范问题。

国际避税指跨国纳税人利用不同国家税制上的不同点和漏洞、经过适当的财务安排以达到逃避或减轻其税收负担的行为。国际避税与国际重复征税的效果正好相反,它不会加重纳税人的税收负担,但却会损害有关国家的税收利益。所以,在当今跨国经营活动十分普遍的情况下,各国都把防范国际避税作为税收管理的一项重要任务。据此,国际税收重点研究跨国纳税人的国际避税手段和方法,并探讨如何建立防范国际避税的有效措施,以维护国家主权利益、公平纳税人的税收负担。

(4) 国际税收协定问题。

由于世界上还没有一种超国家的国际税法或国际税收法律制度,国家间的税收分配和协调关系只能依靠签订双边或多边税收协定来处理和规范。在过去的数十年,国际税收协定一直按几何级数不断增长,现在有3 000多个双边税收协定存在。因此,国际税收在研究现存的发达国家之间、发达国家与发展中国家之间,以及发展中国家之间签订的税收协定的基础上,探索总结解决国际税收问题的有效措施或方法,以及处理和协调国家间税收分配关系的准则和规范,促进国际经济技术合作的发展与交流。

我们知道,国际税收没有独立的征税对象和税种,而各国税收的税类也存在很大的差异性,按照课税对象的性质,一般可以将税收划分为商品税、财产税和所得税。

商品税包括增值税、消费税、营业税、关税等;财产税包括房产税、车船税等。这些流转税和个别财产税的征税对象是某个具体的商品或某项具体的财产,由于在某个时点上,其流转空间或财产存在的空间不是属于这个国家就是属于那个国家,各国对其征税一

---

① 税收外流是指跨国公司通过转让定价手段将应在一国实现的利润转移到税率较低的他国去实现,从而使前者的所得税收入流失。

般都不会越出本国疆界外，不会发生跨国家征税的问题，也就不会涉及其他国家的财权利益。再者，对商品和财产征税一般属于间接税，其税负可以转嫁，一般由商品的购买者或消费者负担税款。所以，一般不将流转税和具体财产税列入国际税收的研究范围。

但是，所得税包括以纳税人的所得额和一般财产价值为征税对象的所得税和一般财产税，如企业所得税、个人所得税、资本利得税、赠与税、遗产税和继承税，等等。这些税种的征税对象，如某一纳税人的工资收入、利润额或一般财产价值等，都是抽象的，它并不与某个具体的物直接联系，而是与这些所得或一般财产价值的所有人直接联系。这些所有人包括跨国个人和法人，从而这种归附于人的所得或一般财产价值也可以是跨国的，并有可能被他们所跨越的国家同时征税，进而产生一系列国际税收问题。

基于此，作者在本书中所谈及的国际税收主要是研究所得税以及一般财产税方面的问题。

1.1.2 国际税收与相关概念的辨析

提起国际税收，人们自然会联系到国家税收、涉外税收等概念，甚至有人将它们混为一谈，造成对国际税收概念的误解。实际上，国际税收与国家税收、国际税收与涉外税收等相关概念既有联系，又有重要区别。

1. 国际税收与国家税收

国家税收是国家凭借政治权力所进行的一种强制课征，是一国政府与其纳税人之间所发生的征纳关系。这种纳税人可以是企业，也可以是个人。一国政府政治权力管辖范围内的纳税人，不仅包括本国人，还包括外国人，所以，国际税收与国家税收之间有着不同寻常的联系和区别。

1）联系

(1) 国家税收是国际税收的基础。

国家税收征纳关系中的征税主体、征税客体、征税对象等税制要素是国际税收赖以存在的基础，如果没有各主权国家在各自国内税法中既定的各种税目、税率等的存在，也就谈不上相关国家在对同一个跨国纳税人的同一笔跨国所得同时征税时所形成的国际税收分配和协调关系，国际税收也就没有存在的土壤和基础了。

(2) 国家税收要受到国际税收的影响。

在全球化经济发展的背景下，任何一个国家税制要素的制定都不得不考虑国际经济环境的影响，特别是当一国制定国内税法时，其税法内容在一定程度上会受到他国税法的影响，特别是受到某些国际税收协定的影响。

2）区别

(1) 含义不同。

国家税收是以国家政治权力为依托的强制课征形式，而国际税收是在国家税收的基础上产生的种种税收问题和税收关系，不是凭借某种政治权力进行的强制课征形式。世界上根本不存在超越一切国家主权的国际政治权力，也没有任何一部国际税法可以被用来进行国际范围内的课征。

(2) 涉及关系不同。

国家税收涉及的是国家在征税过程中形成的国家与纳税人之间的利益分配关系，而国际税收涉及的是国家间税制相互作用所形成的国与国之间的税收分配关系和税收协调关系。

(3) 税种差异。

国家税收按课税对象的不同可以分为不同税种,而由于国际税收不是一种具体的课征形式,没有单独的税种。

2. 涉外税收与国际税收

涉外税收,是指一国政府对外国人(包括外国企业和个人)征税的各种税收的统称,反映为一国政府凭借其政治权力同其管辖权范围内的外国纳税人之间所发生的征纳关系。这种征纳关系并没有超越一国政府的管辖权范围而进入国际范围,因此,涉外税收仍然属于国家税收的范畴,它只不过是把国家税收制度中的涉外部分独立出来,单独设立了税种。而国际税收是指一国税法的国际方面,这类法律法规既可以存在于所谓的涉外税收中,也可以存在于各种非涉外税收中。

在我国,涉外税收一词通常是指专门为我国境内的外国人、外国企业或外商投资企业设置的税种。例如 1991 年开征的外商投资企业和外国企业所得税(该税从 2008 年废止)、1994 年税制改革前的工商统一税和个人所得税均属于我国的涉外税收,它们都属于国家税收的内容。

1.2 国际税收的发展趋势

国际税收与经济发展是密切相关的,其发展趋势也离不开全球经济发展的走向。一些经济学家指出,在国家间经济不断融合的世界经济大潮流中,一方面,国际税收的发展大大推动了全球经济一体化的发展;另一方面,商品、资本、技术、人员的跨国自由流动使税基变成了全球性的,不再固定于某一个国家,这给国际税收提出了新的要求,带来了新的挑战。从国际经济发展的方向来看,未来的国际税收将出现以下几个发展趋势。

1.2.1 在商品课税领域,增值税和消费税的国际协调将逐步取代关税的国际协调成为商品课税国际协调的核心内容

在商品课税国际协调的历史进程中,关税的国际协调一直是一个核心内容。但是,在第二次世界大战后,经过关贸总协定①主持的八轮关税减让谈判,各国的关税税率大幅度下降。从理论上看,国际经济的不断融合要求各国彻底取消进出口关税。但是事实上,越来越多的国家为了弥补关税下降给财政造成的收入损失,开征了增值税并继续完善其原有的消费税,将其作为关税的替代财源。这样一方面可以增加财政收入;另一方面,这些国内税种在一定条件下也可以被用来替代关税充当贸易壁垒。例如,一些欧洲国家过去对从拉美国家进口的香蕉征收高消费税,以及北欧国家对国外进口的葡萄酒征收高消费税,而对本国出产的威士忌酒征收低消费税,这实际上就是在利用消费税充当保护本国产品的工具。然而,在未来国际经济关系十分紧密的情况下,这种用国内商品税替代关税保护贸易的做法是不能被国际社会所接受的,如果出现这种情况,国际社会也应该像协调关税那样协调有关国家的国内商品税。因此,增值税和消费税的国际协调将逐步取代关税的国际协

---

① 关贸总协定即关税及贸易总协定,它既是一个规范国际贸易组织行为的法律框架,又是一个事实上的贸易合作组织,也是一个多边贸易谈判的场所。

调成为商品课税国际协调的核心内容。

1.2.2　在所得课税领域，国与国之间的税收竞争将更为激烈。为了防止"财政降格"的情况发生，国际社会有必要对各国资本所得的课税制度进行协调

在跨国资本可自由流动的背景下，资本的逐利性决定了其必然流向税后利润更高的国家。一国为了把别国的资本吸引到本国以增加其所得税的税基，就必须降低资本所得的适用税率，这实际上是一种"损人利己"的行为。不过，他国一旦发现这种情况发生，也会降低本国的所得税税率，这就造成了所谓的所得税的"国际竞争"。它是国与国之间所得税的一种非合作性协调，会使各国的所得税税率下降到一个不合理的水平，造成国家财政实力的大幅度下降，即出现所谓的"财政降格"。

所得税国际竞争一旦爆发，如果国际社会不加以干预，它就有可能持续下去，给各国造成一定的损失，而且在不久的将来，很有可能使对所得和资本的课税不复存在，政府只能依靠一些国内商品税维持开支需求了。防止所得税国际竞争的最佳办法是对各国所得税的税率和税基进行协调。

1.2.3　随着地区性国际经济一体化的不断发展，区域性的国际税收协调将会有更为广阔的前景。各国之间将加强税收征管方面的国际合作，共同对付跨国纳税人的国际避税和偷税行为

从目前世界经济的发展趋势看，未来的全球经济一体化首会从区域经济一体化开始，而区域经济一体化的发展一定离不开区域范围内的税收国际协调。实际上，没有区域国际税收协调就没有区域国际经济一体化。例如，自由贸易区和关税同盟的建立都要求协调成员国的关税，共同市场的建立要求协调成员国的国内商品税和资本所得税。中国和东盟在 2010 年建立了世界上涵盖人口最多的自由贸易区，双方 90% 的贸易产品将实现零关税。随着今后区域国际经济一体化的发展，不仅会有更多的国家参与到区域性国际税收协调的活动中来，而且区域性税收国际协调的深度和税种范围也会不断扩大。在此基础上，为反制跨国纳税人的避税和偷税行为，并解决跨国纳税人面临的国际双重征税等问题，各国税务部门将进一步加强税收征管方面的国际合作，就税收情报交换、税收事务相互协助等方面进行更为广泛的税务稽查合作。

1.2.4　国际税收由非规范化阶段向规范化阶段发展

很早以前，国际税收问题的解决往往是一国从其国内税法角度出发，单方面从本国税制的修订方面中找出一些解决措施，或是签订一些双边的税收协定进行协调，这属于国际税收发展的非规范化阶段。但是，随着国际经济交流的迅速扩大，以及纳税人所得的国际化和所得税的广泛运用，上述单方面的处理方式和非规范性的双边税收协定已经不能适应形势发展的需要，国际社会迫切需要一个比较完整的规范性的国际税收协调办法，来指导各国处理相互间的税收分配关系。为此，经济合作与发展组织（以下简称"经合发组织"）于 1963 年制定公布，并于 1977 年修订发表了《关于对所得税和资本避免双重征税的协定范本》（以下简称《经合发范本》）；联合国税收协定专家小组也于 1968 年制定，并于 1979 年公布了《关于发达国家与发展中国家间避免双重征税的协定范本》（以下简称《联合国范本》）。这两个国际税收协定范本虽然对各国政府并没有法律上的约束力，但

在事实上已经起到了重要的示范作用，成了各国处理相关税收分配关系的准则。它们的产生使国家间的税收分配关系规范化，是国际税收从非规范化阶段向规范化阶段发展的重要标志。

1.2.5 随着电子商务（数字经济）的发展，国际税收领域将出现许多新的课题，亟待各国政府和国际社会加以研究解决

在电子商务交易中，客户所在国（所得来源国）是否应对国外销售商的经营所得征税；在电子商务交易中，交易所得的性质和类别有时会难以确定，从而给在相关国家之间区分征税权带来了一定困难；在电子商务条件下，纳税人的国际偷税和避税活动会更加隐蔽，从而要求国际社会尽快研究制止纳税人偷税和避税行为的办法。对于这些新的情况，国际社会必须尽快拿出一套有效的解决办法。在经合发组织 2015 年 10 月发布的应对税基侵蚀和利润转移的 15 个行动计划中，第一个就是关于数字经济的，但遗憾的是，这个行动计划并未拿出一个切实可行的解决方案。

复习思考题

1. 什么是国际税收？它的本质是什么？
2. 国际税收与国家税收的联系和区别是什么？
3. 如何辨析国际税收和涉外税收？
4. 国际税收的研究范围包括哪些？
5. 国际税收未来的发展趋势是什么？

第 2 章

所得税的税收管辖权

时政观点

1. 切实维护我国的税收管辖权，国家主权神圣不可侵犯。
2. 纳税主体应当持守纳税信用、合法合规纳税。

学习目标

1. 重点掌握税收管辖权的概念及所得税税收管辖权的类型。
2. 辨析理解各种税收管辖权的判定标准。
3. 区分居民与非居民的纳税义务。
4. 了解各国所得税税收管辖权的实施现状。

课程导入

在英国，一个没有固定住处的流浪汉经常睡在公园里或马路便道上，他是英国的税收居民吗？

2.1 税收管辖权及其确立原则

2.1.1 税收管辖权的定义

国际税收存在的种种问题，诸如国际重复征税的发生，国家间税收分配关系的协调等，都与有关国家的税收管辖权密切相关。研究税收管辖权问题是解决国际税收问题的重要前提。

税收管辖权，是指国家在税收领域中的主权，是一国政府行使主权征税所拥有的管理权力，它表现在一国政府有权决定对哪些人征税、征哪些税以及征多少税等方面。税收管辖权具有独立性和排他性，它意味着一个国家在征税方面行使权力具有完全自主性，在处理本国税务时不受外界的干涉和控制。

2.1.2 税收管辖权的确立原则

一个主权国家的政治权力所能达到的范围主要包括两个方面：一方面，从地域的概念来说，它包括该国领土、领海、领空内的全部空间；另一方面，从人的概念来说，它包括该国所有的公民或居民（包括个人和法人）。由于税收管辖权是国家主权的重要组成部分，国家就有权选择上述两种不同的概念作为其确立税收管辖权的原则，于是就产生了属地主义原则与属人主义原则。

1. 属地主义原则

属地主义原则是以纳税人的收入来源地或经济活动所在地为标准确定国家行使税收管辖权范围的一种原则。

根据属地主义原则，一国政府只能对在其主权范围内来源的所得或发生的经济行为行使其课税权力，即只对纳税人来自本国境内的收入或在本国境内从事的经济活动依照本国税法规定征税，而对纳税人来自国外的收入不予征税。谈到对所得税的征收，根据属地主义原则，一国政府有权对来源于本国境内的一切所得征税，而不论取得这笔所得的是本国人还是外国人。

国家一般对间接税采取属地主义原则，对于所得税则有所不同，对非居民纳税人采取属地主义原则，而对居民纳税人则采取属人主义原则。

2. 属人主义原则

属人主义原则是以纳税人的国籍和住所为标准，对本国的全部公民和居民确立行使税收管辖权范围的一种原则。

根据属人主义原则，一国政府有权对本国居民或公民的一切所得征税，而不论他们的所得是来源于本国还是外国。属人主义原则通常适用于直接税类的所得税、遗产税等。

2.1.3 所得税税收管辖权的类型

对于税收管辖权的确立和行使，国际上并没有统一规定，各主权国家都有权根据本国的政治经济状况和财政政策来自行决定。一国的所得税税收管辖权可以按照属地主义原则和属人主义原则两种不同的原则来确立，从而也就有收入来源地税收管辖权与居民或公民税收管辖权之分，其中收入来源地税收管辖权和居民税收管辖权是两个基本的税收管辖权。

1. 收入来源地管辖权

收入来源地管辖权是按照属地主义原则确立的税收管辖权，指一国政府只对来自或被认为是来自本国境内的所得拥有征税权力，也称地域管辖权。

一国根据税法对所得可以征税的原因，是该国与产生所得的活动之间存在一种联结关系。按照国际用法，基于这种联结的管辖要求权被称为"来源地管辖权"。所有开征所得税的国家都行使来源地管辖权，即对发生于或来源于本国的所得征税。

2. 居民管辖权

居民管辖权是按照属人主义原则确立的税收管辖权，指一国政府对于本国居民（包括个人和法人）的全部所得拥有征税权。

一国可以基于本国与取得所得的人之间存在的联系对居民所得征税。基于国家与被课征人之间的这种联系而对所得提出的管辖要求权被称为"居民管辖权"。一般来讲，受某国居民管辖权管辖的被课征人应就其全球所得纳税，而无论所得的来源如何。也就是说，此人对于来自境内的所得和来自境外的所得都必须纳税。

3. 公民管辖权

公民管辖权是按照属人主义原则确立的税收管辖权，是指一国政府对拥有本国国籍的公民来自国内外的全部所得都拥有征税权。

2.2 收入来源地管辖权判定标准

在实行收入来源地税收管辖权的国家，所考虑的不是收入者的居住地或纳税人的身份，而是其收入的来源地，即以纳税人的收入来源地为依据，确定征税与否，因此，有"从源课税"之说。可见，收入来源地管辖权的特征是只对来自本国境内的收入征税，而不对来自境外的收入征税。由于这一税收管辖权既体现了国际间经济利益分配的合理性，又体现了税务行政管理的方便性，故已得到世界各国公认，并被普遍采用。

收入来源地即纳税人取得收入的地点，它是一国政府对纳税人行使收入来源地管辖权的依据和标准。一国在对某人取得的收入或所得征税时，必须首先明确该项收入或所得是否确实来源于其境内。从某国境内取得收入是指该项收入来源于该国境内，而不论其支付地点是否在该国境内。收入来源地和收入支付地是两个不同的概念，两者有时一致，有时不一致。有些收入虽然来源于一国，但不一定都在该国境内支付。例如，在我国境内工作的外籍人员，其工资、薪金所得来源于我国，但由其雇主在国外支付；我国政府派往国外工作人员的工资报酬，虽然由我国支付，但其来源是国外。针对个人收入来源地与支付地存在着不相一致的情况，各国税法都明确规定，凡从本国境内取得的收入，不论是在本国支付，还是在国外支付，都属于来源于本国的收入，都要依法征收个人所得税。由此可见，对于收入来源地管辖权的行使，关键的问题在于收入来源地的确定，即如何对收入的来源地做出合理与科学的解释，以便确定纳税人与本国有无收入来源地的联结因素，最终确定纳税人取得的收入是否来源于本国境内，若来源于本国境内，则有本国纳税义务；若来源于本国境外，则无本国纳税义务。这个问题不仅投资者、跨国纳税人关注，也是国际税收需要协调规范的核心问题之一。但是，收入来源地的确定，必须借助一定的标准，由于收入的项目不同，如经营所得、劳务所得、投资所得、其他所得等，各国采用的收入来源地判定标准也有所区别。

2.2.1 经营所得来源地的确定

经营所得就是营业利润，它是个人或公司法人从事各项生产性或非生产性经营活动所取得的纯收益。一笔所得是否为纳税人的经营所得，主要看取得这项收入的经营活动是否为纳税人的主要经济活动。例如，一家证券公司因从事证券投资而取得的股息、利息收入属于该公司的经营所得，而一家制造业公司因持有其他公司的股权、债权而取得的股息、利息收入就不属于其经营所得。目前，各国在判定经营所得的来源地时主要使用以下两种标准。

1. 常设机构标准（PE 标准）

常设机构即固定场所或固定基地，是指一个企业进行全部或部分经营活动的固定营业场所。其范围很广，包括管理机构、分支机构、办事处、工厂、车间、矿场、油井、气井、采石场、建筑工地等。属于大陆法系的国家多采用常设机构标准来判定纳税人的经营所得是否来自本国。

一般来说，常设机构必须具备以下三个基本条件。

①常设机构必须是一个营业场所，这种场所并没有任何规模上的限制。通常是指用于从事营业活动的所有房屋、场地、设备或设施，如机器设备、仓库、摊位等，并且不论是其自有的还是租用的。

②常设机构必须是固定的，必须在某个特定的地理位置营业，而且在该地的营业行为要超过一定的时间（一般要超过 6 个月），不包括没有确定地点所进行的营业活动。但在确定地点进行的营业活动有暂时的间断或停顿，不影响其常设机构的存在。因此，这一基本条件是该营业场所具有相对的固定性或永久性，而非临时性，即要足以表明它是常设的。

③常设机构必须是企业用于进行全部或部分营业活动的场所，而不是为本企业从事非营业性质的准备活动或辅助性活动的场所。

根据常设机构标准，如果一个非居民公司在本国有常设机构，而且通过该常设机构取得了经营所得，来源国就可以判定这笔经营所得来源于本国，并对这笔所得征税。反之，如果非居民公司在本国没有设立常设机构，该国就不能认定非居民公司的经营所得是来自于本国，因此也就不能对非居民公司的这笔经营所得行使征税权。可见，在采用常设机构标准的国家，非居民公司的经营所得是否要被征税，关键取决于该居民公司在该国是否设立了常设机构。

不过，这里还有一个问题：如果一个非居民公司在本国设有常设机构，但其经营所得并不是通过这个常设机构取得的，那么该国要不要对这笔经营所得征税？在这个问题上，目前各国主要奉行两种原则：一是实际所得原则（又称归属原则），即一国只对非居民公司通过本国常设机构实际取得的经营所得征税，对其通过本国常设机构以外的途径或方式取得的经营所得不征税。二是引力原则，即如果一家非居民公司在本国设有常设机构，即使它在本国从事的一些经营活动没有通过这个常设机构，但只要这些经营活动与这个常设机构所从事的业务活动相同或类似，那么这些没有通过该常设机构取得的经营所得也要被归并到常设机构的总所得中，在当地一并纳税。

我国判定经营所得来源地实际上也采用常设机构标准。同时，我国在对外国企业征税时不实行"引力原则"。《中华人民共和国企业所得税法》第三条第二款规定："非居民企业在中国境内设立机构、场所的，应当就其所设机构、场所所取得的来源于中国境内的所得，缴纳企业所得税。"第三条第三款规定："非居民企业在中国境内未设立机构、场所的，或者虽设立机构、场所但取得的所得与其所设机构、场所没有实际联系的，应当就其来源于中国境内的所得缴纳企业所得税。"第四条规定："企业所得税的税率为25%。""非居民企业取得本法第三条第三款规定的所得，适用税率为20%。"上述法律表明：如果非居民企业在我国境内没有设立机构、场所，而是直接与我国境内的单位或个人签订合同开展经营活动（如销售产品），其取得的所得就不能认定为是来源于中国境内的经营所得，我国也不能对这种所得行使收入来源地税收管辖权。例如，一家美国公司在中国没有设立任何机构，2018 年，它直接向中国一家企业销售了一台价款为 100 万元的机器，取得销售利润 10 万元。根据常设机构标准，这 10 万元所得的来源地不在中国，因此美国公司不需要向中国政府缴纳企业所得税。但如果该公司在中国设立了办事处，并通过这个办事处向中国这家企业销售了机器，那么这 10 万元的销售利润就应当在中国申报纳税。

2. 交易地点标准

英美法系的国家一般并不采用常设机构标准来确定经营所得的来源地，而是比较侧重用交易地点来判定经营所得的来源地。例如，英国的法律规定，只有在英国进行交易所取得的收入才属于来源于英国的所得。这里的交易泛指各类贸易、制造等经营活动。在确定贸易活动是否在英国国内进行时，主要依据合同的订立地点是否在英国，而对于制造利润则是以制造活动发生地为所得的来源地。加拿大与英国的规定类似，只是以合同签订的习惯性地点作为交易的地点。美国税法也规定，在美国从事贸易或经营活动所取得的利润属于来源于美国的所得。但美国判定贸易利润来源地时是以货物的实际销售地为来源地，并不注重合同签订的地点，这与英国和加拿大等国略有不同。在判定制造利润来源地时，美国与英国一样，也是以产品制造加工活动的地点为所得来源地。

2.2.2 劳务所得来源地的确定

按照劳务所得是否依赖于雇佣或受聘情况，可将其分为独立劳务所得和非独立劳务所得。独立劳务所得，是指自由职业者从事专业性劳务或者其他独立性活动所取得的报酬。"专业性劳务"即个人独立从事非雇佣的各种劳动，包括医师、律师、工程师、建筑师、牙医师、会计师的劳务，也包括独立的科学、文化、艺术、教育或教学活动。独立劳务所得具有独立性和随意性。非独立劳务所得，是指个人受雇于雇主而取得的工资、薪金和其他报酬等。

各国判定劳务所得来源地的标准主要有以下三种。

1. 劳务提供地标准

劳务提供地标准是指跨国纳税人在哪个国家提供劳务或在哪个国家工作，其获得的劳务报酬即为来源于那个国家的所得。该标准对从事独立劳务者而言，主要看其从事活动的固定基地在哪个国家。如果个人在某个国家设有固定基地，如诊疗所、事务所等，并且所得是通过该固定基地取得的，这个国家就可以认定该项所得来源于其境内。对从事非独立劳务者而言，则主要看他们的受雇地点，他们在哪个国家受雇，哪个国家就是非独立劳务所得的来源国。

2. 劳务所得支付者标准

劳务所得支付者标准是指以支付劳务所得的纳税人或固定基地、常设机构的所在国为劳务所得的来源国。如果某跨国纳税人的劳务所得是由某国的居民或设在该国的常设机构、固定基地支付的，该国就是这项劳务所得的来源国。

3. 劳务合同签订地标准

劳务合同签订地标准是指以劳务合同签订的地点来判定受雇劳务所得的来源地。

目前，许多国家采用劳务提供地标准，即按劳务行为的发生地判定劳务所得的来源地。例如，《中华人民共和国个人所得税法实施条例》第五条规定："凡因任职、受雇、履约等原因而在中国境内提供劳务的所得，不论支付地点是否在中国境内，均为来源于中国境内的所得，都应当按照税法规定纳税。"再如，《中华人民共和国企业所得税法实施条例》第七条规定："劳务所得按照劳务发生地确定来源地"。美国税法的规定与中国类似，即只要是在美国境内提供劳务，由此获得的所得就属于来源于美国的所得，而不论雇主和雇员的国籍、居住地或所得支付地是否在美国。但也有一些国家采用劳务所得支付者标准判定劳务所得的来源地。例如，英国的法院就一直坚持就业所得的来源地应为劳务所得的支付地。此外，巴西也使用劳务所得支付者标准来判定劳务所得的来源地。使用劳务合同签订地标准的国家主要包括爱尔兰等国。

2.2.3 投资所得来源地的确定

投资所得是指投资者将其资金、财产或权利提供给他人使用所获取的报酬所得，主要包括股息、利息、特许权使用费和租金所得等。其中，股息是投资者因拥有股权以及其他与股权相似的公司权利而取得的所得；利息是投资者凭借各种债权而取得的所得；特许权使用费是指投资者因向他人提供专利权、商标权、商誉、版权、经销权、专有技术或其他的无形资产的使用权而取得的所得；租金是财产出租人向财产承租人收取的财产使用费。

投资所得具有支付人相对稳定，而受益人比较零散的特点。尤其是在跨国进行间接投资的情况下，投资者并不一定在投资项目所在国活动或居住。当投资所得的取得者和支付者，如债权人和债务人、特许权的提供者和使用者等都在同一个国家境内时，对这类投资所得来源地的确定并不困难，即来源于该国境内。但是，如果这种权利的提供者和使用者并不在同一个国家，而是分别在不同的国家，我们该如何来确定这类投资所得的来源地呢？这在有些国家之间，特别是在发达国家与发展中国家之间，观点极不一致。为了提高资本转移的流动性，发达国家一般主张这类所得的来源地是权利的提供方所在地，应由这类权利的提供方所在国独自征税。但是一些发展中国家则相反，为了强调减少外汇流失，认为这类所得的来源地是这类权利的使用方所在地，主张由支付股息、利息和特许权使用费的国家行使收入来源地管辖权，即由这类权利的使用方所在国征税。

为此，国际社会通常是按利益共享原则合理划分这类权利的提供方和使用方双方国家的征税权。《联合国协定范本》规定投资所得可以由这类权利的提供方所在国征税，也可以由这类权利的使用方所在国行使收入来源地管辖权，即双方国家都有权征税。但是，由这类权利的使用方所在国征税时，要有一个最高额度的规定，以便给这类权利的提供方所在国留有征税的余地。这种最高额度，通常需要通过协定国家谈判加以确定。例如，我国在与日本的税收协定中规定：对于发生在中国，支付给日本居民的股息、利息、特许权使用费所得，如果收款人是实际收益人，则可认为上述各项所得来源于中国，中国政府可以对这些所得征税，但所征税款不应超过各项所得总额的10%。

如果股息、利息、特许权使用费是通过常设机构取得的，则它们应当并入该常设机构营业利润中，按一般企业所得税税率征税。对没有通过常设机构而获得的这类投资所得，一般都由收入来源地所在国按其毛收入征收一笔较低税率的预提所得税。所谓毛收入即指不扣减费用的收入额，较低的预提所得税即指各国单独采取的、比公司所得税税率更低的比例税率。这样，一方面保证了有关国家分享征税的权力；另一方面在确定税率时已考虑了征税时应扣除的成本因素，因此，其税基仍然是对这类投资活动的净收入的征税。

2.2.4 财产所得来源地的确定

财产所得是指纳税人因拥有、使用、转让手中的财产而取得的所得或收益（资本利得）。

对于不动产所得，各国一般均以不动产的实际所在地为不动产所得的来源地，如《中华人民共和国企业所得税法实施条例》第七条规定："不动产所得的来源地按照不动产所在地确定"。

对于动产所得，各国判定其来源地的标准却并不完全一致。有的国家以动产的销售或转让地（动产所有权的过户地点）为来源地（如在 1986 年以前，美国就采用这种规则）；有的国家以动产转让者的居住地为来源地（如目前美国对转让或销售股票、债券、商品和其他投资性动产的收益就采用转让人居住地标准判定其来源地）；还有一些国家以被转让动产的实际所在地为来源地。我国对动产转让所得来源地的判定采用转让地标准和转让者居住地标准。《中华人民共和国个人所得税法实施条例》第五条规定："在中国境内转让其他财产（指建筑物、土地使用权等以外的动产）取得的所得为来源于中国境内的所得。"《中华人民共和国企业所得税法实施条例》第七条则规定："动产转让所得的来源地按转让动产的企业或者机构所在地确定；权益性投资资产转让所得的来源地按照被投资企业所在地确定。"

2.2.5 遗产继承所得来源地的确定

对于跨国取得的遗产继承所得，其来源地的确定，国际上通常视不同情况予以确定。凡以不动产或有形动产为继承物的，以其遗产所在地作为其来源地，并由遗产所在国对遗产所得行使收入来源地管辖权征税；凡以股票或债权为继承物的，则以其发行者或债务人的居住国为其来源地，并由居住国对遗产所得行使收入来源地管辖权，进行征税。

2.3 居民管辖权判定标准

一个国家行使居民管辖权时所考虑的已不再是收入或所得的来源地，而是纳税人的居民身份。它是以纳税人是否居住在本国或拥有居民身份为依据，确定对其是否行使课税权力及征税范围。一般来说，凡是本国的居民（包括个人和法人），不论其收入或所得包括多少种类，也不管其所得或收入来自本国还是外国，居住国政府都有权对其来自世界各地的全部所得进行征税。可见，居民管辖权的特征是对本国居民纳税人来自国内外的所得同等课税。

居民，是指由于住所、居所、管理场所或其他类似性质的标准，在某国负有纳税义务的个人和法人，即在税收领域中，与一个国家发生人身联结关系而负有纳税义务的人。就个人而言，这里所谓的税收居民与居住管理法规中的居民概念是不同的。因为许多国家都有居住管理法，外籍公民要在本国合法居住必须持有本国政府颁发的居住许可证，否则就是非法居住，不是本国的合法居民。但税收征管中的居民概念强调的是纳税人在本国长期居住的事实，它不属于居住管理法的范畴。也就是说，一个纳税人即使没有居住许可证而在本国长期居住，也可以成为税收意义上的居民。为了与居住管理法意义上的居民相区别，人们有时就把税法意义上的居民称为财政居民。后文提到的居民概念都是指财政居民。

居民身份的确定必须借助于一定的标准。世界各国对判定纳税人居民身份的标准不尽相同。

2.3.1 个人居民身份的判定标准

对于个人而言，居民是与参观者或游客相对应的概念。某人是一国的居民，意味着他已在该国居住了较长的时间或打算在该国长期居住，而不是以过境客的身份对该国做短暂的访问或逗留。对个人居民身份的理想判定方法应使个人在适用后可以获得清楚、确定和公平的结果。确定性是非常必要的,因为居民和非居民的税收差别非常大,个人需要知道自己是居民还是非居民。就各国的具体情况来看,个人居民身份的判定一般是通过以下三种标准反映出来的。

1. 法律标准

法律标准也称意愿标准,指纳税人在行使居民管辖权的国家内有居住的主观意愿的,即为该国居民。也就是说,凡在一国有不定期居住意愿,并依法取得入境护照、移居签证和各种居留证明的外国侨民,都属于该国居民。该国政府都有权对其来源于世界各地的全部所得进行征税。非上述范围者则为非居民,该国政府不得对其行使居民管辖权。

教学案例 2-1

在1984年以前,美国判定进入其境内的外国人是过路客还是居民时的决定因素便是个人的居住愿望。1984年后,美国对取得在美永久居留权的外国人,即所谓的"绿卡"持有者,在税收上视为居民。即使该人不在美国居住,从其获得"绿卡"次年的1月1日起,也将成为美国的税收居民。因为持有"绿卡"这一行为本身就表明该人在美国有长期居住愿望。

教学案例 2-2

希腊的税法规定,一个人有在希腊安家的意向,他就成了希腊的税收居民。英国法律也规定,一个成年人的住所要取决于他或她的永久居住意愿。20世纪70年代在英国就有这方面的一个案例。例如,一位先生1910年出生在加拿大。1932年,他加入了英国空军,并于1959年退役,随后一直在英国一家私人研究机构工作,直到1961年正式退休,而且退休后他与英国妻子继续在英格兰生活。在此期间,这位先生一直保留了他的加拿大国籍和护照,并经常与加拿大有金融方面的往来,而且他也希望与妻子一同回加拿大安度晚年,并表示如果妻子比他先去世,自己也要回加拿大度过余生。法院判定这位先生尽管在英国居住了44年,却不是英国的税收居民。

2. 住所标准

住所标准也称户籍标准,指纳税人在行使居民管辖权的国家内拥有永久性住所或习惯性居所的,即为该国居民,该国政府有权对其来自世界各地的所得进行征税。没有在该国拥有住所的人则为非居民,该国政府不能对其行使居民管辖权。

所谓住所即永久性住处,通常是指一个人长期而不是暂时占有的居住场所。住所必须是外表上显而易见的,它一般是一个人的家庭(配偶、子女)所在地或重要财产的所在地。按照住所这一概念,凡是住所在本国境内的个人,均为本国居民,需要承担本国的无限纳税义务;否则,将视其为本国非居民,本国政府对其免予行使居民管辖权。日本、德国等国家都采用了这一标准。

住所也是我国判定个人税收居民身份的一项重要标准。《中华人民共和国个人所得税法》第一条规定:"在中国境内有住所,或者无住所而在境内居住满183天的个人,从中国境内和境外取得的所得,依照本法规定缴纳个人所得税。"另外,《中华人民共和国个人所得税法实施条例》第二条规定:"在中国境内有住所的个人是指因户籍、家庭、经济利益关系而在中国境内习惯性居住的个人。"这表明,我国税法判定个人住所依据的是个人的"习惯性居住地"。这里的"在中国习惯性居住",是指个人在中国以外的学习、工作、探亲、旅游等活动结束后必然要返回中国境内居住,而不一定指个人在中国境内实际居住。也就是说,只要某人的习惯性居住地在中国境内,那么在某个纳税年度中,即使该个人实际并没有在中国境内居住,其在中国境内仍属于有住所,在该纳税年度中,他仍属于中国的居民纳税人。

3. 居所标准

所谓"居所",即习惯性住所,一般是指一个人在某国境内持续停留一段时期而临时居住的处所。它是纳税人不定期居住的场所,即为某种目的,如经商、求学、谋生等而非长期性居住的处所。居所可以是纳税人的自有房屋,也可以是其租用的公寓、旅馆等。由于居所是确定纳税义务的一个重要标志,所以在一些国家税法中又将其称为"财政住所"。采用居所标准的国家主要有英国、德国、加拿大、澳大利亚等国。

与住所相比,居所在许多国家并没有一个严格的法律定义,因而各国对居所的认识和判定标准并不一致。但一般认为,居所与住所至少有两点区别。

(1) 住所是个人的久住之地,而居所只是人们因某种原因而暂住或客居之地。

(2) 住所通常涉及一种意图,即某人打算将某地作为其永久性居住地,而居所通常是指供个人长期有效使用的房产,该标准强调的是人们居住的事实,即某人在某地已经居住了较长时间或有条件长时期居住,但并不强调其在此长期居住的意愿。

教学案例 2-3

英国规定,凡在英国拥有住宅者,不论其居住时间长短,只要在纳税年度内曾在英国停留,就应当确定为英国居民。德国规定,在住所和习惯性居所两项中,只要有一项存在,就足以构成个人的纳税住处而成为德国居民。其中"习惯性居所"规定,只要个人在德国逗留 3 个月以上,便被视为在德国拥有习惯性居所,便可被认定为德国居民。

4. 时间标准

时间标准也称停留时间标准或居住时间标准,指个人在行使居民管辖权的国家内居住或停留超过一定时间的,即成为该国居民,该国政府有权对其来自世界各地的所得进行征税。没有达到规定居住期限的人则为非居民,该国政府不能对其行使居民管辖权。采用时间标准确定个人居民身份的国家则相对较多,如英国、德国、日本、法国、印度、瑞士、中国等。这一标准强调的是当事人在某一纳税年度中是否待在本国及待多长时间,而不论他待在什么地方。正如 1928 年英国某法院在审理一桩纳税案件时指出,一个人即使是没有固定住处的流浪汉,经常睡在公园里或马路便道上,他也可以属于税收居民。

但是,各国在采取时间标准确定个人居民身份时,关于居住时间或期限的具体规定和要求不尽一致。例如英国、德国、加拿大、中国等规定居住超过 183 天的个人,即为该国居民;日本、韩国、阿根廷等规定居住达 365 天以上的个人,为该国居民。然而,即便是在采用同一居住时间或期限的不同国家,在居住时间的计算上也存在着一些差异。这主要表现在以下三个方面。

1) 连续与累计计算居住时间的差别

一些采用时间标准的国家规定,跨国个人只有在本国境内连续居住时间超过税法规定时间,才成为本国居民纳税人。例如,我国税法规定,在中国境内累计居住满 183 天以上的个人，不论属于哪国国籍，均为中国居民个人。有些国家则规定，跨国个人只要在本国境内累计居住时间超过税法规定时间，即为本国居民纳税人。例如日本规定，在日本境内连续或累计居住达 1 年以上的个人为日本居民。

2) 计算居住期间起讫点的差别

一些国家以跨国个人在一个纳税年度内居住在本国境内的时间是否达到本国税法规定的时间为准来判断个人的居民身份。如果一个人的居住时间虽然超过了该国税法规定的时间，但分跨两个纳税年度，而且任何一个纳税年度均未达到规定的时间，则不能将其确认为该国的居民纳税人。如我国税法规定，在我国境内居住满 183 天的个人，是指在一个纳税年度内，在我国境内累计居住满 183 天的个人。在纳税年度内临时离境①的，不扣除离境天数。另一些国家则以个人在本国居住的实际天数达到本国规定的时间为准。只要居住时间达到本国税法规定的时间，即为本国居民纳税人。至于是否在一个纳税年度内住满法定时间则无关紧要，即只要在一个日历年度或一个会计年度以及任何 12 个月内住满法定时间，均可被确认为居民。

3) 各国规定的差别

在使用停留时间标准时，税法必须明确停留天数的计算方法。在这个问题上，各国的规定不尽相同。

多数国家（如美国）规定，在本国停留不足 1 天的按 1 天计算，即只要某人 1 天之中在本国待了几个小时甚至几分钟都要按 1 天来计算；也有的国家（如爱尔兰）规定，只有在本国停留到午夜时分的才按 1 天计算；还有的国家（如英国）以小时为单位计算停留时间，只有在本国停留的小时数相加达到了 24 小时才算停留了 1 天。我国个人所得税法对此也有相关的规定。在计算无住所的个人在中国居住天数时，在中国境内停留当天满 24 小时的，计入在中国境内的居住天数。上述计算在我国境内"停留天数"的规定十分重要，因为这时多算 1 天或少算 1 天很可能会改变在我国无住所个人的居民身份，从而影响其在我国的纳税义务。

在上述 3 种标准中，法律标准（也叫意愿标准）属于主观范畴，难以准确断定，所以各国一般不单独采用这一标准，而是与其他标准结合使用。比如，在巴西，凡是住满 1 年的人均为巴西居民，而不问其居住意愿。但对于已取得长期居住签证的外国人，如果愿意成为巴西居民，其居住期虽不满 1 年，在税收上也可视其为巴西居民。住所标准由于住所具有固定性和永久性，因此易于确定纳税人居民身份。然而，在所得税法中确定一个纳税人的居民身份，应该更多地考虑到纳税人的实际经济活动场所。住所作为一种法定的个人永久性居住场所，并不一定反映一个人的真实活动场所。个人脱离住所而长期在外居住的现象，在科技人员国际交流频繁的今天日益明显。显然，单纯按住所标准确定纳税人居民身份是有明显缺陷的。因此，有些国家采用其他辅助性的规定来弥补住所标准的不足。与住所标准相比，用居所作为确定个人居民身份的标准，在较大程度上反映了个人与其主要经济活动场所之间的联系，所以比住所标准显得更为合理。但是，居所标准的不足之处在于，个人经常居住的场所往往由于缺乏某种客观统一的识别标志，在有关国家的税法中本身是个不甚明确的概念，因而在实际运用中尚有较大的弹性，容易引起纳税人与各国税务当局之间的纷争。相比之下，时间标准显得具体明确，易于在实践中掌握执行，但它所规

---

① 临时离境，是指在一个纳税年度中一次不超过 30 日或者多次累计不超过 90 日的离境。

定的居住时间长短往往与居民管辖权的行使范围成反比。可见，上述 3 种确定个人居民身份的标准各有优缺点。正因为如此，许多国家在实践中往往兼用两种或两种以上标准，将这些标准结合使用，以便准确认定个人的居民身份，更好地行使居民管辖权。我国目前就同时采用住所标准和时间标准判定纳税人的居民身份。《中华人民共和国个人所得税法》第一条规定："在中国境内有住所，或者无住所而在境内累计居住满 183 天的个人，从中国境内和境外取得的所得，依照本法规定缴纳个人所得税。"

2.3.2 法人居民身份的判定标准

法人是与个人相区别又相对应的一种民事法律关系的主体，它一般是指依照有关国家法律和法定程序成立的，有必要的财产和组织机构，能够独立享有民事权利和承担民事义务并能在法院起诉、应诉的社会组织。类似于对个人征税，一个实行居民管辖权的国家在对法人征税时首先也要确定其是否为本国的居民。目前，各国判定法人的居民身份主要有以下几个标准。

1. 注册地标准

注册地标准又称法律标准，即凡是按照本国的法律在本国注册成立的法人都是本国的法人居民，而不论该法人的总机构、管理机构或业务活动地是否在本国境内，公司的注册地也被称为"法律住所"。注册地标准的一个明显的优点是容易操作（因为公司的注册地点是唯一的，并且很容易识别），对政府和纳税人来说既简便又具确定性，它允许纳税人自由选择其最初的居民地。以避税港来吸引投资者的国家一般都提供在他们的法律框架下成立公司的简便和成本低廉的安排，但是它却不利于法人通过移居来进行避税。一般来讲，一个公司不可能随意地变更其公司组建地点而不招致对其资产——包括市场价值很高的无形资产——所产生收益的征税。这就制约了企业通过转换其居民国而避税的能力。因此，许多国家采用注册地标准。

采用登记注册标准的国家有美国、英国、日本、法国、德国、比利时、意大利、挪威、新西兰、澳大利亚、芬兰、瑞典、瑞士、丹麦、印度、泰国、中国等。例如，美国税法规定，凡属按照美国任何一个州的法律向州政府注册设立的跨国公司，不论其总管理机构是否设立在美国，也不论是美国人还是外国人开设的，均为美国居民公司，美国对其来自世界各地的所得均拥有征税权。

2. 管理机构所在地标准

管理机构所在地标准是指在行使居民管辖权的国家内设有管理机构的法人，即为该国的居民法人。只要一个法人的管理机构设在本国，那么无论其在哪个国家注册成立，都是本国的法人居民。公司的管理机构所在地有时也被称为"财政住所"，但是由于公司的管理机构很容易迁移，而且管理机构迁移一般不会引发资产增值的纳税义务，所以管理机构所在地标准容易被公司法人利用进行避税。例如，我们假设 M 公司是在 A 国管理的一家公司，A 国采用管理机构所在地标准。M 公司开发了高市值的无形资产，并打算许可给位于 B 国的纳税人使用。为逃避 A 国对将收取的特许权使用费的税收，M 公司将其管理机构转移至 H 国，H 国是一个低税国家。M 公司的无形资产所产生的大量收益在 A 国无需纳税，因为并没有发生资产的转让。M 公司然后将技术许可给 B 国的使用者。M 公司所取得的特许权使用费逃避了 A 国的税收，因为 M 公司并非 A 国的居民，A 国也不能对外国公司所取得的外国特许权使用费征税。如果上例中的 A 国采用注册地标准的话，M 公司就

189

无法将其居民身份转移至 H 国，除非进行公司重组，将其资产转移至在 H 国成立的另一个公司。此转让使无形资产的累积收益得以实现，从而限制甚至消除了 M 公司避税的机会。

法人的管理机构又有管理和控制的中心机构和有效管理机构两大概念。在实践中，有的国家根据管理和控制的中心机构来判定法人的居民身份，如澳大利亚、加拿大、德国、爱尔兰、新西兰、挪威、新加坡、英国等；也有的国家根据实际管理机构来判定法人的居民身份，如比利时、丹麦、南非、葡萄牙、西班牙等。一般来说，管理和控制的中心机构是指公司的最高权力机构，它负责公司政策的制定和对公司经营活动的控制。这里的公司权力包括公司的财权、公司财产的取得和处置权、公司经营活动的决策制定权以及公司高级管理人员的任免权。一般认为，上述权力的使用地应为掌有这些权力的人的居住地或这些掌权人经常开会以运用公司权力的地方。由于公司的董事往往掌握着公司的上述重要权力，许多国家（如澳大利亚、加拿大、爱尔兰、新西兰、英国等）根据公司董事或主要董事的居住地或公司董事会开会的地点来确定公司的管理和控制中心所在地。此外，有的国家还根据股东大会召开的地点或公司账簿的保管地点来认定公司的管理和控制中心机构所在地。

公司有效管理机构的定义是什么？这个问题比较复杂，目前也没有一个统一的答案。在有的国家（如丹麦、荷兰、西班牙等），有效管理机构是指公司日常业务的管理机构，它负责公司经营决策的执行和具体的运营管理；而在另一些国家（如瑞士），有效管理机构则是指公司的决策机构，它与管理和控制的中心机构实际上是同一概念。

3. 总机构所在地标准

总机构所在地标准，也称户籍标准，是指在行使居民管辖权的国家内设有总机构的法人，即为该国的居民法人。

所谓总机构即企业的总的管理或控制机构，它负责法人的重大经营决策以及全部经营活动和统一核算盈亏，如各类总公司、总厂或被认为是起总机构管理与控制作用的公司。一家公司或企业只要事实上在这些国家内设有总机构，即成为该国的居民公司。采用总机构标准确定跨国法人居民身份的国家有法国、日本、比利时、中国等。

4. 资本控制标准

资本控制标准又称选举权控制标准，是指以控制公司选举权的股东的居民身份为依据来确定该公司的居民身份。如美国税法规定，一家跨国公司虽然在国外注册但只要 50%以上的有选举权的股票为美国股东所掌握，即可确定为美国居民公司，由美国政府对其行使居民管辖权。如果一个法人企业被几个国家的居民股东所共同控股或公司的股票公开上市交易，则资本控制标准就很难采用，这时该公司的利润就应当像合伙企业那样分配，由不同的股东在不同的国家分别纳税。

从上述几种确定跨国法人居民身份的标准以及各国的实践情况可知，许多国家都是兼用两种或两种以上标准来判定公司的居民身份。这样做主要是因为各种标准各有利弊，实行单一标准不利于维护国家的税收权益。我国新的企业所得税法在判定企业居民身份的标准方面与过去相比发生了较大的变化。新的标准为：只要企业满足"注册地标准"和"管理机构所在地标准"两者之一，就属于中国的居民企业。例如，《中华人民共和国企业所得税法》第二条规定："本法所称居民企业，是指依法在中国境内成立，或者在国外成立但实际管理机构在中国境内的企业。"这种做法实际上与英国、爱尔兰、葡萄牙、瑞士等国相同。根据这种判定标准，一家在外国注册成立的公司，如果将实际管理机构设在了中国，该公司也是中国的居民企业。反之，如果一家在中国注册成立的法人企业，即使将有效管理机构迁出了中国，它也是中国的居民企业。

2.3.3 居民与非居民的纳税义务

纳税人对一国政府的纳税义务与该国实行的税收管辖权类型、税收征收制度以及纳税人在该国的居民身份密切相关。在此，我们将结合一些国家的税法来分析居民和非居民纳税义务的区别。

1. 居民的纳税义务

如前文所述，一个实行居民管辖权的国家要对本国居民的国内外一切所得征税，从纳税人角度看，这时该国的居民不仅要就其国内所得向本国政府纳税，而且还要就其境外来源的所得向本国政府纳税。居民纳税人要就其全球所得向居住国政府纳税的义务称为无限纳税义务。在一个实行居民管辖权的国家，无论是个人居民还是法人居民，都要对居住国政府履行无限纳税义务。

在实践中，有些国家还将个人居民分为非长期居民和长期居民，两者都负无限纳税义务，但非长期居民负有条件的无限纳税义务，长期居民则负无条件的无限纳税义务。例如，《中华人民共和国个人所得税法实施条例》第六条规定："在中国境内无住所，但是居住一年以上六年以下的个人（即非长期居民），其来源于中国境外的所得，经主管税务机关批准，可以只就其由中国境内公司、企业以及其他经济组织或者个人支付的部分缴纳个人所得税。"也就是说，这种非长期居民可以不必就其中国境外公司、企业或个人支付的境外来源的所得向中国政府纳税。可见，非长期居民在我国负有条件的无限纳税义务。《中华人民共和国个人所得税法实施条例》第六条同时还规定："个人在中国境内居住满六年后，从第七年起的以后各年度中，凡在中国境内居住满183天的，应当就其来源于境内、境外的所得申报纳税；但在中国境内居住不满183天的，则仅就该年内来源于中国境内的所得申报纳税。"例如，某外籍个人2009年10月底来中国工作，此后一直居住和工作在中国境内。2015年，该外籍个人回国履行职务一次离境了35天，然后又回到中国继续居住和工作。由于我国规定的临时离境天数一次不能超过30天，该外籍个人在2015年已不属于临时离境，也不再属于中国居民。这样，该外籍个人在2015年仅应就该年内来源于中国境内的所得向中国政府申报纳税。

法人居民的无限纳税义务在一些国家也有一定的特殊性。在美国、英国、加拿大等一些发达国家，法人居民与个人居民一样要就其国内、国外的一切所得向本国政府纳税。但这些国家同时又规定，本国居民公司来源于境外子公司的股息、红利所得在未汇回本国以前可以先不缴纳本国的所得税，当这些境外所得汇回本国以后，本国居民公司再就其申报纳税。这时居民公司就其境外股息、红利所得的纳税义务并不是在境外所得产生时而产生，而是被推迟到境外所得汇回国以后才产生，因此上述规定通常被称为"推迟课税"。显然，推迟课税的规定是对居民管辖权所要求的全球所得征税原则的一种暂时的否定。发达国家实行推迟课税规定与其承认外国子公司独立的法人实体地位是分不开的。这是因为，如果不实行推迟课税，母公司居住国对境外子公司的利润无论是否汇回都要课税，这实际上等于撕去了外国子公司头上的"面纱"，把外国子公司与国内母公司视为一体征税，其结果必然是对外国子公司独立法人地位的否定。当然，发达国家实行推迟课税，对本国公司参与国外的竞争也是有利的。因为发达国家的所得税税率过去一直较高，而在推迟课税的规定下，本国的公司到税率较低的一些发展中国家去投资，只要这些境外子公司的利润不汇回，发达国家的母公司的境外投资所得就不必按本国的高税率负担税收，这对于本国公司以较低的税负在发展中国家与当地公司竞争是十分有利的。另外，由于母公司所在国通货膨胀的因素，母公司将从境外子公司取得的股息、红利滞留在境外一段时间以后再汇回，其就这笔境外所得在本国应纳税款的价值会大大下降。曾任美国财政部助理部长的美国哈佛大学法学院教授斯坦利·萨瑞就曾经指出，如果美国公司把受控外国子公司的利润滞留在海外15年后再汇回，则这笔利润不用缴纳任何所得税。需要特别指出的是，我国税法中并没有英、美等国家那种"企业海外投资利润不汇回不对其征税"的推迟纳税的规定。

2. 非居民的纳税义务

在一个实行居民管辖权和收入来源地管辖权的国家，非居民一般只需就该国境内来源的所得向该国政府纳税，这种对该国负有的仅就来源于其境内所得纳税的义务被称为有限纳税义务。无论是个人还是法人，其在非居住国（所得来源国或东道国）一般都负有有限纳税义务。

2.4 公民管辖权判定标准

2.4.1 公民管辖权的概念

公民管辖权是按照属人主义原则确立的税收管辖权，是指一国政府对于本国公民来自国内和国外的全部所得都拥有征税权。

一个国家在行使公民管辖权时，所考虑的只是纳税人的公民身份，而不问其居住在何国。它是以纳税人是否具有本国公民身份为依据，确定对其是否行使课税权力，其特征是对本国公民纳税人来源于境内外的所得同等征税。

2.4.2 公民身份的确定

一个国家在行使公民管辖权时，必须首先考虑纳税人与本国有无人身的公民联结因素。所谓公民亦称国民，通常是指具有某国国籍的、在法律上享有权利和承担义务的个人，但有时也包括按照某国现行法律取得其地位的法人、合伙企业和团体。对于确定某人是否是某国公民，只需要看该人是否具有该国国籍。如果这个人具有该国国籍，即为该国公民，否则为该国非公民。即公民身份的取得必须以拥有国籍为前提条件，各国多以国籍作为判定公民与否的标准。

所谓国籍，是指某人依出生地或血统关系等因素而取得的表明其身份、国别的称号或标志。一国国籍的取得方式主要是由国内法律规定的。各国对原始国籍的确定通常采用出生地主义和血统主义两种原则。

1. 出生地主义

出生地主义即以个人的出生地点为标准确定其原始国籍的一种原则。

按出生地主义规定，凡在本国境内出生的个人，均可取得本国国籍。美国过去曾根据出生地主义立法，规定在美国出生的人即具有美国国籍。《中华人民共和国国籍法》规定："父母双方或一方为中国公民，本人出生在中国，具有中国国籍。"

2. 血统主义

血统主义即以个人的血统关系（父母的国籍）为标准确定其原始国籍的一种原则。

按血统主义规定，凡与本国国民具有血统关系的个人，均可取得本国国籍，享有本国法律规定的一切公民权利，也承担本国的一切公民义务。

一个实行公民管辖权的国家要对本国公民的国内外一切所得征税，从纳税人角度看，这时该国的公民纳税人要就其国内外一切所得向其国籍国政府承担无限纳税义务。

2.4.3 国籍变动与双重国籍的处理

个人因出生地或血统关系而取得国籍之后，还有可能发生国籍变动，如加入国籍、丧失国籍和恢复国籍等。

加入国籍，是指根据一国的国内法，由于婚姻、收养、认领和领土转移等原因，而自然取得该国国籍的自然入籍，以及依照一国的国籍法和移民法，经过申请获准，从原来国籍转变为该国国籍，或者从无国籍转变为该国国籍的申请入籍。

丧失国籍，是指一国国民由于自愿退出，或者已取得其他国家国籍，或者依照该国的国内法被剥夺国籍而丧失其原有国籍的情况。

恢复国籍，是指因某种原因丧失自己原有国籍的个人，按照其原有国籍国的国内法规定的条件提出申请，被获准重新恢复原有国籍。

由于各国国内法有关国籍的规定存在着差异，以及因种种情况所产生的国籍变动，一个人就有可能同时具有两个国家的国籍，即双重国籍。例如，一个根据血统主义立法国家的国民，在根据出生地主义立法的美国所生的孩子，就可能同时具有两个国籍。又如，妇女与外国人结婚，儿童被外国人收养，都有可能在保留原有国籍的同时，也取得其丈夫或收养人的国籍。

对于双重国籍问题，国际上一般都是由有关国家通过协商解决。包括我国在内的大多数国家，都主张采取"一人一籍"的国籍原则，即各国都应将合法取得别国国籍的跨国个人的原有国籍加以取消，同时对保留别国国籍的跨国个人不给予本国国籍。至于对加入或丧失国籍而转入别国国籍的跨国个人，则应自转入别国国籍之日起，作为该（别）国的公民，由所属该国对其行使公民管辖权，而其原有国籍国应同时终止对其行使公民管辖权。对因恢复国籍而从别国转入的跨国个人，也应从转入原有国籍国之日起作为该国公民，由原国籍国恢复对其行使公民管辖权，其转出国应同时终止向其行使公民管辖权。

2.5 各国所得税税收管辖权实施的现状

既然税收管辖权属于国家主权，因而每个主权国家都有权根据自己的国情选择适合自己的税收管辖权类型。几乎所有的国家按属地主义原则实行收入来源地管辖权，即在收入来源基础上"从源征税"。因此，各国对收入来源地管辖权的认识比较一致，要求跨国纳税人对"经济税收事项的发生地"所在国承担有限的纳税义务。但同时多数国家的税收制度，又都是按照属地主义原则和属人主义原则兼用收入来源地管辖权和居民管辖权，即在

"从源征税"的同时,还着眼于纳税人的"居民身份",要求跨国纳税人对其居住国承担无限的或全面的纳税义务。公民管辖权应和居民管辖权等同。

值得一提的是,大多数国家在兼用两种基本税收管辖权的同时,一般都同意并遵循收入来源地管辖权优先的原则。也就是说,对同一笔跨国所得,收入来源国有优先征税的权力,即承认在课税权力方面,收入来源地管辖权优先于居民管辖权。这是因为,投资者从哪个国家赚的钱,理所应当先向哪个国家纳税,如果不允许收入来源国优先征税,而让纳税人居住国优先征税,则收入来源国就不会同意别国的居民在其境内做生意赚钱。同时,世界多数国家,特别是发达国家,既然希望通过技术转让与国际贸易从别国赚取所得,那么,就不能不承认收入来源国在征税上的优先权。不过,优先并不等于独占。这表现在两个方面。一方面,优先是有限制的,收入来源国并不能对一切非居民的所得都从源课税,而只能对在其境内居住一定期限的个人和非居民公司所属的常设机构征税;另一方面优先不能完全排斥纳税人居住国的税收管辖权。居住国在收入来源国优先征税后,仍将分情况对纳税人行使其税收管辖权。因此,对于跨国纳税人的所得,其来源国可以先行征税,然后该纳税人的居住国才能行使其居民管辖权。这在国际税收实践中已被世界多数国家接受。

从目前世界各国的税制来看,所得税税收管辖权的实施主要有三种类型。

1. 同时实行收入来源地管辖权和居民管辖权

在这种情况下,一国要对以下三类所得行使征税权,即本国居民的境内所得、本国居民的境外所得以及外国居民的境内所得。目前,我国和世界上大多数国家都采取这种收入来源地管辖权和居民管辖权并行的做法。

2. 实行单一的收入来源地管辖权

实行单一的收入来源地管辖权意味着一国只对纳税人来源于本国境内的所得行使征税权,其中包括本国居民的境内所得和外国居民的境内所得,但对本国居民的境外所得不行使征税权。目前,实行单一地域管辖权的国家和地区主要有阿根廷、乌拉圭、巴拿马、哥斯达黎加、肯尼亚、赞比亚、马来西亚、中国香港等。另外,还有一些国家和地区的公司所得税仅实行收入来源地管辖权,但个人所得税则同时实行收入来源地管辖权和居民管辖权。当然,这些国家和地区选择实施单一收入来源地管辖权也是从整体利益考虑的。实施单一地域管辖权的多是一些发展中国家,它们在经济发展过程中需要吸收外国资金,因此在所得税的管辖权上选择了单一收入来源地管辖权,以便使外商可以利用在本地建立的机构进行跨国经营而又不必在本地缴纳企业所得税,以此来吸引外商的直接投资。在这种情况下,这些实行单一收入来源地管辖权的国家或地区实际上就成了一种避税港。

3. 同时实行收入来源地管辖权、居民管辖权和公民管辖权

这种情况主要发生在个别十分强调本国征税权范围的国家,其个人所得税除了实行收入来源地管辖权和居民管辖权之外,还坚持公民管辖权。以美国为例,其税法规定,美国公民即使长期居住在国外,不是美国的税收居民,也要就其一切所得向美国政府申报纳税。

复习思考题

1. 什么是税收管辖权？确立税收管辖权的原则有哪些？
2. 所得税税收管辖权分为哪几种类型？
3. 如何确定跨国个人的居民身份？
4. 跨国法人的居民身份的判断标准是什么？
5. 什么是无限纳税义务？哪种纳税人负有无限纳税义务？
6. 目前，各国所得税税收管辖权的实施状况如何？

第 2 篇　国际税收实务

第2章　担保物権の法系

第3章

国际重复征税概述

时政观点

为减轻纳税人负担，避免重复征税，我国实施了"（营业税改增值税）"。我们要深入领会其基本精神及结构性减税对降低企业税负的意义。当前，国家从宏观层面实施大规模的减税降负，帮助企业渡过难关是社会主义制度优越性的体现。

学习目标

1. 重点掌握国际重复征税的概念，认识国际重复征税主要是由国家之间的税收管辖权重叠造成的。
2. 明确国际重复征税是国家之间税收分配关系的焦点，是国际税收理论和实务中的重要问题。

课程导入

一位英语教师从英国来中国任教一年，她在中国期间的收入有可能被英国政府和中国政府同时征税吗？

3.1 国际重复征税的概念

所得的国际重复征税是当今国际税收领域最普遍、最突出的一个问题。由于这一问题的解决必然涉及有关国家的税收权益，其一直是国际税收领域研究的重点课题之一。

重复征税是指同一课税对象在同一时期内被相同或者类似的税种课征了一次以上。这里必须强调重复征税是指相同或者类似税种的重复课征，如果同一课税对象被两个不同的税种重复课征则不属于我们这里讨论的重复征税问题。例如，职工的工资在一些国家既要被课征个人所得税，又要被课征社会保险税（工薪税），但个人所得税与社会保险税的性质不同，所以这两个税种对同一笔工资收入同时课征并不属于重复征税问题。重复征税问题既可以发生在一国之内，也可以发生在国与国之间。

3.1.1 国内重复征税

就所得税而言，国内重复征税问题在联邦制国家最容易发生。这种国内重复征税可以分为纵向的和横向两类。以美国为例，所谓纵向的国内重复征税是指联邦政府和州政府对同一纳税人的同一笔所得同时行使征税权所造成的重复征税。横向的国内重复征税是指两个或两个以上的州政府对纳税人的同一笔所得同时行使征税权而导致的重复征税。

3.1.2 国际重复征税

国际重复征税，有些类似于上述横向的国内重复征税，只不过这时进行重复征税的主体不再是一国，而是两个或多个主权国家。因此，国际重复征税被定义为两个或两个以上主权国家在同一纳税期间内对同一纳税人或不同纳税人的同一所得项目（包括财产）征收相同或类似的所得税。国际重复征税有法律性重复征税和经济性重复征税之分，两者的区别主要在于纳税人是否具有同一性。

1. 法律性重复征税

法律性重复征税是指两个或两个以上国家对同一跨国纳税人的同一所得进行的重复征税，它强调纳税人与课税客体都具有同一性。法律性重复征税比较好理解。例如，A 国居民在 B 国取得一笔所得，A、B 两国都要对这笔所得征税，那么就会发生跨国的法律性重复征税。又如，一个第三国的公司在 A 国设有常设机构，该公司通过这个常设机构在 B 国进行经营活动，取得了一笔所得，如果 A、B 两国都对该经营所得课税，也会发生法律性的国际重复征税问题。但是，对于同一个参与国际经济活动的纳税人来说，他应该承担的税收负担不应大于其仅在一个国家内产生的纳税义务。

2. 经济性重复征税

经济性重复征税是指两个或两个以上国家对不同跨国纳税人的同一所得进行的重复征税。它强调，国际重复征税不仅要包括法律性重复征税，而且还要包括由于纳税人与课税客体的非同一性所发生的国际重复征税，以及因对同一笔所得的确定标准和计算方法的不同所引起的国际重复征税。例如，A 国母公司从其设在 B 国的子公司处取得股息收入，这部分股息收入是 B 国子公司就其利润向 B 国政府缴纳公司所得税后的利润中的一部分。由于母子公司是两个不同的纳税人，而两者的课税对象属于同一税源，这时发生在母、子公司之间同一笔利润（子公司支付给母公司的股息）之上的重复征税就属于经济性重复征税。另外，对合伙公司和合伙人同时征税或者对信托财产和信托的受益人同时征税都会引起经济性双重征税。

3.2 国际重复征税产生的原因

国际重复征税问题是国家之间税收分配关系矛盾的焦点，是国际税收这门学科所必须研究的重要问题。国际上之所以会产生国际重复征税问题，与各国实行的税收管辖权、对企业的收入分配和费用扣除的看法和法律规范存在差异、对关联企业的转让价格看法不一致等原因密切相关。

3.2.1 两个或两个以上国家税收管辖权的交叉重叠

1. 同种税收管辖权交叉重叠

国与国之间同种税收管辖权的相互重叠主要是由有关国家判定所得来源地或居民身份的标准相互冲突造成的。一旦同一笔所得被两个国家同时判定为来自本国，或者同一纳税人被两个国家同时判定为本国居民，两个国家的收入来源地管辖权与收入来源地管辖权或者居民管辖权与居民管辖权就会发生交叉重叠。另外，如果一个纳税人具有双重国籍，而这两个国家又都行使公民管辖权，则两国的公民管辖权也会发生交叉重叠。为了说明国与国之间同种税收管辖权交叉重叠的情况，现举例如下。

1) 收入来源地管辖权之间冲突

收入来源地管辖权之间冲突指两个或两个以上国家都认为同一纳税人的同一所得来源于本国而同时行使征税权。

教学案例 3-1

A、B两国同时认定同一笔经营所得来源于本国，从而两国对这笔经营所得同时拥有收入来源地管辖权。

比如，A国的一家公司在B国有常设机构，B国判定经营所得来源地采用常设机构标准，A国采用交易地点标准。在这种情况下，如果该公司通过其在B国的常设机构向B国的公司销售货物，但销售合同是由A国公司与B国公司直接在A国境内签订，这时A国就可以根据交易地点标准判定这笔经营所得来自本国，并据此对A国公司征税，而B国则会根据常设机构标准判定这笔经营所得来自本国，因而也要对A国公司设在B国的常设机构征税。

教学案例 3-2

A、B两国同时认定同一笔劳务所得来自本国，两国的收入来源地管辖权在这笔劳务所得之上交叉重叠。

比如在判定劳务所得来源地问题上，A国采用劳务提供地标准，B国采用劳务所得支付者标准。这时，如果一B国居民到A国为一家公司提供劳务，但其劳务所得由A国公司设在B国的分支机构向其支付，该居民的劳务所得就会被A、B两国都判定为来源于本国。

2) 居民管辖权之间冲突

居民管辖权之间冲突指两个或两个以上国家都认为同一纳税人是本国的居民，从而对其同一笔所得行使征税权。如果一个纳税人同时被两个国家认定为居民，其通常被称为"双重居民纳税人"。

教学案例 3-3

A、B两国同时判定一个人为本国的居民，两国同时对其拥有居民管辖权，从而造成两国居民管辖权与居民管辖权的交叉重叠。

比如，某人在A国拥有永久性住所，但因公被派遣到B国工作了一年；A国根据住所标准认定该个人为本国的居民，而 B 国根据停留时间标准认为该个人在本年度内属于本国的居民。这样，A、B 两国的居民税收管辖权就发生了重叠。

又如，A、B 两国都采用居民管辖权，且对居民个人的认定都采用时间标准，但有差异。A 国税法规定，凡在 A 国居住满 180 天的个人为 A 国居民，A 国公民离开 A 国满 180 天的为 A 国非居民。B 国税法则规定，凡在 B 国居住满 90 天的个人为 B 国居民，否则为 B 国非居民。A 国某居民离开 A 国去 B 国从事经营活动，在 B 国居住 150 天并取得一笔收入。B 国政府因他在 B 国居住 150 天，已超过 90 天规定，按照国内法判定他为 B 国居民，并对其取得的这笔收入行使居民管辖权。而 A 国政府也因他离开 A 国只有 150 天，不满 180 天，按照 A 国税法规定仍判定他为 A 国居民，并对其行使居民管辖权。这样，由于 A、B 两国对居民居住时间标准规定的内涵不同，双方国家都认为他是本国居民而要对其行使征税权，就产生了居民管辖权之间的重叠，最终导致国际重复征税的产生。

教学案例 3-4

A、B 两国同时判定同一法人为本国的居民，两国的居民管辖权在该法人身上交叉重叠。这主要有以下两种情况：一是 A 国实行注册地标准，B 国实行管理机构或总机构所在地标准。这时，如果一个公司在 A 国注册成立而其管理机构或总机构设在 B 国，则 A、B 两国都要将该公司判定为本国的居民企业。如一家跨国公司在美国注册成立，实际管理机构设在英国。美国以公司注册所在地为标准判定该公司为美国居民公司，英国则以公司实际管理机构所在地为标准判定该公司为英国居民公司。这样，由于两国政府行使居民管辖权所采用的居民公司标准不同，就会出现居民管辖权之间的重叠，从而产生国际重复征税问题。二是 A、B 两国都采用管理机构所在地标准，而一家公司的管理机构一部分设在 A 国，一部分设在 B 国，如董事会在 A 国举行，而总经理部设在 B 国。这时，A、B 两国就有可能根据上述事实判定该公司是本国的居民公司。

3）公民管辖权与公民管辖权重叠

公民管辖权与公民管辖权重叠是指两个或两个以上国家都认为同一纳税人是本国的公民，从而对其同一笔所得行使征税权。

教学案例 3-5

某个纳税人具有美国和加拿大两个国家的双重国籍，而这两个国家又都行使公民管辖权，则该纳税人来自全球的所得都必须向美国和加拿大政府纳税。

2. 不同种税收管辖权交叉重叠

国与国之间不同种类的税收管辖权相互重叠具体分为三种情况：
（1）居民管辖权与收入来源地管辖权的重叠；
（2）公民管辖权与收入来源地管辖权的重叠；
（3）公民管辖权与居民管辖权的重叠。

由于世界上大多数国家都同时实行收入来源地管辖权和居民管辖权，因此这两种税收权的交叉重叠最为普遍。比如，一个 A 国居民在 B 国从事经济活动并在当地有一笔所得，A 国依据居民管辖权有权对这笔所得征税，B 国依据收入来源地管辖权也有权对这笔所得征税。这样，A、B 两国的税收管辖权就在该笔所得上发生了重叠。如果 A、B 两国都行使自己的征税权，则这笔所得势必要受到国际重复征税。公民管辖权与收入来源地管辖权重叠的情况与上述情况类似，这里不再赘述。

3.2.2　两个国家对企业的收入分配和费用扣除的法律规范差异

例如，A 国企业向 B 国企业支付利息，但对这笔利息，A 国不允许企业在税前扣除，但 B 国又要对这笔利息收入征税，这时国际双重征税就会发生。

3.2.3　两个国家对关联企业转让价格看法的不一致

具体内容将在第 8 章中介绍。

复习思考题

1. 法律性重复征税和经济性重复征税的区别是什么？
2. 什么是国际重复征税？为什么会发生国际重复征税？
3. 税收管辖权的重叠有哪些类型？

第 4 章

消除国际重复征税

时政观点

在我国个人所得税计算中，综合所得计税方法的改革、个人专项附加扣除的实行，使个人所得税税负大幅度降低，特别是中等收入人群的减税效果更加明显，老百姓的钱包鼓了、生活水平提高了，幸福感大幅度提升。新个税改革考虑了纳税人生活的方方面面，更体现了社会主义制度的"公平性"。

学习目标

1. 加深理解和领会消除国际重复征税的方式和方法。
2. 全面掌握抵免限额、直接抵免、间接抵免的计算方法。
3. 了解抵免法在税收饶让下的具体运算方法与技巧。
4. 从整体上把握国际税收抵免、抵免限额和税收饶让之间的关系。

课程导入

当同一个人被两个国家根据各国法律同时判定为本国的税收居民，而两个国家都有权对其行使居民税收管辖权时，为避免其被双重征税，两国政府该怎样协调其税收利益？

国际重复征税，不仅直接影响跨国纳税人的利益，而且对涉及的国际经济活动和有关国家的财权利益都会造成不同程度的影响。为了在各国政府之间确立一种合理的税收分配关系，并使纳税人的税收负担合理，使其能充分运用国际资金、合理利用国际资源、发展国际经济，如何就利益对等原则处理国际重复征税问题，也就成了国际税收中的一个重要理论问题。

4.1 消除国际重复征税的方式

对于国际间重复征税问题如何处理，世界各国都相继采取了一些有效的方式。各国多年来的实践表明，在国际重复征税发生前应力求避免，而在其发生后则应力求消除。国际间一般可以通过两条途径来达到解决国际重复征税的目的，一是按照本国国内税法的规定，采用主动限制本国行使的税收管辖权，这是单方面处理国际重复征税问题的方法；二是按照两个或两个以上国家政府间签订税收协定或条约的做法,在国家之间贯彻协定中的一些具体规定,达到解决国际重复征税问题的目的。从发展趋势看,多数国家将会逐渐采用或选择第二种途径来解决重复征税的问题。因此,处理国际重复征税问题的方式通常可分为单边方式、双边方式和多边方式三种。

1. 单边方式

实行居民管辖权的国家为了鼓励本国居民积极从事国际经济活动或到国外投资,大多在其国内税法中单方面地做出一些限制本国税收管辖权的规定,以便解决对本国居民取得来自国外所得的国际重复征税问题。从世界范围内的运用情况看,单方面处理国际重复征税问题的办法大致可划分为免税法和抵免法两种,具体内容将在第4章的4.2中阐述。

2. 双边方式

为兼顾居住国和来源国,以及跨国纳税人的利益,居住国政府和来源国政府通过谈判,签订两国政府之间的双边税收协定,来解决国际重复征税问题,协调两个主权国家之间的税收分配关系。签订双边税收协定的做法,是解决国际双重征税问题的有效途径。自20世纪60年代以来,双边税收协定的缔结已成为国际经济关系的一个显著特征。通过双边税收协定协调两个主权国家之间的税收分配关系,已成为世界各国普遍采用的方式。

3. 多边方式

多边方式是指两个以上的主权国家通过谈判,签订避免国际重复征税的多边税收协定,以协调各国之间的税收分配关系。如丹麦、芬兰、冰岛、挪威和瑞典签订的于1983年12月29日生效的北欧五国多边税收协定,即属于多边方式。由于国际政治经济关系比较复杂,各国的经济结构和税制结构悬殊,采用这种多边方式的国家为数不多。但随着世界经济的不断向前发展,以及区域经济一体化进程的加快,采用多边方式解决国际重复征税问题的国家将会越来越多。

4.2 消除国际重复征税的方法

对于采用什么样的方法来消除国际重复征税,国际社会尚未达成共识,但根据国际重复征税产生的原因,可把消除重复征税的方法分为以下两类。

4.2.1 消除因同种税收管辖权重叠所造成的国际重复征税的方法

两个国家的同一种税收管辖权发生交叉重叠主要是由有关国家判定收入来源地或居民(公民)身份的标准相互冲突造成的。为了防止两个国家同种税收管辖权重叠所造成的国际重复征税,国际社会有必要在判定标准相互冲突的情况下对各国的税收管辖权进行约束,以避免两个国家依照各自的税法对同一笔本国来源的所得或同一个本国居民(公民)同时行使税收管辖权而造成国际重复征税。目前,国际社会在这方面已经具备了比较成熟的规范,这种国际规范主要是由《经合发范本》和《联合国范本》的有关规定形成的。

1. 约束收入来源地管辖权的国际规范

根据所得的种类不同,约束各国收入来源地管辖权的国际规范主要有以下内容。

1) 经营所得

各国判定经营所得来源地的标准有常设机构标准和交易地点标准,但《经合发范本》

和《联合国范本》都主张以常设机构为标准来最终确定一国是否对来源于本国的经营所得具有征税权,即一国企业通过其设在另一国的常设机构进行营业所取得的利润,应在另一国被征税;而交易地点标准并不能成为对非居民来源于本国的经营所得行使征税权的依据。

例如,一家英国居民公司根据合同向我国一家公司销售一批货物,该英国公司在我国设有常设机构,并且这批货物是通过该常设机构销售的,但销售合同的签订地点在英国。根据常设机构标准,这批货物的销售利润应由我国征税,尽管根据英国的司法判例这笔销售利润的来源地在英国。当然,如果这家英国公司在我国没有设立常设机构,我国就不能对这笔销售利润征税,这时英国就可以根据交易地点标准对这批货物的销售利润行使收入来源地管辖权。

2) 劳务所得

《经合发范本》和《联合国范本》都将个人的劳务活动分为独立个人劳务和非独立个人劳务。前者是指个人独立的科学、文学、艺术、教育或教学活动以及医师、律师、工程师、建筑师、牙医师、会计师等的独立活动;后者是指因受雇而提供的各种劳务。

对于独立个人劳务所得到底应该由来源国还是居住国征税的问题,目前国际上并没有达成共识。《经合发范本》目前已将独立个人劳务所得视为一种经营所得,并主张个人独立劳务所得主要应由居住国对其征税,除非他在另一国设有从事这种独立劳务活动的固定基地,否则居住国以外的其他国家不得对这种独立个人劳务所得征税;即使一国居民在另一国设有固定基地,该国(非居住国)也只能对属于该固定基地的所得征税。《联合国范本》则把非居住国对独立个人劳务所得的征税条件放得更宽。除了《经合发范本》规定的固定基地条件以外,《联合国范本》还规定,如果一国居民在另一国因从事独立性劳务而累计停留了183天以上(含183天),或者一国居民在另一国进行劳务活动的报酬是由该另一国的居民支付或由设在该国的常设机构或固定基地负担,并且金额在会计年度中超过了两国协商确定的数额,那么另一国也可以对该居民在本国进行劳务活动所取得的所得征税。

对于非独立个人劳务所得应该由来源国还是居住国征税的问题,《经合发范本》和《联合国范本》有相同的规定,即缔约国一方居民因受雇而取得的工资、薪金等报酬一般应由其居住国征税,除非该居民在缔约国另一方受雇。① 如果一国居民在缔约国另一方受雇,其受雇取得的工资、薪金等报酬在一定条件下就可以被缔约国另一方征税。

3) 投资所得

对于投资所得中的股息所得和利息所得,国际上一般采取所得支付人所在国与所得受益人所在国共享征税权的做法。因为如果两国都按本国规定的税率对股息、利息征税,就会导致一笔所得负担双重的税收,而如果允许实行税收抵免,支付人所在国征税以后受益人所在国就可能无税可征。所以,为了防止同一笔股息、利息负担双重税收,同时又能使支付人所在国与受益人所在国共享征税权,《经合发范本》和《联合国范本》提出由支付人所在国按一个较低的税率对股息、利息征税,以保证受益人所在国实施外国税收抵免以后仍能征到一部分税款。至于支付人所在国具体应按什么税率征税,《经合发范本》还做出了明确规定:对于支付的股息,当受益人直接持有支付股息公司至少25%的资本时,税

---

① 按照《经合发范本》的注释,一国居民在缔约国另一方受雇是指该居民真正停留在缔约国另一方。

率不应超过5%，而在其他情况下，税率不应超过15%；对于支付的利息，税率不应超过10%。各国税法规定的股息预提税税率一般为25%~35%。《联合国范本》没有提出具体的限制税率，只要求有关国家通过谈判确定支付人所在国的税率。

与股息、利息相比，特许权使用费应由哪国征税目前并没有统一的国际规范。《经合发范本》主张由特许权使用费的受益人（即特许权的所有人）的居住国独享对特许权使用费的征税权，除非该受益人在特许权的使用国设有常设机构或固定基地，而且支付特许权使用费的有关权利或财产与该常设机构或固定基地有实际联系，只有在这种情况下，特许权使用费才可归属到该常设机构或固定基地由特许权的使用国对其征税。但《联合国范本》则主张特许权使用费的发生国应享有更大的征税权。除了上述特许权使用费的受益人在特许权使用费发生的国家设有常设机构或固定基地的情况外，《联合国范本》还规定，特许权使用费的发生国可以按照一定的限制税率对支付给另一国受益人的特许权使用费进行征税，具体税率由相关国家协商确定。我国通常是特许权的使用国，所以为了维护税收权益，对外签订税收协定时一般都参照《联合国范本》对企业和单位向境外支付的特许权使用费征收预提所得税，税率一般为10%。

4）财产所得

从民法的角度讲，不动产是指土地和土地上的定着物，包括各种建筑物和生长在土地上的各类植物等。不动产的特点是，它们与土地不能分离或者不可移动，一旦与土地分离或者移动则将改变其性质或者其价值会大大降低。此外，建筑物的固定附属设备也属于不动产。税收协定范本中的不动产不但包括民法意义上的不动产，还包括附属于不动产的财产、农业和林业使用的牲畜和设备、土地财产方面一般法律规定所适用的权力、不动产的用益权①等，但其中不包括船舶、飞机。《经合发范本》和《联合国范本》对不动产所得和不动产转让收益规定的征税权与各国税法一致，即应由不动产的所在国对不动产所得和转让收益征税。

动产是指不动产以外的财产，如机器设备、车辆、动物、各种生活日用品，等等；动产的特点是可以随意移动，而且其价值不受移动的影响。对于动产的转让收益，《经合发范本》和《联合国范本》规定，除以下几种情况以外，动产的转让收益均应由转让者的居住国对其征税。

（1）如果一国居民转让其设在另一国的常设机构或固定基地所拥有的动产，这时其取得的转让收益应由该常设机构或固定基地的所在国征税。

（2）转让从事国际运输的船舶、飞机、内河运输船只或附属于上述船舶、飞机或船只的动产所取得的收益，应由企业实际管理机构的所在国征税。

另外，《经合发范本》和《联合国范本》还规定，转让公司股权取得的收益时，如果该股权主要是由不动产组成，则对该所得的征税权应留给来源国。

2. 约束居民管辖权的国际规范

1）约束对个人行使居民管辖权的国际规范

如果同一个人被两个国家根据本国法律同时判定为本国的居民，从而都有权对其行使居民管辖权时，《经合发范本》和《联合国范本》都要求对这种个人双重居民身份的处理要按照永久性住所、重要利益中心、习惯性居住地、国籍和由双方国家协商解决的习惯顺

---

① 用益权是指对他人的物品有使用或收益的权利。

序来判定其最终居民身份。

2）约束对法人行使居民管辖权的国际规范

在法人方面，根据《经合发范本》和《联合国范本》的精神；如果同一法人被两个国家同时判定为本国的税收居民，则应根据管理机构所在地标准来决定由哪个国家对其行使居民管辖权。根据这种国际规范，当判定法人居民身份的注册地标准和管理机构所在地标准发生冲突时，注册地标准要服从于管理机构所在地标准。当然，对于那些采用注册地标准判定法人的居民身份的国家而言，上述规范是很难接受的，所以，有些税收协定也规定，如果法人被两个国家分别判定为本国的税收居民，则其不应成为任何一方的税收居民。

4.2.2 消除因不同种税收管辖权重叠所造成的国际重复征税的方法

如前所述，不同种税收管辖权的重叠有三种类型，其中最主要、最常见的是两个国家的居民管辖权与收入来源地管辖权的重叠。在国际税收的实践中，大量的问题也是关于如何解决这两种税收管辖权重叠所造成的国际重复征税。这一问题的解决办法大体可以概括为：实行居民管辖权的国家承认所得来源国的优先征税地位，并在行使本国征税权的过程中采取某种方法减轻或免除国际重复征税，这是由收入来源地管辖权的重要性和所得来源国的优先征税地位所决定的。

各国税法和国际税收协定允许采用的消除国际重复征税的方法主要有扣除法、低税法、免税法和抵免法四种。一国可以运用其中一种方法，也可以几种方法并用。

1. 扣除法

扣除法是指居住国允许纳税人列支就外国来源所得支付给外国政府的税收，包括所得税。它意味着采用扣除法的国家对本国居民的全球范围所得征税，但在计算本国应纳税所得额时允许列支外国已纳税额。实际上，扣除法是将已缴纳的外国所得税和其他税收视为纳税人在外国从事经营并取得所得的当期费用予以扣除。扣除法是最不彻底的消除国际重复征税的方法。

为了说明扣除法的计算，我们举一个简单的例子。

 模拟演示 4-1

【背景】A 国居民在某一纳税年度内来自 A 国的所得为 10 万元，来自 B 国的所得为 2 万元。A 国的所得税税率为 40%，B 国的所得税税率为 50%。请计算该居民在 A 国的所得税纳税情况。

【演算】

该居民的居民总所得：$10+2=12$（万元）。

已纳 B 国税款：$2\times50\%=1$（万元）。

在 A 国的应税所得额：$12-1=11$（万元）。

扣除前应纳 A 国税款：$12\times40\%=4.8$（万元）。

扣除后实缴 A 国税款：$11\times40\%=4.4$（万元）。

全部计算为：$(10+2-2\times50\%)\times40\%=(12-1)\times40\%=11\times40\%=4.4$（万元）。

【评述】 采用扣除法时，该居民最多也只能少缴 A 国政府所得税 0.4 万元 ［（1×40%）或（4.8-4.4）］，却仍然重复承担了至少 0.6 万元 ［（4.4+1-4.8）或（1-1×40%）］的所得税税负。因此，仍不能彻底解决国际重复征税问题，只是在一定程度上减轻或缓和了国际重复征税的矛盾。

 模拟演示 4-2

【背景】 假定 A 国一个居民公司在某纳税年度取得总所得 100 万元，其中来自 A 国（居住国）的所得 70 万元，来自 B 国（非居住国）的所得 30 万元；A 国公司所得税税率为 40%，B 国公司所得税税率为 30%。如果 A 国实行扣除法，请分析该公司在 A 国的纳税情况。

【演算】

应缴纳 B 国税款：30×30% = 9（万元）。

来自 B 国的应税所得：30-9 = 21（万元）。

来自本国的应税所得 70 万元。

境内境外应税总所得：70+21 = 91（万元）。

本国应纳税款：91×40% 或（70+30-30×30%）×40% = 36.4（万元）。

【评述】 在上例中，如果该公司只负担 A 国的税收，不存在任何双重征税，其纳税额为 40 万元（100×40%）；如果 A 国不采用扣除法，则该公司境内外应纳税额为 49 万元（100×40%+30×30%），而在实行扣除法的情况下，该公司实际总共负担税款 45.4 万元（9+36.4）。显然，扣除法可以缓解国际重复征税，但不能完全免除国际重复征税。

从上述的分析中可以看出，扣除法不能彻底解决国际重复征税问题，其导致的直接结果是：相对于本国来源所得，居民纳税人的已税外国来源所得会适用更高的税率。因此，扣除法更加有利于本国投资，不利于对外投资，因为对外投资会增加一道外国税收。所以，《经合发范本》和《联合国范本》都不主张在国与国之间签订的双重征税协定中采用扣除法解决国际重复征税问题。但扣除法并没有消失，一些采用抵免法的国家仍然保留着扣除法作为消除双重征税的备选方法，用于抵扣由于一种或多种原因而不能得到抵免的外国税收。此外，有些国家对外国间接投资所得的已纳税额采用扣除法来消除双重征税，比如我国《中华人民共和国外商投资企业和外国企业所得税法实施细则》第二十八条规定："外国企业在中国境内设立的机构、场所取得的发生在中国境外的与该机构、场所有实际联系的利润（股息）、利息、租金、特许权使用费和其他所得已在境外缴纳的所得税税款，除国家另有规定外，可以作为费用扣除。"①

2. 低税法

低税法指居住国政府对其居民国外来源的所得单独制定较低的税率征收标准，对其国内所得则按正常的标准税率征税，以达到减少重复征税的目的。低税法只能在一定程度上降低重复征税的数额，即在某种程度上缓和了实际重复征税的矛盾，但不能根本解决重复征税问题。

---

① 新的企业所得税法对这些发生在境外的所得已改用抵免法来解决国际双重征税问题。

模拟演示 4-3

【背景】A 国某居民来自国内所得 80 万元,来自 B 国所得 20 万元,A 国的所得税税率为 35%,但对本国居民来源于国外的所得规定适用 10% 的低税率征税,B 国的所得税税率为 40%。如果 A 国采用低税法,请计算该居民在 A 国的纳税情况。

【演算】

应缴纳 A 国税收:(80+20)×35%=35(万元)。

已缴纳 B 国税收:20×40%=8(万元)。

A 国实征税收:80×35%+20×10%=30(万元)。

该居民纳税总额:30+8=38(万元)。

A 国放弃的税款:35-30=5(万元)。

【评述】如果国际重复征税存在,该居民需纳税:35+8=43(万元),而在低税法条件下,则要纳税 38 万元,即少缴纳 5 万元税款。

从上述的分析中可以看出,低税法只是居住国对已缴纳外国税款的国外所得按减低的税率征税,而不是完全对其免税,所以它与扣除法一样,也只能减轻而不能免除国际重复征税。因此,《经合发范本》和《联合国范本》也都没有推荐低税法作为避免双重征税的方法,只有个别国家在国内税法中使用这种方法来缓解国际重复征税。例如,比利时的相关法律规定,对本国公司从国外分支机构取得的所得减征 75% 的公司所得税。

3. 免税法

免税法是指居住国对于纳税人来源于外国的所得给予免税。按照免税法,居住国只对本国居民的本国来源所得征税,对于外国来源所得不再征税。也就是说,来源国拥有唯一的征税权。由于只有来源国征税,免税法可以完全消除居民管辖权与收入来源地管辖权的重叠所引起的国际重复征税。

只有个别的国家或地区对本国或本地区居民取得的所有外国来源所得给予免税。这些国家或地区实际上只对本国或本地区来源所得征税,相对于全球征税原则,这种征税原则通常被称为"属地征税原则"。大多数采用免税法的国家只对有限的几种外国来源所得免税,如最普遍的经营所得和从外国关联公司取得的股息所得。而且,免税法也往往局限于外国已纳税所得或者至少在外国按照某种最低税率已纳过税的所得。

在实际应用中,根据各国实行的所得税制,是采用比例税率还是累进税率,以及是否通过双边税收协定的途径免税,都是需要协商的问题。免税法又分为全额免税法和累进免税法两种形式。

(1)全额免税法是指居住国政府对其居民来自国外的所得全部免予征税,只对其居民的国内所得征税,而且在决定对其居民的国内所得所适用的税率时,也不考虑其居民已被免予征税的国外所得。由于全额免税法对居住国政府造成的财政损失较多,所以采用全额免税法的国家只有法国、澳大利亚及部分拉美国家。

(2)累进免税法是指居住国政府对其居民来自国外的所得不征税,只对其居民的国内所得征税,但在决定对其居民的国内所得征税所适用的税率时,有权将其居民的国外所得汇总到国内所得中加以综合考虑。这种免税方法主要适用于实行累进所得税制的国家,而

第4章 消除国际重复征税

且是通过签订双边税收协定的途径实现的。

为了说明免税法的计算，举例如下。

 模拟演示 4-4

【背景】A 国某居民在某一纳税年度内，来自 A 国所得 10 万元，来自 B 国所得 5 万元，来自 C 国所得 5 万元。A 国个人所得税税率为 4 级全额累进税率，即：所得额在 5 万元（含）以下的，适用税率为 5%；所得额在 5 万元至 15 万元的部分，适用税率为 10%；所得额在 15 万元至 30 万元的部分，适用税率为 15%；所得额在 30 万元以上的，适用税率为 20%。B 国和 C 国的所得税税率分别为 15% 和 20%。如果 A 国采用免税法，请计算该居民的纳税情况。

【演算】

按全额免税法，该居民在 A 国的应纳税额为 1 万元（10×10%）。

按累进免税法，A 国对该居民的国外所得 10 万元（5+5）也不征税，只对来自 A 国的所得 10 万元征税，但对其国内所得征税时，其适用税率已不再是按国内所得 10 万元所对应的税率 10% 征收，而是要对其国内所得 10 万元与国外所得 10 万元加以综合考虑，按 20 万元的所得所对应的税率 15% 征收，因此该居民的税收负担情况为：

居住国（A 国）税收：10×15% = 1.5（万元）。

来源国（B 国）税收：5×15% = 0.75（万元）。

来源国（C 国）税收：5×20% = 1（万元）。

居民的税收总负担：1.5+0.75+1 = 3.25（万元）。

【评述】可见，按累进免税方法，A 国税务当局可较全额免税方法多征税收 0.5 万元（1.5-1）。

 模拟演示 4-5

【背景】在模拟演示 4-4 中，如果 A 国个人所得税税率不是全额累进税率，而是采用 4 级超额累进税率（税率表和其他情况同上），按全额免税法和累进免税法，又该怎样计算该居民的纳税情况呢？

【演算】

按全额免税法：

该居民应向 A 国纳税：(10-5)×10%+5×5% = 0.75（万元）。

采用累进免税法：

居住国（A 国）税收：(20-15)×15%+(15-10)×10% = 1.25（万元）。

来源国（B 国）税收：5×15% = 0.75（万元）。

来源国（C 国）税收：5×20% = 1（万元）。

居民纳税总额：1.25+0.75+1 = 3（万元）。

【评述】同样，采用累进免税法时，A 国税务当局较全额免税方法可多征税收 0.5 万元（1.25-0.75）。

一些国家能够实行免税法，与其国情和经济政策密切联系。采用免税法的国家大多是发达国家，这些国家有着大量的相对过剩资本，为给这些资本寻找出路，因而采取了一系列税收方面的政策，以鼓励本国资本的输出。这些税收鼓励措施的一个重要内容，就是对这些输出资本所带来的跨国所得或收益不予征税。因此，免税法鼓励本国居民投资于税率低的国家，特别是避税港，还会刺激纳税人将本国所得转移到国外。例如，某纳税人居住在一个实行免税法的国家，如果纳税人在本国存款并取得利息，需缴纳本国利息所得税；这样，纳税人就会千方百计地将资金转移到利息税率较低或不征利息税的国家。因此，为了避免免税法的实施违背税收中性的原则，实行免税法的国家对本国居民国外来源的所得免税往往有严格的限定条件；可以免税的外国来源所得必须是外国已纳税所得，而且外国的适用税率及其他有关情况必须与本国类似。对来源于不征所得税或税率很低的避税港的所得一般不给予免税。目前，世界上一些国家对于本国居民通过外国分公司或常设机构取得的营业利润给予免税，也有一些国家对于本国居民从外国公司（本国居民公司所占股份比例不能少于最低限度，一般为5%或10%）取得的股息给予免税。对股息的免税通常称为"参股免税"。

当然，税务当局采用免税法使得税收征管更加简单、便利，也可以有效消除纳税人的双重税收负担。鉴于此，《经合发范本》和《联合国范本》都将免税法列为避免国际重复征税的推荐方法之一。

4. 抵免法

抵免法是指居住国允许纳税人将支付给外国政府的所得税冲抵本国的纳税义务。在有些情况下，抵免法也适用于支付给外国地方政府的所得税。抵免法的全称为外国税收抵免法，即一国政府在对本国居民的国外所得征税时，允许其用国外已纳的税款冲抵在本国应缴纳的税款，从而实际征收的税款只为该居民应纳本国税款与已纳外国税款的差额。显然，抵免法可以有效免除国际重复征税。外国税收抵免法是以承认收入来源地管辖权优先地位为前提条件的，而不是独占的。也就是说，对跨国纳税人的同一笔所得，来源国政府可以对其征税，居住国政府也可以对之征税。但是，来源国政府可以先于居住国政府行使税收管辖权，即在形成这笔所得的时候，就将征税，而后，在这笔所得汇回其国内时，居住国政府方可对之课税，并采取抵免的方法来解决双重征税问题。鉴于抵免法的重要性以及实施的复杂性，我们将从以下几个方面对其进行详细介绍。

1）抵免限额

前文已经指出，抵免法是指居住国允许本国居民用国外税款冲减本国应缴税款的一种方法。但居住国与来源国的所得税税率并不相同。根据抵免法，如果来源国的税率低于居住国，居民需要就外国来源所得缴纳本国税收，本国税收额等于国内外税率差乘以外国来源所得额；如果居住国税率与来源国税率相同，则纳税人可以用来源国税款完全抵免这笔外国所得应缴纳的本国税款，居住国也不需要再对其补征税款。现在的问题是，如果纳税人支付的外国税收的实际税率高于本国实际税率，实行抵免法的国家会不会就外国税收高于本国税收的部分给纳税人退税呢？如果这样，就是全额抵免；反之，如果本国应纳税款的抵免额不能超过国外所得按照居住国税率计算的应纳税额（即抵免限额），就是普通抵免。下面用一个模拟演示来说明这两者的区别。

模拟演示 4-6

【背景】 A 国总公司在 3 个国家设立了分公司，其某一纳税年度的纳税情况如表 4-1 所示。

表 4-1　分公司的纳税情况

公司	所得额/万元	国外税率/%	国外税额/万元	国内税率/%	国内税额/万元	差额税款/万元
A 国总公司	100	—	—	35	35	—
B 国分公司	100	30	30	35	35	+5
C 国分公司	100	35	35	35	35	0
D 国分公司	100	40	40	35	35	−5
总公司合计	400	—	105	—	140	—

【演算】 由表 4-1 可见，在 B 国的分公司所得应向 A 国补缴差额所得税款 5 万元（35-30）；在 C 国的分公司所得已纳 C 国的所得税可得到全部抵免；在 D 国的分公司所得所缴纳的 D 国政府所得税，已超过居住国所允许的抵免数额 5 万元（40-35）。

【评述】 在这种情况下，如果不规定抵免限额，允许高税率国家的税收可以全部抵免，等于允许外国政府用高税率挖走本国政府的财政收入，即本国政府代纳税人向外国政府缴纳差额税款。这种将跨国纳税人的税收负担从高税率国家转移到低税率国家的做法显然是有失公平的。所以，为了维护居住国的税收权益，对居民纳税人来自国外并承担了国外税负的所得，更有必要规定抵免限额了。

在实践中，各国为了保证本国的税收利益，都实行普通抵免。因为如果实行全额抵免，低税国居民会到高税国去进行投资，低税国政府不仅得不到任何税收上的好处，从该居民国内所得中本应得到的税收还会受到损害；更有甚者，假如低税国的居民只有来源于国外的所得，在居住国没有任何所得，那么在全额抵免的情况下，居住国政府还要从其他居民缴纳的税收收入中拿出钱来给他一定的补偿（即退税）。上述两种情况是各国都不愿看到的，所以实行抵免制的国家都规定本国纳税人只能在抵免限额以内进行抵免。我国的税法也有这种规定。《中华人民共和国企业所得税法》第二十一条规定："企业取得的国外所得已在境外缴纳的所得税税额，可以从其当期应纳税额中抵免，抵免限额不能超过国外所得依照本法规定计算的应纳税额。"

抵免限额是指居住国政府允许其居民纳税人抵免国外已纳所得税款的最高额，它一般不超过外国来源所得按照本国税法计算的应纳税额。在此限度内，跨国纳税人在国外的已纳税款可全额抵免，超过此限度，则只能按此限额抵免。需要指出的是，抵免限额是允许纳税人抵免本国税款的最高数额，它并不一定等于纳税人的实际抵免额。纳税人被允许的实际抵免额为其在来源国已纳的税额与抵免限额相比的较小者。例如，一居住国的纳税人取得的国外所得在来源国实际负担了 10 万元税款，而这笔国外所得应在居住国缴纳的税款（抵免限额）为 15 万元，则居住国允许该纳税人的实际抵免额为 10 万元。在这种情况下，该纳税人的抵免限额大于实际抵免额，我们可以把两者之间的差额称为抵免限额余额。相反，如果该纳税人在国外缴纳的税款为 20 万元，而在居住国的抵免限额为 15 万元，则该纳税人的实际抵免额只能为 15 万元。在这种情况下，该纳税人就有 5 万元的外国税款不能用于冲抵居住国的应纳税额。我们把外国税款大于本国抵免限额的差额称为超限抵免额,在本例中,超限抵免额为 5 万元。许多国家允许当年不能抵免的外国税收(超限抵免额)可以向以后年度结转并冲抵国内税收,以后年度的抵免限额余额可以冲抵以前年度的超限抵免额。但各国规定的结转期限并不相同。如加拿大规定为 7 年,美国规定为 5 年,日本规定为 3 年,我国规定为 5 年。

假设 R 是 A 国居民,A 国税率是 30%。第一年,R 取得外国来源所得 100 万元,缴纳外国税收 50 万元,50 万元用于抵免 A 国税收 30 万元,剩下 20 万元不能抵扣,R 有 20 万元的超限抵免额。第二年,R 又取得外国来源所得 100 万元,缴纳国外税收 25 万元,由于 A 国允许抵免 30 万元,这样,当年的外国税收 25 万元和从第一年结转的超限抵免额 5 万元将被抵扣,R 剩下 15 万元的超限抵免额可以结转到以后年度。

从完善税收政策的角度,抵免法被公认为是最好的消除国际双重征税的方法,但是抵免法的实施并不容易。最重要的是,抵免法的采用无论给政府还是纳税人都会带来难题。其中,必须解决的难题之一是:如何计算抵免限额?是按所得来源抵免、分项抵免,还是分国抵免?抑或是对不同类型所得采用不同规定的综合抵免?或者几种抵免方法并用?为了有效实施抵免法,必须就上述问题及其他相关情况制定详细的、技术性强且非常复杂的法律规定。复杂的法律条款虽然会导致税务当局和纳税人征纳成本的提高,但从防止利用避税港避税的角度讲,这也是合理。否则,居民通过转移本国来源所得至避税港就可能逃避本国税收。

各国对抵免限额的具体规定各不相同,因此在实践中,抵免限额可分为综合抵免限额、分国抵免限额和分项抵免限额三种类型。

(1) 综合抵免限额。

综合抵免限额,亦即全球抵免制,允许所有外国税收汇总计算抵免限额,也就是说,首先比较纳税人已纳外国税额总和与全部外国所得按照本国税法计算的应纳税额,二者中较小的数额就是抵免限额。综合抵免制可以在限额内使高税国的高税与低税国的低税相互抵补均衡。

其计算公式为:

综合抵免限额=国内外应税所得按居住国税法计算的应纳税总额×(国外应税所得额÷国内外应税所得额)

在公式中,国内外应税所得按居住国税法计算的应纳税总额即为抵免前按国内外应税所得总额计算的应缴本国(居住国)政府所得税。在居住国所得税税率为比例税率的情况下,综合抵免限额的计算公式还可以简化为:

综合抵免限额=全部国外应税所得额×本国税率

但必须指出,如果居住国所得税的适用税率为累进税率,抵免限额的计算公式就不能简化了。

模拟演示 4-7

【背景】同模拟演示 4-6

【演算】参见表 4-1,A 国政府首先要给其总公司计算一个综合抵免限额,即:400×35%×(300÷400)= 140×(300÷400)= 105(万元)。

也可以写成 300×35%=105(万元)。

由于总公司在国外已纳税额（各外国分公司所纳税额之和）共为 105 万元，与上式计算的抵免限额相等，所以已纳国外所得税额可得到全额抵免，便可抵免 105 万元，A 国政府实际入库税款为 35 万元（140-105）。而在采用分国抵免限额下，B 国分公司应补缴差额税款 5 万元，D 国分公司则有 5 万元不能得到抵免，这样，A 国政府的实际入库税款即 40 万元（35+5）。可见，综合抵免限额实际上是允许把外国高税率国家（如 D 国）的超抵免限额与低税率国家（如 B 国）的抵免限额余额拉平后进行抵免。如此，在应补缴 5 万元和不能抵免的 5 万元部分拉平冲抵后，总公司可获全额抵免，在综合抵免限额环境下，较分国抵免限额可多抵免 5 万元。

【评述】从上述计算及抵免效果来看，综合抵免限额对于计算国内居民纳税人来自国外所得可抵免已纳所得税额，确实提供了方便，而且方法比较简单，克服了分国抵免限额计算烦琐的弊病。所以，这一方法自 20 世纪 70 年代以来为多数国家所采用。例如，美国在 1975 年以前曾经实行过分国抵免限额，自 1975 年开始，为了简化征纳手续，已改为实行综合抵免限额。

从上面的分析中可以看出，当跨国纳税人在某一外国的所得税超过了抵免限额，而在另一外国的所得税不足抵免限额的情况下，采用综合抵免限额，对跨国纳税人来说是有利的。因为他可以用一国的抵免限额余额去弥补另一国的超限抵免额，使一部分甚至全部超限抵免额的外国所得税，也能在当年得到抵免。这种方法的好处是其他限额抵免方法所享受不到的。但是，综合抵免限额对一主权国家来说，在上述情况下，却会影响该国的财权利益，因为这样会减少居住国政府的税收收入。然而，如果跨国纳税人在某一外国有经营所得，而在另一外国有经营亏损的情况下，采用综合抵免限额，就会把其来自外国的所得总额冲销一部分，使公式中的分子、分母同时减少相同数额（即亏损额），从而使抵免限额减少，这对跨国纳税人是不利的，而对居住国政府则是有利的。针对上述综合抵免限额的缺陷，有些国家采用了另一种抵免限额的方法，即分国抵免限额。

(2) 分国抵免限额。

分国抵免限额是比较纳税人在国外每一个国家的已纳税额与从该国取得的所得按照本国税法计算的应纳税额，二者中较小者为抵免限额。这种方法不允许各国间税负高低的相互抵补，但允许同一国家的不同类型所得之间的税率高低保持均衡。

其计算公式为：

分国抵免限额=国内外应税所得按居住国税法计算的应纳税总额×（某一外国应税所得额÷国内外应税所得额）

同样，在居住国税率为比例税率的情况下，分国抵免限额的计算公式也可以简化，即：

分国抵免限额=某一外国应税所得额×本国税率

按照上述计算公式，可逐一计算纳税人在各个外国的抵免限额，与纳税人在各外国实际缴纳的所得税进行比较，确定纳税人在每一个外国的可抵免税额，并在此基础上进行实际税收抵免。

模拟演示 4-8

【背景】同模拟演示 4-6。

【演算】在 A 国采用分国抵免限额的情况下，总公司抵免限额的计算及纳税情况如下：

B 国分公司抵免限额：400×35%×（100÷400）= 35（万元）。或 100×35% = 35（万元）。

可抵免税额：实缴 B 国税额 30 万元，小于抵免限额，即可抵免 30 万元。

C 国分公司抵免限额 = l00×35% = 35（万元）。

可抵免税额：实缴 C 国税额 35 万元，等于抵免限额，即可抵免 35 万元。

D 国分公司抵免限额 = l00×35% = 35（万元）。

可抵免税额：实缴 D 国税额 40 万元，超过抵免限额，超过部分不能抵免，故可按抵免限额抵免，即可抵免 35 万元。

A 国允许总公司的抵免总额 = 30+35+35 = 100（万元）。

总公司抵免后应缴 A 国税款 = 400×35%−100 = 40（万元）。

【评述】由上述计算可以看出，在纳税人国外所得来自多国的情况下，分国抵免限额公式适用国外所得税率高于国内所得税率的情况。当国外所得税率低于或等于国内所得税率时，只需将各国外所得承担的外国政府所得税额直接相加，作为抵免数额即可。

分国抵免限额可以避免综合抵免限额用纳税人在某一外国的超限抵免额与另一外国的抵免限额余额拉平抵免的弊端，这对居住国政府来说是有利的。然而，当纳税人在某一外国有所得，而在另一外国有亏损的情况下，采用分国抵免限额则对跨国纳税人有利，所计算的抵免限额也是合理的。因为它可以避免综合抵免限额在相同情况下，把所得与亏损相互抵消，使公式中的分数的值减少，从而减低抵免限额的弊病。

从总体上说，采用分国抵免限额能够较为合理地兼顾居住国政府与纳税人的双方经济利益，它根据各个国家的具体情况来确定抵免限额和实际抵免额，更接近于实际情况。所以，在实行抵免制的国家中，采用分国抵免限额的比较多。例如英国、德国、芬兰等国家都实行分国抵免限额。美国最早也实行分国抵免限额，但从 20 世纪 70 年代起，除一些指定的所得项目以外，其他所得开始实行综合抵免限额。不过，由于综合抵免限额存在的缺陷会促使纳税人寻找一个税负较低甚至无税的国家或地区进行投资，这等于是刺激纳税人不在本国投资，而到低税国投资。显然，这与美国倡导的资本输出中性理念是相悖的。美国一些学者据此主张废除综合抵免限额，重新回到分国抵免限额中。

由此可见，分国抵免限额和综合抵免限额在不同情况下的作用是不一致的。两种方法各有利弊，优缺点是互补的。不过，这些优点与缺点都是相对于居住国政府和跨国纳税人的利益而言的。任何一个主权国家，都有权在其税收制度中规定采用何种限额抵免方法。《中华人民共和国企业所得税法》规定：企业所得税采用分国抵免限额。

(3) 分项抵免限额。

分项抵免限额是比较每一项所得的已纳外国税额与该项所得按照本国税法计算的应纳税额，二者中较小者为抵免限额。这种方法可以避免不同所得之间的税率高低的相互抵补。虽然只有很少的国家实行分项抵免限额，但在理论上它是最好的方法。分项抵免限额中的所得"项"是指某一所得类型，如利息所得或海运所得等。原则上讲，一国可以将在外国适用特殊税收规定的某类所得定义为一个所得"项"。例如，如果 B 国对营业利润按 50% 征税，对利息所得按 10% 征税，A 国在计算本国居民支付给 B 国税收的抵免限额时，可能将发生于 B 国的营业利润和利息所得分别视为不同"项"的所得。

20 世纪 70 年代以前，大多数国家采用分国抵免限额，而在这之后综合抵免限额逐渐取代了它。值得注意的是,由于许多国家对股息、利息、特许权使用费等投资所得规定较低的所得税率,也有一些国家对农业、林业、渔业或矿业收入采取低税优惠的办法。因而一些国家在已采用综合抵免限额的同时,为了防止跨国纳税人以某一外国低税率所得税的抵免限额余额冲抵另一外国高税率所得税的超限抵免额而进行国际间的税收逃避活动,明确规定对上述国外来源的单项收入采用单独计算抵免限额的方法。

其计算公式为:

分项抵免限额=国内外应税所得按居住国税法计算的应纳税总额×(国外某一单项应税所得额÷国内外应税所得额)

当然,在居住国所得税率为比例税率的情况下,上述抵免限额的计算公式也可以简化。分项抵免限额作为综合抵免限额的一种补充,其目的或作用在于弥补综合抵免限额之不足。其实,上述问题不仅存在于综合抵免限额之中,而且在分国抵免限额中也同时存在。

我国目前对企业和个人外国税收抵免限额的计算主要采用分国抵免限额。我国的有关税法规定,企业如果能全面提供境外完税凭证的,可采取分国不分项的办法计算企业的外国税收抵免限额。我国的个人所得税也允许采取分国抵免限额,但与企业所得税分国不分项的办法不同,它要求采用分国分项的办法计算抵免限额。

计算抵免限额的三种方法之间并不排斥,一国可能同时采用实行两种或三种方法。例如,有的国家以综合抵免限额为基础,同时对于某些类型的所得(如利息和海运收入)采用分项抵免限额。美国就是实行这种混合方法计算限额的,对于不同类型的所得分别计算出不同的抵免限额,通常称为"分篮限额法"。

2) 直接抵免与间接抵免

由于外国税收抵免方法涉及面广,对不同经济关系的公司、企业、个人等的不同所得可以有不同的处理方式,因而在计算上显得较为复杂。在实际应用中,抵免方法又可分为直接抵免和间接抵免两种方法。

(1) 直接抵免。

所谓直接抵免,是指居住国的纳税人用其直接缴纳的外国税款冲抵在本国应缴纳的税额。一国居民直接缴纳外国税款,可以是个人居民到国外从事经济活动取得收入而向当地政府纳税,可以是居住国的总公司设在国外的分公司(总公司与分公司在法律上属于同一法人实体)向所在国缴纳税款,也可以是居住国母公司从国外子公司取得股息、利息等投资所得而向子公司所在国缴纳预提税。可见,直接抵免是一种适用于同一经济实体的跨国纳税人的税收抵免方法,其基本特征在于允许抵免的外国税收必须是跨国纳税人直接向非居住国缴纳的所得税,非直接缴纳的所得税款则不能直接冲抵居住国应纳所得税款。所以,直接抵免一般适用于个人的所得税抵免、总公司与分公司之间的公司所得税抵免以及母公司与子公司之间的预提所得税抵免。

用直接抵免计算应纳居住国税额的公式为:

应纳居住国税额=(居住国应税所得+来源国应税所得)×居住国税率−实际抵免额=纳税人全部应税所得×居住国税率−实际抵免额

 模拟演示 4-9

【背景】假定 A 国一个居民公司在某纳税年度获得总所得 10 000 万元。其中,来自本国所得 8 000 万元，来自 B 国（来源国）分公司所得 2 000 万元。现计算该公司在采用直接抵免法时应向 A 国缴纳多少税款。

【演算 1】

当 A 国适用税率为 30%、B 国为 30%，即两国税率相等时，A 国政府允许该公司用已纳全部 B 国所得税冲抵 A 总公司的应纳税额。

总所得按 A 国税率计算的应纳税额：10 000×30% = 3 000（万元）。

分公司已纳 B 国税额：2 000×30% = 600（万元）。

实际抵免额：600 万元。

总公司得到抵免后应向 A 国缴纳的税额：3 000-600 = 2 400（万元）。

国内外应纳税合计：2 400+600 = 3 000（万元）。

【评述 1】

这种情况表明，当两国税率相等时，对分公司已纳 B 国税额，总公司可以享受全部抵免。总公司与分公司的税收负担之和仍然是 3 000 万元，没有因有国外所得而发生变化。

【演算 2】

当 A 国税率为 30%、B 国税率为 20%时，该总公司仅能按实纳外国税款进行抵免，在实行税收抵免后，还要就 B 国所得按照两国税率差额，向 A 国补缴其税收差额。

总所得按 A 国税率计算的应纳税额：10 000×30% = 3 000（万元）。

分公司已纳 B 国税额：2 000×20% = 400（万元）。

B 国税收抵免限额：2 000×30% = 600（万元）。

实际抵免额：400 万元。

总公司抵免后应向 A 国缴纳的税额：3 000-400 = 2 600（万元）。

国内外应纳税合计：2 600+400 = 3 000（万元）。

【评述 2】

这种情况表明，当居住国税率高于分公司所在国税率时，该居民公司就其来自 A 国、B 国所得抵免后缴纳的全部税额，也等于该公司的全部所得应承担的本国（A 国）税负。

【演算 3】

当 A 国税率为 30%、B 国税率为 40%时，该居民公司在 B 国已纳税额在 A 国得不到全部抵免，其可以用于抵免的数额仅为其 B 国所得按照 A 国税率计算的税额。

总所得按 A 国税率计算的应纳税额：10 000×30% = 3 000（万元）。

分公司已纳 B 国税额：2 000×40% = 800（万元）。

B 国税收抵免限额：2 000×30% = 600（万元）。

实际抵免额：600 万元。

总公司抵免后应向 A 国缴纳税额：3 000-600 = 2 400（万元）。

该居民公司缴纳的税收总额：2 400+800 = 3 200（万元）。

【评述 3】

这种情况表明，当外国税率高于居住国税率时，由于居住国规定有抵免限额，纳税人在国外缴纳的税款就有一部分不能用于冲减本国的应纳税额，纳税人的实际税收负担就要重于前两种情况（该居民公司比前两种情况多负担 200 万元税款）。

(2) 间接抵免。

许多抵免制国家提供间接抵免。间接抵免是指本国公司可以间接抵免其外国关联公司所支付的外国所得税,当国内公司从其国外关联公司取得所分配的股息时即可获得该项抵免。抵免额为支付股息的所得所承担的由外国关联公司支付的外国税收,也就是说,间接抵免的基本特征是外国税收只能部分地、间接地冲抵居住国的应纳税款。

间接抵免发生在这种情况下,即一国的母公司在国外拥有子公司,子公司在当地缴纳公司所得税,并将税后利润按母公司的股权比重分配给母公司。由于母公司分得的股息来自子公司的税后利润,因此这部分股息必然会负担子公司所在国的税款。又因母子公司是两个不同的法人,所以子公司缴纳的而由母公司负担的那部分子公司所在国税款并不是母公司的直接缴纳,而是一种间接缴纳。这样一来,母公司用这笔国外税款冲抵本国的应缴税款就属于间接抵免。需要指出的是,母子公司之间的间接抵免只适用于子公司所在国课征的公司所得税,如果母公司取得的股息必须向来源国缴纳股息预提所得税,该预提税也可以在抵免限额内冲抵母公司的应纳税额。但由于母公司是预提税的纳税人,对股息预提税的抵免属于直接抵免,而不属于间接抵免。而且,由于母公司收到的股息只是子公司所得税后利润的一部分,无法确切或直接知道这部分股息已经负担了多少子公司所在国的所得税,以及原所得额(即税前所得)为多少,必须通过推算才能知道。所以,居住国政府对其母公司从国外子公司处取得的股息汇总计征所得税时,只能用母公司取得的子公司股息的相应利润(即还原出来的那部分子公司税前所得),作为母公司来自国外子公司的所得,并入母公司总所得内进行征税。允许抵免的税额也只能是这部分股息所应分摊的那部分子公司所得税额。

一般而言,外国税收抵免只限于本国居民纳税人直接缴纳的外国税收,而间接抵免出于抵免目的忽略了本国公司和外国关联公司作为两个独立公司的法律存在形式。并且,本国公司拥有的外国关联公司股份必须达到最低比例,通常为10%,才允许抵免关联公司所缴纳的外国所得税。

在间接抵免的情况下,母公司向居住国的纳税额应分两步计算。

第一步,计算母公司来自国外子公司的所得额。

母公司来自子公司的所得=母公司股息+母公司股息承担的子公司所得税

当外国子公司所得税适用比例税率时,母公司来自子公司的所得,还可按下列简化公式计算:

母公司来自子公司的所得=母公司股息÷(1-子公司所得税率)

第二步,计算母公司间接缴纳的子公司所在国的税款。

母公司股息承担的子公司所得税=子公司所得税×(母公司股息÷子公司税后所得)

同样,当外国子公司所得税适用比例税率时,母公司应承担的子公司所得税的计算公式也可以简化,即:

母公司应承担的子公司所得税=母公司股息÷(1-子公司所得税率)×子公司所得税率

按照上式计算出来的应属母公司承担的外国子公司所得税,还必须特别注意与抵免限额进行比较(抵免限额的计算与直接抵免情况下相同)。在没有超过抵免限额的情况下,可以允许母公司从其应缴纳的居住国政府所得税中全部扣除,否则只能按限额进行抵免。

间接抵免的基本运作可以通过下面的例子来阐释。

 模拟演示 4-10

【背景】A 国母公司在 B 国设立一子公司(该子公司并非是母公司的全资子公司),A

国公司所得税率为35%，B国为30%。在某纳税年度，该子公司所得为1 000万元，缴纳B国所得税300万元（1 000×30%），并从其税后利润700万元（1 000-300）中分给A国母公司股息100万元。（假设母公司并无来自A国的所得）

【演算】

母公司来自子公司的所得：100+300×［100÷（1 000-300）］=142.8571（万元），

或：100÷（1-30%）=142.8571（万元）。

母公司间接缴纳的子公司所得税：300×［100÷（1 000-300）］=42.8571（万元），

或：100÷（1-30%）×30%=42.8571（万元）。

间接抵免限额：142.857l×35%=50（万元）。

实际抵免额：42.8571万元。

母公司实缴A国所得税：50-42.8571=7.1429（万元）。

【评述】从上述计算结果可知，母公司向A国缴纳的7.1429万元所得税，实际上就是母公司抵免后补缴的差额税款。

在通常情况下，子公司所在国不仅对子公司的所得课征公司所得税，还要对支付给境外母公司的股息课征预提所得税。因此，母公司所在国还要对这两种税采用直接和间接相结合的方式进行税收抵免。

模拟演示 4-11

【背景】在模拟演示 4-10 的情况下，B国预提所得税率为10%，子公司在付给母公司100万元股息时，就要缴纳预提所得税10万元（100×10%）。

【演算】

母公司国外税款总额（=直接抵免+间接抵免）：10+42.8571=52.8571（万元）。

抵免限额：142.857l×35%=50（万元）。

实际抵免额：50（万元）。

母公司实缴A国所得税：50-50=0（万元）。

【评述】可见，经过抵免后，母公司并未向A国缴纳任何税款。换而言之，A国政府并未从母公司征到税。

模拟演示 4-12

【背景】A国母公司在B国设立一子公司，并拥有子公司50%的股票，在某一纳税年度内，母公司来自A国的所得为1 000万元，子公司来自B国的所得为500万元，A国所得税率为40%，B国为35%，并且B国允许子公司保留税后利润（即未分配利润）10%，并对其汇出境外的股息征收10%的预提所得税。

【演算】

子公司纳税情况：

子公司已纳B国所得税：500×35%=175（万元）。

子公司税后收益：500-175=325（万元）。

子公司可保留的未分配利润：325×10%=32.5（万元）。

子公司可分配股息：325-32.5=292.5（万元）。

应分给 A 国母公司的股息：292.5×50%＝146.25（万元）。
母公司股息预提所得税：146.25×10%＝14.625（万元）。
母公司纳税情况：
母公司来自子公司的所得：146.25+175×（146.25÷325）＝225（万元）。
或：146.25÷（1-35%）＝225（万元）。
母公司应承担的子公司所得税：175×（146.25÷325）＝78.75（万元）。
或：146.25÷（1-35%）×35%＝78.75（万元）。
抵免限额：225×40%＝90（万元）。
母公司国外税款总额（直接抵免+间接抵免）：14.625+78.75＝93.375（万元）。
实际抵免额：90（万元）。
母公司实际缴纳的 A 国所得税款：（1 000+225）×40%-90＝400（万元）。

【评述】在上述计算抵免时，必须按间接抵免的两个重要公式进行操作，不能直接以已知控股比例等条件进行计算。

间接抵免不仅适用于母公司来自其外国子公司的股息所应承担的外国所得税的抵免，而且还可适用于母公司通过子公司来自其外国孙公司，以及外国孙公司下属的外国重孙公司等多层外国附属公司的股息所应承担的外国政府所得税来解决子公司以下各层"母子公司"的重复征税问题，但具体计算步骤要更加复杂些。

3) 费用的分摊

一国无论是采用免税法还是抵免法消除国际双重征税，都应制定一些规则，合理地分摊纳税人取得外国来源所得和本国来源所得所发生的费用。多数国家承认，在对非居民纳税人的本国来源所得征税时，有必要制定上述费用分摊规则。这些国家通常允许非居民扣除与取得应税本国来源所得有关的费用，不允许扣除其他费用。然而，似乎没有哪一个国家意识到同样有必要合理地分摊本国纳税人取得本国来源所得和外国来源所得所发生的费用。

对外国来源所得免税的国家，不应扣除取得外国来源所得所发生的费用。例如，纳税人用于取得免税外国来源所得的借贷资金所发生的利息费用是不应扣除的。如果一国允许扣除取得免税外国来源所得所发生的费用，就相当于对取得外国来源所得提供税收优惠，鼓励取得免税的外国来源所得，而不鼓励取得应税的本国来源所得，实际上，这个国家不仅对外国来源所得免税，而且对一部分本国来源所得也准予免税。

许多国家并没有制定具体的规定用以计算归属于外国来源所得的费用。通常可以采用两种方法，即追溯法和分摊法。

追溯法需要据实查询费用与外国来源所得的联系；分摊法需要根据公式计算分摊费用，公式的确定要么按照纳税人国外资产占其总资产的比重，要么按照外国来源毛收入占其全部国内外来源毛收入的比重进行计算。与追溯法不同，分摊法所依据的假设前提是，相关费用的发生是为了均等地支持纳税人的所有资产或取得收入的经营活动。

由于居民纳税人就其全球范围的所得在本国纳税，因而实行抵免法的国家应允许居民纳税人扣除取得外国来源所得所发生的费用。然而，由于存在抵免限额，外国税收抵免额始终受限于外国来源应税所得按照本国税法计算的税额。为此，必须正确计算纳税人外国来源的应纳税所得额，如果计算不当，没有扣除相关费用，就会增大抵免额。为了正确计算外国来源的应纳税所得额，应允许纳税人从外国来源的毛收入中扣除与取得收入有关的费用。

制定费用分摊规则的必要性可以通过一个简单例子作进一步阐述。

模拟演示 4-13

【背景】假设某居民公司借入资金 1 000 万元,年利率是 8%,现将这笔贷款用于外国分公司的经营活动,外国分公司获得毛收入 280 万元,扣除利息支出 80 万元后,得到净收入 200 万元,净收入按外国税率 50% 纳税,须交税 100 万元。如果该公司本国来源所得是 2 000 万元,则全部国内外来源所得为 2 200 万元,假设本国税率是 40%,该公司抵免前的应纳税额为 880 万元(2 200×40%)。由于受到抵免限额的限制,允许该公司抵免的外国税收是 100 万元和 80 万元(880×200/2 200)中的较小者,这样,80 万元就代表了纳税人外国来源的应税所得按照本国税法计算的税额,如表 4-2 所示。

表 4-2 某居民公司纳税情况　　　　　　　　　　　　　　　　单位：万元

项目	金额
外国分公司毛收入	280
利息费用	80
外国净收入	200
外国税收(税率是 50%)	100
本国净收入	2 000
国内外所得总额(200+2 000)	2 200
按 40% 税率计算的应纳税收	880
外国税收抵免额	80
应纳税总额	800

【评述】在上例中,80 万元的利息费用完全由外国来源所得摊销。如果利息费用完全由本国来源所得摊销,由于抵免限额是 140 万元(280×50%)和 112 万元(880×280/2 200)中的较小者,则外国税收 140 万元能在本国税收中抵免 112 万元(高于 80 万元)。假设利息费用合理地分摊到外国来源所得,在计算外国税收抵免限额时也应当按此分摊原则,否则按照本国税法,外国税额超出就外国来源所得计算的本国税额部分也会被抵免。总之,在保护本国税基方面,将利息和其他费用合理地分摊到本国来源所得和外国来源所得至关重要。

计算间接抵免限额时,也应当将合理的费用额分摊到外国来源所得。此外,间接抵免还会涉及居民母公司从外国关联公司取得所得所发生费用扣除时间的确认问题。居民国对通过外国关联公司取得的外国来源所得征税,通常要等到居民母公司实际得到股息(或其他已税分配利润)时才确认征税时间,相应地,至少从理论上讲,母公司取得该项所得发生的利息和其他费用支出也只有在确认征税后才能扣除,即费用扣除时间应确认为母公司从外国关联公司取得已税分配利润的时间。但实际上,很少有国家采用这种费用扣除时间的确认方法。

4) 税收饶让抵免

税收饶让抵免是指居民国对于根据来源国一般税收法规本应缴纳但实际没有缴纳的外国税收给予抵免。通常实际没有缴纳税收的原因是来源国为了吸引外资而对外国投资者提供了免税期或其他税收优惠措施。如果没有税收饶让,由于投资者在来源国税收的减少将会导致居民国税收的增加,因此,来源国税收优惠的真正受益者将是居民国而不是投资者。对于居民国来说，税收饶让不是一种消除国际重复征税的方法，而是居住国对从事国际经济活动的本国居民采取的一种税收优惠措施。

 模拟演示 4-14

【背景】A 国是发展中国家，法定企业所得税率是 30%，如果外国公司在 A 国设立生产性企业，可以享受 10 年免税期。B 公司是 B 国居民公司，在 A 国设立了一个加工厂。B 国企业所得税率为 40%，实行外国税收抵免制。

【演算】如表 4-3 所示，B 公司第一年在 A 国取得收入 1 000 万元，如果没有免税期优惠，A 国要对 B 公司征税 300 万元（1 000×30%），B 国按税率征税 400 万元（1 000×40%），减去外国税收抵免额 300 万元，补征 100 万元，B 公司全部应纳税额为 400 万元（300+100）；由于免税期的存在，A 国税收由 300 万元变为 0，由于 B 公司在 A 国没有纳税，B 公司在 B 国的应纳税额变成等于 400 万元（400-0），B 公司全部应纳税额仍然为 400 万元（0+400）。这样，B 公司由于享受免税期待遇在 A 国少缴税收 300 万元导致了 B 国税收增加 300 万元，而 B 公司没有真正受益。

如果 B 国愿意就 A 国少征的税收给予 B 公司税收饶让抵免，B 公司就会得到免税期实惠。B 公司在 A 国取得收入 1 000 万元，在 A 国不缴税，在 B 国法定应缴税 400 万元，但允许抵免 A 国少征的税收 300 万元后，最终全部应纳税额为 100 万元。

表 4-3 外国公司在 A 国和 B 国的纳税情况　　　　　　　　　　单位：万元

A 国	
从 A 国取得的收入	1 000
没有免税期的 A 国应纳税额	300
免税期免税额	300
A 国实际缴纳的税收	0
B 国	
从 A 国取得的收入	1 000
B 国法定应纳税收	400
饶让抵免额	300
B 国应纳税额	100

【评述】上例阐明了在没有税收饶让的情况下来源国的税收优惠收益如何从外国投资者那里转移到居民国。也就是说，发展中国家牺牲本国税收利益做出的减免税，将会变成投资者居住国（大多是发达国家）的税收收入，减少了发展中国家的财政收入并相应地增加了发达国家的财政收入。因此，税收饶让是发展中国家和发达国家签署税收协定的一个主要特征。一些发展中国家传统上一贯坚持：如果发达国家不给予饶让，就不与其签署税收协定。许多发达国家也将给予发展中国家税收饶让作为协定常规条款，有些发达国家出于鼓励向发展中国家投资的考虑自愿给予饶让，但其他发达国家只是勉强给予发展中国家税收饶让。

美国强硬地反对税收饶让，在已经签署的税收协定中都未规定税收饶让条款，其结果是在过去的很长一段时间内美国与发展中国家签署的协定很少。美国的立场是，给予虚幻税收（实际未缴纳的税收）抵免与外国税收抵免的效率与公平目标相悖，会导致发展中国家纷纷展开恶性税收优惠竞争。尽管这一立场被认为是"傲慢的""帝国主义的"和"骄傲自大的"，但它是对税收饶让负面影响效果的评价。近年来，发展中国家坚持索要税收饶让的强硬立场有所改变，美国与发展中国家签署协定的数目也迅速上升。

评价税收饶让抵免离不开它所鼓励的税收优惠。尽管税收优惠在政治领域得到了一些支持者的热情支持，但在税收政策原则方面却很难自圆其说。为实现特定目标而设计的特定税收优惠可能是合理的，但这些优惠规定为了防止滥用的目的往往局限在很窄的范围内，通常得不到多数政治支持。从大量的关于税收优惠的文献中得出的一般结论是，税收优惠成本太大，受益不确定，潜在的受益很难与可能花费的成本相匹配。

税收饶让带来的另一个问题是通过滥用税收饶让来避税。例如，如果协定中的税收饶让抵免条款规定得较宽泛，往往会诱导第三国居民在税收饶让给予国设立传输公司，借以享受协定的税收饶让待遇。此外，由于税收饶让会刺激纳税人将利润转移到来源国，因此税收饶让对居民国的转让定价操作也形成压力。

1998年，经济合作与发展组织（OECD）发表了题为《税收饶让的再思考》的报告，对税收饶让提出了质疑。报告认为，税收饶让应只给予那些经济发展水平明显低于OECD成员国的国家。此外，报告还就如何制定饶让抵免条款、确保税收饶让仅适用于真正的经营性投资活动并防止税收饶让滥用提出了有价值的建议。

4.3 消除国际重复征税不同方法的比较

关于国际重复征税问题的处理方法，包括扣除法、免税法和抵免法等，各有利弊。采用哪种方法比较适当，取决于各国的税制结构和税收政策，最根本的还在于居住国和收入来源国的税收管辖权是否都得到考虑和维护，以及跨国纳税人的国际重复征税问题是否得到基本解决。

1. 扣除法与免税法的比较

扣除法与免税法的区别在于免税法承认收入来源地管辖权的独占地位，而扣除法只是有限度地承认收入来源地管辖权的优先地位。免税法是对跨国纳税人来自国外的所得免予课税，扣除法则仅对其来自国外的所得已纳所得税款部分免予课税。所以，扣除法的税收负担高于免税法，也就是说，免税法是对国际重复征税问题的彻底解决，而扣除法则至多是一种酌情照顾而已。故扣除法对跨国纳税人进行国际投资和国际贸易不利。

2. 抵免法与扣除法的比较

抵免法完全承认收入来源地管辖权的优先地位，对国外已征本国居民的所得税款，在税法规定限度内给予抵免，而扣除法并非完全承认收入来源地管辖权的优先地位，对国外已征本国居民的所得税款，仅给予部分扣除照顾。抵免法可基本解决跨国纳税人的国际重复征税问题，而扣除法则不能完全解决这种问题，但两者在充分考虑居住国居民管辖权的行使方面，具有共性。

3. 免税法与抵免法的比较

免税法是对本国居民来自国外的所得，完全放弃居民管辖权，而抵免法则是照样行使居民管辖权，只不过在课税时对其居民已缴国外所得税款给予抵免。但是，由于免税法在实践中又有全额免税与累进免税两种不同做法，对于全额免税法，居住国政府完全承认了收入来源地管辖权的独占地位，放弃了居民管辖权。而对于累进免税法则不然，虽然在表面形式上它也承认了收入来源地管辖权的独占地位，放弃了居民管辖权，但由于其独特的计算方法与效果，居住国政府在对其居民国外所得全部免税而仅对其国内应纳税所得额征税时，还可从适用较高税率上取回一部分收益，实际上也是对居住国税收权益的一种维护。在同样情况下，其效果与抵免法基本相同，甚至还可能会优于抵免法。此外，抵免法与免税法在承认收入来源地管辖权的独占或优先地位，以及解决跨国纳税人的国际重复征税问题方面，效果也基本相同。

复习思考题

1. 消除国际重复征税的方式有哪些？
2. 消除国际重复征税的方法有哪些？
3. 什么是抵免限额？如何计算抵免限额？其合理性何在？
4. 什么是直接抵免？什么是间接抵免？
5. 母公司应如何在采用抵免法的情况下缴纳本国税款？
6. 什么是税收饶让？其有何意义？

第 5 章

国际避税

📝 时政观点

关税具有涉外性，对货物征收关税，势必提高纳税人的经营成本，直接影响国际贸易的开展。这不仅是一种经济关系，更是一种政治关系。同学们应结合当前我国经济形势和主动履行大国担当的事实，认可中国对世界人民作出的重大贡献，特别是对于发展中国家的援助。

📖 学习目标

1. 全面把握避税与偷税、节税的区别与联系。
2. 重点掌握国际避税的概念和产生的原因。
3. 了解避税港的概念和类型。
4. 掌握避税港的特征。

🔍 课程导入

避税港在不同国家有不同的名称：英语国家称其为"避税港"，法国称其为"财政天堂"，德国则习惯称其为"税收绿洲"。作为避税港的国家和地区往往自称"金融中心"。它们的本质是什么呢？

📖 5.1　国际避税的概念

众所周知，任何事物都有正反两个方面，国际税收也不例外。作为国际重复征税的对立面，国际避税同样也是一种普遍而有趣的社会经济现象，它是商品经济发展到一定阶段的必然产物。国际重复征税会损害跨国纳税人的切身经济利益，从而不利于国际经济活动的发展；而国际避税虽可以减轻跨国纳税人的税收负担，但却会影响相关国家的税收利益，扭曲国与国之间的税收分配关系。所以，各国政府以及国际社会不仅要采取措施避免所得的国际重复征税，也要采取措施防范跨国纳税人的国际避税。

1. 避税的含义

要弄清什么是国际避税，自然要先弄清什么是避税。避税历来是各国税收征管工作中的一个重要问题，它与节税、偷税、漏税等活动不同，但又有一定的联系。避税究竟是合法的还是违法的？要回答这个问题，还必须对避税和节税、偷税、漏税等有关问题进行全面分析和比较。

1）节税

节税也称税收筹划，在西方国家几乎早已家喻户晓，但在我国却鲜为人知。税收筹划是指纳税人在法律规定许可的范围内，根据政府的税收政策导向，通过对经营活动的事先筹划与安排，进行纳税方案的优化选择，以尽可能减轻税收负担，获得正当的税收利益。

税收筹划的特点在于合法性、筹划性和目的性。此外，在社会化大生产的历史条件下，税收筹划还反映出综合性和专业性的要求。特别是20世纪50年代以来，税收筹划的专业化趋势十分明显。面对社会化大生产和日益扩大的国际市场以及错综复杂的各国税制，许多企业、公司都聘用税务顾问、税务律师、审计师、会计师、国际金融顾问等高级专门人才从事税收筹划活动，以节约税金支出。同时，也有众多的会计师、律师和税务师事务所纷纷开辟和发展有关税收筹划的咨询业务，因此作为第三产业的税务代理便应运而生。由此可见，节税是一种合法的行为，在税务上不应反对，而应予以保护。

2）偷税、漏税

偷税是指纳税人通过非法的手段不缴或少缴税，通常都要采用虚报、瞒报和故意欺骗的做法。对于偷税的这一基本含义，人们已达成某些共识，即偷税是一种非法行为，是以非法手段减轻纳税义务。但是，人们并没有说明使用非法手段是否有意识。实际上，偷税可包括无意识违法行为和故意违法行为两种。前者主要是指纳税人因无知或无意识地违反税法规定而单纯不缴纳或少缴应纳税款的行为，即漏税。例如，纳税人由于不熟悉税法规定和财会制度或工作粗心大意，漏报应税项目，少计应税产品数量，错算销售金额或经营利润，错用税种、税目、税率等原因，再加上征收人员政策、业务知识水平等原因，发生的漏交税款。而偷税则是指纳税义务人以欺骗、隐瞒等手段，故意不缴或少缴应纳税款的行为，但要证明纳税人故意不缴或少缴应纳税款，有时也不是一件很容易的事情。所以，两者又可以统称为偷、漏税。

综上所述，偷税的基本特征是非法性和欺诈性，所以也可称为税收欺诈。偷税与节税相比，二者的区别是非常明显的，前者违反法律，后者是法律规定所许可的；前者是对已确立的纳税义务隐瞒作假，后者则是在纳税义务确立之前所做的经营、投资、理财的事先筹划与安排。

3）避税

避税是个常常引起人们争议的概念。一般认为，避税是指通过合法的途径延迟、规避或减少纳税。当代著名经济学家萨缪尔森在分析美国联邦税制时指出："比逃税更加重要的是合法地规避赋税，原因在于议会制定的法规有许多'漏洞'，听任大量的收入不上税或者以较低的税率上税。"

以上叙述表明：避税与偷税无论是从动机还是最终结果来看，两者之间并无绝对明显的界限，共同之处在于两者都是纳税人有意采取的减轻自己税收负担的行为，但它们毕竟是两个不同的概念。一般认为，两者之间存在以下区别。

（1）偷税是指纳税人在纳税义务已经发生的情况下通过种种手段不缴纳税款；而避税则是指纳税人规避或减少纳税义务。

（2）偷税直接违反税法，是一种非法行为；而避税是钻税法的空子，并不直接违反税法，因而从形式上看它是一种不违法的行为。

（3）偷税不仅违反税法，而且往往要借助犯罪手段，比如做假账、伪造凭证等，所以偷税行为应受到法律制裁（拘役或监禁）；而避税是一种不违法行为，并不构成犯罪，所以不应受到法律的制裁。

避税与节税相比，主要的区别在于前者虽不违法，但有悖于国家税收政策导向和意图；而后者则是完全合法的，甚至是税收政策予以引导和鼓励的。

面对纳税人的避税行为，政府可以采取两种措施：一是完善税法，堵住税法中的漏洞，使纳税人没有可乘之机；二是在税法中引入"滥用权利"或"滥用法律"的概念，即一方面承认纳税人有权按使其纳税义务最小化的方式从事经营活动；另一方面对纳税人完全是出于避税考虑而进行的交易活动不予认可，并将其视为纳税人滥用了自己的权利，税务机关可以根据真实商业目的原则不承认纳税人的避税安排，并对避税造成的后果进行调整。

2. 国际避税的含义

国际避税，是避税活动在国际范围内的延伸和发展，是指跨国纳税人利用各国税法规定的差别和漏洞，以种种公开的合法手段规避或减轻其税负的行为。对于上述国际避税的概念，可从以下两点把握。

1）国际避税不同于国内避税

国内避税是指一国纳税人利用本国的税法漏洞进行的避税，它不通过纳税人跨越国境的活动，其所规避的纳税义务仅为居住国的纳税义务。而国际避税则是利用国与国之间的税法差异，钻涉外税法和国际税法的漏洞而进行避税。这种避税活动需要纳税人从事一些跨越本国国境的活动，或者纳税人跨越本国国境进行自身的流动，或者纳税人将自己的资金或财产转移出本国，使其在国际间进行流动；国际避税所要规避的纳税义务不仅限于纳税人的居住国，还包括所得的来源国；纳税人进行国际避税的目的往往不是减轻其在某一国的税收负担，而是减轻其全球总税负。

2）国际避税不同于国际偷税

国际偷税是纳税人在跨国经营活动中利用非法手段逃避其在有关国家已负有的纳税义务，它与国内偷税活动一样，是一种违法行为。而国际避税则是纳税人利用公开、不违法的手段进行的，一般并不违反有关国家的税法，所以总体上说它不属于非法的行为。由于国际避税和国际偷税的性质不同，所以对两者的处理方法也有所不同。对于国际偷税，有关国家要像对待国内的偷税活动一样对违法者进行法律制裁；而对于国际避税，有关国家一般只能通过完善本国的涉外税收法规或修订本国与他国签订的税收协定堵塞法律漏洞，不给跨国纳税人提供国际避税的可乘之机，但并不能像对待国际偷税那样对跨国纳税人进行严厉的法律制裁。

5.2 国际避税产生的原因

避税最初产生的缘由是纳税人为抵制政府过重的税收负担，维护既得利益而进行各种偷税、逃税受到严厉的法律制裁之后寻求更为有效的躲避税负方法的结果，国际避税的出现也不例外。第二次世界大战以后，国际避税之所以能够广泛产生并在世界范围内得到迅猛地发展，其原因不外乎有其内在动机和外部条件两个方面，即国际避税存在主客观两方面的原因。

1. 从主观上看，跨国纳税人追逐最大利润是产生国际避税的内在动机

利润最大化是所有从事生产、经营、投资活动的纳税人都追求的共同目标，跨国纳税人更是如此。减轻纳税义务的方式很多，包括隐蔽式的非法偷税、逃税和公开式的避税。但是，如果跨国纳税人以偷税、逃税的方式来减轻税负，不免会遭到有关国家的严厉打击，使其声誉扫地，钱财受损，结果得不偿失。因此，许多跨国纳税人都不愿以这种风险太大的方式来减轻税负，而乐意以避税的方式来实现这一目标，因为避税既不违反税法规定，不致遭到法律的严厉打击，又可获得额外收益。可见，减轻税负最有效而又风险不大的方式莫过于避税了。

2. 从客观上说，各国税收制度的差别和缺陷是产生国际避税的外部条件

人们常说，内因是动力，外因是条件，只有内因和外因的结合，才能有结果。概括起来，国际避税产生的客观原因主要有以下几个方面：

（1）有关国家（地区）税收管辖权的差异以及判定居民身份的标准和判定所得来源地的标准存在差异，可以为跨国纳税人提供税收管辖权的真空，从而有可能使跨国纳税人避开任何国家（地区）的纳税义务。

历史上著名的朗勃避税案就是利用税收管辖权真空进行的。朗勃是英国一种汽轮机叶片的发明人，他将这项发明转让给卡塔尔的一家公司，得到47 500美元的技术转让费。朗勃根据技术转让费的获得者不是卡塔尔居民不必向卡塔尔政府纳税的规定，避开了向卡塔尔政府纳税的义务。同时，朗勃又将其在英国的住所卖掉，迁居到中国香港，以住所不在英国为由避开了向英国政府的纳税义务。而香港仅实行地域管辖权，不对来自香港以外地区的所得征税。这样，朗勃虽取得了一笔不小的技术转让费收入，但因处于各国（地区）税收管辖权的真空地带，可以不就这笔收入负担任何纳税义务。

（2）税率的差异。税率是税法的核心，它的高低直接关系到纳税人的税收负担。如果世界上所有国家和地区所征收的税率高低一致，没有一个可供其进行国际避税的场所，则纳税人一般也就没有可能通过人或财物的跨国流动进行避税。然而，现实中国家之间的税率差异很大，有的税率高，有的税率低，甚至有的国家根本不征所得税。这就为纳税人将所得从高税国转移到低税国进行避税提供了可能。特别是避税港的存在，是跨国纳税人进行国际避税的重要前提条件之一。

（3）国际税收协定的大量存在。为避免所得的国际重复征税，目前世界上存在着大量的国际税收协定。然而，税收协定中的有关规定很容易被跨国纳税人用来进行国际避税。例如，目前各国对本国居民向外国居民支付的股息、利息、特许权使用费一般要征收较高的预提税。但如果一国与他国签订了税收协定，则对向对方国家居民支付的股息、利息等课征的预提税税率就会大为降低。这时，一个第三国居民企业为了从上述两国的税收协定中得到预提税方面的好处，就可以在其中一国建立中介性质的附属公司，以便利用两国间的税收协定减轻预提税的纳税义务。这就是我们后面要谈到的滥用国际税收协定的问题。滥用国际税收协定是跨国公司进行国际避税的重要方式，而国际税收协定的大量存在，则为跨国公司进行国际避税开了方便之门。

（4）涉外税收法规中的漏洞。一国涉外税收法规中存在漏洞，也可以为纳税人进行国际避税创造有利条件。这方面的典型例子是一些发达国家实行的延迟课税规定。延迟课税是指一国政府对本国居民从国外分得的利润在汇回本国以前不征税，只有当这笔利润汇回

本国时再对其征税。实质上，发达国家制定延迟课税的规定是为了支持本国居民公司海外子公司的发展，增强其与当地公司的竞争能力，但这一规定后来被许多跨国公司用来从事国际避税。它们在低税国或国际避税港建立自己的子公司，通过种种手段把利润转移到这些子公司，并将分得的利润长期滞留在海外子公司。由于可以享受推迟课税待遇，这些跨国公司就凭借这种手段成功地避开了居住国较重的税收。

此外，跨国避税活动的形成，客观上还有一些非税原因。例如，外汇管制方面的宽严程度，以及公司法、移民法、银行保密条例、通货膨胀等方面的差异，也都会对跨国纳税人的国际避税行为具有重要影响，即可能引起纳税人或课税对象由一国向另一国转移。

 ## 5.3 避税港

在现实社会经济生活中，有相当一部分国家和地区出于一定的经济目的，采取以无税或低税为基本特征的税收政策，制定优惠的税收制度，为跨国投资者提供了合法逃避国际税收的便利条件。这些国家和地区对跨国投资者有着十分强烈的吸引力，即所谓的"避税港"。跨国投资者为了减轻税收负担，经常利用这些国家和地区从事国际避税活动。

5.3.1 避税港的概念

当人们谈论避税港时，还有自由港、和平港以及安全港之说。在这种情况下，所谓的"港"字往往可以泛指某一国家或某一地区，超出了"港口"或"港区"原有的狭窄含义。

避税港，亦称国际避税地，是指对所得（或某些形式的所得）或实体（或某些形式的实体）征收低税或不征税的国家和地区。从实质上说，避税港就是指外国人可以在那里取得收入或拥有资产，而不必支付高税率税款的地方，它的存在是跨国纳税人得以进行国际避税活动的重要前提条件。

尽管人们对"避税港"一词已十分熟悉，但截至目前，它还没有一个被普遍接受的定义。根据 OECD 的报告，一个对流动性经营活动无税或仅有象征性税收的国家，只要满足三个附加条件之一，就会被视为避税港。

（1）它不与别的国家有效地交换税收信息。

（2）它以非透明的方式向纳税人提供税收优惠。

（3）非居民不用在避税港从事实质性经营活动便能享受税收优惠。因此，一些国家并不给避税港下定义，而是依赖于国家名单。

避税港的一般定义是基于外国和居民国所征收的税收的比较上，如果外国实际征收的税率与居民国大体相同，则该外国不应被视为避税港，因为它不会被用于延迟纳税或规避居民国的税收。国内和外国税率的比较可以基于名义税率、平均实际税率或特定的受控外国公司支付的实际外国税收。

使用名义税率来划分避税港会带来一些问题，因为它忽视了外国慷慨提供的扣除、免税、抵免或补贴，使用名义税率唯一的好处是易于确定。一个国家的平均实际税率是确立避税港地位的较好指标，但是，实际税率常常很难确定，它需要每年对居民公司的受控外国公司所在的每一个国家来逐一确定。另外，一个国家的实际税率高并不意味着设立于该国的受控外国公司就不能适用低的外国税收。一些国家，如芬兰、德国和西班牙，利用实际税率法来定义避税港。例如，按照德国受控外国公司法，受控外国公司是指设在实际税率低于25%的低税国家的公司；在芬兰和葡萄牙，受控外国公司法适用于设立在实际税率低于芬兰和葡萄牙税收的60%的国家的受控外国公司。然而，大多数国家将重点放在受控外国公司支付的实际外国税收上。例如，法国和挪威规定，如果受控外国公司就其相关所得实际支付的外国税收低于其为法国和挪威的居民所应支付的法国或挪威的税收的三分之二，就适用受控外国公司法。将受控外国公司实际支付的外国税收和其作为居民所应支付的国内税收相比较，在理论上是正确的方法。它将焦点集中在每一特定的受控外国公司的具体情况上。但是，这种方法给纳税人在计算相应的国内税额方面带来了沉重的执行负担。

由于定义避税港存在一定的困难，大多数国家用列举避税港国家或非避税港国家的名单来代替避税港的定义。该名单可以包括在国内法律中，或者由税务机关发布，这一名单旨在向纳税人和税务官员提供具体的指南。名单体现在法律上的重要性千差万别，在一些情况下，一个国家是否出现在名单上这一事实便成为其是避税港或非避税港的决定因素。在另一些情况下，名单只是用来作为判定一国是否是避税港的假定条件。

5.3.2 避税港的类型

一般认为，避税港可以分为以下几种类型。

（1）不征收任何所得税的国家和地区。其中，有的国家和地区不仅不征收所得税，而且也不征收任何财产税。这类避税港通常被人们称为"纯避税港"或"典型的避税港"。目前，这类纯避税港主要包括巴哈马、百慕大群岛、开曼群岛、瑙鲁、瓦努阿图、特克斯和凯科斯群岛、汤加等。

（2）征收所得税但税率较低的国家和地区。这类避税港包括瑞士、爱尔兰、列支敦士登、海峡群岛、英属维尔京群岛、所罗门群岛等。

（3）所得税课征仅实行收入来源地管辖权的国家和地区。这类国家和地区虽然征收所得税（一般税率也较低），但对纳税人的境外所得不征税，在一定条件下也为跨国公司的国际避税提供了方便。许多拉美国家过去属于这类避税港，如巴拿马、哥斯达黎加等。另外，中国香港也属于这类避税港。

（4）对国内一般公司征收正常的所得税，但对某些种类的特定公司提供特殊税收优惠的国家和地区。这类避税港包括卢森堡、巴巴多斯等。

（5）与其他国家签订有大量税收协定的国家和地区。根据国际税收协定，缔约国双方要分别向对方国家的居民提供一定的税收优惠，主要是预提税方面的税收优惠。如果一个国家有广泛的国际税收协定，就可能被一个第三国居民通过滥用国际税收协定的手段进行国际避税，所以许多人主张这类拥有大量国际税收协定的国家也应列为避税港，如荷兰。

5.3.3 避税港的特征

综观国际上大大小小、形形色色的避税港，通常具有税收和非税的相关特征。

1. 税收特征

1）独特的"低税"结构

低税负是避税港的基本特征，不仅占国内生产总值的税收负担低，而且直接税的负担不高。直接税的征收对象是一般财产、资本、利润、所得，而且直接税的负担难于转嫁。

直接税负担轻这一基本特征,可以像磁铁一样吸引外部资源。

2) 以所得税为主体的税制结构

避税港国家和地区除了少数消费品外,一般不征流通税,商品的进出口税收也放得很宽。

2. 非税特征

避税港之所以对跨国投资者具有巨大的吸引力,是因为它除了无税或低税以外,还具有其他一些有利条件。这些有利条件实际上正是避税港所具有的一些非税特征,只有具备了这些特征,避税港才能真正成为跨国投资者的"避税天堂"。

1) 政治和社会稳定

作为一个避税港,政治和社会稳定是前提条件,否则就不能吸引跨国公司来这里投资。目前,世界上一些著名的避税港多是一些小国或半自治地区,它们的政局较稳定,其中许多国家和地区没有军队,一般认为这些国家和地区的政局稳定奠定了基础(政变和内战的可能性极小)。相反,过去亚洲著名的避税港黎巴嫩由于战火不断,许多跨国公司撤走了,从而失去了避税港的地位。

2) 交通和通信便利

交通和通信便利是避税港应具备的"硬件"之一。大多数成功实行了避税港政策的国家和地区都重视这一条件。从避税港在全球的分布情况不难看出,避税港主要分布在靠近南北美洲的大西洋和加勒比海地区、欧洲地区以及远东和大洋洲地区这三大区域。通常,那些重要的避税港,不是靠近美国,就是靠近西欧、东南亚和澳大利亚。它们与主要的资本输出国在地理位置上都很接近,这就为避税港吸引跨国公司前来投资创造了便利条件。另外,避税港与主要投资国的交通一般也很发达。例如,百慕大群岛距离美国的纽约只有1 247千米,从百慕大群岛到纽约每隔2个小时就有一趟航班,飞行时间不到2个小时;开曼群岛到美国的迈阿密飞行时间仅为1个小时,每天都有几趟航班;泽西岛和根西岛到伦敦的飞行时间也仅有1个小时。

3) 银行保密制度严格

跨国集团公司利用避税港避税主要是人为地将集团公司的利润从高税国的关联公司转移到避税港的基地公司,这无疑会损害高税国的税收利益,所以高税国对本国公司向境外转移利润的问题会十分关注。在这种情况下,如果避税港没有银行为客户存款严格保密的法律或制度,跨国公司向避税港转移资金的行为就会暴露在光天化日之下,高税国的反避税措施也就比较容易收到成效。为了吸引避税公司,避税港国家或地区一般都很重视银行的保密问题。有的制定了银行保密法,对银行职员的泄密行为要给予严惩。

4) 对汇出资金不进行限制

跨国公司利用避税港进行国际避税经常要与避税港的基地公司之间调出调入资金,这就要求避税港政府对跨国公司的资金调出不能加以限制。目前,世界上存在的主要避税港基本上都满足跨国公司的这一要求。这主要有两种情况:一是根本没有外汇管制,大多数避税港都属于这种情况。比如,开曼群岛、巴拿马、瑞士、卢森堡、列支敦士登、中国香港等。二是虽然实行外汇管制,但这种外汇管制不适用于非本地居民组建的公司,如百慕大群岛、荷属安第列斯、巴哈马等就属于这类避税港。

复习思考题

1. 避税与偷税有何区别？
2. 什么是国际避税？国际避税产生的主客观原因是什么？
3. 什么是避税港？它有哪几种类型？具有哪些特征？
4. 一个国家若想成为避税港，应当具备哪些条件？

第 6 章

国际避税的一般方法

时政观点

所得税是对所得征税，即有所得者缴税，无所得者不缴。我国对于企业所得税的征收不是让企业所有者权益减少，而是促进企业加强其经营管理活动，提高企业的营利能力，更有利于调节产业结构，促进经济发展。因此纳税人应积极依法纳税，某些明星偷逃税事件让我们意识到依法纳税的重要性。另外，企业缴纳所得税时享受的优惠政策也体现了国家对高新技术企业、软件企业等的大力扶持。

学习目标

1. 全面了解国际避税的一般方法。
2. 重点掌握课税主体、客体转移性避税的常见方法。
3. 了解课税主体、客体非转移性避税的内容。

课程导入

高税居住国（国籍国）跨国公司的一种常见经营模式，其在国外经营初期，以分支机构形式从事经营活动，而当分支机构由亏转盈之后，再及时转变为子公司。你如何看待这种现象？

在某个拥有税收主权国家的统一国内法管辖下，一定课税主体的课税客体所承担的税负是既定的。但是，如果这个课税主体和课税客体在空间上发生了向另一个不同税收主权国家的转移，由于这两个不同课税权主体国家的国内法不一样以及它们在处理各自的国际税收关系方面所遵循的国家之间的协议规定也互有差异，这就势必会带来税负的不同程度变化。因此，当跨国纳税人有意识地利用这一点来为其减轻国际税负目的而服务时，课税主体和课税客体的国际转移，也就成了国际避税的主要方法。这里所说的国际转移，包含了跨越国境和税境两方面的含义，在实践中，课税主体（以下简称"主体"）和课税客体（以下简称"客体"）的转移既可分别进行，也可以结合进行。

6.1 主体转移性避税

主体转移又称人的流动。在国际税收领域中，主体限于跨国纳税人，它包括跨国个人和跨国法人在内，主体转移包含了极其广泛的内容，并不仅仅限于个人和法人的国际迁移，而且还包括个人在一国中设法改变其纳税人身份（从居民变化为非居民）和设法避免成为任何一国居民等做法。一般说来，主体转移是以摆脱或回避高税国居民（公民）管辖权，从而减轻税负为主要目的。

6.1.1 主体转移性避税的方法

跨国纳税人为了实现主体转移性避税，通常会根据有关国家在实施税收管辖权时是适用法律标准还是户籍标准而采取不同的手段。此外，还可以采用其他手段进行变相转移。

1. 在适用法律标准的国家

1) 跨国个人变更国籍

在适用法律标准的国家，跨国个人的无限纳税义务是由其国籍或公民身份决定的，国籍或公民身份的存在，犹如无形的绳索，紧紧地将跨国纳税人与国籍国的公民管辖权联在一起，无论这个人走到哪里，总也走不出国籍国的"税境"，可见，在引致无限纳税义务的诸多连结因素中，国籍最具有刚性。跨国个人想转移或规避其高税国籍国的税负，摆脱公民管辖权的制约，唯一的途径就是放弃其原国籍，获得别国国籍。鉴于国籍变更要受有关国家国籍法和移民法的制约，手续繁杂，加之实行公民管辖权的国家对企图以改变国籍方式避税有所防范，因此，以变更国籍方式进行国际避税，一般是较难奏效的。

2) 跨国法人变更国籍

在适用法律标准的国家，跨国法人的"国籍"是因在该国依法注册而获得，因此，一个跨国法人为了国际避税而变更其国籍国，则只要撤销在该国的登记注册、改在其他国家登记注册即可实现，由此可消除公民管辖权下的无限纳税义务。然而，不论是个人还是法人，转移或规避其国籍国，并不意味着就此必然全部消除在该国负有的无限纳税义务。因为实行公民管辖权的国家，往往同时还行使居民管辖权，如果纳税人在那一国家的某些连续因素和活动，仍会落入居民管辖权的范围，无限纳税义务就不可能避免。

2. 在适用户籍标准的国家

在适用户籍标准而实行居民税收管辖权的国家，住所和居留天数等构成无限纳税义务的连接因素。位于高税居住国的跨国的纳税人，为国际避税目的而转移或规避其居住国，就得通过各种方式消除在高税居住国中的这些连接因素。

1) 跨国个人住所与居所的转移或规避

对于适用户籍标准的国家，一个跨国个人为了国际避税目的而转移或规避其居住国，没有在法律标准下转移或规避其国籍国那样困难，它可以选择，因为其所在国关于判断居民身份的标准是多种多样的。

（1）住所的真正迁移。

高税居住国的跨国个人，若在国内外拥有大量的收入和财产，为减轻居住国无限纳税义务的负担，可以直接将其住所迁往低税国，这是一种移居国外的行为，可以有效地中止在原居住国的无限纳税义务。对于这种纯粹为了躲避高税负而真正移居国外的现象，国际上称之为"税收流亡"。所谓"税收流亡"指为了躲避纳税而放弃居民身份，常年不断地从一个国家迁移到另一个国家的现象。这种做法主要有两类人采用：一是已经离退休的纳税人，这些人从原高税国搬到低税国或特定的低税区以便在支付退休金税收和财产、遗产税收方面获得好处（如迁移至避税港或自由贸易区、经济开发区、特区等）；另一类是在某一国居住而在另一国工作（如居住在日本，在新加坡工作等）以躲避高税负。从总的情况来说，以迁移住所的方式避税不会涉及过多的法律问题，只要纳税人具有一定的准许迁移的手续就可以了，因此很难认定其主要目的是为了避税，而赠与税和遗产税的有效规避则要涉及一些技术问题和法律问题。例如，向避税港或自由港的公司转移财产和赠与遗产，然后再以避税港或自由港公司的名义实现赠与和遗留等。

(2) **住所的短期迁移。**

这是指高税居住国跨国个人，为了某项特定的避税目的，移居国外一两年，待实现特定的避税意图之后，再迁回原居住国，故又称为假移居。

 例 6-1

加拿大在 1971 年 12 月税制修改前，对资本利得完全不征税。比如，一个荷兰人为了既能出售他在某个荷兰公司的大量股份，又能躲避荷兰的资本利得税，可以移居加拿大，在加拿大出售股份。由于荷兰与加拿大的税收协定中没有限制这种做法的特殊条款，这类收入就只能由居住国征税。由于他的居住国是加拿大而不是荷兰，就可以完全规避荷兰的资本利得税了。

(3) **缩短居住时间和临时离境。**

由于确定居所的标准在很大程度上与居住时间有关，跨国个人就可以采用例如不住满半年或一年这样一些认定居民身份的居住天数来规避居所。而针对连续居住半年或一年的判断标准，则可以采用临时离境一段时间再重新入境，使居住日达不到连续计算的一定天数来进行避税。尽管各国判定居所标准的规定很严格，使跨国纳税人要想长期在某国停留而又规避居所难以成功，但是，在一年或一段更长的时间里，跨国个人还是有可能规避在某一国家的纳税义务的。比如，纳税人通过在各国间的旅行，或在不同的旅馆中只逗留不长的时间，甚至有时住在船上或经常住在私人游艇上，来避免在任何一国形成居所而受居民税收管辖权的制约。在国外的相关文献中，使用"税收难民"一词来称呼这些为躲避居民管辖权而东奔西走的人。

但是，对于以上述方式来实现避税目的个人，他必须使自己成为，至少在名义上、形式上成为"真正"的移民，避免给政府一个虚假移民或部分迁移的印象。对这种旨在规避纳税义务的移民，许多国家都有一些相应的反避税措施。如荷兰政府明确规定凡个人放弃荷兰居所而移民国外、并在一年内未在国外设置住所而返回荷兰的居民应属荷兰公民，在此期间发生的收入一律按荷兰税法纳税。其他国家虽然在具体规定上与荷兰不尽相同，但在基本精神上是一致的，因此跨国避税必须尽量避免给政府留下这种不彻底迁移的证据。否则，将冒双重纳税的风险。

(4) **成为临时纳税人。**

当个人被派到他国从事临时性工作，常常可以享受某些优惠税收待遇。提供这些优惠的国家往往是根据这些被派出人员的临时性和非居住性来决定优惠的内容。有些国家对临时性和非居住性的确定是以这些人员在这些国家逗留的时间长短为标准，有些则是以是否拥有固定住所为标准。各国为临时入境者和非居民提供的税收优惠很多，免税项目占很大比例。

 例 6-2

美国政府规定，凡外来者在美国居住期不超过三个月，对其所获的收入免征所得税。

巴基斯坦规定，凡在巴基斯坦居住期限少于九个月者一律免征其所得税。还有一些国家对没有本国正式居民或公民身份的人一概称为"临时入境者"，这些人在被确认为"完全"的居民或公民之前概不负担纳税义务。比如美国对居民实行绿卡制，未获得绿卡的均为"临时入境者"，美国税法对"临时入境者"并未规定任何纳税义务，所以，以"临时入境者"身份进入美国境内的外国人可以不对其在美国获得的收入纳税。

此外，还有一些国家为吸引更多的外国专家来本国工作，便采取提供税收优惠的办法，以补偿其出国工作的额外费用。但是，这些税收优惠很容易被利用作为国际避税的方法。

 例6-3

比利时属高税国之列，但该国对外国公司派往比利时常设机构工作的管理人员，尽管在比利时已经居住了5~8年，仍可视其为"非居民"；对以外国科学工作者身份来比利时工作的人，尽管在比利时无限期地居住下去，也仍然可以被视为"非居民"。对于这些管理人员和科学家，比利时规定只就他们的薪金所得征税，除享受一般扣除之外，还可以享受应税薪金所得30%的特别扣除等优惠，这种扣除可以高达150万比利时法郎。而且，如果这些纳税人在任何一个纳税年度里，有一半工作时间是在比利时境外进行的，还将给予他们所得50%的免税照顾。

(5) 部分移居。

这是指跨国个人没有完全放弃和摆脱构成住所或居所的全部因素，而是依然保留着与原居住国的某些社会或经济上的依附或联系。例如，本人迁出，家属并不迁出；或将构成居民身份的一部分财产转出，但在该国仍有劳务活动和保持银行账户等。一方面，由于各国税制之间的差异和税务机关配合不够，这种部分移居会给纳税人机会，利用在住所判断与非居民税收待遇界线划分上的模糊点，加以逃税。另一方面，由于与原居住国仍保持着藕断丝连的联系，部分移民也可能会给跨国个人带来国际重复征税的风险。

2) 跨国法人居所的转移与规避

(1) 虚假迁出与转移。

在实行户籍标准的国家，比如大多数欧洲国家，判定一个公司是居民公司还是非居民公司，是看它在本国有无居所，但是判断居所的重要标准，是公司实际控制和管理的地点，这是一个基于事实的标准。比如在英国可以看到这样的情况：一家在英国注册的公司可以是别国的居民公司，而在别国注册的公司则可能是英国的居民公司。因此，利用居所变化规避纳税义务的核心就是消除使其母国或行为发生国成为控制和管理地点的所有实际特征，实现公司居所"虚无化"。

 例6-4

法国斯弗尔钢铁股份有限公司以下列手段和方法避免在英国具有居所及成为英国纳税义务人：该公司中的英国股东不允许参与管理活动，英国股东的股份与影响和控制公司的管理权力分开，他们只享受收取股息、参与分红等权利；选择非英国居民做管理工作，如经理、董事会的成员等；不在英国召开董事会或股东大会，所有与公司有关的会议、等均在英国领土外进行，档案工作也不放在英国国内；不以英国电报、电讯等有关方式发布指示、命令；为满足应付紧急情况或偶然发生的交易等特殊需要，该公司在英国境内设立一个单独的服务性公司,并按照核准的利润率缴纳公司税,以免引起英国政府的特别注意。事实证明,这些做法是十分正确有效的。据报道,1973—1985年,该公司成功规避了78 137万美元的对英国政府的应纳税款。

此外,还可以采用管理机构虚假迁出的做法,即通过变更登记而将总机构改变为分支机构,或改变公司体制,将公司管理体制从原来的总经理制改为董事制,或者反过来操作。与此同时,将新的董事会或总经理处设在低税国。

(2) 居所的真正迁移。

居所的真正迁移即一个跨国法人的管理机构或实际有效管理中心,真正从高税居住国迁往某一低税国。这是跨国法人摆脱高税居住国税收管辖权的最彻底的方式,但要真正实行起来是比较困难的。从财务上看,将一个公司的居所转移到低税或无税居住国一般是劳民伤财之举,一个公司真的想拔营起寨,有许多东西是无法带走的,有些虽能带走但因拆装、运输成本及停工损失太高而不合算,这就要在当地加以变卖,税务当局就企业因变卖资产而产生的资本利得而核定征收的大量税款也是企业所无法避免的,除非公司有大量财务损失可冲抵资本利得。这种因素有效地抑制了高税国中的居民公司进行财政性迁移。同样的道理,也正是这一点导致公司在移民过程中伪造财务损失、冲抵总资本利得来避税。但总的来看,对于法人来讲,通过居所转移来避税的方法有得有失。

6.1.2 主体非转移性避税方法——滥用税收协定

在寻求国际避税的过程中,跨国纳税主体并不一定非要进行转移不可,还可以借助其他手段进行。即从表面上看,跨国纳税人并没有发生税境之间的转移,而是待在本国不动。与此同时,指使别人在另一国为其创造某种媒介形式,通常是采取信托的形式,借此来转移部分所得或财产,造成法律形式上所得或财产与原所有人分离的现象。此举目的在于,在最终所有人的居住国避免就这部分所得或财产缴纳所得税、继承税和赠与税。这种手段被称为"虚设信托资产",是典型的避税活动之一。

例 6-5

新西兰的一家公司曾为躲避本国的所得税,将其年度利润的70%转移到巴哈马群岛的某一信托公司。由于巴哈马群岛是世界著名的避税港,税率比新西兰低(35%~50%),因此,该新西兰公司每年就可以有效地规避300万~470万美元的税款。

1. 滥用税收协定的客观条件

各国普遍采用缔结双边税收协定方式来解决国际双重征税问题和调整两国间税收利益分配关系,为了达到消除国际双重征税的目的,缔约国双方都要作出相应的约束和让步,从而形成对缔约国双方居民适用的优惠条款。例如,降低来源国对居住国居民投资所得的预提税税率,或对某些所得项目免税等。但是,根据税收协定,只有缔约国一方的居民和国民(有些情况下)才能享受协定待遇。然而,由于世界上大多数国家都在不同程度上采取了允许资本自由进出国境的政策,这就使得出于经营的目的,跨国个人和法人可以自由地在另一国家建立新的实体。以上客观条件的存在,为跨国纳税人的避税活动开辟了一个新的领域,使原本无资格享受协定待遇的第三国居民,可以利用种种巧妙手段,从另两个国家之间所签订的税收协定中捞到好处。税收专家把这种情况称为"滥用税收协定"。

一种比较常见的做法是并非为缔约国一方居民或国民的纳税人经常通过在缔约国一方

（或另一方）设立公司或其他法人实体的形式获取协定规定的利益，因为该公司或实体会成为其在缔约国另一方（或一方）取得的所得的导管。显然，滥用税收协定会减少有关缔约国的正常税收收入，是主体变相转移的一种特殊避税方式。应当指出，虽然纳税人可能通过滥用税收协定来获取本不可能得到的任何协定利益，但大多数滥用税收协定的情况都包括纳税人企图获取按照限制税率对股息、利息和特许权使用费征收预提税的好处。

2. 滥用税收协定的常见方式

滥用税收协定避税的手法，是以设置中介体为主要特征，大体可以归纳为以下三种方式。

（1）设置直接导管公司。

这是协定滥用的一种传统形式，是指利用缔约国一方境内的非关联财务公司作为中介，来帮助本身不能享受协定待遇的纳税人开展投资活动。

 例 6-6

假设 T 是 TH 国居民，TH 国是避税港，与 A 国没有税收协定。A 国与 B 国之间有税收协定，根据该协定，对于支付给 B 国居民的利息，A 国将预提税的税率从正常的 30% 降为 0。T 在 B 公司投资 100 万美元，B 公司是一个独立的财务中介，是 B 国居民。B 公司用这 100 万美元购买非关联的 A 国某制造商发行的债券，制造商向 B 公司支付 10 万美元的利息。B 公司提出，按照 A 国与 B 国之间的税收协定，这 10 万美元的利息在 A 国应予免税。然后，在扣除一些佣金后，B 公司将 10 万美元利息所得支付给 T，作为其原始投资的回报。这个例子是用通常被称为"倒手贷款"的方法来降低税负的。作为财务中介的 B 公司，按照协定在 A 国避免了纳税，又在 B 国极大地降低了税负，因为其从 A 国取得的 10 万美元利息所得的大部分都支付给了 T，并得以税前扣除。

在 B 国建立的这种公司，犹如一条从非缔约国伸出去吸取缔约国低税所得的管道，故被形象地称为"直接导管公司"。

（2）设置踏脚石导管公司。

滥用税收协定的另一种传统形式是利用在缔约国一方设立受控公司。

 例 6-7

比如，上述案例中的 T 在 C 国设立了一个独资子公司 C。T 由于拥有 C 公司的股权而为其注入资金 200 万美元，C 公司用这笔款项来购买 A 国证券交易市场上市的多家 A 国公司的股票，并由于拥有这些股票而取得 40 万美元股息。A 国与 C 国之间有税收协定，根据该协定，A 国对支付给 C 国居民的股息征收的预提税税率从 30% 降为 15%。作为 C 国居民，C 公司提出其取得的 40 万美元股息应享受协定规定的减税待遇，而 C 公司的所得在 C 国又可以免税，因为根据 C 国的税法，对境外股息所得不征税。

在 T 公司从 C 国获取所得的过程中，C 公司如同一块供过渡用的踏脚石。故被形象地称为"踏脚石导管公司"。

（3）直接利用双边关系设立低股权控股公司。

由于一些国家对外签订的税收协定都明确规定，缔约国一方居民公司向缔约国另一方居民公司支付股息、利息或特许权使用费，享受协定优惠的必要条件是：该公司由同一外国投资者控制的股权不得超过一定比例（比如全部股权的25%）。这样，外国投资者就可以精心组建一个外国低股权的控股公司，以谋求税收利益。

例如，一种被称为"五分结构"的安排，就是一个典型例子，该结构被用于同德国签订税收协定的某些国家。根据德国签订税收协定的惯例，如果某德国公司股息的受益者是一个外国公司，而该公司至少持有分配股息的德国公司25%以上的股份，德国的税收协定通常对这一德国公司分配的股息不给予税收协定优惠。针对这种情况，一个拥有德国公司股份的公司，为了获取税收协定的优惠，就可以依本国法律在本国境内先组建五个子公司，然后由这五个子公司分别持有德国公司的股份，使每个子公司持有德国公司的股份少于25%，从而受惠于与德国之间的税收协定。

与此同时，在跨国避税过程中，许多法人总想通过在海外建立自己的办事机构和分支机构来实现避税。但是，事实表明，相当一些海外办事机构和分支机构在行政管理上有许多不便，耗资多且效率低。因此，不如在海外业务中转国或其他地区找一个具有居民身份的银行来帮助处理业务。这样，公司就可以利用银行居住国与借贷方双边所在国签订的税收条约来获取税收利益。

 例 6-8

一国纳税人与某一银行签订信托合约，该银行受托替该纳税人收取利息。当该受托银行所在国与支付利息者所在国签订有双边税收条约时，利息预提税享有优惠待遇，则该纳税人即可获得减免税的好处。

再比如，日本与美国签有互惠双边税收协定，日本银行从美国的居民手中获取的利息可以减轻50%的税负。因此，当一个中国公司贷款给一个美国公司时，可以委托一个日本银行作为代理向美国公司收取贷款利息，这样就可获得少纳税的好处。

6.2 客体转移性避税

客体转移具有从动性，它是伴随纳税人作出的经营安排和所从事的交易进行的，离开主体的经营活动，客体转移就无从谈起。

6.2.1 客体转移性避税的方法

客体转移性避税通常会涉及跨越国境、在同一主体的不同部门或两个主体之间移动。客体转移性避税的方法多种多样，涉及的国家和纳税人也不尽相同。

1. 避免成为常设机构

在确定对非居民的营业利润是否课税上，一些欧洲国家一直沿用"常设机构概念"，即对构成常设机构的经营组织征税，否则就不征税。因此，对纳税人来说，规避了常设机构身份，也就随之避免了承担在该非居住国的有限纳税义务，当非居住国税率高于居住国税率时，这一点显得尤为重要。

根据《经合发范本》和《联合国范本》第五条，常设机构一般是指"企业进行全部或部分营业的固定场所"，这一定义涉及对一国地域的有形依附因素。例如，两个范本都列举了以下一些构成常设机构的场所：管理场所、分支机构、办事处、工厂、作业场所、矿场、油井或气井、采石场或任何其他开采自然资源的场所。但在有些情况下，可能难以找到上述有形依附因素,为此,两个范本引入了第二个判定要素。即《经合发范本》对常设机构的定义包括了企业的非独立代理人,这些代理人有权并经常代表企业签订合同。大多数税收协定都将这种非独立代理人认定为常设机构。《联合国范本》对这种代理人的规定范围更广,延伸到包括仅仅为企业储存并代表其交付商品的代理人。在这一点上,有些税收协定采纳《联合国范本》的规定。一些评论家认为,常设机构的定义应进一步扩大到包括代表企业进行实质性经营的大多数非独立代理人,而不管其是否有权代表企业签订合同。他们指出,有权签订合同在商务上的重要性微乎其微,因为现代通信方式使代理人能在瞬间与其外国委托者取得联系。这第二个判定要素与前面列举的有形因素交织在一起,使得非居民要避免常设机构身份可能是件很困难的事情,但这并不是毫无可能的。由于各国税法(尤其是税收协定)中有一些免税经营规定的例外存在,而这些例外就为避税活动提供了可乘之机。

上述内容为跨国纳税人提供的好处是:他们可以根据所从事的一项或多项免税活动实现避税,也可以利用服务公司避税。如果跨国纳税人的公司是建立在避税港或另一个设有税收条约或协定的国家,这些做法产生的效果就会更为明显。

例 6-9

1973 年,西班牙利尔德纺织服装有限公司(以下简称"利尔德公司")在荷兰鹿特丹建立了一个机构,其作用是为该公司搜集北欧国家纺织服装信息。根据西班牙政府和荷兰政府签订的双边税收协定,这种专门用于搜集信息、情报的办事机构不属于常设机构,因而不承担纳税义务。然而,该公司仅一年就根据其在荷兰的机构提供的信息为利尔德公司成交了两笔生意,价值 2 120 万美元。尽管该鹿特丹的办事机构承担了所有有关供货合同和订货数量的谈判和协商,但是由于该办事机构最终没有在合同和订单上代表利尔德公司签字,荷兰税务部门也毫无办法,只得眼睁睁地让其避税。

近几年,不需要设置常设机构的经营活动越来越多,随着技术水平的提高和生产周期的缩短,相当一些企业可以在政府规定的免税期内实现其经营活动,并获得相当可观的收入。这种短期经营方式给各国税务部门带来很大的麻烦。

例 6-10

韩国的一些海外建筑承包公司在中东和拉美国家承担了数量很大的建筑工程。由于中东和拉美国家规定,非居民公司在半年以内获得的收入可以免税,韩国的海外建筑承包公司常常设法在半年以内完成其承包工程,这样就可免交这些国家的所得税。

例 6-11

日本在 20 世纪 70 年代兴建了许多海上流动的工厂车间,20 世纪 80 年代,这些流动工厂先后到亚洲、非洲、南美洲等地流动作业。海上工厂每到一地,就地收购原材料就地加工,就地出售,整个生产周期仅为一两个月。加工出售完毕之后,开船就走,无须交纳一分税款。仅税款一项,海上工厂就获得了数以百万美元计的额外收益。这方面的资料数据日本从未公布过,估计从 20 世纪 70 年代到 80 年代末,日本海上工厂规避各国税款可能达数十亿美元之巨。例如,1981 年,日本一公司到我国收购花生,该公司派出来的一个海上流动车间在我国港口停留 27 天，把收购的花生加工成花生酱，又把花生壳压碎后制成板再卖给我国，结果我国从日本获得的出售花生收入中又有 64% 返还给日本，而且日本公司销售花生壳制板获得的收入分文税款未交。造成这一现象的直接原因就是我国和其他多数国家都对非居民公司的存留时间作了规定，而该日本公司就是善于利用这一规定实现了合理、合法避税。

2. 利用常设机构进行收入与费用的转移

在无法避免常设机构的情况下，巧妙地安排总机构与常设机构、常设机构与常设机构之间的交易，也可以达到避税的目的。

如果一个跨国法人作为投资者，决定采用常设机构形式在国外投资，该常设机构就成为总机构。如何在总机构与国外常设机构之间分配企业全部经营成果（包括盈利和亏损两个方面）呢？在实践中，这类问题主要体现在总机构与分支机构，以及分支机构之间的利润分配上。

在各国间的税收协定中，一般实行利润归属原则，即常设机构所在国对归属该常设机构的利润有权征税。对此，国际上有两种通行方法：第一种方法称为直接法。从法律上讲，常设机构并不是一个独立的法律实体，但直接法却将其视为独立的企业，按独立核算原则或公平交易原则与总机构和其他常设机构进行交易，直接法的特点是常设机构的利润实行独立核算。第二种方法称为间接法。它是考虑到法律上的事实，认为总机构与国外常设机构是在全球范围内产生共同利润（或损失）的一个实体，所以按一定的规则和计算公式，将其经营损益在总机构与国外常设机构之间进行分配。

直接法和间接法在实践中常常产生不同的结果。直接法寻求市场条件下的正常交易等客观标准，可以根据成本加成法或类似方法来确定常设机构的"正常"利润率，为此要求常设机构保存独立完整的账册，从而反映真实的收入与费用情况。间接法则通常使用一些公式来计算分配企业的全部经营成果，计算公式一般要考虑到反映整个企业财务状况的重要变量，比如总收入、营业额、资本结构、投资比例、员工比例等。根据企业经营的不同特点，间接法可选择其中若干适合的变量作为计算分配损益的客观依据。比如，加工业可以根据一定成本比率，如生产成本或工资额来分配利润，银行业可以营运资金或贷款额比率作为分配依据；保险业则以投保额多少来划分利润。

从直接法和间接法所要求的条件和分配形式上看，存在着国际避税的广泛可能性。因为在各国的税法及税收协定中，很难找到有关"正常"营业活动的参考条款。工商业活动是多形式、多变化的，常常没有"正常状态"，税务当局在确定有关活动或常设机构的"正常盈利率"时，主要是以本国经验为基础，最终的利润率通常是由纳税人与税务当局协商确定，这一切都为跨国纳税人施展避税技巧提供了机会。跨国纳税人利用常设机构转移收入与费用进行避税的常见方式有以下几种。

（1）利用常设机构转让营业财产。

总机构与常设机构之间，或两个常设机构之间转让营业财产有两个重要问题要解决。一个是财产转出机构是否由此而产生一笔资本利得，在账面上是否反映出就此负有的纳税义务，对这笔资本利得应如何进行估价。另一个是财产转入机构对财产价值的计算，以便确定今后计提折旧的基础。这种计算有两种方法：一种以账面价值为基础，即以原始成本价，减去转出机构已提的折旧费；一种是按重置成本价，即按财产转入时该财产的真实市场价格计算。因此，一个跨国法人通常可以利用转出方与转入方所在国对营业财产评估计算以及税率规定上的差异，通过总、分机构或两个常设机构之间财产的转移，尽量减少当期或将来的纳税义务。

（2）利用常设机构转移利息、特许权使用费和其他类似的费用。

这些费用既可能发生在企业与第三方之间，也可能发生在总机构与常设机构之间，许多国家的税法和税收协定对此进行了严格区分：纳税人向第三方企业的支付，如被认为是"真实"的支付则可以在纳税时作为费用扣除；而总机构与常设机构之间或常设机构之间的这种支付，则被认为是"虚假"的支付，对支付方不准作为纳税扣除，对收取方也不予计入利润。

然而，这些原则性的规定，在实际工作中有时很难精确把握，在不予扣除和允许扣除项目之间存在许多模糊之处，跨国纳税人对此加以巧妙利用，就可以达到减轻税负的目的。

（3）利用常设机构转移管理费用。

尽管设在国外的常设机构或多或少都有一些重要的决策自主权，但一个跨国法人的主要管理工作往往是集中在居住国的总机构进行的，这样就产生了一个有关总机构管理费用如何在总机构和常设机构之间分配的问题。在采用直接法确定常设机构利润的国家，税务当局要了解总机构是否以及在多大程度上对常设机构进行了实际管理。如果常设机构的确受益于这种管理活动，则可以相应负担总机构的有关管理费用，并从它的利润中予以扣除。

那么，常设机构支付给总机构的这种费用除了弥补成本之外，是否应包含利润呢？假如常设机构与总机构真的是彼此相互独立的实体，而且它们各自的经济职能也不一样，那么这样一种利润加价是可以接受的，因为一个独立的第三方提供这类管理服务，其收取的费用，肯定有高于实际成本的利润因素在内。然而，常设机构与总机构实际上是一个法律实体，常设机构仅是被视为独立分设企业而已。常设机构从其利润中应拿出多少钱作为总机构管理服务的报酬才算合理呢？实际上很难找到统一的答案，只能视有关国家税法和协定而定，有的税收协定对这一点规定得很明确。比如，瑞士与荷兰之间的税收协定认为常设机构利润的固定比例是由从事管理活动的总机构创造的，即常设机构净利润的 10%～20% 归总机构，不过，根据《经合发范本》中的意见，在确定常设机构应税所得额时，不应考虑理论上的所谓管理利润额。

正是因为在总机构管理费用分配上的巨大弹性、各国税制之间又存在着差异，跨国法人可以利用这一点达到减轻税负的目的。比如，尽量给高税国中的常设机构多分配一些费用，这样就减轻了总机构的利润和税负。

（4）利用常设机构转移劳务费用。

在实践中，常设机构常常为其总机构提供某些辅助性服务，这一类服务可能是技术性或管理性的，反过来，总机构也可能为常设机构提供类似服务。此外，常设机构可以为其总机构所生产的产品做广告，但常设机构本身并不生产和经营这些产品，对于这类劳务该不该收费？是否在收费中包含佣金这类的利润因素？对此，各方有不同的看法和认识。在采用直接法的情况下，常设机构为总机构提供服务而发生的费用开支应算作它的利润。但在实际费用之外，是否还应包含佣金呢？显然，独立企业间的服务交易应计入佣金收入，但常设机构与总机构毕竟是一个法律实体，通常无法精确计算象征性佣金的百分比，难以寻找出佣金重新记在常设机构的账目上。所以《经合发范本》的意见认为对这类服务的佣金不应计入常设机构利润；相反，如总机构为常设机构提供服务，常设机构为此付出的佣金在计算利润时也不予列支。

利用这些规定，跨国公司可以将一部分劳务活动从高税国转向低税国的常设机构，这就意味着一部分利润随之转入了低税国。

(5) 利用常设机构的亏损策略转移税负。

虽然跨国公司通常都要将其利润连同其国外常设机构的当年损益一起汇总向居住国或国籍国申报纳税，但发生在高税国中的亏损和发生在低税国中的亏损，有时会产生大为不同的结果。由于各个国家对待企业亏损的税务规定相差很大，设法在最有利的国家使某个常设机构在最有利的时间列明亏损，这为跨国纳税人减轻税负提供了很大的回旋余地。

3. 利用关联公司间转让定价转移收入与费用

一个跨国公司在进行对外投资经营活动时除了采用常设机构形式外，更常见的形式是建立具有独立法人资格的子公司，通过合资，参股等形式取得对其子公司的控制权，这些子公司便成为集团公司的成员。在子公司与子公司、母子公司之间，因特殊的经济利益和联系而形成了国际税收上所称的关联公司。随着各国间经济交往的扩大，许多跨境交易实际上都是在公司集团内部复杂的关联公司之间进行的。集团公司可以利用这种特别的关系，通过转让定价来影响关联公司的收入与费用的分配，进行国际避税甚至偷漏税活动，进而影响到有关国家之间的税收分配关系，这已成为各国税务当局极为关注的重大问题。转让定价作为实现客体转移性避税的最重要手段之一，涉及面广，内容复杂。这里先举一个简单的例子进行初步说明。

 模拟演示 6-1

【背景】某国的 M 集团公司的三个子公司 A、B、C 分别设在 X、Y、Z 三国，三国的公司所得税税率分别为：50%、40%、25%。A 公司为 B 公司生产组装电视机用的零部件。

【演算】A 公司以 100 万美元的成本生产了一批零部件，加上利润 30 万美元，本应按 130 万美元的价格直接卖给 B 公司，经 B 公司组装成品后按 160 万美元的总价格投放市场。事实上，A 公司并没有直接把这批零部件卖给 B 公司，而是按成本价 100 万美元卖给了 C 公司，C 公司又转手按 150 万美元的高价卖给 B 公司，B 公司组装成品后仍以 160 万美元的价格售出。这样一来，各公司及 M 集团公司实现的利润、应纳税额及税收负担就会发生重大变化，具体变化如表 6-1 和表 6-2 所示。

表 6-1 转让定价转移利润前

项目	利润/万美元	纳税/万美元	税负/%
A 公司	30	15	50
B 公司	30	12	40
C 公司	0	0	0
M 集团公司	60	27	45

表 6-2　转让定价转移利润后

项目	利润/万美元	纳税/万美元	税负/%
A 公司	0	0	0
B 公司	10	4	40
C 公司	50	12.5	25
M 集团公司	60	16.5	27.5

很明显，M 集团公司在转让定价转移利润后要比转移利润前少纳税款 10.5 万美元（27-16.5），税负减轻 38.89%〔（45%-27.5%）÷45%〕。

【评述】由此可见，跨国公司与转让定价关系密切。跨国公司可以借助转让定价这一工具，利用有关国家税负轻重的差异，对跨国收入和费用进行扭曲分配，进而实现利润由高税国向低税国大量转移，达到减轻其全球税负之目的。

综上所述，转让定价是某纳税人与其关联人在销售、购买和共享资源时所确定的价格。例如，如果 A 公司将在 A 国生产的产品卖给在 B 国的外国关联 B 公司，所定的销售价格即是转让定价。转让定价通常与市场价格形成对照，市场价格是在非关联人之间进行商品或服务交易时由市场确定的价格。

1）转让定价的常见表现形式

跨国公司在集团内部销售商品或服务的过程中使用转让定价，集团内部各公司之间的价格是转让定价中最重要的种类。个人与他们所控制的公司或其他机构，或与他们关系密切的家庭成员进行交易时，同样也会使用转让定价。在实践中，转让定价的表现形式多种多样，我们可以从以下五个方面对之加以归类分析。

(1) 货物的购销。

在跨国集团公司的内部交易中，货物购销占有极其重要的地位，涉及原材料、燃料、低值易耗品、零部件、半成品、产成品等有形货物的买卖。这些货物内部交易定价的高低对购销双方起着相反的影响。

①控制原材料和零部件的进出口价格来影响关联公司的产品成本。例如，为降低子公司的产品成本，使其获得较高利润，母公司可向子公司低价供应原材料，或由子公司高价向母公司出售零部件产品。反之，通过母公司高价向子公司出售原材料，或子公司向母公司低价出售零部件产品来提高子公司的生产成本，就可以减少子公司的利润。这种现象在我国称为"高进低出"，是造成某些三资企业亏损的重要原因之一。

②母公司利用掌握的国际营销网，操纵子公司产品的销路，压低或提高对子公司产品的收购价格。反之，在利用子公司系统内的销售机构推销母公司的产品时，则可以通过提高或压低佣金支付的形式影响子公司的销售收入，从而影响子公司的纳税情况。

③在货物购销过程中，利用母公司控制的运输系统，通过向子公司收取较高或较低的运输装卸费和保险费用来影响子公司的销售成本。

④在母子公司之间人为制造呆账、损失赔偿等，以此来增加子公司的费用支出。

⑤当集团公司内部交易采取来料加工形式时，压低支付给子公司的工缴费，借此来降低子公司的利润以避税。

(2) 贷款的往来。

通过控制贷款利率的高低来影响子公司的产品成本是转让定价的又一种表现形式。例如，母公司利用本系统的金融机构向子公司提供优惠贷款，不收或少收利息，可使子公司减少产品成本。相反，也可以通过高昂的利息费用来增加子公司的成本。

在集团公司内部以借贷方式循环使用资金，有些交易是通过预先支付利息方式避税，有些则利用利息差额来达到避税目的。前一种情况是，当一个公司预期本年度将赚取巨额利润而要缴纳较多税款时，该公司会赶在其会计年度结束之前，从关联公司借入一大笔贷款，借款条件是需要就该贷款预先支付整个贷款期的利息，由此将利息支出列入当期纳税扣除，缩小了利润额；在这一会计年度结束后，该公司即偿还贷款。后一种情况是，一个盈利公司通过借入一笔按市场利率计算的巨额贷款，然后转贷给关联公司，并按象征性的低利率计算利息，等以后年度再调整为按市场利率计算。这一借入贷出利息之间的较大差额，会造成用当期亏损来冲抵利润，从而推迟当年的纳税义务。

（3）劳务的提供。

劳务涉及的范围很广，关联公司之间提供的设计、维修、广告、科研、咨询等劳务活动中，均存在收费与否和劳务收费标准的高低问题。甚至总机构管理活动的存在也被视为一种劳务，要按一定比例向各分支机构分摊管理费用。跨国公司通过控制这些劳务费用的高低，进而可以控制集团公司不同成员的成本与利润。比如，向子公司索取过多的管理费，将母公司自身的管理费（例如母公司经理人员的年金）摊入子公司的管理费用，以此来减少子公司的利润。

（4）无形资产的使用与转让。

通过对专利、专有技术、商标、商誉、版权等无形资产的使用与转让，控制收取特许权使用费高低的方式，母公司对子公司的成本和利润可以施加影响。这类费用的支付有时影响集团公司资本构成的变动，有时影响收入及成本费用的分摊。以提供专利使用权为例，母公司可能对其全资子公司索取较低的专利使用费，而向少数股权控制的子公司索取较高的专利使用费。

（5）固定资产的购置与租赁。

在以固定资产作价投资的情况下，固定资产购置额的高低，既影响公司的股权份额，也影响折旧费的摊销。例如，母公司向子公司提供设备的价格直接影响摊入子公司的产品成本，提高固定资产原值，意味着加大折旧费，必然增加子公司的生产成本；反之，则会减少成本。

2）转让定价的动机

跨国公司通过对转让价格的控制，使它设在国外的各子公司或分支机构服从其全球战略目标，以获取最大的利润，这是其利用转让定价的基本目的。如果我们对此作进一步的分析，则可以在跨国公司转让定价活动的背景下发现其如此安排的税务动机和非税务动机。

（1）税务动机。

转让定价的税务动机主要出自减轻税负方面的考虑，而且与公司税的关系最为密切。由于跨国集团公司的各成员分布在不同的国家中，集团公司常常利用各国间税率和税收规则方面的差异，使其高税国一方的实体降低对低税国一方相关联实体的售价，压低收费和费用分配标准；反过来，低税国一方的实体可提高对高税国一方相关联实体售价，提高收费和费用分配标准，借此手段把一部分应在高税国实现并纳税的利润转移到低税国。高税国因此而减少的税收收入一部分转化为低税国的税收收入，另一部分直接增加了整个集团公司的税后所得。在税率差异较大的两个国家，关联公司间的转让定价，常常表现出极为明显的税务动机。

①减轻公司税税负。

世界上绝大多数国家对公司的营业利润征收公司所得税，因此，减轻公司税税负在转移定价的税务动机中首居其位。我们用一个简单的例子对此加以说明。

 例6-12

M集团公司的三个子公司A、B、C分别设在X、Y、Z三国。X、Y、Z三国的公司所得税税率分别为50%、40%和20%。A公司为B公司生产组装录像机用的零件，A公司生产了一批零件，成本为200万美元，本应以240万美元的价格直接出售给B公司，经B公司组装可按300万美元的价格投入市场。那么A公司的税负应为20万美元［(240-200)×50%］；B公司的税负应为24万美元［(300-240)×40%］，这样集团公司的总税负为44万美元。

然而，为了减轻税负，A公司没有直接对B公司供货，而是以210万美元的低价卖给了C公司，C公司转手以280万美元的高价卖给B公司，B公司仍以300万美元的总价格出售，这样一来，各公司的税负情况如表6-3和表6-4所示。

表6-3 转让定价转移利润前

项目	利润/万美元	纳税/万美元	税负/%
A公司	40	20	50
B公司	60	24	40
C公司	0	0	0
M集团公司	100	44	44

表6-4 转让定价转移利润后

项目	利润/万美元	纳税/万美元	税负/%
A公司	10	5	50
B公司	20	8	40
C公司	70	14	20
M集团公司	100	27	27

显然，经过转让定价后，M集团公司的总税负为27万美元，减少纳税17万美元(44-27)。X国国库损失15万美元(20-5)，Y国国库损失16万美元(24-8)，Z国国库增收14万美元(0+14)。可见，在这种转让定价安排中，M集团公司与低税国从中受益，而高税国蒙受损失，前者受益之和31万美元(17+14)刚好等于后者受损之和(15+16)。所以，在各国税率有较大差异的情况下，转让定价可以作为一种有效的避税手段。

②规避预提税。

各国对外国公司或个人在本国境内取得的消极所得（如股息、利息、租金、特许权使用费等），往往征收较高的预提税，在两国间没有税收协定的情况下，税负是不容忽视的。但是通过转让定价，可以在一定程度上减轻预提税的影响。

例 6-13

X 国 A 公司是 Y 国 B 公司的母公司，B 公司应从当年盈利中向 A 公司支付 100 万美元的股息。Y 国预提税税率为 20%，应纳预提税 20 万美元。为了规避这笔预提税，B 公司不是直接向 A 公司支付股息，而是将一批为 A 公司生产的价值 300 万美元的配件仅以 200 万美元的价格卖给 A 公司，以低价供货来代替交付股息。

③增加外国税收抵免额。

当母公司所在国实行外国税收抵免法，并全额抵免的情况下，利用转让定价可以起到增加当年外国税收抵免额的作用。

（2）非税务动机。

除了纳税上的考虑外，我们可以更多地看到转让定价中存在的非税务动机。在税率相近的国家之间，转让定价多半是出于经营管理方面的其他动机，即使在税率差异较大的国家之间，从转让定价背后也可以寻觅到许多重要的非税务动机。

①打入与控制市场。

如果打入某一国外市场是公司的一定目标，那么通过转让定价的手段，公司可以按低价把产品卖给国外关联公司，然后国外关联公司可以按当地竞争者无法匹敌的价格出售产品。即使该国外关联公司所在国对成品进口有反倾销法规限制，也不会产生很大影响，公司可以低价向其国外关联公司出售零部件和半成品，由国外关联公司进行装配或完成最后加工，然后按照如果直接进口将被当作倾销的价格出售，因产品的最后工序是在国外关联公司所在国完成的，属于国内生产而不能被视为倾销。

②调节利润，改变子公司在当地的形象。

当一个母公司为了使其新建的子公司在竞争中具有较高的信誉、易于在当地发行股票和债券或取得信贷以便扩大经营规模、占有更多的市场份额时，往往通过低价提供原材料、零部件、劳务，而高价回购其产品的做法，使子公司显示出较高的利润率。反之，如果母公司希望掩饰某一子公司的盈利能力时，就可以提高向子公司的供货价格而压低回购价格。因为当一个子公司经营顺利，盈利丰厚时，可能会带来一系列母公司不希望发生的问题。比如，子公司的工人会提出增长工资或更多分享公司利润的要求，东道国中会滋长要求没收外国公司高额利润的政治压力，新的竞争者受到高利润的吸引而打入本行业从而加剧竞争，等等。因此，通过抬高转让定价而适当地给子公司盈利"降温"是母公司的一种经营策略。这一点在合营公司中表现得极为明显。

③转移资金，多得补贴和退税。

出于国际收支平衡的考虑，有些国家实行严格的外汇管制，对当地子公司以股息形式汇出利润有所限制。然而，外国母公司向处于该国的子公司发运货物或提供服务时定高价，则可以间接地从该国调出资金。另外，有些子公司因当地投资法令等原因的限制，难以在当地取得资金，外国母公司就可以通过转让定价使它的子公司得到资金融通。并且，有些国家为了鼓励出口，往往以出口货物的价值为基础给予补贴或退税，因而，出口货物的转让价格越高，获得的补贴或退税也就越多。

④避免外汇风险。

在跨国经营活动中，外汇风险无处不在，汇率的狂涨或暴跌会直接影响跨国公司的盈利水平高低，为了避免汇率波动的风险或获取汇率差价的利益，跨国公司往往利用转让定价使子公司提前或延缓支付利润，或把损失转移给特定的关联公司。此外，低价转让可以使更多的产品进入一个实行外汇管制或对进口货物价值实行限额控制的国家。例如，一个子公司可按半价从其外国母公司那里购买产品，这样就可以获得多出一倍的所需产品。

⑤加速成本回收和利润汇回。

为了加速对子公司投资成本的回收和利润汇回，母公司可以提高对子公司的供货价格和劳务收费，压低子公司对母公司的收费；为加速在合资公司中投资的回收和多得收益，母公司也可以提高对合资公司的供货价和收费标准，压低回购价。当子公司所在国政局不稳、投资前景暗淡时，常常会出现这种情况。

⑥从合资公司中多捞好处。

以合资形式建立的子公司，必然会涉及东道国的当地合作者，所以对外方母公司就存在实行转让定价的诱因。例如，在合营双方各占 50% 股份的情况下，合资公司经营得再好，外方母公司充其量只能分得一半的税后利润。但是，当地合作者有权分享子公司的利润，却无权分享外国母公司的利润，外国母公司正是抓住这一点，在子公司最终利润形成之前，通过高转让定价提前获取利润。这种做法往往不仅拿走了母公司应分得的一半利润，而且顺手牵羊将子公司当地合作者应分得的部分利润也拿走了。

只有明白了这个道理，我们才能理解在对外经济合作中许多令人迷惑不解的现象：为什么在我国实行较低税率，而且在经济特区给予许多税收优惠的情况下，某些母公司位于高税国的跨国公司还要通过转让定价来从设在我国的合营公司中向外转移利润？为什么一些合资公司长期处于亏损状态，而外商还愿意继续干下去？一个重要的原因，就是转让定价发挥着妙不可言的作用。在外商实行转让定价的情况下，许多合资公司虚亏实盈，造成我国税收利益的外流。

综上所述，一国政府对转让定价应持的正确态度可以总结为以下两方面：一方面，不能因为转让定价有避税功能或在客观上可以产生避税的效果就否定它存在的合理性和合法性，并对纳税人的任何转让定价行为都实施严厉的惩罚措施。另一方面，也不能因为转让定价在跨国公司的内部经营管理中有重要作用而对其放任不管、忽视它对本国税收收入可能造成的不利影响。

4. 利用避税港实现客体转移性避税

高税居住国中的跨国纳税人，如想从客体转移中获得更大的收益，一般都会考虑对避税港的利用。跨国纳税人采用在避税港建立各类信箱公司，虚构避税港的不同营业活动，虚构信托资产和利用转移定价等手段，将资金、货物和劳务等客体引入避税港。在跨国纳税人实现其避税目的的过程中，避税港的关联企业和业务活动会发挥一种"分离"和"隔绝"的功能，即将一部分所得从高税国纳税人的收入中分离出来，隔绝高税居住国对此行使居民管辖权。因为流向避税港的客体，已经落在具有法人资格的另一实体手中，这些转移来的客体所形成的利润，可以在低税甚至无税的条件下在避税港积累起来，当跨国纳税人需要时再用于新的投资，这就是所谓的避税港积累功能和资金转盘作用。由于避税港不但吸引着客体流入，也是主体转移时常光顾之处，因此形成了特殊的避税港避税模式，对此，我们将在第 7 章中进一步讨论。

6.2.2 客体非转移性避税的方法

客体非转移性避税就是客体在形式上并没有发生跨越国境或税境的移动，但通过跨国纳税人的精心安排，仍可起到客体转移的避税作用。它属于客体转移的一种特殊形式。

1. 利用延迟纳税的规定

在客体非转移性避税方面，跨国纳税人采用的有效方法之一，是利用各国税法有关延迟纳税的规定，通过在低税国或避税港组建的一个实体（通常具有法人资格，比如一个子公司）进行所得和财产的积累。延迟课税，是指一国政府对本国居民从国外分得的利润在汇回本国以前不征税，只有当这笔利润汇回本国时再对其征税。实质上，发达国家制定延迟课税的规定是为了支持本国居民公司海外子公司的发展，增强其与当地公司的竞争能力，但这一规定后来被许多跨国公司用来从事国际避税。它们在低税国或避税港建立自己的子公司，通过种种手段把利润转移到这些子公司，并将分得的利润长期滞留在海外子公司。由于可以享受推迟课税待遇，这些跨国公司就凭借这种手段成功地避开了居住国较重的税收。

 例 6-14

日本居民公司 A 拟在避税港设立一家子公司，并拥有该子公司 40% 的股份，60% 的股权由日本居民公司 B、韩国公司和新加坡公司各拥有 20%。依据日本税法的规定，设在避税港的公司，如 50% 以上的股权由日本居民所拥有，这家公司则被视为日本的基地公司，其税后利润即使没有作为股息汇回日本，也要向日本政府申报纳税。为此，如果将日本 B 公司所拥有的 20% 的股权转让给非居民公司所拥有，该子公司就可以享受到推迟纳税的优惠待遇。

从高税居住国的角度看，滥用延迟纳税的规定是一种避税行为，推迟了在居住国（国籍国）纳税义务。利用延迟纳税有前提条件，那就是跨国纳税人要先在合适的低税国或避税港建立一个子公司（一般为其全资子公司），再利用其他客体的转移性手段，使利润在该子公司得以形成和积累。这些利润可能根本就不汇回给母公司，也可能在拖延一段时间后再以股息形式汇回。对于高税居住国（国籍国）中的跨国纳税人来说，延迟纳税就等于获得了一笔无息贷款，可以增加集团公司的流动资金。

2. 不合理保留利润避税

跨国公司可以通过不合理保留利润达到避税目的，当然，这种情况也可能发生在国内公司。通常，各国政府都允许公司保留一定的税后利润，这种合理的留利为企业发展提供了重要的内部资金来源。但是，这种保留的利润若超过了合理的界限（即政府规定的正常需要），就很容易被视为不合理保留利润。跨国公司往往以不合理保留利润的方式，即把应分给股东的一部分股息暂时冻结起来不予分配，而是以公积金的形式积存起来，然后将这部分利润转化为股东所持有的股票价值的升值额，从而达到少纳税的目的。

模拟演示 6-2

【背景】某跨国公司 2019 年的全球销售收入为 1 000 万美元，销售成本为 500 万美元，核定扣除额为 50 万美元，国外来源所得承担的外国税款可抵免额为 50 万美元（也等于外国实纳税款），该公司居住国的公司所得税率为 34%，假定税后留存利润不能少于 20%。

【演算】

销售利润：1 000-500=500 万（美元）。

应税所得：500-50=450 万（美元）。
应纳公司所得税额：450×34%=153 万（美元）。
实纳公司所得税款：153-50=103 万（美元）。
税后利润：450-(103+50)=297 万（美元）。
按规定应分配股息：297×80%=237.6 万（美元）。

即应将237.6万美元作为股息在各股东之间按其股权比例进行分配，并缴纳预提税（在股息汇出该居住国时），然后各股东又按其获得的股息数额依其所在国税法规定缴纳个人所得税。

【操作】 出于避税目的，该公司可以有意识地降低应分配股息的比例，甚至不分配股息。假定该公司决定分配股息59.4万美元（297×20%），这就意味着几乎只有极少部分的利润作为股息分到了股东的手里，因而仅负担这部分利润的预提税，各股东缴纳的个人所得税也相应减少了，从而达到减少股东税收负担的目的。

【评述】 少分配的那部分股息并非意味着股东权益的损失，而是可以转化为股东持有股票的价值，当以后年度生产因之扩大、效益因之提高的时候，每股股息也随之增加，从而股票行市也可能随之上升。当股东需要用钱的时候，他们可以出售这些股票取得高额收入，而在一般情况下，出售股票取得收入所纳的资本利得税要比个人所得税少得多，或者当以后年度股东所在国的税率有所降低的时候再进行股息分配，也可以减轻股东的税收负担。

3. 精心选择国外经营方式

1) 分支机构与子公司的选择

在前面我们已经提到，当一个跨国法人决定在国外投资和从事经营活动时，可以在两种方式中择一而行：建立常设机构或组建子公司。而经营性的常设机构又多以分支机构形式为主，诸如分公司、分行、分店等。事实上，在一个国家从事大量经营活动的外国公司通过经营活动或将公司资产用于与那些活动有联系的经营中所获取的收入通常是要在那个国家纳税的。这个公司在该国的存在一般被称为"分支机构"。税收中谈到分支机构时经常像谈论一个独立存在的实体。这是为了方便讨论诸如怎样向分支机构征税、怎样计算其收支和保留其会计账簿等问题。然而，在所有这些情况中，"分支机构"的用语只是一个比喻。与子公司相比，一个分支机构不是一个法律实体，不能自主行动。分支机构的财产和活动实际上是公司的财产和活动，分支机构只是公司的一部分。出于减税的目的，如何在分支机构与子公司这两种经营方式之间作出选择便取决于许多财务性和非财务性条件。

在实践中，分支机构与子公司各有利弊。

从税务角度分析，分支机构有如下优点：可以不缴纳资本注册税和相应的印花税；可以避免对利息、特许权使用费或股息征收的预提税；有机会利用消除国际重复征税方法中的免税法。并且，在一项新的投资经营活动初期，外国分支机构往往会出现亏损。作为惯例，跨国纳税人总机构所在国一般允许其用国外分支机构的这些损失冲抵其总机构利润，这种做法也可以用来处理由于货币兑换而产生的利润或损失，这一点正是使用分支机构的主要长处。

分支机构的缺点如下：由于其在东道国没有独立的法人地位，无资格享受当地政府为子公司提供的诸如免税期或其他投资奖励的税收优惠政策；假如分支机构今后转变为子公司，可能要产生资本利得税，并且这种转变也许还要事先征得税务和外汇管制当局的同意；分支机构一旦取得利润，总机构在同一纳税年度内要就这些利润向其居住国（国籍国）纳税。如果来源国税率低于居住国（国籍国）税率，分支机构就无法获得延期纳税的好处。

相比之下，子公司与分支机构恰好相反，分支机构的优点和缺点对子公司说来，却是缺点和优点。跨国纳税人往往反复权衡利弊，然后作出他们认为最有利的选择。高税居住国（国籍国）跨国纳税人的一种常见选择方案，就是在国外经营初期以分支机构形式从事经营活动，产生的亏损可以及时冲抵总机构的利润，以减少在居住国（国籍国）的纳税。而当分支机构由亏转盈之后，再及时转变为子公司，从而享受延期纳税的好处。针对这种避税方式，有些国家制定了相应的限制措施，以防跨国纳税人"两头受益"。

 例 6-15

M 国一家跨国公司欲在我国投资兴建一家芦笋种植加工企业，该公司派遣了一名经济顾问来我国进行投资政策考察。在选择中外合作经营企业还是中外合资经营企业形式投资时，他向我国有关部门进行了涉外税收政策方面的咨询，并且建议这个项目应采用中外合作经营企业的形式，并不应由该公司投资，而应改由该公司设在 H 国的子公司投资。

他的建议是基于这样的考虑：芦笋是一种根系植物，在新的种植区域播种，达到收获期大约需 4 年至 5 年，这样就使企业在开办初期面临着较大的亏损。如果采用中外合资经营企业的投资形式，在 M 国和 H 国被视为子公司，其亏损只能在中外合资经营企业内部弥补。但如果是中外合作经营企业，该企业将被视为 M 国或 H 国公司的分公司，其亏损可以在 M 国总公司内弥补。这样不仅可以减轻企业开办初期的压力，还可以减轻总公司的税收负担。

2) 合伙企业与公司的选择

跨国个人在选择经营方式时常常会遇到在合伙企业与公司之间作出抉择的问题。许多国家税法规定，合伙企业的营业利润不缴纳公司所得税，而是按合伙出资比例缴纳个人所得税。从避免公司所得税方面来说，合伙企业对跨国个人颇具吸引力。

 例 6-16

A 国的某先生计划去 B 国经营热带水果商店，预计年盈利 4 万美元。如果该店作为合伙企业，则个人所得税税率为 40%，该先生可净得税后利润 2.4 万美元；如果该店作为公司，则公司所得税税率为 30%，该先生可净得税后利润 2.8 万美元，如果全部作为股息分配给该个人，则该个人还要缴纳个人所得税 1.12 万美元（2.8×40%），这样，他净得税后利润就只有 1.68 万美元。与前者相比，他多负担了 0.72 万美元的所得税款。从减轻税负的角度考虑，该纳税人会采用合伙企业而不会去组建公司进行经营。

然而，这仅仅是从减轻双重征税的角度去考虑问题。实际上，影响这种经营决策的因素还有很多，合伙企业并不一定是一种最佳经营形式。合伙人要负无限责任，合伙份额不能自由转让，不能自由发行股票以扩大经营规模，利润一旦产生就直接反映在合伙人当年的纳税义务中。在大多数国家中，合伙企业不具有独立法人资格，这会影响到它对税收协定待遇的享有权，在许多国家享受不到对公司提供的各类税收优惠，等等。相比之下，公司则可以克服这些缺点。所以，在投资经营决策中税收是一个重要因素，但并不是唯一的决定性因素。

4. 利用税收优惠，选择投资经营中的低税点

受各自政治体制、经济发展水平、总体经济发展战略和产业政策等诸多因素影响，各国税制之间必然存在很多差异，这些差异的存在，使税收负担在不同纳税人、不同征税对象之间难以均衡一致，这就给跨国纳税人提供了选择的机会，使其能够巧妙地利用合适的税负较轻的投资经营形式或获取税负较轻的收入项目，我们将这些有助于减轻税负的投资经营形式和收入项目，称为低税点。

1）充分利用税收优惠

低税点大量存在于各项税收优惠中。出于不同的经济目的甚至政治目的，许多国家在税收上实行某些优惠措施，尤其是对投资提供的税收鼓励，不仅在发展中国家盛行，在发达国家也不鲜见，诸如加速折旧、投资抵免、差别税率、亏损结转、免税期等。这些优惠措施，旨在引导纳税人在指定方向上进行投资经营活动，然而却很可能导致税收漏洞扩大。

比如，国家为开发国内某些落后地区、加速某些新行业的建设以及扩大出口等，可能有意识地在这些方面降低税率或给予一定的免税期，借此吸引投资者，从而实现国家的预期计划。跨国纳税人可以合法地利用这些低税点，减轻其在非居住国的税负。

例 6-17

某玻璃公司打算更新一套供水装置。具有循环或节水功能的，每套需要 100 万美元；普通功能的，每套需要 80 万美元。如果公司购买前一种，就要多花钱，但税法规定，节水装置可享受 40% 的投资抵免。另外，节约水耗后，每年还可以少开支水费 2 万美元。经过对比，这家公司决定购买有节水功能的供水装置。

2）从税务处理方式中寻找低税点

当居民公司向非居民支付利息时，支付人可以在计算所得时扣除利息支出（除非有特殊规定）。一般情况下，对支付给非居民的利息不征税或者依据税收协定按照预提税的降低税率征税。如果非居民贷方也为居民公司的股东，居民国的公司税基则会因为利息而非股息的支付而受到严重的侵蚀。与利息不同的是，居民公司支付的股息一般不予抵扣。因此，居民公司取得收入并支付给股东将适用两级税收：对公司取得的收入征收的公司税和对分配给股东的股息征收的股东税。如果股东是非居民，股东税一般以预提税方式征收。相比之下，居民公司取得的收入以利息形式分配给为公司股东的非居民贷方只适用一级税收，因为公司可以扣除利息支出，且来源国仅对支付给非居民的利息征收预提税。向非居民支付利息优于支付股息使非居民投资者倾向于向居民公司借贷融资，这种现象称为"资本弱化"。

模拟演示 6-3

【背景】某新办企业 2020 年全部所得为 1 000 万元，扣除项目数额为 50 万元，可抵免的外国税款为 10 万元，所在国企业所得税率为 40%。请计算该企业 2020 年在其居住国的纳税情况。

应纳税所得额：1 000－50＝950（万元）。

应纳所得税款：950×40%＝380（万元）。

实纳所得税款：380-10=370（万元）。

【操作】该企业为了减轻税负，在股东未交足本企业所需资本的情况下，向本企业海外股东借款，并发生150万元利息支出，假定该公司所在国预提税税率为20%。计算该企业2020年在其居住国的纳税情况。

应纳税所得额：1 000-（50+150）=800（万元）。

应纳所得税款：800×40%=320（万元）。

实纳所得税款：320-10=310（万元）。

利息的预提税：150×20%=30（万元）。

【评述】可见，在有不正常借款的情况下，该企业可以少缴纳税款30万元[370-（310+30）]。

【结论】从上例可知，用负债形式资助居民公司在降低来源国税收方面比权益融资更有效，主要原因在于利息可以扣除而股息不能。此外，居民公司可以在任何时候偿还贷款而不用发生税收事项，而公司要偿还权益投资（如回购股份或降低资本）就必然产生应纳税股息。

复习思考题

1. 跨国纳税人进行国际避税的一般方法有哪些？
2. 主体转移性避税的方法有哪些？客体转移性避税的方法有哪些？
3. 什么叫滥用税收协定？滥用国际税收协定有哪些方式？
4. 转让定价的常见表现形式有哪些？
5. 转让定价的税务动机和非税务动机分别是什么？
6. 什么叫延迟纳税？它对纳税人有何意义？
7. 分支机构与子公司的利弊各是什么？
8. 转让定价对跨国公司的经营有何重要意义？

第 7 章
避税港避税模式

> **时政观点**
>
> 中国香港回归祖国以后，政治稳定、经济繁荣，我国企业要更好地利用中国香港的"国际金融中心"地位，在将国际贸易业务做得更大、更好的同时，更加坚定中国特色社会主义制度和文化。
>
> **学习目标**
>
> 1. 着重理解与领会避税港的两种避税模式。
> 2. 重点掌握虚构避税港营业和虚构避税港信托财产避税的具体方式。
> 3. 正确评价避税港的作用。
>
> **课程导入**
>
> 中国香港作为"国际金融中心"，应如何在中国企业"走出去"的过程中发挥积极作用？

避税港的存在，是当代世界经济中一个引人注目的现象。避税港所实行的政策，对国际资本流动、投资分布状况、跨国公司收入与费用的分配格局以及有关国家的税收收入，有着不容忽视的影响。在过去 50 年里，避税港的增加及对其利用的扩大是惊人的。许多形势变化也有助于避税港及其应用的发展，包括：

（1）外汇管制的取消和国际贸易与投资的自由化。
（2）通信、交通及金融服务的改进。
（3）避税港采取的灵活的商务体制和严格的银行秘密与保密要求。
（4）积极进取的营销行为。

早先形成的避税港，可就人们设想的任何税收筹划提供服务，经验已经十分丰富；较年轻的避税港也跻身尝试以占一席之地。

对于从事跨国经营的跨国纳税人而言，通常把有效利用避税港作为其国际税务筹划的重要组成部分。对避税港的利用，几乎涉及主体转移性避税和客体转移性避税的各个方面；汇集了国际迁移、变相转移、滥用税收协定和转让定价等诸多避税手段，是一种综合避税模式。跨国纳税人利用避税港进行避税的基本模式可以归纳为两种：虚构避税港营业和虚构避税港信托财产。

7.1 虚构避税港营业

跨国纳税人利用避税港从事避税活动的一个常用方式，就是虚构避税港营业。某些设在避税港境内的公司，其经营活动很少甚至完全没有真正在避税港内进行。虚构避税港营业的基本途径，是通过总公司或母公司将销售和提供给其他国家和地区的商品、技术和各项服务，虚构为设在避税港受控公司的转手交易，从而将所得的全部或一部分滞留在避税港，再通过贷款和投资方式重新回流至居住国，以躲避其原应承担的高税率国家的税负。

在虚构避税港营业中起中介作用的，是以避税港为基地的各种性质的受控公司。这些公司通常分为信箱公司和各种专业性的公司，包括控股公司、投资公司、金融公司、租赁公司、航运公司、保险公司、专利公司、贸易公司和其他劳务服务公司等。其中有不少属于外国基地公司性质。

外国基地公司，是指以避税港为基地而建立的、为了从事转移和积累与第三国营业或投资而产生利润的公司。例如 A 国某公司希望向 C 国投资，首先，它在避税港 B 国建立一个外国基地公司，然后通过 B 国基地公司向 C 国投资，这就是典型的从事"第三国营业"的外国基地公司。现实生活中还有非典型的外国基地公司。例如，A 国公司希望在本国进行再投资，但它先在避税港 B 国建立一个外国基地公司，再通过该公司向本国进行投资。下面着重介绍各种受控公司的建立及其避税特点。

1. 信箱公司

信箱公司，是指那些仅在所在国完成必要的注册登记手续、拥有法律所要求的组织形式的各种"文件"公司。这种公司往往只存在于文件之中，只拥有一个信箱和一个常务董事，公司从事的商业、制造、管理等活动都是在别处进行的。这些公司一般设在避税港，是典型的避税港公司，也是外国基地公司最重要的形式。

 例 7-1

澳大利亚所属的诺福克岛曾是避税港。1972 年，在岛上注册的公司有 1 450 家，同岛上的居民人数几乎相等，基本上一个居民就拥有一家公司，在这么一个小地方集中这么多的公司，怎么可能真正开展实际的营业活动呢？又如百慕大群岛，土地面积仅 53.3 平方千米，人口仅 6 万，如果要真正设立工商企业，仅美国一国的百余亿美元的投资也是容纳不下的。可见，真正在百慕大群岛的只不过是用来投资的"户头"而已。

2. 控股公司

控股公司，是指在一个或多个子公司里控制着大量股份和拥有举足轻重表决权的公司。这种控股比例可以高达 100% 或低至 50% 以下，控股公司的收入主要是股息和出售股份的资本利得。在避税港建立控股公司是避税手法之一，因为在那里可能对股息收入和资本利得不征税或只征很少的税。事实上，许多避税港都为控股公司提供特别优惠的税收待遇，如荷兰、荷属安的列斯群岛、卢森堡、新加坡和瑞士等。

模拟演示 7-1

【背景】一个高税率国家的母公司在若干个低税率国家拥有子公司,母公司想用这些子公司的利润在其他国家再设立一些子公司。但现有的子公司在向母公司支付股息后,母公司所在的居国要对之征收所得税。在国外再成立子公司,就要设法避免缴纳过高的所得税,否则就得付出高额的代价。

【操作】假定母公司所在的居住国并未就利用避税港问题在其税法中做出反避税规定,那么事情就好办了:母公司只需建立一个避税港子公司来控制那些外国子公司的股权就可以了。

【评述】由于股权转移到避税港子公司,母公司无须就股息向其居住国缴纳所得税了。

3. 投资公司

投资公司,是指专门从事有价证券投资的公司,这些有价证券包括股票、公司债券或其他证券,它们在某个公司的股份中只占很少或极少的比例,在企业经营决策中并不拥有任何重要的表决权,这是投资公司与控股公司的不同之处。但其目的都是为了消除或减轻在股息、利息、租金、运输、保险、特许权使用费和营业所得项目上的税负,以及对处理财产取得的资本利得的税负。另外,有些国家之间的税收协定中对投资所得不征或少征预提税的规定,也给投资公司提供了重要的有利条件。

投资公司的组建有三种不同的方式:一种是集团公司在避税港建立金融公司,另一种是私人在避税港建立投资公司,还有一种就是所谓的"离岸投资基金"。

离岸投资基金,即高税率国家的公司和个人在避税港建立的一种互助投资的基金,换言之,是指公司和个人在避税港建立的外国投资公司,它流动性很大、非常灵活而又相当复杂。这种离岸投资基金可以使居民纳税人延迟缴纳就其消极投资所得征收的国内税。离岸投资基金也可允许纳税人将一般性所得转化为处理基金股份所取得的财产收益。这种基金一般都是在像巴哈马、荷属安的列斯群岛、中国香港这样的避税港建立。例如,荷兰的劳伦多基金就是建立在荷属安的列斯群岛的库拉索,这样可以逃避荷兰对基金分配给其成员的财务利益征收股息预提税。

4. 金融公司

金融公司,是指在一个集团公司里充当借贷中介人或向第三方提供资金的机构。为了不缴纳或少缴纳利息所得税,或取得高税国对集团公司支付利息进行税收扣除的许可,或利用有利的税收协定、不缴纳或少缴纳利息支付国的预提税,跨国纳税人通常可在避税港设立金融公司。因此,集团公司在进行证券投资或购置不动产时,暂时需要的大量资金往往可以通过其设立在避税港的金融公司解决。

例 7-2

比如,美国公司常常把金融子公司设立在荷属安的列斯群岛,这是因为美国与荷属安的列斯群岛签有税收协定,并规定荷属安的列斯对其公司支付给美国债券持有人的利息免征预提税。由于荷属安的列斯不开征所得税,在这种情况下,就可以将大量利息集中到金融公司账上,可以获得少纳或不纳税的好处。又如,德国公司常在卢森堡建立金融公司;而像巴拿马、利比里亚、新加坡、中国香港等这类避税港也常被利用来建立金融公司以逃避税收。

5. 租赁公司

租赁公司，是指专门从事租用、租赁贸易和租购等项活动的机构。由于许多国家和地区为跨国纳税人提供特别优惠的税收待遇，如加速折旧和投资税收减免以鼓励企业取得和拥有工业设备或财产。根据一般规定，这些由税收带来的好处将由那些拥有财产所有权的纳税人获得，而那些很快就要出卖这些财产的人是不能获得这些好处的。因此，当一个纳税人利用信贷资金购进一批设备，并立即将设备转让给另一个纳税人时，确认该项转让契约是销售合同还是租赁合同，就相当重要了。若是租赁合同而不是销售合同，则转让者才可有权获得上述税收优惠。因此，跨国纳税人就可以利用这些规定，在避税港设立租赁公司，通过租用、租赁贸易和租购定价进行避税。

 例 7-3

A 国母公司在 C 国和避税港 B 国分别设立子公司，A 国母公司用借来的钱购买了一批设备，然后以尽可能低的价格租赁给 B 国子公司，B 国子公司又以尽可能高的价格再转租赁给 C 国子公司。在这一过程中，A 国母公司作为法律上的租赁财产所有者，可以对出租设备提取折旧；而避税港 B 国子公司作为经济上的租赁财产所有者，也可以对租入设备提取折旧。除了租赁定价和设备折旧以外，租赁公司还可以享受税务当局有关投资鼓励的好处，这样就达到了避税目的。

6. 航运公司

跨国纳税人躲避税收的另一种手段，是在避税港建立国际航运公司，包括国际船舶运输公司和航空公司等。由于这类航运公司的所有权和经营权可以不在同一国内，总管理机构可以位于第三国（通常是避税港），其船舶、飞机还可以在别处重新注册，使其能逃避高税国行使税收管辖权，从而可以躲避或减轻所得税和资本利得税。

 例 7-4

第二次世界大战刚结束时，美国、英国、荷兰和瑞典都是世界上主要的造船大国。当时，工业企业面临着来自强有力的工会的压力，对于工作方式和生活条件的规定限制了其盈利能力，于是船运公司开始到巴拿马和利比里亚注册。这些国家不仅仅是避税港，而且还为公司躲避各自原居住国法律和工会对经营活动的限制提供了条件。例如，利比里亚是西非西南部的一个小国，人口只有 170 万，生产橡胶。由于实行低税政策，吸引外国公司在那里办了许多种植园，目前橡胶产量居非洲首位。另外，该国还凭借濒临大西洋的地理优势，对外国商船征税低微，因此，国际商船悬挂利比里亚国旗的总吨位数居世界前列，这也是所谓的"方便旗"。

从减轻税负的角度考虑，跨国纳税人往往还可以通过高税国船舶运输公司或飞机公司的大量亏损，或船舶、飞机等运输工具的租赁、出租和转租等，达到躲避所得税之目的。巴拿马、利比里亚、巴哈马、百慕大、开曼群岛、中国香港、荷属安的列斯群岛等避税港，都有许多国际船舶运输公司或飞机公司。希腊、塞浦路斯等避税港也是国际避税者乐于前往建立航运公司的好地方。

7. 保险公司

保险公司，主要是指为包括其自身在内的集团公司成员提供经营活动的保险和分保，并完全由该集团控制的一种组织。

通常，在企业的经营活动中，每年都会发生大量的保险费支出，而且有时一般的保险公司不太愿意接受跨国集团公司所需的保险项目，因此跨国集团公司有必要成立自己的受控保险公司，并由其承担集团公司经营活动的风险保险。在这方面，避税港能为保险公司提供许多方便，所以近二十年来，许多跨国集团公司纷纷在避税港建立自己的受控保险公司。与支付给独立的保险公司的保险费相比，在避税港建立自己的受控保险公司，有许多好处：一方面，可以减少要缴纳的保险费用；另一方面，还可以承担第三方保险公司所不能承担的部分损失，甚至承担全部损失。此外，受控保险公司还常常被认为是利润的积累中心，它可以调节母公司的经营成本。例如，受控保险公司可以对母公司的资产像其他独立的保险公司一样进行正常保险，但索取的保险费率却低于或高于其他独立的保险公司，从而降低或增加母公司的经营成本。像巴哈马、百慕大、开曼群岛、中国香港、荷属安的列斯群岛和巴拿马等避税港，就成了受控保险公司的"乐园"。其中，百慕大已成为世界上保险公司和再保险公司最集中的避税港。

8. 专利公司

专利公司，是指专门从事专利、商标、版权、牌号或其他工业产权的取得、利用或使用特许等活动的公司。由于一些国家（如低税国或避税港）在与其他国家签订的税收协定中，对特许权使用费的支付所征收的预提税有优惠的规定，如免征或减税，这样，跨国纳税人为了不缴或少缴预提税，就可以在具备上述特征的国家建立专利公司，从事专利等的取得、利用或特许使用等项活动。而从事这些活动的最好"乐园"，莫过于避税港了。

例 7-5

A 公司拥有一项价值高昂的专利技术，准备通过许可证贸易方式将该项专有技术转让给中东某国的使用者，而该中东国家对支付给外国公司的特许权使用费不征收预提税。为避免就出让专有技术而取得的所得缴纳所在国的税收，A 公司可以在避税港设立一个专利公司，并指使其与中东的使用者签订转让合同，造成转让活动并不发生在 A 公司所在国的假象，就可以避免缴纳其所在国要求的税收。

9. 贸易公司

贸易公司主要是指从事货物和劳务交易的公司，它只不过是为集团公司进行的购买、销售和其他交易活动开具发票而已。跨国纳税人往往通过在避税港建立贸易公司进行虚假的营业，把高税国公司的利润转移到避税港贸易公司。然而，跨国纳税人并不把有税收协定的避税港作为其建立贸易公司的最佳选择。这是因为其购销交易等活动常涉及进出避税港，税收协定的情报交换条款往往给其带来麻烦，所以，从保密性角度考虑，跨国纳税人往往选择那些没有税收协定的避税港作为建立贸易公司的好地方，如巴哈马、百慕大、中国香港、巴拿马。

10. 服务公司

服务公司是指从事部分管理、卡特尔协定组织、离岸投资基金管理或其他类似劳务的公司。跨国公司常常通过在避税港建立服务公司进行费用分配，即通过向避税港服务公司支付劳务费用把高税国公司的利润转移到避税港服务公司中，从而可以避免缴纳高税国公司的所得税。而高级管理人员还可以通过在避税港服务公司工作避免缴纳个人所得税。

综上所述，跨国纳税人为躲避税收而在避税港建立的各种公司，有许多属于外国基地公司。通过外国基地公司，特别是信箱公司进行国际避税活动，能形成一个介于所得来源同所得最终获得者之间的积累中心。通过积累股息、利息、特许权使用费收入，或来自不动产、证券的所得，纳税人可以在不纳税或尽量少纳税的情况下进行再投资，从而避免了缴税。

7.2　虚构避税港信托财产

目前，国家除了所得税以外，遗产税、继承税、赠与税、资本转让税、对个人征收的一般财产税等也是跨国个人不可忽视的税负。赠与税和遗产税的税率一般都在50%左右，有的甚至高达70%到90%。跨国个人可以通过一系列主体非转移性与客体转移性相结合的方式利用避税港进行避税，其中虚构避税港信托财产是一种较为常见的手法。

所谓信托，是指某人（委托人）将其资产或权利（信托财产）托付给另一个人（受托人），并由受托人按照委托人的要求加以管理和使用，以利于受益人的行为。这个受益人可以是委托人指定的第三者，也可以是委托人自己。

信托是一种法律关系而不是一个像公司之类的法人实体。信托的存在通常有一定的时间限制，但在避税港，由于允许建立信托而又无信托法规约束，实际上信托也就可以无限期地存在下去。建立信托有许多好处，如为继承财产提供条件、为财产保密、便利投资和从事经营风险活动、免除或降低财产和所得的税负等。所以，许多避税港国家和地区都允许外国人在其境内成立信托组织。同时，跨国纳税人也都乐于利用信托方式从事避税活动。虚设避税港信托财产的方法主要有以下几种。

1. 设立个人持股信托公司

个人持股信托公司，是指消极投资收入占总收入60%以上，股份的50%以上被5个或5个以下的个人所持有的公司。这种公司很容易被跨国个人利用其亲属的化名来顶替，因而实际上就是他一个人所控制的公司。这样，跨国纳税人就可以利用避税港不征所得税和遗产税的特殊条件避税了。

 例7-6

一个高税国A国的跨国个人，在避税港B国设立一个个人持股信托公司，把其在A国或远离避税港B国千里之外的财产虚设为避税港的信托财产，委托给这家公司经营管理，然后，把这部分财产及其经营所得以及在A国或其他任何地方积累下来的财产及其经营所得，都挂在该公司的名下，并逐步转移到避税港B国。这样，首先可以规避掉这部分财产经营所得的所得税款的全部或大部分。接着，该公司用这部分转移来的信托资本在当地进行股票买卖，从事消极投资牟利，又可以获得不缴资本利得税的好处。而且，当这个A国跨国个人死后，该公司还可以按死者生前事先确定好的办法，把这笔财产或信托基金分给他指定的受益人（如指定给其亲戚、朋友等），这样还可以再躲避掉巨额遗产税的全部或大部分。

第7章 避税港避税模式

2. 设立受控信托公司

跨国纳税人不仅可以利用在避税港建立信托财产从事消极投资的避税活动，而且还可以利用建立信托财产来掩盖股东在公司的股权，进行积极投资的避税活动。例如，一个高税国 A 国的跨国纳税人可以在避税港 B 国设立一个受控信托公司和一个受控持股公司，通过持股公司进行投资活动，然后把持股公司委托给信托公司。这样，持股公司的股权就合法地归信托公司所有，并由信托公司管理持股公司，而这些财务利益的真正所有者却是委托人兼受益人的高税国 A 国的跨国纳税人。这是一种典型的虚设避税港信托财产的方法。

  例 7-7

新西兰朗伊桥公司为躲避本国的所得税，将其年度利润的 70% 以信托形式转移到巴哈马群岛上。由于巴哈马群岛是一个避税港，税率比新西兰低 35%~50%。因此，该公司每年可以有效规避 300 万~470 万美元的税款。

3. 订立信托合同

在国际经济活动中，许多公司想通过在海外建立自己的办事机构和分支机构来实现避税。但事实表明，相当一部分海外办事机构和分支机构在行政管理上有许多不便，耗资多且效率低。因此，不如在海外中转国或其他地方找一个具有居民身份的公司来帮忙处理业务，利用该公司居住国与他国签订的税收协定，为双方提供方便。

  模拟演示 7-2

【背景】日本和美国签有互惠双边税收协定，日本银行从美国居民手中获取存款可以少付 50% 的税款（美国规定利息税率为 20%，日本银行可以按 10% 支付）。中国某家公司与美国某一公司发生了借贷关系：中国公司是贷款提供方，美国公司是贷款需要方。

【操作】中国公司可委托日本某一银行代替中国公司向美方公司收取贷款利息。

【评述】上述做法可获得少缴纳 50% 税款的好处。

总之，避税港的作用可谓积极性和消极性兼而有之。

第一，国际避税港可以为投资者提供少纳税以获得更多利润的好处，导致资金不断地从高税国流向国际避税港。外国的积极投资，可以加快避税港国家和地区的资金集中和积聚，促进生产规模扩大和进一步社会化；外国的消极投资也能够增加这些国家政府或企业手中的外汇资金；外国企业机构的注册登记、租房用地和办公营业等，多少也可以使这些国家和地区增加一定的收入；为躲避高税而来定居的外国人，也能给避税港带来为数不少的外汇；所有这些国际投资者的活动，还会促进避税港的金融国际化，由此产生一个易于筹集外资的金融市场。第二，国际避税港能够吸引外国先进技术和设备的流入，以促进这些国家和地区的技术革命。第三，国际避税港外籍人员的密集，外国工厂的兴建、公司商号的设立和外国移民的定居，往往需要增加一批工人、店员和服务人员，这就提高了这些国家和地区的就业率。

当然，我们在谈论国际避税港的积极作用的时候，也不能无视它消极的作用。

第一，虽然外国公司在国际避税港开办了成千上万的各种公司或机构，但其中有相当一部分是虚构的，其目的仅仅是避税。像这样的公司，有形资产方面的投资很少，不会给国际避税港国家和地区带来具有实际意义的先进设备和先进技术，它们往往只是一些挂着一块招牌的公司，而且一有风吹草动，或者有更好的避税港便马上转移，因此也缺乏稳定性。第二，即使是从事真正营业活动的各种银行和金融公司，它们所进行的也往往是消极投资，一旦投资业务衰落、利润菲薄、当地或国际资本市场发生波动，这些公司就会很快把资金转移到其他国家去寻求更大的利润，从而给避税港已形成的金融系统造成极大的影响。第三，由于国际避税港大多数是发展中国家和地区，文化技术水平比较低，外国公司往往宁愿雇佣本国或来自其他发达国家的移民当职员，所以并不能很好地解决国际避税港人员的就业问题。第四，也是最重要的一点，国际避税港用来吸引外资的税收优惠，往往因为资本输出国单方面采取的反避税措施而被抵消掉一部分，甚至完全不能发挥作用。

复习思考题

1. 跨国纳税人是怎样利用避税港进行国际避税的？
2. 如何利用避税港信托财产避税？
3. 如何评价国际避税港行为？

第 8 章

国际反避税的方法与措施

时政观点

《中华人民共和国企业所得税法》和《中华人民共和国个人所得税法》都增加了对于跨国纳税人的反避税条款，这对于维护我国的税收主权具有重要意义。

学习目标

1. 全面理解和领会防范国际避税的重要意义。
2. 主要了解各种国际避税的防范措施。
3. 重点掌握受控外国公司法及转让定价税制的内容。

课程导入

据媒体报道，1995 年，美国一家全球著名的跨国公司在北京设立了一家外商独资企业，而后经过两次增资，其注册资本达到 2 000 万美元，但是长期以来，这家在京的美资企业一直亏损，其平均利润率为 −18%，而在北京，该行业的平均利润率为 12%。如何看待我国外商投资公司的避税问题？

近几十年来，国际避税活动花样翻新，规模有增无减，形形色色的避税港的存在，更助长了这一势头。这种情况与国际偷漏税交织在一起，必然造成竞争条件的扭曲和引起国际资本的不正常流动，对许多国家的财政收入产生了不利的影响。收入和财富被重新分配转移给了那些成功地进行了避税和偷漏税的人们，这些人支付的税款低于他们本应缴纳的数额，而那些奉公守法的纳税人却实实在在地缴纳了税赋。然而，事情并非到此为止，因为政府为了确保事先确定的预算，不得不提高税率或开征新税，这又可能给那些诚实的纳税人压上新担子，这显然有失公道。因此，努力减少国际避税和偷漏税，是一件大事。为此，大多数国家都制定了对付各种国际避税类型的反避税条例。在长期的实践中，某些发达国家已逐渐形成了一套值得借鉴的反避税措施，其重点是运用法律手段，在立法和执法上下功夫。当然，扩大和加强政府间的双边合作，酝酿和探索在更大的国际范围内进行反避税多边合作也很重要。

8.1 国际反避税的一般方法

由于各国国情不同,必然导致反避税措施的多样化。本节侧重介绍国际反避税的一般方法并阐述了国际反避税措施的概况。

8.1.1 加强单边反避税立法措施

高质量税收立法将为其本身的实施奠定基础。完整的条文、严谨的措词、明确的解释,是高质量税收立法的重要标志,也是保护税法免遭蛀蚀的"铠甲"。完善税收法律、堵住漏洞,增强各国税法的防护能力,是税务当局赢得反避税斗争的一个重要方面。因此,立法是反避税的基本出发点。同时,为了有效地加强税务当局在反避税和反偷漏税斗争中的地位,税收立法还应从多方面做出有利于税务当局进行工作的规定。各国的单边反避税措施大致有以下几种。

1. 制定反避税条款

各国税法中的反避税条款,通常可以分为四大类。

1) 一般反避税条款

一般反避税条款主要集中在税法对课税客体的表述方面。各国税法对课税客体的表述有两种方法:一种是以民法概念为基础来表述课税客体;另一种则是以广义的和一般的经济概念来表述课税客体。以所得税为例,前一种方法是规定一项制度,据此可用其独立的法律形式来定义可扣除的营业成本;后一种方法是明确规定可扣除成本为正常营业过程中发生的全部成本,这是一个总的综合应税所得概念,如税法中的"应税所得是来自企业的任何种类所得"等类似说法。

显然,第一种方法法律用语虽然准确、严密,但以法律概念表述课税客体会束缚税务当局的反避税能力,在法律措词上纠缠不清。后一种方法,即用经济的而不是法律的概念来表述课税客体,增强了税务当局对避税行为的应变能力,并增加了税务当局对国际避税习惯做法采取行动的机会。税法中广泛存在的经济性规定显然比刻板的民法措词能体现出更大的灵活性和适应性。但是,由于这种方法规定不够具体,在执行中难免存在着某种不确定性,需要与其他反避税条款相配合,才能发挥更好的作用。

2) 特殊反避税条款

在实践中,纳税人利用不断更新的法律手段和解释方式,通过防止导致纳税义务的基础的存在,避免落入税收法令的范围内。针对这种情况,特殊反避税条款规定了明确具体的课税客体,也就是在法律上把某些活动或所得规定为征税对象,在法律解释上不给纳税人留下钻空子的机会。比如,美国、法国、比利时和英国税法中的许多条款,都是以这种方式拟定的。

3) 特殊与一般相结合的反避税条款

特殊与一般相结合的反避税条款是指在税法条款里对某种交易行为及其纳税义务作出具体规定的同时,并附以一般性的规定。例如,《美国国内收入法典》第367节对公司以股份交换财产以及其他的交换作了具体的规定,同时还规定,必须向税务部门证实:逃避联邦所得税并不是这种交换的主要目的。这种方法的好处在于:立法机关在采取立法手段的同时,通过授予税务当局广泛的处理权可以防止一些精明的纳税人钻特殊条款的空子。

4）综合反避税条款

综合反避税条款是指针对有相似性或可比性的避税行为，所列入的可以适用于不同类型的反避税条款。比如，《美国国内收入法典》第482节、《法国税收总法典》第57条和《比利时税法》第24条中对关联公司转移定价所作出的规定，以及《美国国内收入法典》F分部针对避税港营业所作出的规定等，都属于这一类的反避税条款。

2. 强化纳税义务

强化纳税义务的措施通常包括三方面内容。

1）税法规定纳税人有延伸提供税收情报的义务

各居住国（国籍国）的税务当局，一般不能直接掌握居民（公民）纳税人的国外活动资料，也不能去国外进行实地调查，因为这超出了它所管辖地域的范围。为了解决这个问题，各国税法一般都规定，居民（公民）纳税人有向居住国（国籍国）提供其在国外从事经营活动情况的义务。至于提供税收情报的义务人，可以是居民纳税人，可以是与纳税人有业务关系的第三者，还可以是非居民纳税人。

当然，这种义务不利于保护纳税人的商业秘密从而可能对当事人造成损害。因为根据税法规定的报告义务，纳税人必须向税务当局公开一部分营业秘密，而税务官员的保密义务并不是无懈可击的。

2）税法规定纳税人对某些交易行为有事先取得政府同意的义务

在反避税条款中，最严厉的立法就是规定对某些交易行为纳税人要事先取得税务当局的同意，否则，就是违章行为，应予以处罚。它不仅包括居民纳税人，有时还包括与这类交易进行合作的外国人。

例 8-1

英国的所得税法和公司税法就规定，居民法人将英国境内住所迁移至国外，或将国内资产转移到由其支配的外国法人名下，必须由财政部事先同意，否则就要受到以下处罚：首先，必须像没有迁出之前一样，继续向英国政府履行无限纳税义务；其次，还要受到一定的惩罚制裁。美国税法也规定有类似的条款。例如，美国的跨国纳税人在进行某些交易时，有义务事先向税务当局提出证据，证明它们此举的主要目的不是避税和逃税。

3）税法规定纳税人对国际避税案件有事后提供证明的义务

依各国诉讼法的一般原则，诉讼中的举证责任是由原告一方承担。换言之，原告必须提供充足证据，法院才能在诉讼中判定被告有罪。然而，当国际逃税避税案件发生时，由有关国家的税务当局来提供证据是一种繁重的负担。为了摆脱这种被动局面，一些国家开始在税收立法中放弃诉讼法的这一传统原则，而是通过税法特别规定纳税人有事后向税务当局提供证据的义务。一般要求纳税人至少要对下列两种情况提供证据：案件涉及的国外事实；跨越税境交易的正常营业。比利时所得税法和法国税收总法典就曾有过这样的法律规定。除非纳税人能够提供相反的证据，否则他的某些支付（特别是对国际避税港的支付）都将被认为是虚构的，不能从应税利润中予以扣除。这种做法被称为举证责任的倒置。有些国家虽然没有明确纳税人的举证责任，但也规定纳税人有配合税务当局的调整提供所需资料的义务。

8.1.2　加强单边税务行政管理

上述单边反避税立法措施，还必须通过加强以下几方面的税务行政管理才能奏效。

1. 收集有关信息资料

各国税务当局往往结合实际情况，利用税法赋予的权力，设计不同用途的各类报表，由纳税人填报，以便从中获得反避税所需的资料。美国在这方面做得最多，现将美国财政部设计的一些表格名称列举如下。

① 针对外国控股公司中的高级职员、董事或股东的第 957 和 958 号表格。（第 957 号表格要求详细说明营业性质和全部股票种类，并且规定股东必须是记名的。第 958 号表格则要求详细说明总所得和扣除项目。）

② 针对受控外国公司的第 2592 号表格。

③ 针对创建或转让某些外国信托的第 3520 号表格。

④ 申报关于外国银行账户、证券账户和其他财务账户的情况的第 4683 号表格。

⑤ 针对通货或货币证券的国际交易所设计的第 4790 号表格。

此外，从国际反避税需要出发，各国税务当局还注意加强与其他政府部门（如海关、外汇管制局等）之间的联系与合作，以求掌握较全面的信息资料。

2. 加强税务调查与税务审计

加强对税务人员的培训是保证税收调查行之有效的有力措施。美国国内收入局对跨国公司使用的基本避税手段，为其税务稽查人员开设特别课程，传授发现偷漏税和避税的大量技术方法。这包括同离任的和在职的公司高级职员，特别是那些被解雇的职员进行谈话；与公司的领导人谈话；检查董事们在旅行中途停留地（主要是避税港）的活动等。

税务部门除了进行税务调查，还必须进行税务审计。与其等待不情愿的外国政府提供协助，税务机关更愿意自己对纳税人进行审计，包括雇用私人的国际会计师事务所来对跨国纳税人提供的情况进行审核。这种审计往往是有重点地集中在几种主要的国际避税和偷漏税手法上，审计对象一般也是选择问题比较多的私人企业和较大的跨国公司。但是按照国际惯例，一个国家的税务机关不能到另一个国家去审计纳税人的财务记录，除非受到该另一国政府这样做的邀请。一些国家的政府认为，如果没有同时得到相关纳税人的同意，这样做也是不合适的。有些国家通过联合审计项目来解决问题，根据这样的项目，某个特定的纳税人（及其子公司）可以受到两个国家的税务机关的联合审计。

各国的实践表明，通过税务调查和税务审计所查补的税款，要远远高于税务部门为此所花掉的费用。

 例 8-2

例如，美国的"净值法"是利用对跨国纳税人年初资产负债表上的所得净值与年末资产负债表上的估计所得增减净值进行比较，扣除一定的生活费用和其他费用，推算出这个时期大致的应税所得，以检查纳税人是否隐瞒了应税所得的一种方法。又如，美国的"银行存款法"，是参照银行账户的存取，对跨国纳税人实际和估计的收支进行比较，以检查是否存在少报所得的一种方法。

3. 争取银行的合作

几乎所有国家的法律都允许银行为客户严格信息，有些国家（地区）对泄露客户信息的银行职员，还给予刑法上的制裁。不过，也有些国家通过在其法律条文中规定本国银行必须履行义务的方式来破除这种保密封锁。例如，美国税务当局查看有关银行账目多半是通过一份法院的决定进行的。当本国银行客户被怀疑涉嫌纳税欺诈案时，银行将自觉服从法院的指令，但是对外国银行则无计可施。大多数国家的税务当局只能积极争取外国银行的合作，以便打击国际避税行为。这种合作，至少要通过两方面的努力才能实现。第一，通过国与国之间签订反对有组织犯罪条约来实现税务当局与外国银行的合作。第二，税务当局对了解到的所有事实和情报必须予以严格保密。

例8-3

瑞士银行有着极其严格的保密制度，但是美国国内收入局还是通过美国与瑞士签订的双边税收条约享受特殊待遇，争取到了瑞士银行的合作。在一定的情况下（或案件中），如发生伪造有关财务文件的骗局时，该条约允许美国国内收入局查阅瑞士银行账户。除此之外，瑞士一般不允许各国税务当局接近瑞士银行的账簿。通过这样的合作，美国国内收入局已查出了一些重大的国际偷漏税案件，给予国际偷漏税活动以一定的打击。

8.1.3 积极开展国际协作

防止国际间的避税和偷税，如果仅仅依靠一国的单边措施，其效果是有限的。因此，加强有关国家政府之间在税务领域中的合作就显得十分重要。目前，各国之间通过有关条约或协定达成的防止国际避税的措施主要有两方面的内容：一是建立有关情报交换制度；二是在税款的征收方面进行征管合作，以下分别说明。

1. 情报交换

一个国家的税务机关在获取其居民在境外活动的信息方面，经常遇到极大的困难，更无法证明信息的准确性。比如，包括所有避税港在内的许多国家和地区，都有严格的银行保密法。避税港国家很少与发达国家签署含有情报交换内容的税收协定。在20世纪80年代，美国与避税港国家达成了一些进行情报交换的协议，但这些协议主要用来发现贩毒者洗钱的资金，对发现较为普遍的避税或偷税现象效果不大。最近，为了适应OECD反对有害税收竞争的举措，许多避税港国家与OECD成员国之间签署了更具有实质意义的情报交换协议。即使在未涉及避税港的情况下，就居民纳税人申报的境外所得收集情报并进行审计也是非常困难的。为了解决情报收集问题，许多国家在其税收协定中都包含了情报交换条款。

《经合发范本》和《联合国范本》第26条规定，缔约国双方主管当局应交换"为实施本协定的规定所必需的情报、或缔约国双方关于本协定所涉及的税种的国内法律的情报"。《联合国范本》更明确指出，情报交换的目的不仅是为了实施缔约国的税法，也是为了打击避税。根据《经合发范本》和《联合国范本》，情报交换可以是应缔约国一方的特别要求，或由缔约国一方自发而主动进行。具体的税收协定中，对情报交换范围的规定或大或小。比如，有的协定表明，情报交换的范围包括所有国内税种。与此相反，其他一些协定规定，情报交换的内容仅限于为实施协定本身的规定所必需的情报。

当然，缔约国一方税务机关对通过情报交换条款获取的情报必须保密，但一般可在法院审理程序中披露。情报交换条款的规定不应被理解为缔约国一方有义务代表缔约国另一方，采取与本国法律或行政惯例不相一致的行政措施，或提供泄露商业秘密的情报或类似情报。该条款中，一个摆脱性规定是，允许缔约国一方拒绝提供泄露后将"违反公共政策"的情报。对于银行保密法严格的国家来说，情报交换条款形同虚设，因为按照这些国家的法律，其主管当局都无权获得关于纳税人财务活动的有价值信息。

例 8-4

　　某日本人在中国居住已满 6 年，按《中华人民共和国个人所得税法》的规定，该日本人为中国税收居民，应就其从中国境内和境外取得的全部收入向中国政府纳税。为了妥善处理该日本人的涉税事项，中国政府必须向日本政府或日本税务当局了解他的收入情况。根据中国与日本缔结的双边税收协定，日本政府和税务当局有责任为中国政府了解核实该日本人的收入情况提供情报资料。就情报交换的内容而言，主要有三个方面：一是交换为实施税收协定所需要的情报。如纳税人在居住国或收入来源国的收入情况，关联企业之间的交易作价，利息和特许权使用费的支付人与受益人之间的关系，分公司或子公司的开业、营业、关闭，以及市场价格、商业活动等。二是交换与税收有关的国内法律，如有关税法的实施细则，为防止国际偷漏税和国际避税而单方面采取的法律措施等。通过情报的交换与协调，缔约国各方在执行法律时不至于与协定的要求冲突。三是交换防止税收欺诈和偷漏税的情报。

2. 征管合作

　　征管合作的主要内容包括缔约国一方代表另一方执行某些征税行为。例如，代为送达纳税通知书，在纳税责任未确定前对有关纳税人及其财产代为实施某种保全措施等。在这种情况下，征管合作能有效地制止避税和逃税行为。

　　基于互惠和防止国际逃税、避税的需要，在一些国家间签订的税务行政协助协定中也达成了有关征税方面的安排。如在 OECD 和欧洲理事会起草的多边协定范本《税收征管互助公约》中，有对核定的税款征收活动提供广泛合作的规定。这个公约还规定，缔约国在提供公约所涉及税种的法律文件方面，也应互相协助，其已经由生效所需数目的国家签署。1995 年签署的《加拿大－美国税收协定议定书》中有一项新的规定，即本应由缔约国一方征收的欠税，可以由缔约国另一方征收，就像是属于该另一方的欠税那样。这个大胆的突破早就该出现，它将防止纳税人通过将居住地改变到另一国的方式来避免承担在一国的纳税义务。

8.2　国际反避税的特别法律措施

　　世界上并无一部通用的国际税法，国际税收领域中的各种反避税措施往往体现有关国家各自的特点。但是，其中的一些措施和方法，由于其合理性与实用性，已被越来越多的国家所借鉴和采用，于是就逐渐演变成为具有广泛意义的国际惯例。

8.2.1　限制避税性移居

　　跨国纳税人进行国际避税的手段之一，是从高税国移居到低税国或避税港，以摆脱高税国的居民身份，免除向高税国政府负有的无限纳税义务。为了防范本国居民出于避税目的而向国外移居，一些国家（主要是发达国家）采取了一些立法措施，对个人或法人向国外移居加以限制。

1. 限制个人移居的措施

在许多国家，公民移居国外与出国旅游一样，是个人的自由，政府一般不加干预。所以即使发现公民有移居避税的企图，政府往往也不能限制其离境，只能从经济上对其采取一些限制措施，使移居给政府造成的税收利益损失降低到最低程度。一些发达国家在立法上采取了有条件地延续本国向外移居者无限纳税义务的做法。

 例 8-5

德国在 1972 年公布的《涉外税法》中就规定，凡移居到避税港的前德国公民，若从其移居的当年算起，往前 10 年中有 5 年是德国税收上的居民或公民，符合三个条件之一者，税务当局就将认定他们与德国保持有实质的经济联系，在未来 10 年内仍视其为国内的税收居民，对其德国境内外的全部所得仍要课税。这三个条件如下。

① 纳税人在移居地不缴纳所得税，或虽缴纳所得税，但其适用的税率不足德国税率的 2/3。

② 纳税人在移居后与德国公司保持实质性的经济联系，具体标准为，以合伙人的身份取得有限合伙公司不少于 25% 的所得额，或在德国的一家居民公司中拥有 25% 及以上的股票。

③ 该纳税人在移居后取得来源于德国的净所得占其世界范围所得的 30% 以上，或在某一纳税年度中达到 12 万德国马克。

高税国居民为了逃避无限纳税义务，有的彻底切断了与原居住国的联系，真正移居到他国，但有的只是采取虚假移居的手段。对于这种行为，一些国家也采取了严格的限制。

 例 8-6

瑞典在 20 世纪五六十年代曾是世界上个人税收负担最重的国家之一。为了防止人们以移居为名逃避瑞典的无限纳税义务，瑞典在 1966 年实施的《市政税法》中规定，瑞典公民在移居到别国后的 3 年内，一般仍被认定为瑞典税收上的居民，仍要在瑞典负无限纳税义务，除非他能够证明自己与瑞典不再有任何实质性联系，而且这种举证责任由纳税人承担。又如，1999 年意大利公布了一项反避税措施，规定从该纳税年度开始，凡意大利居民移居到一个避税港国家，即使该人的名字已经从市政户籍登记处删除，仍然要被认定为意大利居民，并继续向意大利政府负无限纳税义务。与此同时，意大利经济和财政部还公布了一份避税港名单，列出了瑞士、列支敦士登、安道尔等 59 个国家和地区。另外，美国的所得税法中也规定，如果美国公民以避税为目的放弃美国公民身份，则该纳税人必须像美国公民一样再向美国政府负 10 年的无限纳税义务。芬兰、挪威、西班牙等国也有类似的规定。澳大利亚、加拿大、法国等还对移居国外的个人开征"移居税"，即对其没有实现的资本利得征税。

此外，为了防止人们用临时移居、压缩居留时间的办法躲避本国的居民身份，许多国家都规定纳税人的临时离境不扣减其在本国的居住天数。例如，我国税法规定，纳税人在一个纳税年度中在我国境内居住满 365 日的，要就从我国境内和境外取得的所得缴纳个人所得税；临时离境一次不超过 30 日，或多次累计不超过 90 日的，不扣减在我国居住的天数。

2. 限制法人移居的措施

各国判定法人居民身份的标准不同，限制法人移居的措施也就不同。如果一国采用注册地标准判定法人居民身份，则该国的居民公司若要移居他国，只能在本国注销而改在他国重新注册。为了防止本国的居民公司迁移到低税国，许多国家（如美国、英国、爱尔兰、加拿大等）规定，如果本国居民公司改在他国注册或总机构、有效管理机构移到国外，不再属于本国居民公司时，必须进行清算，其资产视同销售后取得的资本利得，要在本国缴纳所得税。也就是说，政府要对将财产转移至境外取得的转让收益征税，即在增值财产被转让给非居民关联方的情况下，一些国家视该财产已按公平交易价出售以便对增值收益征税。否则，对该收益征收的国内税收可能会被全部逃避。此外，一些国家在纳税人不再成为居民时，即对增值收益征税。这些规定可能十分复杂，因为移民的纳税人实际上并未处理财产，纳税人可能没有必需的资金就增值收益缴纳税款。因此，可以制定特殊条例允许纳税人在提供最终付税担保的前提下延期支付税款。

8.2.2 限制利用改变公司组织形式避税

跨国公司国际避税的方式之一，是适时地改变国外附属机构的组织形式——当国外分公司开始盈利时，即将其重组为子公司。为了防止跨国公司利用这种方式避税，有些国家在法律上也采取了一些防范措施。

 例 8–7

美国税法规定，外国分公司改为子公司以后，分公司过去的亏损所冲减的总公司利润必须重新计算清楚，并就这部分被国外分公司亏损冲减的利润进行补税。英国则用限制本国居民公司向非本国居民公司转让经营业务的方法阻止本国公司将国外的分公司改组为子公司。如英国税法就明确规定，除非经财政部同意，否则一个英国公司将自己一部分贸易或经营业务转让给国外的非居民公司就是违法。由于国外分公司是英国公司的一部分，并不具有外国居民公司的身份，所以这条法律并不限制英国公司将自己的一部分业务通过国外分公司去开展。但如果国外分公司改建为子公司，子公司就具有了外国居民公司的地位。这样，由于有上述规定，英国公司的业务就不能再通过该外国子公司开展，这就在客观上限制了英国公司用改变国外机构组织形式的方式避税。

8.2.3 防止滥用税收协定

第三国居民滥用其他两国之间的税收协定，主要是为了规避有关国家的预提税。目前，除了奥地利、芬兰等极少数国家以外，绝大多数国家都把滥用税收协定的行为视为一种不正当的行为，并主张加以制止。为了防止本国与他国签订的税收协定被第三国居民用于避税，一些国家已开始采取防止滥用税收协定的措施。这些措施主要包括以下几方面。

1. 制定防止税收协定滥用的国内法规

目前，采取这种做法的国家主要是瑞士。前文已经提到，瑞士是一个有广泛税收协定的国家，其公司所得税之低，在发达国家中是不多见的。根据其签署的税收协定，协定国对向瑞士居民支付的股息、利息和特许权使用费征收较低的预提税；瑞士对支付给协定国居民的股息、利息征收的预提税也可以降到很低。此外，瑞士对特许权使用费还不征收预提税。由于这些优越条件，瑞士过去经常被第三国纳税人选为建立中介控股公司、中介金融公司和中介许可公司的地点，利用瑞士与其他国家签订的税收协定享受其他国家给予的预提税优惠。瑞士与美国签订税收协定较早，所以当时美瑞两国之间滥用税收协定的情况比较严重。迫于压力，瑞士议会于1962年12月颁布了《防止税收协定滥用法》，决定单方面严格限制由第三国居民拥有或控制的公司适用税收协定。《防止税收协定滥用法》规定，除非特别条件得到满足，否则瑞士与他国签订的税收协定中的税收优惠不适用于股息、利息和特许权使用费。这以后，瑞士滥用税收协定的情况有所改善。

2. 在双边税收协定中加进反滥用税收协定条款

为防范第三国居民滥用税收协定，可以在协定中加进一定的防范条款，例如，美国坚持在税收协定中加入优惠限制条款以防止滥用协定。具体有以下几种方法。在实践中，各国一般选择同时使用多种方法，很少只局限于使用某种方法。

1) 排除法

排除法即在协定中注明协定提供的税收优惠不适用于某一类纳税人。

 例8-8

美国1962年与卢森堡签订的税收协定条款中规定，在卢森堡注册成立的控股公司不属于该协定适用的纳税人。这样，第三国居民就不能借助在卢森堡成立的中介控股公司来享受美国的预提税优惠。又如，加拿大对外签订的一些税收协定条款中也规定，在巴巴多斯、塞浦路斯、以色列、象牙海岸、牙买加和斯里兰卡注册成立的公司，如果可以在当地享受特别税收优惠，则不能得到加拿大根据税收协定提供的税收利益。除了美国和加拿大以外，澳大利亚、奥地利、比利时、塞浦路斯、丹麦、法国、德国、卢森堡、荷兰、西班牙、瑞典、英国等国也都使用排除法。总的来看，排除法所限制受益的公司都是那些容易充当中介的公司。使用这种方法时，税务部门并不需要具体核查被限制的公司是否是外国投资者为避税而建立的中介公司，只要不能排除其受限制的性质，就不能享受税收协定的好处。

2) 真实法

真实法即规定不是出于真实的商业经营目的、只是单纯为了谋求税收协定优惠的纳税人，不得享受协定提供的税收优惠。

 例8-9

英国与荷兰、荷属安第列斯签订的税收协定条款中规定，如果债务和特许权交易只是纳税人为了利用协定而不是由于真正的商业原因而发生，则该协定对利息、特许权使用费规定的预提税减免就不对其适用。英国与瑞士缔结的税收协定中也规定，如果拥有股权只是为了取得本协定提供的税收利益而没有真实的商业原因，则凭借该股权得到的股息就不能享受税收优惠。除英国外，澳大利亚、丹麦、荷兰、瑞典、瑞士、美国等国也采用真实法。我国对外签订一些税收协定时也采用真实法来防止滥用税收协定。

3) 纳税义务法

纳税义务法即一个中介性质公司的所得如果在注册成立的国家没有纳税义务，则该公司不能享受税收协定的优惠。

例8-10

比利时、法国、德国、意大利与瑞士缔结的税收协定中规定，由瑞士非居民大量控股的瑞士居民公司从缔约国另一方取得的利息、特许权使用费和资本利得只有在公司所在地有缴纳州所得税的义务才能享受税收协定提供的优惠。此外，比利时与英国、加拿大与马来西亚、加拿大与新加坡、丹麦与瑞士、丹麦与英国、德国与英国、荷兰与新西兰、西班牙与德国签订的税收协定中也有纳税义务法的相关条款。

4）受益所有人法

受益所有人法即规定协定提供的税收优惠的最终受益人必须是真正的协定国居民，第三国居民不能借助在协定国成立的居民公司而从协定中受益。

 例8-11

美国从1980年以后对外缔结的税收协定或协定议定书中都有限定受益人的条款，包括美国与澳大利亚、巴巴多斯、塞浦路斯、法国、意大利、加拿大、牙买加、新西兰等国签订的协定。美国与我国税收协定的备忘录中也有类似条款。例如，美国与塞浦路斯签订的税收协定条款中规定，美国的税收优惠只给予下列公司。

①75%以上的股份由塞浦路斯居民个人所有。
②公司的大部分股票在塞浦路斯证券市场上市。
③公司的所得没有被大量用于支付给美国和塞浦路斯以外的第三国居民。

除美国外，加拿大、丹麦、法国、意大利、荷兰、英国也采用受益所有人法。

5）渠道法

渠道法即如果缔约国的居民将所得的很大一部分以利息、股息、特许权使用费的形式支付给一个第三国居民，则这笔所得不能享受税收协定提供的预提税优惠。

 例8-12

某美国公司试图利用中国和巴巴多斯税收协定规避股权转让预提税的案例如下。

某美国公司2006年5月在巴巴多斯注册成立了D公司。6月，D公司出资3 380万美元从我国B公司手中购买新疆一家从事液化天然气生产和销售的公司（A公司）。同年7月，D公司与B公司又签署了股权转让协议，将其持有的A公司24.99%的股权转让给B公司，转让价格为4 596.8万美元。至此，D公司仅在一年的时间里，仅从我国A公司股权的一买一卖中，就取得财产转让收益1 217万美元。

在此案例中，某美国公司显然是想利用巴巴多斯与我国税收协定"财产收益"中的条款13规避我国的预提税。在2010年2月之前，该条款规定我国对巴巴多斯居民转让我国居民公司股份取得的收益（财产转让所得）不能课征预提税。最终，某美国公司的避税企图没能得逞，原因是D公司拿不出巴巴多斯的居民身份证明。而且我国启动了税收情报交换机制，结果确认D公司不是巴巴多斯的税收居民（根据巴巴多斯的税法，只有公司的管理和控制中心设在巴巴多斯才属于巴巴多斯的居民公司，而D公司仅在巴巴多斯注册成立，其三名董事都是美国人，且常年居住在美国，所以D公司的管理和控制中心不在巴巴多斯）。这样，D公司就没有资格享受中巴税收协定中的优惠待遇。

6）禁止法

禁止法即不与被认为是国际避税港国家或地区缔结税收协定，以防止跨国公司在避税港组建公司作为其国际避税活动的中介性机构。澳大利亚、奥地利、比利时、丹麦、法国、德国、意大利、卢森堡、荷兰、新加坡、西班牙、瑞典、瑞士、英国和美国实行禁止法，不与避税港签订税收协定。

8.2.4 资本弱化条例

一些国家针对纳税人对借贷形式的偏爱，制定了资本弱化条例以防止居民公司的非居民股东以可抵扣的利息而非不可抵扣的股息形式，利用超额借贷资本抽取公司的利润。根据这些条例，当居民公司的资本过度地依赖于负债时，对其支付给非居民股东的利息就不允许扣除。"资本弱化"一词较贴切，因为只有当公司权益资本小于借贷资本时才适用这些条例。

一些国家制定了法令性的资本弱化条例，一些国家依赖于管理性指南或实际操作规程，也有一些国家试图用一般的反避税条例来处理资本弱化问题。不同国家的法令性资本弱化条例大不相同，但大体上有如下的结构特征。

①非居民债权人：资本弱化条例一般仅适用于拥有居民公司重要股权的非居民债权人，股权控制水平由占股份的15%到控制居民公司不等。

②国内实体：大多数国家的资本弱化条例仅适用于居民公司，然而，对于居民合伙公司和信托企业或非居民公司的分支机构，仍然可以产生通过支付超额的利息而获取利润的现象。

③超额利息的确定：资本弱化条例一般只适用于居民公司支付给非居民股东的某些超额利息，超额利息的确定取决于国内公司负债与权益的比率。换句话说，其只是相对权益而言，人为加大的负债利息，实际上是伪装的权益，不能扣除。

根据资本弱化条例，可以按如下方法确定负债与权益比率。

①固定的负债与权益比率。

②参照所有居民公司或从事某个工业或商业行业的所有居民公司的平均负债与权益比率。

许多国家使用固定的负债与权益比率，如 2∶1 或 3∶1，有时金融机构比率较高，如我国规定金融企业的这个标准为 5∶1，其他企业为 2∶1。将负债与权益作为比率因素来计算使得许多附带的税收政策成为必然。例如，是考虑非居民所有的负债，还是仅仅考虑重要的非居民股东所持有的负债？权益是否包括分配的盈余，还是仅仅包括股本和留存收益？混合证券（如优先股）应归类为负债还是权益？

OECD 推荐了一种可选方法，即根据实际情况将负债和权益归类，包括居民公司的负债与权益的比率。这种方法与用于转让定价的公平交易原则一致，避免了运用固定的负债与权益比率所造成的死板和专断。但是，其较难以管理，且在运用上缺乏明确性。另一种方法是以美国为代表的收益剥离原则，依据利息和公司所得的关系确定超额利息。如果利息超过公司所得的 50%，公司就不能扣除支付给某些非居民或免税居民股东的利息。美国的收益剥离原则包括有安全港规定，即负债与权益比率低于 1.5∶1 的公司不适用该原则。

总之，运用资本弱化条例的结果就是不能扣除超额利息。在一些国家，将该超额利息视为股息；在另一些国家，超额利息可以向前结转，并在以后的年度中扣除。

8.3　受控外国公司法

许多国家的税收居民就其全球所得纳税，并可以抵免对外国来源所得征收的外国税收。然而，由于缺乏补救性的立法，对外国来源所得征收的国内税收可以轻而易举地通过成立外国公司或信托达到延迟纳税的目的，因为外国公司或信托一般被视为独立的纳税实体，公司的控股股东或者信托的受益人在未获得分配前免于征税。当对外国公司或信托取得的所得征收的外国税收很低或为零时，这种延迟纳税的好处为最大。因此，如果受控的外国公司或外国信托建立在避税港，延迟纳税将会成为最严重的问题。这一问题明显地表现在消极投资所得上，因为这些所得很容易被转移至或聚集在设在避税港的海外实体。例如，假设位于 A 国的公司取得有价证券利息所得 1 000 元，A 国的税率为 40%，假如该公司在没有税收的避税港设立了一家全资子公司，通过转让证券给该子公司就可以推迟缴纳税款 400 元，且不必就利息缴纳 A 国的预提税，因为利息不来源于 A 国或者利息在 A 国免于征收预提税。即使利息适用于 A 国的预提税，该公司也能就公司税率和预提税率差额部分延迟缴纳 A 国的税收。

许多国家制定了详细的法令以防止或限制利用受控外国公司来推迟或避免国内税收。根据这些法令，受控外国公司本身不适用居民国税收，而受控外国公司的居民股东按照其在受控外国公司部分或全部所得中所占的比例份额来缴纳当期的税收。该所得必须是按照国内税法条例并以国内货币来确定。美国在 1962 年率先采用受控外国公司法，即著名的 F 部分（Sub-part F）。F 部分的原则基于美国 1937 年条例：即在 1937 年制定的专门针对个人利用外国避税港问题的外国个人控股公司条例。在最终颁布时，该条例代表了要求取消受控外国公司所有收入延迟实现的初始建议和仅取消消极投资所得延迟实现的美国跨国公司的立场之间的妥协。基本妥协表现为对多数类型的消极投资所得和某些类型的易被转移至避税港的积极经营所得当期予以征税。自 1962 年以来，美国陆续做了修改，使得该条例日趋严格，并填补了执行中的一些漏洞。自从美国于 1962 年采用 F 部分以来，许多其他资本出口国也颁布了受控外国公司法以保护其税基。

受控外国公司立法的基本框架反映了两大竞争性基本政策。一方面，旨在防止避税，并促进公平和经济效益的传统目标的实现；另一方面，各国一般不想无缘由地干涉居民公司在外国市场中和他国居民公司的竞争能力。尽管各国受控外国公司法的特性迥异，但就多数国家而言，条例的一些基本框架内容是相同的。有关受控外国公司法的主要框架性内容将在下文中介绍。

8.3.1　受控外国公司的定义

除一些例外情况外，各国一般均将受控外国公司立法的范围限制在如下类型实体取得的所得。

①非居民。
②与其拥有者分别纳税的公司或类似实体。
③由国内股东控制的或者国内股东拥有实质性利益的实体。

受控外国公司法不适用作为管道或过渡性征税的实体。例如，合伙企业，因为外国合伙企业的居民股东已按照其在合伙企业所得中的份额缴纳了居民国税收。

大多数受控外国公司立法仅仅适用于被某些国内股东控制的外国公司。控制一般是指拥有50%以上的已发行的选举股。一些国家将控制的概念扩展到拥有相等于已发行的股票总价值50%以上的股票。一些国家规定即便居民拥有外国公司少于50%的选举股权，该居民仍被假设为控制该外国公司。例如，澳大利亚和新西兰的相关条例规定，如果居民拥有外国公司的40%或以上的选举权股，并且没有其他非居民拥有选举控制权，则视为该居民控制该外国公司。一些国家，如法国、葡萄牙和丹麦将受控外国公司法适用到居民具有实质性所有权利益的外国公司。葡萄牙和丹麦规定所有权限定比例为25%，法国为10%。

控制也包括间接控制。拥有同时被另一个受控外国公司拥有的避税港公司的股份并不能逃避受控外国公司法。例如，如果一居民拥有一外国公司60%的选举权股，且该外国公司拥有第二个外国公司的选举权股的50%以上，该第二个外国公司被视为该居民的受控外国公司。许多国家也采用推定拥有条例以防止关联人之间通过分解股份拥有比例来逃避受控外国公司法。例如，如果一居民公司拥有一外国公司40%的选举权股，且另一居民公司拥有同一外国公司选举权股的20%，假设该两个居民公司是相关联的，如它们是同时为另一居民公司全资拥有的子公司，该外国公司即被视为该两个居民公司的受控外国公司。在一些国家，控制必须集中在少数的居民股东身上，例如，澳大利亚、加拿大和新西兰要求五个或以下居民控制一外国公司。在另一些国家，被居民股东广泛拥有的外国公司甚至也被视为受控外国公司。

8.3.2　归属所得的定义

归属所得是指受控外国公司应分配给股东且不再享受股东居住国推迟课税规定的某些类型的所得；这种所得虽没有支付给居住国股东，但仍要归属到国内股东应税所得之中一并申报纳税，这类所得又称受污所得。受污所得一般包括消极投资所得和基地公司所得。

消极所得包括股息、利息、租金、特许权使用费和资本收益。所有制定受控外国公司法的国家尽管对消极所得有不同的定义，但均视消极所得为受污所得，因为不同类型的消极所得极易通过新金融工具转变为其他类型的所得。为填补避税漏洞，必须给予消极所得最广泛的定义。或许在受控外国公司法中定义消极所得的最难点是分清一种一般被视为消极所得但因来源于积极经营活动而不再适用受控外国公司法的收入类型。例如，一家真实的金融机构从事正常的银行业务取得的利息收入一般被视为积极所得，而在许多国家不适用受控外国公司法。租金和特许权使用费也能类似地产生于积极经营活动。例如，来源于汽车租赁业务的所得不应适用于专门针对滥用避税港而设定的税收。积极和消极所得的区别没有一定之规。例如，对于好的税收筹划者而言，他们会将易于转入避税港的海外租赁业务表面上设计成积极经营活动。如果一国的受控外国公司法不适用于海外租赁所得，该国的国内税基就可能被侵蚀。也很难区分金融机构取得的属于积极所得的银行业务利息和金融机构取得的属于消极所得的投资性收入。

基地公司所得一词用于指消极所得以外的被受控外国公司法视为受污所得的所得。基地公司所得的概念常常十分复杂，并且各国在其受控外国公司法中所作出的定义范围都大相径庭。基地公司所得的一项重要组成部分是受控外国公司向其所在的国家境外销售财产或提供劳务，或向关联方销售财产或提供劳务所取得的所得。在这些情况下，利用受控外国公司取得该项所得的主要目的可能是逃避国内税收，而非出于国际竞争所需的正当理由。

总之，归属于国内股东的受控外国公司所得应按照国内税条例并以国内货币计算和纳税。

8.3.3 受控外国公司法适用的国内纳税人

受控外国公司法适用的纳税人是指该法规所要打击或限制的对象。正是这些纳税人企图利用推迟课税的规定，逃避从外国受控公司取得的所得本应向本国缴纳的税收。受控外国公司法就是要限制纳税人通过延期纳税的手段进行国际避税。

在多数国家，对受控外国公司征税的规定适用于个人和公司股东。在少数国家，这些规定仅适用于居民公司。受控外国公司法要打击的对象一定是在外国受控公司中拥有股权的本国居民股东，并且在大多数国家，受控外国公司的居民股东只有在符合最小股份拥有要求（一般是10%）时，才会按照其在外国公司的未分配收入的份额来计算征税。豁免小股东税款，是因为他们没有足够影响力来要求外国公司分配其收入或获得必要的资料计算其所占外国公司所得的份额。

20世纪90年代后期，许多国家加强了对受控外国公司的立法，主要是将打击的范围从受控外国公司扩大到了受控外国合伙企业。

8.4 转让定价税制

利用转让定价转移利润是关联公司（特别是跨国公司）从事避税活动最常见的手段之一，它严重影响了国家的税收权益。因此，许多国家制定了公司集团内或转让定价税制，以防止关联纳税人通过人为地抬高或降低关联交易价格向不同管辖区转移所得和费用。目前，对于该税制是确切地归类为国际反避税法规还是属于一国基本税制的一部分尚值得商榷。不过，建立转让定价税制，通常需要国家的配合，甚至要通过政府间协商来达成协议，即通过税收协定加以实施。

8.4.1 关联公司的判定

转让定价税制针对的是跨国关联公司之间的交易作价。正确运用转让定价税制进行反避税，首先就要准确地判定交易双方是否是关联公司。如果交易双方之间不具有关联关系，则转让定价税制对该笔交易就根本不适用。如果交易双方属于关联公司，则税务部门就有权对交易作价进行审核，如果发现交易作价不合理，明显偏离正常的市场价格或合理价格，税务部门就要依据转让定价税制对不合理的转让定价进行调整。

一般来说，两个或两个以上有共同利益的相互直接或间接拥有或控制的人为关联人。这种关系的明显标志是具有制定不同于市场价格的转让定价的能力。在实践中，公司之间的关联关系主要反映在三个方面，即管理、控制和资本。《经合范本》和《联合国范本》都规定，凡符合下述两个条件之一者，便被视为具有跨国关联关系。

①缔约国一方公司直接或间接参与缔约国另一方公司的管理、控制或资本。

②同一人直接或间接参与缔约国一方公司和缔约国另一方公司的管理、控制或资本。

这里的参与管理是指对公司经营管理权的控制，即如果一家公司对另一家公司在经营、购销、筹资等方面拥有实际控制权，这两家公司之间就具有关联关系。这里的参与控制是指一个公司有权任命另一个公司的董事或高级管理人员，或者有权为另一个公司制定基本的或主要的经营决策。而参与资本是指拥有对方公司一定的股本，掌握其一定的股权。对于股份制公司来说，如果能对其控股，就能够掌握其经营管理和经营决策权。但持有一个公司多大比例的股本才算控股并无一定之规。在股权十分分散的情况下，拥有一个公司5%或5%以下的股份就可能控制这个公司，并不需要拥有其50%以上的股权。所以在实践中，从参股的角度来判别公司间的关联关系必须由税务部门统一规定一个控股比例的标准。目前，制定了转让定价法规的国家一般都有这方面的规定，但各国制定的控股比例标准却不尽相同。例如，美国、瑞士、新西兰、新加坡、韩国等规定为50%，挪威规定为30%，德国、西班牙规定为25%；葡萄牙甚至规定为10%。另外，持股比例通常是指直接和间接持有的某公司的股份比例。间接持股比例一般按连乘方法计算。例如，A公司持有B公司60%的股份，B公司又持有C公司40%的股份，则A公司间接持有C公司24%（60%×40%）的股份。

我国在制定关联公司的标准方面有类似的规定。《中华人民共和国企业所得税法实施条例》第一百零九条规定，关联方是指与公司有下列关联关系之一的公司、其他组织或者个人。

①在资金、经营、购销等方面存在直接或者间接的控制关系。
②直接或者间接地同被第三者控制。
③在利益上具有相关联的其他关系。

2016年6月29日，中华人民共和国国家税务总局发布了《关于完善关联申报和同期资料管理有关事项的公告》，该文件对企业在资金方面的控制（包括直接控制和间接控制）关系进行了详细说明：如果一方直接或间接持有另一方的股份总和达到25%以上（含25%），或者双方直接或间接同为第三方所持有的股份达到25%以上，则两方之间具有关联关系。此外，该文件还规定，若一方通过中间方对另一方间接持有股份，只要一方对中间方持股比例达到25%以上，则一方对另一方的持股比例按照中间方对另一方的持股比例计算。

8.4.2 转让定价调整的方法

在一个设计完善的所得税制度里，税务当局应该具有在适当的案例里调整关联人所制定的转让定价的权力。这种权力应当包括对关联企业之间的毛收入、扣除额、减免税和其他折让进行重新分配的权力，以使国家可以从在其境内所进行的经济活动中征收到合理的税收份额。根据国际惯例，一个适当的转让定价应符合公平交易原则。也就是说，纳税人在与关联人的交易中制定的转让定价应相当于在可比非关联交易中所制定的价格。具体到对转让定价的调整方法来说，一般有以下方法。

1. 传统方法

1）可比非受控价格法

可比非受控价格法，是指参照非关联人在类似的情形下销售相似的产品所制定的价格来确定公平交易价格。如果这样的可比销售存在的话，它就是优先的选择方法。在公共市场上销售的油类、铁矿、小麦和其他商品都广泛地使用这个方法确定价格。该方法也适用于给那些自身价格并不主要依赖于特殊技能和品牌的制成品进行定价。该方法并不十分适用于对很多中间产品的定价，如一般不卖给非关联方定做的汽车零件。它也不适用于销售价主要依赖于生产者的品牌价值的产品定价。此方法的操作由以下示例说明。

模拟演示 8-1

【背景】A国母公司在B国设立了一子公司，A国公司所得税税率为50%，B国则为20%。现在，A国母公司把其生产的一批产品以120万美元的转让价格销售给B国子公司。A国税务当局检查发现，当时市场上同样数量的这种产品的成交价格是170万美元。

【操作】A国税务当局可以按照可比非受控价格法对其转让价格进行调整，向A国母公司就调整后所增加的50万美元（170-120）所得补征公司所得税25万美元（50×50%）。

【评述】可比非受控价格法适用于跨国关联公司之间有形资产的交易、贷款、劳务提供、财产租赁和无形资产转让等交易，是调整跨国关联公司转让定价的一种最合理、最科学的方法。这种方法要求受控交易（关联交易）与非受控交易（非关联交易）具有严格的可比性，否则非受控交易使用的价格就不具有参照性。

2）再销售价格法

再销售价格法是从最终卖给非关联方的价格中适当减去加价部分，以此作为关联方之间销售商品的公平交易价格。应用该方法的范例是，纳税人将产品卖给作为分销商的关联方，然后分销商将没有任何进一步加工的商品再卖给非关联顾客。适当的加价即毛利，也就是再销售价格中的一个百分比，是分销商与非关联方进行类似交易时要赚取的那部分钱。根据再销售价格法，公平交易价格的计算公式为：

公平交易价格＝再销售价格×（1-合理销售毛利率）

例 8-13

A国的母公司把一批产品以10 000美元的价格销售给B国子公司，B国子公司再以15 000美元的市场价格将这批产品在当地销售。B国的独立公司销售同类产品可实现的销售毛利率为20%。在这种情况下，按照再销售价格法，A国的税务部门要把母公司的销售价格调整为12 000美元。其计算公式为：公平交易价格=15 000×（1-20%）=12 000（美元）。

模拟演示 8-2

【背景】在某一纳税年度，A国M汽车制造公司在B国设立一子公司，A国公司所得税税率为34%，B国则为17%。M公司的汽车制造成本为每辆10万美元，在A国市场上还未销售过，现以12万美元作价销售给B国子公司一辆汽车，B国子公司最后以19万美元的价格在当地售出了这辆汽车。

【演算】

M公司的利润：120 000-100 000＝20 000（美元）。

B国子公司取得的利润：190 000-120 000＝70 000（美元）。

但是，这种集团公司内部作价是不符合公平交易原则的。根据B国税务当局调查证明，当地无关联公司同类汽车的销售毛利率为20%。

按照再销售价格法，A国M公司向B国子公司销售汽车的价格应调整为152 000美元

［190 000×（1-20%）］。

调整后，M 公司取得的利润为 52 000 美元（152 000-100 000），B 国子公司取得的利润为 38 000 美元（190 000-152 000）。

现在，我们不妨对调整前后母、子公司的获利及纳税情况进行比较，见表 8-1 和表 8-2。

表 8-1　调整前

公司	利润/美元	纳税/美元	税负/%
母公司（M 公司）	20 000	6 800	34
子公司	70 000	11 900	17
集团公司	90 000	18 700	—

表 8-2　调整后

公司	利润/美元	纳税/美元	税负/%
母公司（M 公司）	52 000	17 680	34
子公司	38 000	6 460	17
集团公司	90 000	24 140	—

【评述】再销售价格法一般适用于跨国关联公司之间工业产品销售收入的分配，是通过进销差价倒算出来的市场价格。其核心是产品的市场再销售价格与合理销售毛利率的确定。

3）成本加成法

成本加成法用生产成本和关联销售者的其他成本作为制定公平交易价格的起算点，用一个适当的利润百分比乘以销售者的成本，使成本上增加了适当的利润额。这个百分比的确定是参照与非关联方交易或非关联方之间可比交易的销售者赚取的毛利百分比。应用成本加成法的范例是纳税人将其制造的产品卖给关联方，关联方在商品上附加上自己的品牌后卖给非关联顾客。

例 8-14

X 国 A 公司向 Y 国的关联公司 B 提供了一批特制零部件，这批产品的生产成本为 10 000 美元，A 公司向 B 公司的销售价格也为 10 000 美元。由于市场上没有同类产品，X 国税务部门决定按照成本加成法审核和调整这笔关联交易的转让定价。根据 X 国税务部门掌握的资料，当地合理的成本利润率为 20%。因此，这批产品调整后的价格应为 12 000 美元［10 000×（1+20%）］。根据这种情况，X 国税务部门按 12 000 美元的价格计算 A 公司的销售收入，并相应调整其应税所得。

成本加成法是可比非受控价格法的延伸。它一般适用于在既无可比非受控价格，又无再销售价格的情况下，跨国关联公司之间缺乏可比对象的某些工业产品销售收入和特许权使用费收入的分配。例如，当关联公司之间发生有关专利、专有技术和商标等无形资产的转让时，必须收取一项符合公平交易原则的特许权使用费收入。而无形资产种类很多，所涉及的技术、性能、成本费用和目标效益等的差异也比较大，常常缺乏具有可比性的同类产品市场价格或再销售价格作为分配的依据，也很难对其收费依据做出统一的规定。因此，必须更多地采用成本加成法。

4）成本法

成本法，是按实际发生的成本作为分配标准。这是一种性质完全不同的分配标准，它并不包括利润因素在内，反映了跨国关联公司之间的某种业务往来关系，而不是一般的商品交易关系。所以，成本法一般只适用于跨国关联公司之间非主要业务的费用分配，以及一部分非商品业务收入的分配。非商品业务包括贷款、劳务提供和财产租赁等，其相应的业务收入是利息收入、劳务收入和租赁收入。成本法要求转出公司必须把与该交易对象有关的成本费用正确地记载在账册上，并以此为依据进行分配。而该项交易又必须与转入公司的生产经营有关，并使转入公司真正受益。

 模拟演示 8-3

【背景】A 国 M 汽车制造公司在 B 国设立一子公司。2019 年，M 公司为其 B 国子公司垫付的有关成本费用如下：

①为其子公司培训业务技术人员和财会人员费用 50 000 美元。
②广告费 7 000 美元。
③购买器材所支付的运费和保险费 1 000 美元。
④调查原材料采购和产品销售的国际市场行情所支付的调查费用 8 000 美元。
⑤为审计子公司的会计报表聘请高级会计师花费 3 000 美元。
⑥向关联集团公司外的银行借入一笔贷款，年利息为 2 000 美元，再转贷给子公司。
⑦为子公司与其他外国公司的合同纠纷支付 15 000 美元诉讼费。

【操作】按照成本法，M 公司为子公司垫付的这些费用，都可以按账面上实际记载的金额，分配给子公司承担。

【评述】成本法要求转出方准确记载与该项交易对象有关的成本费用，并以此为依据分配。

2. 其他方法

1）利润分割法

利润分割法可以计算从事共同生意的关联方在世界范围内的应税所得。应税所得是在关联方之间根据他们对获取所得的贡献比例进行分配的。在传统方法都不能运用时，就会使用这个方法。该方法最显著的特点是它适用于一系列交易的总利润而不是个体交易。相反，传统方法都是基于个体交易。下面的例子阐述了如何使用利润分割法。

 例 8-15

P 公司和 S 公司是从事生产和销售药物制品的关联公司。P 公司从事广泛的研究活动，并用专利制作方法生产药物制品，所制药品销售给 S 公司。S 公司对药品进行了零售再包装，附上了有附加值的品牌，并通过大量的市场运作将它们卖出。P 公司没有将产品卖给非关联方，也不存在其他非关联方的同样产品的可比销售。S 公司重新包装并出售的产品与非关联方销售的产品也没有可比性。

在这些条件下，一些国家可能会使用利润分割法为药物制品制定适当的转让价格。假设，P 公司的成本是 300 美元，S 公司的成本是 100 美元。再假设，S 公司销售给非关联顾客的总收入是 600 美元。在这种情况下，集团公司的净利润是 200 美元［600－（300+100）］。

如果 P 公司对于企业的贡献被证明大约占总净利润的 75%，那么对利润应按 75：25 的比例进行分割。这样，使用利润分割法，P 公司将获得利润 150 美元，S 公司获利 50 美元。

利润分割法可以有很多的变化。一个变化就是将它与一个或多个传统方法相结合。传统方法可以对日常活动的平均利润进行分配，利润分割法可以将企业生产经营的利润从开发高附加值的无形资产中分割出来。

例 8-16

在上述例子中，假设 P 公司从事日常生产活动，S 公司从事日常销售活动。P 公司的生产总成本是 300 美元，非关联公司从事可比制造活动时可获得成本 20% 的回报。鉴于此，根据成本加成法，P 公司可获得分配给它的利润 60 美元（300×20%）。S 公司拥有总销售收入 600 美元，从事同样活动的非关联公司的总毛利润率是 10%。根据再销售价格法，S 公司应该获得分配给它的利润 60 美元（600×10%）。剩下的利润 80 美元［200-（60+60）］应该使用利润分割法进行分配。假设，可以同样运用 75：25 进行分割，那么在利润分割法下，P 公司的利润是 60 美元（80×75%），P 公司的总体利润是 120 美元（60+60）。S 公司在利润分割法下的利润是 20 美元（80×25%），总体利润是 80 美元（60+20）。

为了公平、有效地运用利润分割法，必须使用某些公平有效的方法以确定适当的利润分割。由 OECD 推荐的一个方法是观察那些从事可比活动的非受控人之间的利润是如何分割的。遗憾的是获得这样的信息特别困难，因为只有当涉及有附加值的无形资产时，才最有可能应用利润分割法。基于关联方在开发无形资产方面的有关贡献而进行的利润分割应该是适当的。

2）交易净利润法

交易净利润法有时称之为可比利润法，是在某种情况下确定销售有形和无形资产的转让价格时可以采用的方法。在交易净利润法下，纳税人必须为自己或关联方（被检验方）对一组交易的利润建立公平交易的范围（交易净利润法范围）。如果被检验方所报告的那些交易的利润虽有下降但仍是在该范围内，它的转让价格将被税务当局所接受。如果它的利润低到超出了该范围，税务当局将可以对转让定价进行调整，以使利润保持在该范围内，一般是保留在范围的中心点。

一般来说，在交易净利润法下，确定被检验方的利润先要确定非关联人的某些经济指数的利润率，然后用该利润率计算出被检验方的利润。例如，假设非关联人有应税所得 80 美元和投资资本 800 美元，投资资本是在应用交易净利润法时需要使用的经济指数。非关联人的应税所得与投资资本的比率是 80：800。如果被检验方有投资资本 500 美元，在交易净利润法的简易形式下，它的公平交易利润将是 50 美元（500×10%）。

为了完善对交易净利润法的应用，必须要求纳税人或政府对不止一个非关联人的交易净利润法进行计算。这样的计算越多，结果可能越可靠。被检验方的公平交易利润应该是由几个计算所确定的利润范围内的数额，在该范围内进一步确定被检验方的公平交易利润时可以采用统计方法。应用交易净利润法时，纳税人必须确定一个非关联人在从事可比交易中有希望能获得的利润范围，纳税人可以各种方法建立这个范围。一个方法是确定两个或更多的从事与纳税人大体相似的活动的非关联方所投入资本的回报率，然后用纳税人的资本数额乘以每一个非关联人的资本回报率。第二个方法是由纳税人为两个或更多的可比受控人的总销售收入计算出营业利润率,并将该营业利润率用于它自己的销售。第三种方法是以两个或更多的关联人的经营支出确定毛利润率,并将该毛利润率用于它自己的经营支出。也可以运用其他经济指数来确定利润范围。

 例 8-17

假设被检验方 T 公司所从事的经营活动在复杂性和特性上与 A 公司和 B 公司差不多,A 公司和 B 公司与 T 公司是非关联公司,A、B 两公司之间也没有关联关系。A 公司和 B 公司毛收入的营业利润率分别是 0.2 和 0.3。T 公司的毛收入是 200 000 美元。在交易净利润法下,T 公司的公平交易利润范围应该为 40 000 美元(200 000×0.2)~60 000 美元(200 000×0.3)。假设应用交易净利润法的各种条件具备,T 公司的公平交易利润就应该被看作 40 000~60 000 美元。

一旦交易净利润法范围确定,就需要在该范围内选定一个数额,作为被检验方的公平交易利润。如果纳税人使用的那些价格所确定利润在交易净利润法范围内的话,税务当局一般会接受纳税人账册中所显示的转让价格。假如纳税人报告的利润在范围之外,税务当局将视范围的中间点为公平交易利润。如果在建立交易净利润法范围时使用了两个以上的非关联人的数据,那么范围的中间点应为计算出的利润额的加权平均数。

8.4.3 转让定价调整中的国际重复征税问题

当一个公司在两个或更多的国家与关联公司进行跨境交易,而这些国家都具有对关联公司转让定价进行调整的权力时,该企业有可能被双重征税。

 例 8-18

假设在 D 国的 D 公司以成本价 60 美元将自产的产品卖给关联 E 公司,E 公司在 E 国将该商品以零售价 150 美元出售。D 公司须在 D 国为其生产利润纳税,E 公司须在 E 国为其销售利润纳税。这个关联组织(D 公司和 E 公司)的净利润为 90 美元(150-60)。假设 D 国认为 D 公司向 E 公司销售的适当转让价格应该是 130 美元,而 E 国认为那笔销售的适当价格应该是 65 美元。这样一来就产生了双重征税,造成两家公司的所得总和只有 90 美元,却要为 155 美元的所得纳税,具体见表 8-3。

表 8-3 政府调整转让定价后产生的重复征税

项目	D 国	E 国
(1) D 公司向 E 公司销售产品的价格	130 美元	65 美元
(2) D 公司生产成本	60 美元	60 美元
(3) D 公司所得	70 美元	5 美元
(4) 产品在 E 国的零售价格	150 美元	150 美元
(5) E 公司所得 [(4)-(1)]	20 美元	85 美元
(6) D、E 公司所得总和 [(3)+(5)]	90 美元	90 美元
(7) 总应税所得 [D 国(3)+E 国(5)] =70+85=155(美元)		

为了防止这种对所得的经济性重复征税，一国调整了本国公司的转让定价从而增加了其应税利润以后，该公司的境外关联公司所在国就应相应调减这个关联公司的应税利润，并在税额上进行相应的变动。如果一国对转出利润课征了预提所得税，为了避免出现国际重复课税，对方关联公司所在国也应允许本国公司就这种预提所得税办理税收抵免。但这都需要有关国家在转让定价调整问题上意见一致，并相互协调。

根据《经合发范本》第 9 条第 2 款和第 25 条，大多数签署协定的国家承诺，如果协定签约国对方已根据公平交易标准对纳税人的价格进行了调整，就要考虑对用于计算纳税人的应税所得的转让价格进行相应调整。例如，假设 A 公司生产的产品成本为 20 美元，以 40 美元出售给外国关联 B 公司，B 公司以 60 美元再销售给非关联人。A 公司须在 A 国纳税，B 公司须在 B 国纳税。A 国判定卖给 B 公司的合适价格应该是 50 美元，A 公司应税所得就增加了 10 美元。如果 B 国在判定适当转让价格上与 A 国相同，就应允许 B 公司将成本增加 10 美元，并相应将 B 公司应税所得减少 10 美元。修正某个纳税人的转让价格时要考虑到对其关联纳税人转让价格的变更，这被称为"关联调整"。

8.4.4 预约定价协议

近年来，一些国家探索在转让定价纠纷实际引发之前，便与纳税人就确定转让价格的方法达成协议。预先认可制度的主要目的是减少转让定价纠纷所引起的诉讼给纳税人和税务当局双方带来的高额开支。纳税人希望预先得到关于他们进行的一项或多项交易定价方法的承认，要向税务当局签署一个"预约定价协议"（APA），纳税人必须提供其希望在执行 APA 的交易中使用的定价方法的详细资料。同时，纳税人还必须解释为什么这个方法能够制定出合理的价格。在某些情况下，两个或两个以上的政府对纳税人使用的定价方法可以利用税收协定中的争端解决机制达成一致意见。OECD 于 1999 年发布了为多国开发联合预约定价协议的指南。

1. 预约定价协议的概念

预约定价协议，是指纳税人事先向税务机关提出未来年度可能发生的关联交易的定价原则和计算方法，经过税务机关审核同意后，双方就定价原则和计算方法达成的协议。其目的主要是解决未来年度的转让定价问题。预约定价协议可以分为三种类型，即单边协议（纳税人与某个税务当局之间的协议）、双边协议（两个国家的税务当局与纳税人之间的协议）和多边协议（涉及多个国家的税务当局的协议）。预约定价协议是目前国际税务管理中的一个重大课题，是随着各国税务当局不断强化转让定价税务管理、税企矛盾增多而产生的。

2. 预约定价协议的优点和不足

预约定价协议可以给各方带来利益，如纳税人可以确切地知道今后税务部门对自己经营活动中的转让定价行为会作何反应；预约定价协议可以提供一种非常好的环境，纳税人、税务部门可以相互合作，以确定纳税人的转让定价活动适用于哪种转让定价方法；可以大大减轻纳税人保留原始凭证、文件资料的负担，而且能使纳税人避免一些冗长的诉讼程序。

尽管预约定价协议可以给纳税人带来一定的利益，但其申请的复杂程度之高，信息披露的要求之严，给纳税人带来的成本之大，确实使许多纳税人望而生畏。据美国 1996 年的一项调查，在受访的美国跨国公司中，只有 10% 签订了或准备签订预约定价协议。众多公司不愿签订预约定价协议的原因主要是担心其申请材料要求填报的内容过于详细从而很容易泄露公司的机密。另外，预约定价协议申请的成本也过高，而且费时费力。

尽管预约定价协议存在一些不足之处，但随着经验的不断积累以及使用方法上的更加灵活，相信预约定价协议今后会有更加广阔的前景。

综上所述，国际社会针对跨国纳税人的避税活动，已经行动起来，采取了一系列的防范措施。应当指出的是，上述各种国际反避税措施虽然可以从不同角度起到防范作用，但是，并不能完全消除国际避税，有时甚至收效不大。其原因主要在于：第一，国际避税对各国造成的财政利益损失不同，有些国家或地区还可能因此而获得好处，因此各国对反避税的态度不尽一致；第二，反避税的国际合作目前主要采取双边形式，而世界上还无任何一国同所有国家均签订双边税收协定，这就使跨国纳税人绕过协定签订国避税成为可能，即使是多边税收协定，也仅限于某一国际性或区域性组织内部，仍然存在避税漏洞；第三，有些反避税条款在原则确定与运用上存在差距，在实践中难以贯彻。因此，如何防范国际避税，改善征纳关系，处理国家之间的税收分配关系，推动国际经济向前发展，仍然是世界各国迫切需要研究和解决的重要问题。

复习思考题

1. 如何通过制定和完善税收立法来防止国际避税？
2. 如何防止滥用税收协定？
3. 为什么要规定资本弱化法规？各国资本弱化法规的主要内容是什么？
4. 发达国家受控外国公司法的主要内容是什么？
5. 转让定价税制包括哪些内容？
6. 关联公司的判定标准有哪些？
7. 转让定价的调整方法有哪些？
8. 什么是预约定价协议？它存在的主要目的是什么？
9. 预约定价协议可以给征纳双方带来什么利益？

第 9 章

国际税收协定

> **时政观点**
>
> 作为负责任的大国,我国在维护国家主权的基础上积极遵守国际税收协定,为世界经济的发展做出了重大贡献。
>
> **学习目标**
>
> 1. 了解国际税收协定的法律特征和目的。
> 2. 掌握《经合发范本》和《联合国范本》的区别。
> 3. 了解典型国际税收协定的主要内容。
>
> **课程导入**
>
> 自改革开放以来,我国非常重视对外缔结国际税收协定。从 1981 年 1 月至 2022 年 6 月,我国已正式签署了 109 个避免双重征税的协定,其中 105 个已经生效。如何看待《经合发范本》和《联合国范本》对我国签订国际税收协定的影响?

在大多数国家,国际税收协定都是其国际税收规则的重要内容。目前,世界上共有 2 000 多个关于所得税的双边税收协定在有效执行,而且这个数字还在不断增加。这些协定大多数以《经合发范本》为基础。《联合国范本》与《经合发范本》相似,但有一些条款不同,下面将对两者进行具体讨论。

9.1 概况

国际税收协定一般是指国与国之间签订的避免对所得及资本双重征税和防止偷逃税的协定。

9.1.1 国际税收协定的法律特征

协定是主权国家间达成的协议。《维也纳协定法律公约》的第 2 条规定:协定是国家间达成的并受国际法约束的国际协议(不管采用的是一个或多个名称)。国际税收协定给缔约国赋予权力或施加义务,在大多数国家,除非在国内立法中明确列入协定的内容;否则,国际税收协定对缔约国的公民或居民不赋予权力。

在许多国家，国际税收协定与国内立法之间的关系颇为复杂。一个基本的原则就是，在协定与国内法的规定发生冲突的情况下，协定应该优先。在有些国家，比如法国，这条原则具有宪法性的地位。但是在许多国家，根据国内法的规定，政府明显有权推翻税收协定的规定。例如，在许多议会制民主国家，一条基本的法制原则是，立法机关有最高权威。许多国家的法院要求立法机关要首先明确表示推翻一个协定的意愿，然后再使与该协定冲突的国内法生效。法院还可以尽力找到一个折中的方法，来解决协定与国内法之间显而易见的矛盾。在国内税法与国际税收协定的关系问题上，我国与大多数国家持有相同观点。《中华人民共和国企业所得税法》第五十八条规定："中华人民共和国政府同外国政府订立的有关税收协定与本法有不同规定的，依照协定的规定办理。"显然，我国是主张国际税收协定应优先于国内税法的国家。

一般来说，国际税收协定适用于缔约国征收的任何所得税，包括省（州）政府、地方政府和其他区域性政府征收的所得税。然而，在一些联邦制国家，宪法规定或约定俗成的传统不允许中央政府在其签署的税收协定中限制地方政府的征税权。因此，在这些国家，税收协定只适用于中央税，加拿大和美国即为其中两例。在这种情况下，区域性政府可以不管中央政府的规定而自行征税。比如，美国的一些州政府（已知的最好范例是加利福尼亚州）对跨国公司征税按照统一的计税依据（合并申报和按公式进行比例分配），全然不顾美国政府在税收协定中关于使用公平交易原则的承诺。

绝大多数国际税收协定并不产生新的税种。正相反，它们往往限制一国对税收的征收，国际税收协定在本质上主要是减轻纳税义务。但是也有例外，最显著的例子就是法国和奉行法国做法的几个非洲国家之间的税收协定。根据这些协定，即使缔约国国内法没有该税种，也可以由协定规定并据以征收。

需要指出的是，无论是《经合发范本》还是《联合国范本》，对各国都不具有法律约束力。这些范本的作用只是为未来签署税收协定的双方指明一个方向，其目的是为各国谈签税收协定创造一个便利的条件，以免人们对每项条款所述及的所有问题都从头开始进行详细的分析和长时间的讨论。但在具体谈签双边税收协定时，应当灵活机动，以便在协定中加进一些适合本国情况的特殊规定，不能完全照搬范本的条款。

9.1.2　国际税收协定的目的

大致来说，国际税收协定的目的是通过消除税收障碍来促进跨国贸易和投资。这一总体目标是通过几个具体的、操作性的目标来实现的。

国际税收协定最重要的操作性目标就是消除双重征税，典型双边税收协定的绝大部分实质性内容都以此为目的。比如，国际税收协定中有加比规则，使本来具有双方居民身份的纳税人只成为一方的居民。另外，国际税收协定还限制或取消来源国对某些种类所得的征税权，或要求居住国对纳税人在来源国缴纳的税收给予抵免或对其境外所得完全免税。二战后的早期，国际税收协定的核心目标几乎完全放在消除双重征税的问题上。那时，处于萌芽阶段的跨国公司面临着双重征税的巨大风险，没有什么国家愿意单方面采取措施消除双重征税，协定的谈签也才刚刚起步。大多数双重征税问题的解决方法主要是在20世纪50年代和60年代初制定的。然而在今天，这些方法已经被谈签税收协定的国家习以为常地接受了。一个重要例外就是在对关联人之间的交易制定转让定价时，各缔约国对公平交易原则的适用还不尽相同。

消除双重征税这一历史性着重点不应掩盖大多数国际税收协定的另一个同样重要的操

作性目标——防止偷漏税,后者是对前者的制衡。正如双重征税对国际贸易构成不适当壁垒一样,容忍偷漏税会形成对国际贸易的不适当补贴。但是,尽管大多数国际税收协定都将防止偷漏税明确列为目的之一,却很少有条款规定实现该目的的具体措施,甚至连偷漏税这一概念在典型的国际税收协定中也没有清晰的定义。有些国家(如瑞士),对其进行很窄范围的定义,仅涵盖构成犯罪的偷税,而大多数缔约国都以更宽的范围将其定义为包括偷税犯罪在内的各种形式的逃避税行为。

除了以上两个主要目的之外,国际税收协定还有一些辅助性目的。一个是消除对外国国民和非居民的税收歧视,另一个是在缔约国之间进行情报交换。最后,大多数缔约国还在协定中为解决税收争议提供了方法。

9.1.3　国际税收协定范本

影响较大的国际税收协定范本有两个——《经合发范本》和《联合国范本》。此外,许多国家还有各自的税收协定范本,这些范本一般不予公开发布,而主要用来在谈判时提供给对方国家。《联合国范本》和各国的税收协定范本都在很大程度上借鉴了《经合发范本》。

《经合发范本》历史悠久,始自 19 世纪的一些早期外交条约,这些外交条约的有限目的是为了保证在另一国工作的一国外交官不会受到歧视。20 世纪初,所得税刚刚成为举足轻重的税种,就立刻被包括在这些外交条约的范本之内。第一次世界大战后,国际联盟就开始了制定专门处理所得税问题的协定范本的工作。这项工作以 1943 年和 1946 年的两个协定范本而告终。当时,这两个协定并未得到各国的一致认可。于是,起草一个能为大家广泛接受的协定范本的工作就被 OECD 承担下来。截至 2022 年,OECD 有 30 多个成员国,包括许多主要的发达国家。《经合发范本》草案在 1963 年首次公布,并在 1977 年和 1992 年进行了两次修订。之后,决定将其改装为活页形式,以方便随时增删修改。后来的几次修订分别是在 1994 年、1995 年、1997 年、2000 年和 2002 年。主要由各成员国资深税务专家组成的财政事务委员会负责协定范本的修订和其他有关国际税收合作的事项。该委员会通过常设秘书处和几个工作小组展开工作。负责处理税务问题的常设秘书处官员现在已成为税收政策和管理中心的一部分,该中心是 2001 年建立的。工作小组由各成员国的代表组成,第一工作小组负责《经合发范本》,随时对与协定有关的事项加以密切关注。与《经合发范本》共同发布的是一个详细的注释《经合发范本注释》,该注释以协定条款为顺序编排。在税收协定的解释和适应方面,《经合发范本注释》的作用越来越大,对于一些并非 OECD 成员国家之间的协定,也是如此。为了把一些非成员国的意见考虑在内,OECD 于 1999 年将该注释向包括阿根廷、巴西、中国、以色列、俄罗斯和南非在内的主要非成员国开放纳言。

对于资本输出国和资本输入国来说,《经合发范本》更有利于前者。根据该范本,消除或减轻双重征税的方式经常是要求来源国对缔约国另一方居民的所得免征部分或全部税收。几乎从名称本身就能确定,发展中国家是资本净输入国。另外,大多数发展中国家还适用免税法来为其国内的公司消除双重征税。这样的结果就是,如果发展中国家与发达国家签署税收协定并按照《经合发范本》以牺牲来源地管辖权来换取居民管辖权,将是不利的。认识到《经合发范本》的这些缺点之后,发展中国家就在联合国的领导下制定了自己的税收协定范本。

《联合国范本》在 1980 年首次发行,并于 2001 年做出了修改,尽管没有什么实质性的变动。《联合国范本》是由联合国发达国家与发展中国家之间税收协定专家组起草的，这个专家组于 1967 年由联合国经社理事会建立。专家组成员都是各自政府指派的税务专家和实际管理工作者，但他们以独立的身份参加小组工作；有 15 名成员来自发展中和经济转型期国家，10 名成员来自发达国家。《联合国范本》按照《经合发范本》的体例编排，许多条款的规定与《经合发范本》完全相同或基本相同。因此一般来说，可以不把《联合国范本》认为是一个完全独立的范本，而是对《经合发范本》有限的但是很重要的修改。

两个范本的主要区别就是《联合国范本》较少限制所得来源国的税收管辖权。比如，《联合国范本》没有对股息、利息和特许权使用费的预提税税率进行限制性规定，而是将其交由谈判中的两个缔约国去商定，并且《联合国范本》的规定使得纳税人更容易在所得来源国构成常设机构，这样也使来源国对经营所得具有更大的征收权。

9.2　典型国际税收协定的内容

本部分将讨论建立在 OECD 和《联合国范本》基础上的典型的双边税收协定的一些主要规定。

9.2.1　范围和法律效力

签署双边税收协定的两个国家称为"缔约国"。根据典型税收协定的第 1 条（人的范围），协定的规定适用于为"缔约国一方或双方居民"的人。该协定的第 4 条（居民）具体说明，为了协定的目的，"居民"一语的定义取自各缔约国国内法的规定。在第 3 条（一般定义）中，"人"被定义为包括"个人、公司和任何其他团体"。《经合发范本注释》中写道，慈善基金就属于第 3 条"人"的含义范围之内。的确，为了税收协定的目的，很可能将经缔约国国内法认可的任何法人实体作为"人"对待。对于典型的税收协定来说，一个合伙企业虽然可能成为一个"人"，但如果在缔约国内的纳税义务由各合伙人而非企业承担，该合伙企业就不可能是缔约国一方的居民。

典型的税收协定明确列举了适用于协定的由各缔约国（有时也包括地方）征收的税种，每个国家的个人所得税和企业所得税都无一例外地列入。大多数协定还规定，协定也将适用于日后增加或者代替所列税种的相同或实质相似的税收。有的协定列举了不适用于协定的所得税或财产税种。比如，许多税收协定就把政府因筹集养老金而对工资征收的工资税排除在外。

虽然新签署税收协定的国家都认为双方的关系会无限期的保持不变，但几乎总是应对方的要求而在协定中设定终止条款。根据同为终止条款的《经合发范本》第 30 条和《联合国范本》第 29 条，缔约国一方可以在任何日历年度年底 6 个月以前，书面通知对方单方面终止协定。一个最新的发展趋势是，缔约各方一般都同意，协定在互换照会生效执行后，应至少经过 5 年才能终止。当然，缔约双方也可以通过协议在任何时间终止协定。

9.2.2　经营所得

关于对经营所得征税的规定在《经合发范本》和《联合国范本》的第 3 条、第 5 条和第 7 条。第 7 条（营业利润）指出："缔约国一方企业"的利润应仅在该国征税，但该企业通过设在缔约国另一方的常设机构在该另一方进行营业的除外。如果缔约国一方企业在缔约国另一方设有常设机构，来源国对其征税应仅限于归属于该常设机构的利润。《经合发范本》和《联合国范本》的第 7 条第 2 款规定，常设机构的利润应按公平交易原则确定。在确定常设机构的利润时，《联合国范本》第 7 条第 1 款采纳了有限引力原则。根据该原则，如果企业在缔约国一方设有常设机构，不仅通过常设机构取得的所得应该征税，而且在两种情况下，即企业在该方销售的商品与通过常设机构销售的商品相似，或在该方从事的经营活动与通过常设机构从事的经营活动相似的，企业从该销售或经营活动中取得的所得也应在该方纳税。对于尽力减少在来源国的税负的企业来说，《联合国范本》的方法增加了某种不确定性。从政府的角度来看，该规定的好处就是简化了税收征管并减少了避税的可能性。

根据《经合发范本》和《联合国范本》第 5 条，常设机构一般是指"企业进行全部或部分营业的固定营业场所"。该定义几乎在所有的协定中都是相同的。《经合发范本》和《联合国范本》还列举了以下一些构成常设机构的场所：管理场所、分支机构、办事处、工厂、作业场所、矿场、油井或气井、采石场或者任何其他开采自然资源的场所。企业如果在缔约国一方构成"固定的营业场所"，就必须在某个特定的地理位置进行营业，并且在该地的营业行为必须超过一定的时间（一般定为 6 个月）。在使用采油机等设备的场所，即使没有企业的人员操作设备，也会构成常设机构。营业场所如果成为"固定"的，有特定的地理位置就足够了。比如，企业如果经常性地在集市中经营一个移动性摊位，那么该集市也会成为企业的常设机构。至于企业是租赁还是拥有其场所，对判定是否构成常设机构并不重要。

根据《联合国范本》第 5 条（联合国范本注释），如果企业在缔约国一方的海域使用渔船进行商业性捕鱼，该渔船也构成常设机构。但是，这个观点还有争议。对于在缔约国一方从事电子商务的企业，如何判定其是否构成常设机构有很多难点。《经合发范本》对常设机构的定义包括企业的非独立代理人，这些代理人有权并经常代表企业签订合同。大多数税收协定都将这种非独立代理人认定为常设机构。《联合国范本》对这种代理人的规定范围更广，延伸到包括仅仅为企业储存并代表其交付商品的代理人。在这一点上，有些税收协定采纳《联合国范本》的规定。一些评论家认为，常设机构的定义应进一步扩大到包括代表企业进行实质性经营的大多数非独立代理人，而不管其是否有权代表企业签订合同。他们指出，有权签订合同在商务上的重要性微乎其微，因为现代通信方式使代理人能在瞬间与其国外委托者取得联系。

除此之外，《联合国范本》还规定，在缔约国一方从事保险销售的企业如果在该国收取保费或对发生在该国的风险进行保险，应认为企业在该国构成常设机构。但是，在保险活动是由独立代理人进行的情况下，该规定不适用。

大多数协定都规定，建筑工地、钻井作业或其他临时性工程的场所在持续达到一定期间的情况下，将构成常设机构。《经合发范本》规定的期限为 1 年，《联合国范本》规定的期限为 6 个月，并把适用范围扩展到包括装配工地和与建筑、装配工地相关的监督管理活动在内。发展中国家在谈签协定时，一般都采纳 6 个月的期间甚至更短。比如，印度和美国的协定就规定为 4 个月。而一些发达国家之间的税收协定将此期间延长为 1 年以上。比如，日本和美国的协定规定为 24 个月。

根据《联合国范本》，如果企业在缔约国一方通过雇员或其他人提供个人劳务并且在任意 12 个月中达到 6 个月，企业在该一方构成常设机构。这条规定主要是为了保证，如果管理和咨询活动在来源国持续达到一定时间，则该项活动的所得可以在来源国征税。

《经合发范本》没有类似的规定。

按照《经合发范本》和《联合国范本》的一般规定，一个设施，如果主要被企业用来购买供出口的商品、储存或陈列商品，或者为另一企业加工的目的而储存商品，则该设施不构成企业的常设机构。《经合发范本》还规定，用来交付商品的设施不构成常设机构。《联合国范本》没有这项例外，是为了允许来源国对经营仓库取得的所得征税。根据两个范本，其他一些用来进行"准备性或辅助性"活动的设施也不构成常设机构。

子公司不会仅仅因为其受控于母公司而成为母公司的常设机构。同样，母公司也不会因此成为子公司的常设机构。这些重要的规定，会促使大多数跨国公司在境外业务可能具有实质内容的情况下，通过设立子公司来开展活动，而不是通过分支机构或常设机构。如果跨国公司认为与某个国家的联系无足轻重，一般会通过独立经销商来开展业务，而避免在该国构成常设机构。

根据《经合发范本》和《联合国范本》的第8条（海运、内陆水运和空运），对海运或空运活动所得的征税有更多的限制性规定。《经合发范本》和《联合国范本》的第8（A）条都把对该项所得的征税权排他性的赋予海运或空运的实际经营地国家，即使海运或空运企业在来源国构成常设机构也是如此。许多协定把这种独家征税权给予企业的居民国，相当多的协定允许来源国对海运或空运纯粹来自于国内的经营所得征税。《联合国范本》第8（B）条规定，如果海运或空运活动是"经常"的，就允许来源国对其所得征税。

根据《经合发范本》，从动产取得的租金视为经营所得。所以，只有在纳税人在一国构成常设机构并且该租金归属于该常设机构的情况下，该国才能对其征税。《联合国范本》第12条规定，允许来源国对特许权使用费征税，并将设备租赁取得的租金包括在特许权使用费的定义之内。《联合国范本》还把来自胶片的所得视为特许权使用费。

根据《经合发范本》和《联合国范本》第6条，来自不动产的租金所得可以在来源国征税。比如，从公寓租赁中取得的租金可以在公寓所在国征税。

9.2.3　受雇和个人劳务所得

根据《联合国范本》第14条（独立个人劳务），缔约国一方的居民在缔约国另一方从事"专业性劳务或其他独立性质的活动"，不在该另一方征税。除非其在该另一方拥有经常性的"固定基地"。《经合发范本》也曾包括该条款，直到2000年修订时删除为止。《经合发范本》这一变化导致的结果是，在缔约国一方提供个人劳务的个人和公司，只有在该方构成常设机构且其所得归属于该常设机构的情况下，才能在该方就其所得征税。"专业性劳务"一语既包括医生、律师、工程师、建筑师、牙医师和会计师的劳务，也包括独立的科学、文学、艺术、教育和教学活动。按照《联合国范本》，一般来说，对于专业人员和其他人提供的独立个人劳务的所得，只要他们在一个纳税年度中在来源国停留时间超过183天，或他们的所得在来源国是可扣除的，来源国就可以对该所得征税，而不管是否存在固定基地。

根据《经合发范本》第15条（非独立个人劳务），在缔约国一方受雇取得的所得可以在该国征税，而不管该雇员是否拥有固定基地。然而，如果雇员的所得由境外雇主支付，也不被来源国雇主作为费用在税前扣除，并且该雇员在任何12个月中在来源国停留时间不超过183天，则该所得应在来源国免税。

对专业人员和雇员提供劳务取得的所得在来源国给予免税的规定，不适用于表演家和运动员（及其随员）。上述免税规定也不适用于在居民公司中担任董事的非居民因其服务而取得的报酬。还有一些例外就是，代表缔约国一方从事受雇服务的个人的所得仅在该国征税。当然，作为政府外交代表而在外国工作的政府雇员，可以根据特别协议或国际法的规定享受免税待遇，税收协定不会影响其效力。

根据《经合发范本》第18条（退休金），个人因以前的受雇活动而取得的退休金一般仅在居民国征税。《联合国范本》为来源国对退休金征税提供了一些机会。对为政府服务而取得的退休金一般可在支付退休金的缔约国征税，除非取得退休金的个人既是缔约国另一方的居民又是其国民。

根据《经合发范本》和《联合国范本》第20条（学生），学生和企业学徒或接受培训的人员，由于接受教育或培训的目的停留在缔约国一方，其为维持生活、教育或培训收到的来源于该国以外的款项，该国一般不应征税。有些协定还包括了对访问学者和教师免税的互惠规定。

9.2.4 不动产所得和收益

每个国家都希望对来自不动产销售、境内自然资源开发、国内农业等的所得保留征税权。作为这一观点的反映，《经合发范本》和《联合国范本》第6条（不动产所得）把对"不动产"所得的征税权保留给了来源国。"不动产"一词的定义遵循不动产所在地国家的规定，尽管根据通常的理解，该词特别包括来自农业、林业、矿产和其他自然资源的所得。第13条（财产收益）明确规定，处置不动产取得的收益也可在来源国征税。

由于来源国既有权对不动产所得征税，也可对处置不动产的收益征税，因此对税收协定来说，将处置不动产取得的收益认定为所得还是财产收益也就无关紧要了。对该收益性质的认定留待国内法解决。

有些国家在其税收协定中特别规定，转让公司股权取得的收益，如果该股权主要是由不动产组成，则对该所得的征税权应保留给来源国。《联合国范本》第13条第4款也包括了这样的规定。这种规定的目的，是为了防止纳税人不直接处置不动产，而是通过将其不动产先转让给受控公司，然后再转让所持的该公司股权的方式来逃避在来源国的税收（如果协定规定该种所得在来源国免税）。在《联合国范本》和一些协定中，关于对合伙企业和信托中股权的处置所得，都适用这条规则。为了防止纳税人很轻易地规避这条规则，缔约国应该在国内法和协定中规定，如果公司、合伙企业或信托的股权的价值主要来自不动产，那么转让该股权的收益应予征税。

9.2.5 以限制税率对某些投资所得征收预提税

大多数税收协定的一个主要目的，就是在来源国按限制税率对支付给缔约国另一方居民的股息、利息和特许权使用费征收预提税。设定限制税率的目的是为了在来源国和居民国之间分享税收收入。

根据各自对国家利益的理解，强烈建议缔约国按表9-1中的最高额提税税率来确定在来源国征税的限制税率。

表9-1 《经合发范本》认可的最高预提税税率

支付给关联公司的股息	支付给其他人的股息	利息	特许权使用费
5%	15%	10%	0%

资料来源：《经合发范本》（2000年版）第10条（股息）、第11条（利息）和第12条（特许权使用费）。

《经合发范本》中建议的最高额提税税率，特别是特许权使用费的零税率，对于大多数发展中国家来说是不能接受的。为了反映发展中国家的利益，《联合国范本》并没有对预提税的限制税率给出特定的建议，而是希望由缔约国双方协商确定。发展中国家签署的大多数税收协定中，对预提税的限制税率，都超过了《经合发范本》建议的最高额提税税率。比如，对于发展中国家来说，同意将特许权使用费的最高预提税税率限定为15%，是不常见的。

许多税收协定中对最高预提税税率的限定，要比《经合发范本》中建议的模式复杂得多。比如，很常见的情况是，一个税收协定中规定，对工业产权的特许权使用费、为文学著作版权而支付的特许权使用费和为电影而支付的特许权使用费分别适用不同的税率。最新的许多税收协定还包括一些特殊规定，来处理为使用计算机软件而支付报酬的征税问题。《经合发范本注释》中有关于此类报酬如何征税的具体建议，但许多国家都表示至少在某些方面不愿遵照执行。

9.2.6 其他所得

对于上述各类所得之外的其他所得，许多税收协定都把征税权给予取得所得的纳税人为其居民的居民国。《经合发范本》和《联合国范本》的第13条（财产收益）都规定，除归属于常设机构的利润或转让不动产取得的收益外，对财产收益的征税权都保留给居民国。《经合发范本》第21条（其他所得）关于对其他所得的规定中提出，协定中其他条款未做规定的各项所得，都由居民国独占征税权。《联合国范本》第21条（其他所得）把对未规定的各项所得的征税权，保留给来源国。最近几年来，随着来自新金融产品的所得种类的增加，第21条的重要性越来越大。按照《经合发范本》签订的税收协定，对于类似于传统所得却又经协议界定为税收协定中未规定的所得的，一般都限制来源国对其征税。

对于缔约国一方居民支付给缔约国另一方居民的赡养费和子女抚养费，一些协定中有如何征税的规定。通常的规则是，接受方的居民国对赡养费征税，而支付方的居民国对子女抚养费征税。

9.2.7 公平待遇与合作

典型的税收协定中都有一些促进缔约国之间互相给予公平待遇和进行合作的规定。为了减少缔约国一方居民和国民在缔约国另一方受到不公平待遇的风险，大多数协定都规定，各缔约方同意，不歧视缔约另一方的居民和国民。虽然无差别待遇这一目的高尚而有价值，但并非能轻易获得。

为了解决双方税法或协定本身适用中出现的问题，缔约国双方还试图建立一种争议解决机制以促进公平待遇与税收合作。几乎所有的税收协定都规定，缔约国双方应在税收征管中互相合作。《经合发范本》和《联合国范本》第26条（情报交换）规定，缔约国双方应交换"为实施本协定的规定所需要的情报，或缔约国双方关于本协定所涉及的税种的国内法律的规定所需要的情报"。目前，《经合发范本》和《联合国范本》都没有强制规定缔约双方为税款征收互相提供协助，尽管在不久的将来，双方完全有可能这样做。

第 9 章 国际税收协定

复习思考题

1. 国际税收协定与国内税法的关系是什么?
2. 《经合发范本》和《联合国范本》的主要区别有哪些?
3. 典型国际税收协定的主要内容有哪些?

参考文献

[1] GLAUTIER M E N. A Reference Guide to International Taxation [M]. Toronto：Lexington Books，1987.

[2] EI-AGRAA A M. International Economic Integration [M]. Hampshire：The Macmillan Press，1988.

[3] GINSBERG A S. Tax Havens [M]. New York：New York Institute of Finance，1990.

[4] TANG Y W. Transfer Pricing in the 1990s [M]. Santa Barbara：Praeger，1992.

[5] Dept. of Economic, Social Affairs Staff. United Nations Model Double Taxation Convention between Developed and Developing Countries [M]. New York：United Nations Publications，2001.

[6] ARNOLD B J. International Tax Primer [M]. Amsterdam：Kluwer Law International BV，2019.

[7] 刘佐，刘铁英. 中国涉外税收指南[M]. 北京：法律出版社，2002.

[8] LARKINS E R. International Applications of US Income Tax Law：Inbound and Outbound Transactions [M]. Hoboken：John Wiley & Sons，Inc，2004.

[9] CRACEA A. International Bureau of Fiscal Documentation, Organisation for Economic Co-operation and Development. OECD Model Tax Convention on Income and on Capital [M]. Amsterdam：IBFD，2013.

[10] 王铁军. 国际避税与反避税[M]. 北京：中国财政经济出版社，1987.

[11] 葛惟熹. 国际税收学[M]. 北京：中国财政经济出版社，1994.

[12] 杨志清. 国际税收[M]. 北京：中国人民大学出版社，2007.

[13] 经济合作与发展组织. 跨国企业与税务机关转让定价指南（2010）[M]. 北京：中国税务出版社，2015.

[14] 经济合作与发展组织. G20税基侵蚀和利润转移（BEPS）项目2014年成果[M]. 北京：中国税务出版社，2015.

[15] 朱青. 国际税收[M]. 10版. 北京：中国人民大学出版社，2021.